Pilgrims through the Years

Pilgrims through the Years

A Bicentennial History of
First Baptist Church, Savannah, Georgia

George H. Shriver

PROVIDENCE HOUSE PUBLISHERS

Franklin, Tennessee

Printed in the United States of America

03   02   01   00   99   1   2   3   4   5

Library of Congress Catalog Card Number: 99-66969

ISBN: 1-57736-156-3

Cover design by Gary Bozeman

Sketches by Frances Mills depict architectural details of the choir and baptistery

Illustration for pages ii–iii is photo of the tidal creek located on the property of the Bethesda Home for Boys, Savannah, Georgia. A plaque placed on the bluff reads as follows:

Nicholas Bedgegood

In the creek below the bluff bordering these grounds Nicholas Bedgegood, first ordained Baptist minister in Georgia, and for sometime Whitfield's [sic] agent at Bethesda, in the year 1765 baptized Benjamin Stirk and his wife, Mary, Thomas Dixon, and a Mr. Dupree, and subsequently Mrs. Hannah Barksdale Polhill, and others now unknown. Stirk and Dixon, and probably others of these, were employed at the orphan house. To these Bedgegood also administered the Lord's Supper on these grounds, which with their baptism, constituted the first known administration of the ordinances among Baptists in Georgia, thus identifying this spot as the location of the first known activity of Baptists in Georgia.

Committee on Baptist History
Georgia Baptist Convention
1954

PROVIDENCE HOUSE PUBLISHERS
238 Seaboard Lane • Franklin, Tennessee 37067
800-321-5692
www.providencehouse.com

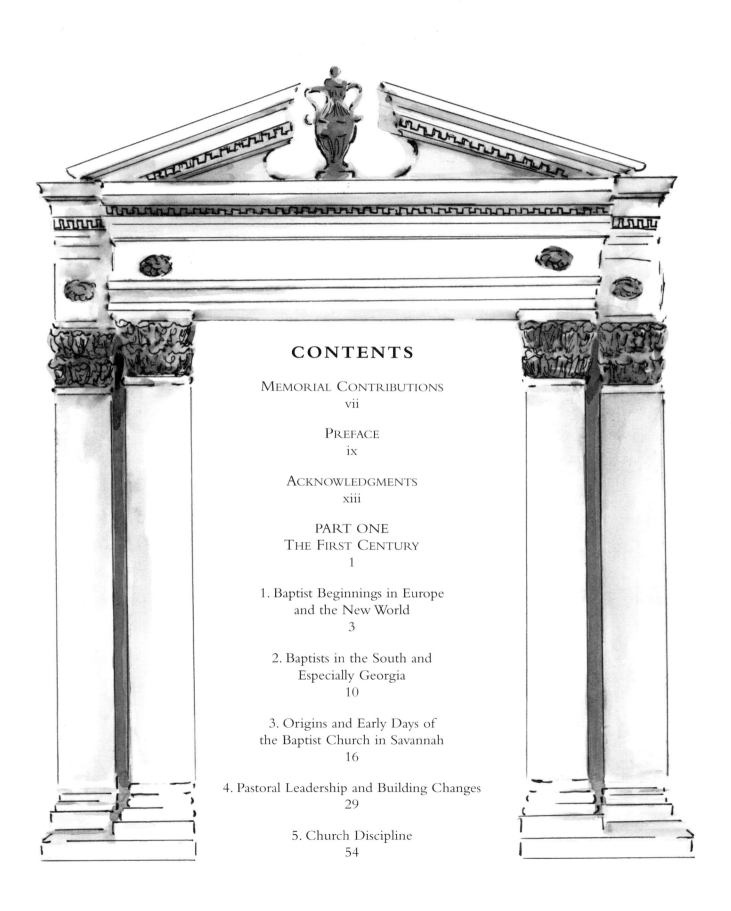

CONTENTS

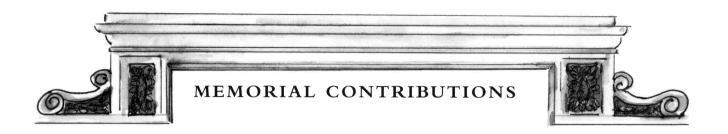

MEMORIAL CONTRIBUTIONS

The following persons have made significant contributions which make the publication of our two-hundred-year history a reality for all our past, present, and future generations.

In memory of Dr. Thomas D. Austin
by Jane B. Jennings, M.D.

In memory of Ralph F. Crutcher
by Eleanor H. Crutcher

In memory of All the Saints of First Baptist Church
who from their labors rest
by Allene and Vreeland George

In memory of J. Curtis Lewis
by J. Curtis Lewis Jr.

In memory of John B. Rabun, M.D.
by Mrs. John B. (Alsie) Rabun

In memory of Mr. And Mrs. Frank M. Huff
and Mrs. Frankie Huff Winn
by Mr. and Mrs. (née Lucile Huff) William C. Sutton Jr.
and John Wallace Winn

In memory of Rosa (Rose) Smith Usher
from the Rosa Smith Usher Memorial Fund

All proceeds from the sale of this history book will go into the Heritage and Hope Fund. Heritage and Hope is a project for the preservation and renovation of our facilities to demonstrate our gratitude for the blessing of our Heritage and Hope for the future.

Young ladies and young gentlewomen too

Do no small kindness to my Pilgrim show:

Their cabinets, their bosoms, and their hearts,

My Pilgrim has; 'cause he to them imparts

His pretty riddles in such wholesome strains

As yield them profit double to their pains

Of reading; yea, I think I may be bold

To say, some prize him above their gold.

The very children that do walk the street,

If they do but my holy Pilgrim meet,

Salute him well; will wish him well, and say,

He is the only stripling of the day.

They that have never seen him, yet admire

What they have heard of him, and much desire

To have his company, and hear him tell

Those Pilgrim stories which he knows so well.

Yea, some that did not love him at the first,

But called him fool and moody, say they must,

Now they have seen and heard him, him commend,

And to those whom they love, they do him send.

—John Bunyan, *The Pilgrim's Progress*

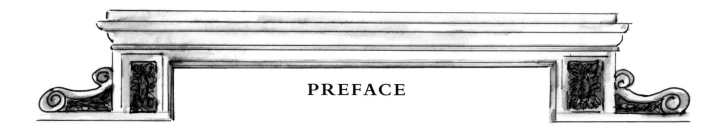

PREFACE

The story of the Baptists on the American religious scene as well as in Savannah involves the most fractured tradition within all of Protestantism. For this reason even the story of a single church inscribed in that larger context is a terribly difficult one to write. Exceptions within this larger tradition can be found for every generalization made in this book. True, this is challenging as well as frustrating at one and the same time. The task is never completed and one shies away from simplisms in the never ending search for truth. Baptists are pilgrims all and also illustrate numerous instances of wayfaring along the route. (Throughout this volume the words "pilgrim" and "pilgrimage" are used to describe the people of God on the main road to the City of God. The words "wayfarer" and "wayfaring" are used to describe the people of God who at times stray and wander a bit before returning to the commitments of the main road. Indeed, all Christian pilgrims and institutions at times become straying wayfarers.) This multifaceted movement has largely been due to two major factors—ecclesiology (the autonomy of the local church) and the priesthood of every believer (each with Bible in hand with slightly different interpretations and at times too eager to found another "truly biblical" church). The saying that "a Baptist is a Baptist is a Baptist" has very little truth except for the above two commitments.

The present volume attempts to describe the two hundred years of history of First Baptist Church, Savannah, Georgia, both thematically and chronologically. Neither the themes nor the chronological matters are all inclusive. But I would argue that all that is presented here is a vital part of the whole story. Granted, many things are left out of the story in this approach. Later, the reader will certainly want to fill in some of the gaps with additional reading and study from the numerous primary and secondary sources. Pointers for this additional study are inherent in the thematic aspect of the structure. Each theme presented here can be expanded many times over in the search for additional illustrations. As well, each theme is suggestive of yet other themes which can be explored. In other words, even a history of only one congregation is simply a "starter." Pilgrimage in heritage and hope is a continuing process. The pilgrim never finally arrives; the pilgrim is always on the road.

The congregation under consideration here is only one of over two million Christian congregations with probably one-and-a half billion members in over twenty thousand denominations worldwide. Though Baptist, the congregation is associated with only one of over fifty different Baptist denominations in the United States. All this points to a very important though often overlooked component of our culture—the local religious congregation. Further, there is general ignorance of congregational histories. One pragmatic reason for such a history is so that forgetfulness might be replaced by remembrance, to the end that we will better know where we are if we have an awareness of where we have been. As well, if we know where we are we are better prepared to use that "terrible freedom" in relation to where we want to go. In this experience, then, the gown of history past, present, and future is seamless.

This historian, as an "insider" (member of the church), was invited several years ago to write a history of the First Baptist Church of Savannah, Georgia, which would celebrate its first two hundred years of history. Frankly, this would have been a virtual impossibility without the careful Minutes (with a few lapses and lost records) of the congregation and diaconate done by dozens of secretaries. In addition, the contemporary church produced an excellent historian in the person of Mabel Freeman LaFar. Her articles and hundreds of pages of culled-out material from the records of the church were invaluable to the research. Every congregation should be so fortunate as to have such an historian. It must also be said that every member of the History Book Committee has made valuable contributions to the project. Special mention must be made, however, of Dr. George Pruden and Lynne Davis. Their careful and creative work as copy editors is deeply appreciated. In addition, Joan Usher and Alsie Rabun uniquely contributed to the book in a variety of ways and are hereby sent a card of thanks. James Richardson and Kristin Andreason, associate and assistant minister, respectively, at First Baptist Church, made important contributions to the content of the volume. The present senior pastor, John Finley, has been helpful beyond the call of duty and the historical sermons of Tom Austin have been useful and enlightening. Finally, deep appreciation is extended to Peggy Smith who has labored so long and creatively over several editions of the typed manuscript.

As an "insider," I believe that I have been able to give far more than superficial interpretations. I have read far more material than could have been included and made numerous selective decisions, for the whole story could never be told. I have attempted to retain my objectivity as an historian while writing at the same time an "inside history" as a professing Christian and long-time Baptist by choice. I have attempted to discover the true congregational identity of First Baptist Church but as set within the community, denomination, and national context. I have discovered multiple identities, for this church has been variously oriented toward missions, civic responsibilities, activist projects, and liturgical as well as evangelistic sanctuary expression, and has been ecumenical from the start.

In setting forth the story, necessity has required selectivity. Vital and creative history is not simply listing all the names, dates, and events—though some of this is necessary. Hopefully, more essential matters have been selected. Too many congregational histories are full of deception as if "nothing bad ever happened here." Pilgrims are always wayfarers at times—they are human and subject to mistakes. These moments must be related as well. So, a congregational history must not be life seen through rose-colored glasses or only positively devotional nor must it be a chronicle of persons, pastors, committees, and budget contributions. Such pseudohistories must be conscientiously avoided. Some "preferred identity of the congregation" must not be invented. This would be the "history that never was." The true identity of the congregation must be described as it zig-zagged across the years. Local congregational history best illustrates one of the favorite sayings of the great nineteenth-century church historian, Philip Schaff: "God writes on a crooked line." This truthful story is at the same time full of grace and graceful experience.

Self-knowledge is absolutely necessary in our rapidly changing contemporary world. Toward this goal the present history dedicates itself. A longer memory thereby will be provided and a correct and true tradition be recovered. May this congregation by looking backward rediscover the moorings which in the present will lead to more creative, diversified, and complete ministry. May the present ministry be more spacious, truly Baptistic, and ecumenical and lead this local congregation into a brave new world of creative Christian witness.

A FESTSCHRIFT

Festschriften are celebration writings. The present Festschrift celebrates the first two hundred years of history of the First Baptist Church of Savannah, Georgia. It is a holistic celebration of men, women, whites, blacks, liberals, moderates, fundamentalists, ministers, laypersons, statesmen, politicians—these and others, pilgrims all, in process and progress down their own particular part of the Christian road called Baptist.

Chippewa Square, the present location of the church, appropriately presents a scene of major features of American life and culture. The square is graced by a statue of James Edward Oglethorpe and each day joggers, bikers, tourists, and street-people appreciate in different ways this small piece of real estate in downtown Savannah. This oldest church building in Savannah surveys daily a cross section of American life and culture—from a nearby bed-and-breakfast to an old movie house which now serves as a community theater. In the near distance are steeples of other denominational buildings reminding us of the broader Protestant world and this church's own ecumenical beginnings and commitments.

Although certainly no longer a point of concern, for much of its tenure on Chippewa Square the First Baptist Church congregation resented the presence of a theater directly across the square, feeling it was a focal point of sinful activity in Savannah. The 1818 building, designed by William Jay, burned in 1948. Photo courtesy of the Georgia Historical Society.

In the midst of downtown secularism, this building and the pilgrim people of God who make tracks toward it on weekdays as well as on weekends stand as witnesses to other than secular values—offering an alternative message in a downtown setting. While so many others have fled to the suburbs, this congregation has remained as a lively witness to the self-giving love of Jesus the Christ. All the warts of their history notwithstanding, this pilgrim people has been intrinsically committed to this supreme value throughout their history.

This history divides itself chronologically in a simplistic manner—the two centuries of existence. The founding days are set within the context of Baptist beginnings in the Old World and continuings in the New World and more especially in the South. Georgia was a Johnny-come-lately colony as were the Baptists themselves. Episcopalians, Lutherans, Jews, and others were already parts of the religious scene in Savannah prior to the founding of a Baptist congregation. Soon enough, however, the growth pattern and the roles played in Savannah's life by the Baptist congregation were formidable and remained so. Within each century, the multifaceted story of this congregation is told by means of themes arranged within themselves chronologically. As well, these themes form an interesting mesh with numerous intertwining threads relating to congregational life.

Every written history is an interpretation, for the sources do not automatically speak for themselves. The selection of materials themselves is an act of interpretation, for the whole story is never told. If one told all that is found just in the records here, the volume would be an absurdity of several thousand pages. Hopefully, the essence of the heritage and hope of this congregation has been captured in a limited number of themes and illustrations. The attempt to do this has been an exhilarating experience for the writer; if readers find parts of the volume to be similarly rewarding, then my efforts have been worthwhile. In this case, one pilgrim calls to others to join with him in the thrilling experience of searching for truth on the road. Our prayer is that all those who "take up and read" will discover the true heritage and hope of First Baptist of Savannah—as a witness and testimony of her total history.

ACKNOWLEDGMENTS

More than ten years ago Dr. Walter B. Shurden suggested in a letter to Jeryl Davis: "get a scholarly, first-class book-length history of your church written. . . . Yours is one of the most historic churches of the South. It deserves a first-class history. . . ." In late 1991, Jack H. Usher, Chair of the Diaconate, appointed a committee to undertake the project. Work began in earnest with the arrival of Dr. John M. Finley, who has been a constant source of encouragement through active involvement in every aspect of the work. We are most fortunate that a member of our congregation, Dr. George H. Shriver, agreed to write the book. He is Professor of History, Emeritus, at Georgia Southern University and a prolific author and editor of books on Baptist history. We have benefited also from the interest and contributions of present and former church members who are not on the committee as well as people outside of our congregation. They helped us by providing oral histories and taking on tasks which were instrumental in producing this book, and we want to acknowledge their assistance.

Art and layout:	Frances Mills	Typing:	Shirley Allen
Videotaping:	Billy Sutton		Jeanne Lawhorne
Photography:	Joseph Byrd		Carol Scott
	Hunter Photography		Karen Jerald
	Jeanne Papy (jacket cover)		Cathy Parrish
	Adam Weathersby (title page)		
	Doug Curie		

We thank the members of First Baptist Church for their confidence in entrusting us to oversee this book. It has been an awesome undertaking, but also a rewarding one. Our heritage has been blessed and challenges us as we enter the third century of our church's history and the new millennium. Thanks be to God.

History Book Committee
Co-chairs: George Pruden and Joan Usher,
Members: Edith Bennett, Lynne Davis, Chris Hendricks,
Bob Miller (a valuable member until his passing),
Alsie Rabun, Lucile Sutton, and Betty Waldrop

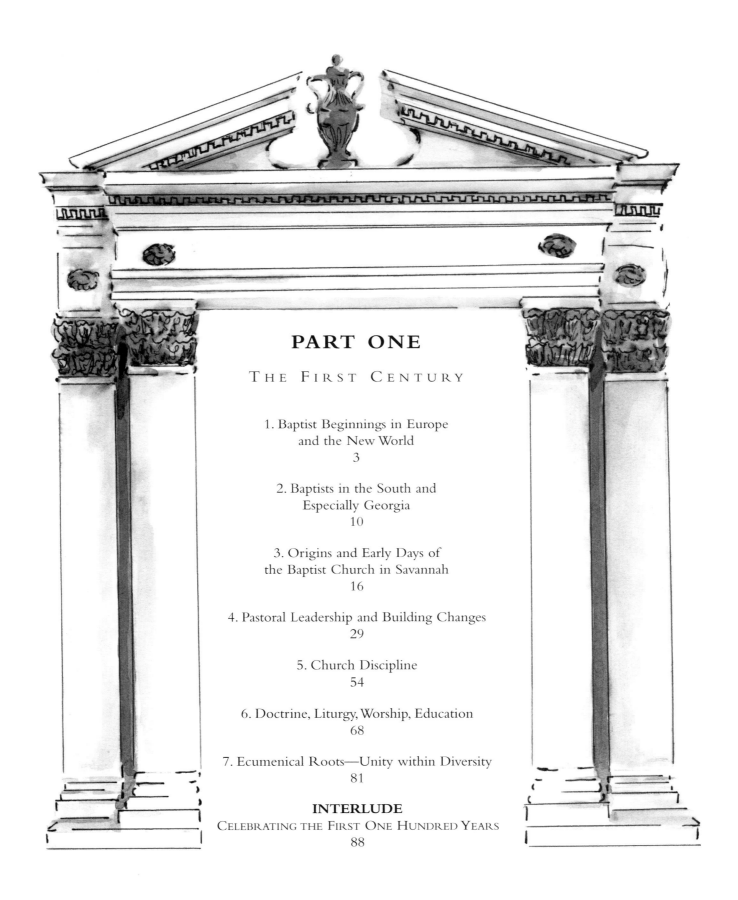

PART ONE

THE FIRST CENTURY

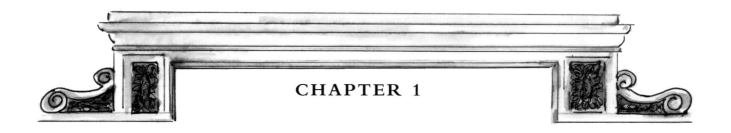

CHAPTER 1

BAPTIST BEGINNINGS IN EUROPE AND THE NEW WORLD

> *This mountain is not one we climbed once upon a time; it is a well-known peak we never wholly know, which must be climbed again in every generation, on every new day.*
> —Richard Niebuhr

First Baptist Church of Savannah, Georgia, has a long and distinguished history itself that merits a careful recounting, but this church is also an important part of a much more extensive historical context. Its own unique story deserves the enhancement of at least a brief survey of that tradition from which it evolved in the year 1800. The way Baptists have "done" their history, their emergence in seventeenth-century England, their early growth and expansion in the New World, and their own pluralistic evolution in the South—all these topics add deeper insight into the life, ministry, and mission of that group which had its formal beginnings in the first year of the nineteenth century in Savannah. As no human is an island, so is no institution an entity to itself. Each institution has its own longer *traditio* and a knowledge of this *traditio* results in a more complete and sensitive understanding of the meaning and significance of the singular institution. The church of 1800 must be seen as inscribed in this more involved story of Baptists. Given such attention, then, these matters will spotlight to even a greater degree the rich and varied two-hundred-year story of the Baptists of First Baptist Church.

ON WRITING BAPTIST HISTORY

Presently the search for roots by individuals as well as by interest groups seems of paramount importance. Denominations and their congregations are no different in this need than the rest of society. How did we come into existence? Where have we been? Where are we? Where do we want to go? All these and more questions are being asked by those most qualified to answer. And a variety of answers has been forthcoming all the way from biographies to heavy classroom texts.

Certainly the people called Baptist have participated in this endeavor as much as any other group and have produced their pathways of knowledge concerning their own roots. Most Baptists have never had a course in historiography (unless they were history majors on the university level), but any history student knows that the search for roots involves itself, in part, in addressing oneself to the history of the writing of history in that particular subject area. First off, this requires "detached attachment" to one's own denomination. "Attachment" is obviously found in the confessional commitment of the denominational historian. "Detachment" is absolutely necessary for the objective historian who carefully uses the norms of historical research. Objectivity on the one hand is not ruined by "attachment"; it really involves his/her being "open" to new information coming in, from whatever source. All Baptist historians have illustrated "attachment." Not all of them have shown "detachment" and objectivity in approach.

What can be said of the unique character of Baptist history, then? Quickly put, the difference is not one of method or approach but, rather, content. The subject matter is said to be the denominations called Baptist. But where are the Baptists and what is the Baptist denomination(s)? The subject matter itself must be defined. Practically defined it would include all the outward, observable, and institutionalized manifestations of the Baptist movement in the history-that-happens. It would then include all those who have called themselves or been called by others, "Baptist." And the approach to this history must be informed openness.

The discipline of Baptist history, especially in the United States, covers a wide range of manifestations—from denominations such as the Southern Baptist Convention (SBC) (founded in 1845 and the denominational "Mother" of First Baptist Church of Savannah) to small bodies that might even be called "sects." In the past (as well as somewhat in the present), in some Baptist-sponsored colleges, seminaries, and religious training schools, church history was presented as a rapid survey of inconsequentials until the birth of the particular denomination sponsoring that school. Then the study of church history became a study of that particular group as if it were the most authentic continuation of the church. In some schools even the survey of early, medieval, and reformation periods became a study of minority sect groups as if they were the "trail of blood" of that particular Baptist denomination back to the days of Jesus. In some Baptist circles on the grassroots level even today, such views are strongly entertained.

But at least in most Baptist schools this situation has changed. Most Baptist historians are reflective of the "detached-attached" methodology. They have come to stand and do research within the whole Christian tradition, to study the renewal and pilgrimage of a people called Christian and then the Baptist movement as inscribed within this larger context.

Baptist historiography was unfortunately at first grounded in *a priori* reasoning and within an apologetic and polemical context of denominational rivalry. This earliest approach has usually been designated as the successionist theory of Baptist history. Though no longer accepted in educational circles, it continues nevertheless to have a following in certain grassroots contexts. The view essentially says that there has been an authentic succession of Baptist churches since apostolic times, each one making its Baptist witness and generally persecuted by the dominant culture, both secular and religious (popularly called "the trail of blood"). Among others who set forth this position are the following: Thomas Crosby, *The History of the English Baptists* (1738–40);

G. H. Orchard, *A Concise History of Foreign Baptists* (1855); and J. M. Cramp, *Baptist History: From the Foundations of the Christian Church to the Close of the Eighteenth Century* (1868). The little red booklet by J. M. Carroll, *The Trail of Blood*, setting forth this view, is still in print and widely circulated. Historians of a minority and often persecuted denomination thus found a way to legitimate their tradition and to give answer to the problem of authority. Their view of church succession obviously parallels the Roman Catholic legitimation by means of apostolic succession.

A second historiographical approach held to a viewpoint generally known as the Anabaptist spiritual kinship theory. This view, too, found comfort and satisfaction in locating a succession of Baptist believers among the minority and persecuted sects of centuries past, such as the Anabaptists (who were really the forefathers of contemporary Mennonites). While this view did not insist on historical proof of this connection, it did point to those "spiritual" qualities and principles shared by all these groups. Admittedly and from the start, then, this position was more confessional than historical in a scientific way. It is problematical as to whether the difference between these two views could be understood on the grassroots level. However, both certainly lent themselves to anti-intellectualism and obscurantism in final analysis. Those historians who urged this position included the following: David Benedict, *A General History of the Baptist Denomination in America* (1848); Richard B. Cook, *The Story of the Baptists in All Ages and Countries* (1884); Thomas Armitage, *A History of the Baptists*; and Albert H. Newman, *A History of Anti-Pedobaptism* (1897). Even the distinguished Walter Rauschenbusch is remembered by some of his students as having suggested this position in classroom lectures.

The third approach, and one followed in contemporary educational circles, is sometimes referred to as the English Separatist descent theory. According to this position, Baptists originated from the religious turmoil of seventeenth-century England—the Baptist movement being inscribed in the much larger Puritan situation, and especially in the Congregationalist wing of Puritanism. More specifically, the Baptists' moment of truth and birth came in circa 1641 when believer's baptism by immersion began to be practiced by a group in London that had withdrawn over a comparatively short period of time from the mother church of Congregationalism at Southwark, England. In addition, this splitting off was a rather friendly one and not described by anger and extreme judgmentalism. Baptist beginnings were actually ecumenical in spirit. This description of Baptist origins was set forth by William H. Whitsitt in his *A Question in Baptist History* (1896). Another American Baptist historian, Augustus H. Strong, agreed with Whitsitt in an address which he delivered in 1904. With refinements, these scholars' conclusions survive to the present time. The Calvinistic Baptists of 1641 are then generally agreed as being the genuine forebearers of the early Baptist bodies in the New World. For one, this view does not run counter to the principles of historical research as do the other two theories, for it is all too obvious that modern Baptists have no historical continuity with ancient and medieval sects nor with sixteenth-century Anabaptists.

In addition, seventeenth-century Baptist beginnings cannot be separated from the context in which they appeared, that is, from the larger context of reform groups coming into existence out of the Reformation movement. From the start, their emphasis was on freedom of religious expression for all persons. They went beyond the Congregationalists in their insistence on the separation of church and state (this idea was certainly hand-in-glove with the concept of adult believer's baptism as opposed to infant baptism). These emphases on personal freedom and the separation of church and state have been at one and the same time a blessing and a curse to the Baptist cause. The blessing is obvious—religious liberty; the curse is just as obvious—fragmentation. The very birth and early rise of the Baptist movement explain the variant strands of tradition which have developed through the years, resulting in so many different Baptist bodies in the United States in the twentieth century. The largest of these is the Southern Baptist Convention and even there one finds potential fragmentation presently. The metaphor utilized in this book involves wayfaring, renewal, and pilgrimage. The Baptists and their denominational expressions are all *en route*, on the way, on a journey, pilgrims all.

SPECIFIC HISTORICAL BEGINNINGS

The sixteenth and seventeenth centuries in Europe were marked by dramatic changes in the body politic. Economic, national, social, and religious revolutions, reformations, and wars were rampant. Many of these occurrences were caused by the Protestant Reformations of the sixteenth century with numerous aftershocks in the seventeenth. The scene of one church in one world in the Middle Ages of western Europe ceased to be. Martin Luther and other reformers dared to open the religious Pandora's box with their ideas of the priesthood of every believer and *sola scriptura* (scripture alone as a guide to truth instead of papal authority and tradition). By the end of the sixteenth century, Lutherans, Reformed (Calvinists), Anglicans, and numerous radical minority groups competed with Catholicism throughout Europe for the religious support of individuals and, in the case of the majority groups, for the support of the state as well. One church in one state was still the belief of the major reformers as well as of Catholics. The concepts of the separation of church and state and religious liberty were considered heretical as well as the beliefs of seditionists. Each ruler determined the religious denomination of his/her territory and all other views were deemed heresy and sedition. Those of a minority position in a particular territory moved (the beginning of the modern religious refugee problem), converted, or were persecuted. Protestant and Catholic territories practiced persecution of one another, and both persecuted the truly minority groups such as the various kinds of radical reformers (for one, the Anabaptists later known as Mennonites).

In other words, long before the founding of the earliest English-speaking colonies in the New World, Christianity had become fragmented throughout western Europe. Numerous social and economic upheavals as well as outright wars added to the unrest and the search for economic, social, and religious "place." This European religious variety predetermined the rich religious diversity in the early American colonies. Even in the thirteen colonies, however, there would be state churches in most (the exceptions being Rhode Island and Pennsylvania) with some persecution and the reduction of some colonists to a kind of second-class citizenship due to their different religious affiliation. Eventually, of course, in the national period no one denomination would ever be strong enough to mount a serious or successful campaign for appointment as the state church, though Congregationalists and Anglicans certainly had ambitions in that direction. And even though at first in the national period some states retained a state church, eventually by the fourth decade of the nineteenth century, even Massachusetts yielded to the principles of separation and liberty. The religious variety and diversity of the colonial period dictated this "lively experiment" of the early national period of United States history.

The beginnings of Baptist history in the period of turmoil in Europe are inscribed in the English phase of the Reformation and more specifically in the context of Puritan agitation within and without the Anglican Church during the period of the Stuart kings as well as during the period of Cromwell's Protectorate, when his policy of religious toleration encouraged denominational growth. These beginnings of Baptist life took two forms—General Baptists, more separatistic and Arminian (especially in relation to opposition to predestination), and Particular Baptists, more ecumenical and Calvinistic (especially in holding firmly to predestinarian belief).

Puritan is a "blanket term" covering a king-sized bed. Some Puritans wanted just a few changes of the English church upon separation from papal authority and they remained Anglican. Others, however, desired numerous and radical changes and due to the political climate were forced to become separatists from the stated Anglican Church. These separatists were radically divided even among themselves and this led eventually to numerous persecuted sects and minority denominations.

Late in 1607 one of these separatist groups left Gainsborough due to real and potential persecution, and in the search for greater freedom of expression settled in Holland. John Smyth and Thomas Helwys were the religious leaders of this group in Amsterdam, which formed a religious covenant with one another. By late 1608 or early 1609 Smyth became convinced of adult believer's baptism, baptized himself and Helwys by affusion (pouring), and then baptized the rest of the church group. This can probably be named the birth of the Baptist movement. A bit later Smyth and some of the members joined with the Dutch Mennonites and Helwys and other members returned to England in late 1611 or early 1612 to form the first Baptist Church on English soil at Spitalsfield near London. In theology this group was Arminian and the mode of baptism practiced was by affusion rather than immersion. These General Baptists grew slowly but by the end of the century had moved in one of two directions—toward the Calvinistic Baptists or toward the Unitarians. One of their major contributions was certainly their plea for liberty of conscience, a hallmark of Baptists from that point on.

The origin of Particular Baptists was quite different. Their background is actually with the "mother church" of the Congregationalists. In 1616 Henry Jacob founded a church group at Southwark, London, committed to a congregationalist ecclesiology and the concept of a church covenant. This group was Puritan as well, but their Puritanism led them to a different position about church government than the Anglican episcopacy. They still believed in one church in one state but a congregational one. They could even refer to the Anglican as "mother church"; therefore, their beginnings can be said to be ecumenical. By the 1630s, however, some members of this church were beginning to interpret certain Biblical passages in a different way and over a period of years a number left the Congregationalist church to form another, however friendly, congregation. Sometime between 1638 and 1641 this new church began to insist on religious liberty, separation of church from state, and a mode of baptism that was by "dipping ye body into ye water"—immersion. In addition, the person dipped would be an adult believer. John Spilsbury, William Kiffin, and Hanserd Knollys were the ongoing leaders of this new group. They were known as "particular" Baptists due to their Calvinistic belief that only the "particular" ones were preordained to go to heaven and to enjoy the atonement offered by Jesus the Christ. By 1644 their number had increased to seven churches in the London area, and they produced the famous London

Confession of Faith of fifty separate articles reflecting Calvinistic belief, requiring adult believer's baptism by immersion, and urging religious liberty. Early in their history Baptists committed themselves to the idea of association for a variety of purposes, and one result was certainly the growing sense of denominational awareness and self-consciousness.

The background and beliefs of the earliest Baptists in the New World were definitely British. The Puritan-Congregationalist context is also clearly the most immediate context. Baptist life in the colonies officially began with Roger Williams, the heretic of Massachusetts Bay Colony. In addition to his growing belief in religious liberty, Williams also began to criticize a paid ministry (he called them "hirelings") as well as to insist that Native Americans should be paid for their land illegally given to colonists by the English king. Exiled from the Bay area in midwinter 1636, Williams purchased land from Narragansett Indians and founded Providence Plantation. Briefly convinced of Baptist beliefs, in 1639 Williams was baptized by Ezekiel Holliman, a former Congregationalist Puritan himself. Then Williams baptized Holliman and a small group of others who formed what is generally believed to be the first Baptist church on New World soil, in Providence, Rhode Island. Soon thereafter, Williams became a seeker or disaffiliated from any formal church body, never believing that he had ever found the true church of Jesus the Christ. Another Baptist congregation was formed in nearby Newport (some contending it to be the first Baptist church in the New World though such records are extinct) under the leadership of John Clarke, a medical doctor. Calvinistic as well as Arminian views were held by different Baptist members at this time, and in the 1650s an early schism took place illustrating from the start that the Baptist understanding of freedom of conscience would lead to numerous schisms throughout the centuries.

Always in the minority in New England, Baptists soon formed themselves into churches in other colonies and found themselves persecuted by state-church authorities—imprisonments, whippings, fines, banishment, and loss of positions followed them everywhere. Two examples alone are vivid enough: Obadiah Holmes was whipped and imprisoned for preaching against infant baptism and the erudite Henry Dunster, the president of Harvard College, was removed from office for refusing to have his infant child baptized. The state-church rigidity of New England would result in numerous illustrations of persecution of minority bodies. Baptists in New England were treated like heretics and dissenters.

More religious tolerance and some religious liberty in the Middle Colonies attracted Baptists as well as numerous other minority religious bodies. Indeed, Pennsylvania colony would become a cross section of religious life in the colonial period much like that of the United States of later years. This more favorable context resulted in rapid growth patterns and certain important aspects of denominational self-consciousness such as cooperative units and confessional affirmations. The first Baptist association in the New World was founded in Philadelphia in 1707, and in turn this association published the first Baptist confession of faith in the New World in 1742. Later it was often referred to as "the Baptist Confession." Printed by Benjamin Franklin, the title page is significant and revelatory of early Baptist emphases: "A Confession of Faith Put forth by the Elders and Brethren of many Congregations of Christians (Baptized upon Profession of their Faith). Adopted by the Baptist Association met at Philadelphia, Sept. 25, 1742. To which are added, Two Articles, viz. Of Imposition of Hands, and Singing of Psalms in Public Worship. Also A Short Treatise of Church Discipline." A

Calvinistically oriented document, it also suggested the laying on of hands at baptism as well as the singing of hymns. Its addition of the treatise on church discipline set the stage for the next 150 years of an emphasis in local church discipline on moral as well as theological matters. Though it did become the Baptist confession, other associations which accepted it did not receive it as a papal pronouncement. Indeed, the Separate General Association of Virginia adopted it in 1783 but stipulated that its adoption did

> not mean that every person is to be bound to the strict observance of everything therein contained, nor do we mean to make it, in any respect, superior or equal to the scriptures in matters of faith and practice: although we think it the best composition of the kind now extant. . . .

The Philadelphia Association not only produced a useful confession of faith, but it also provided a forum for theological and political discussion, financial support of matters of a common interest, and a context for numerous cooperative ventures. Indeed, when religious liberties were curtailed and infringed upon, such associations became proactive on behalf of complete religious liberty for all groups, including themselves.

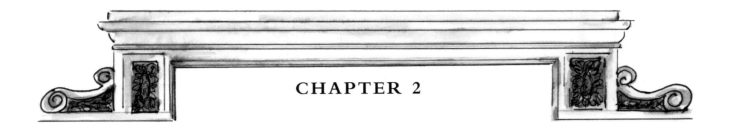

CHAPTER 2

BAPTISTS IN THE SOUTH
AND ESPECIALLY GEORGIA

The state church of every Southern colony was Anglican. Some colonies were more accepting of dissenters than others, the colony of Georgia being one of them. Virginia, on the other hand, from the early start had been much less accepting of religious dissenting positions. Before the Great Awakening of the 1720s and 1730s, Baptists were far more numerous in the North than in the South. A scattering of congregations and individual Baptists were located in Virginia and the Carolinas and after 1733 a bare sprinkling existed in Georgia.

The earliest institutional presence of Baptists in the South was located in the vicinity of Charleston in the 1690s when a small group of Baptists from Kittery, Maine, settled on the Cooper River at present-day Charleston. The Reverend William Screven led them in becoming an organized religious body and Baptist church. There were certainly General as well as Particular Baptists in this church as Screven was more flexible and accepting in his outlook. By 1699 these Baptists owned real estate in Charleston and before 1701 an actual building in which to worship.

Baptist growth and expansion in the South were actually very slow until the period of the Great Awakening. Then turmoil and controversy as well as growth entered the picture of Baptist life. Baptists prior to the Awakening can be designated as Regular Baptists. They were more Calvinistic, promoted orderly worship and the singing of psalms, and urged higher education for their ministry. Great Awakening emphases among Baptists led in different directions—moderated Calvinism (in the direction of Arminianism), uninhibited worship, the singing of hymns, and an insistence on "God's call" of ministry rather than on an education.

The Separate Baptist movement had its birth in the "fire and light" of the revivals of George Whitefield. This movement originally came from a Congregationalist context. At times entire churches and ministers separated from staid Congregationalism. It was only a short step then to the Baptist position. Separate Congregationalists could take a little side step and adopt adult believer's baptism as a way toward truly regenerate church membership—and they did. These grassroots folk were noisy and sometimes crude, urged using the Bible alone rather than creedal affirmations, and criticized

10

Regular Baptists for their lack of strictness in relation to membership and church discipline. They were intensely individualistic and described by their critics as crude, rude, ignorant, and backward. The Regular Baptists of the then urban centers and the Separate Baptists of the frontier, rural areas often conflicted and numerous controversies and schisms took place. By the early part of the nineteenth century, however, these two strains of Baptist life had in the main united their efforts—there was unity in the midst of diversity and at least "family" acceptance.

No doubt about it, the Separate Baptist movement in the South was the source of rapid Baptist growth. The leaders of the revivalism which spread like wildfire in the South were Shubael Stearns, Daniel Marshall, and Samuel Harriss. These men itinerated through Virginia, the Carolinas, and even Georgia. Stearns and Marshall founded in 1758 the famous Sandy Creek Association in North Carolina as well as the Sandy Creek Church, which in a seventeen-year period had become the "mother" church of forty-two others. Indeed, it was Daniel Marshall who in 1771 or 1772 founded the first Baptist church in Georgia, the Kiokee Baptist Church now located near Appling in Columbia County. Soon enough other churches sprang up in Georgia. There had certainly been a scattering of individual Baptists before this but no organized church.

The last three decades of the eighteenth century were beset by tremendous political ferment and social change. Though the original charter of the colony of Georgia offered religious liberty to all but Catholics, when it became a royal colony, this situation changed. The Second General Assembly of the colony met in Savannah in the winter of 1758 and among other actions declared the Church of England as the state church of the colony. Though all other religious bodies were thereby declared rather second-class and subject to legal action, the ever weakening royal situation actually resulted in no severe punishments for these other groups. Baptists in other colonies had already paid a sometimes high price for their religious commitments and were very outspoken in their advocacy of religious liberty and the separation of church and state. Jailings, mob violence, and beatings did not silence these Baptists in other colonies, and some of them made creative contributions to these two principles being written into the founding documents of the new United States. Baptists in Georgia enjoyed the fruits of Baptist labor in these other colonies and due to the timing of the Revolution never suffered very much simply because of their religious faith. They were, of course, supportive of both of these principles in due time. Georgia was much more tolerant and flexible in relation to other denominations than the Church of England. After the Revolution the greater transition was on the shoulders of the formerly established church for now it was simply one of many "free churches"—free from state entanglement but also from state monetary support. The state constitution of 1798 recognized only voluntary support of all religious bodies.

All religious bodies suffered during the Revolution and were in disarray at its conclusion. The Baptists and Methodists were best situated to succeed, however, and in the 1780s and 1790s they experienced a great deal of numerical growth. Both these grassroots movements spoke the religious language of common folk and were best suited to frontier conditions. Baptists with their love of liberty, congregational emphases, and fiery preaching and Methodists with their committed circuit riders would eventually outgrow all the other denominations.

As of the beginning of the last decade in the eighteenth century, Baptists in Georgia could count at least forty-two churches with thirty-three ministers and over thirty-two hundred members. The need for some kind of organization for missionary as well as for other purposes was early sensed following the Revolution; therefore, and probably in 1784, the Georgia Baptist Association was formed, separating itself in a friendly way from the South Carolina Association. The growth pattern of other denominations was much slower. It should also be pointed out that slaves usually worshiped in the churches of their masters in a separated fashion (balcony or otherwise) or in a special kind of service, always under the watchful eye of white masters. There were few exceptions to this rule, but one occurred in Savannah. In 1778 the first "colored" Baptist church was founded, in this case later under the watchful eye of the white Baptist Church of Savannah, which was organized in November 1800.

With the expansion and growth of the Baptists, new associations were founded. In 1806 the Savannah Association, with churches on both sides of the river in two different states, changed its name to the Savannah River Association. By late 1818 the Baptist churches on the Georgia side of the river accomplished a friendly separation and became the Sunbury Association. The Savannah Baptist Church was a creative and contributive member. Growth and self-consciousness led to the founding of the Georgia Baptist Convention (GBC) at Powelton in 1822. Local, associational, and state organizations were now in place to assist Baptist work in every phase of the interest of the people themselves who were adult baptized believers.

It is important to note the beginnings of national Baptist organizational life as well as that of the denomination of which the Baptist Church of Savannah has always been a part. These two organizations were respectively known as the General Missionary Convention of the Baptist Denomination in the United States for Foreign Missions and the Southern Baptist Convention.

By the late eighteenth and early nineteenth centuries, a number of religious bodies in the United States became more self-conscious of the value of unitive efforts on the state and then national level. These efforts ranged from benevolence activities to missions. State missionary societies were formed everywhere and then missionizing interests led to national cooperative ventures. In 1810 the Congregationalists formed the American Board of Commissioners for Foreign Missions. Missionaries were sent to other countries including Luther Rice, Adoniram Judson and his wife, Ann Haseltine Judson. On board the ship bound for India (1812) these three became convinced of Baptist views and upon arrival decided that they could not accept funds for their work from a Congregationalist body. So, Luther Rice returned home to generate support among Baptists for such a missionary venture. Rice traveled widely among churches and associations galvanizing interest in creating a national Baptist society committed to foreign missions with affiliate state societies supporting this effort financially. The founding of the General Missionary Convention in Philadelphia's First Baptist Church on May 18, 1814, resulted from his efforts. It became known as the "Triennial Convention" due to its national meetings during each three-year period. This body was the first national organization of Baptists in the United States. Baptists now had national visibility and self-consciousness and expressed unity toward, at first, the single purpose of missions. Luther Rice remained the main agent for this body and was especially successful in his tours of the South. The founding of this national body was not without opposition, of course. The freedom of conscience enjoyed by Baptists in so many positive ways could also have its "dark side," which often led to controversy and fragmentation.

Staunch Calvinistic Baptists opposed this national organization and started the "antimission movement." "Why meddle with the divine plan for the elect?" they questioned. Also, they urged, the Bible does not speak of such organizations—they are human inventions and not biblical! Daniel Parker and Alexander Campbell were two of the most vocal opponents and their efforts led to greater schism. Such opposition as well as Baptist fear of any kind of hierarchy led in the short run to the founding of single-interest societies, hopefully without any danger of a national ecclesiastical bureaucracy. Separate societies were founded for foreign missions, home missions, education, Bible translation, Sunday Schools, evangelism, printing, and social welfare. No society had direct connections with another. Each society could receive support from individuals, churches, or associations. What was involved was the contribution of funds to a specific cause and membership based on financial support. Cooperation toward worthy goals could be practiced without any fear of ecclesiastical control. Baptists could have their cake and eat it, too, with no compromise of individual, local, or state autonomy. Still retaining one of their distinctives—autonomy—Baptists now joined other denominations in their search for identity on the national level.

Slavery questions prompted the most grievous denominational schisms and foundings of new groups on the religious scene in the United States. This "peculiar institution" in the South was the major cause of the beginnings of the Southern Baptist Convention, the first truly comprehensive Baptist organization in the United States.

The practice of slavery had been sanctioned even in religious circles early on in the history of the New World. The "heathen" had been given to the settling Europeans as an inheritance! Or so they reasoned. Even some Congregationalist ministers owned slaves. The institution grew but with an ever enlarging group of critics, many of them within religious communities and with religious principles fueling their criticism. Quakers were among the most perceptive of the critics, especially John Woolman. Humanitarianism and liberal ideas from the Revolution also contributed to opposition. There were even some antislavery societies in the South following the Revolution among Methodists and Presbyterians, as well as Baptists. By the 1830s, however, two significant things had taken place. First, a very aggressive abolitionist movement had developed in the North led by such charismatic figures as William Lloyd Garrison, Wendell Phillips, and John Greenleaf Whittier. Southerners had pressed for antislavery legislation in the distant future while the abolitionists called for immediate action. This "outside interference" was resented and resisted in the South. Second, numerous agricultural changes were taking place in the South between 1790 and 1830. New cotton markets and the new cotton gin of 1792 had truly made cotton "king" in the South. The slavery issue was now terribly complicated by regional economics, and even religious leaders in the South were subject to being "acculturated" by these new developments. Agitation in the North for "freedom now" and critical economics in the South resulted in southern clergy adopting proslavery sentiments even in their sermons. Lecterns became "bully pulpits" for these proslavery preachments. Among numerous others from all the major religious bodies in the South, the Baptist Richard Furman claimed that the right of holding slaves was "clearly established in the Holy Scriptures both by precept and example."

As shown above, Baptists in the United States had organized for missions and other purposes along the lines of more loosely administered societies rather than structured organizations. This gave national visibility to Baptists and an opportunity for cooperation toward common purposes. Among other societal organizations, the General Missionary Convention of 1814 was followed by the American Baptist Home Mission Society of 1832.

Due to the above two factors, tension was bound to be experienced within the two national mission societies. Abolitionism was certainly making inroads within these two societies and the South was definitely going to be resentful of this. By 1840 the Alabama Baptist Convention had adopted resolutions to the effect that they believed abolitionism to be unscriptural and would therefore withhold money from the General Missionary Convention until it was assured that the body had no connection with abolitionism whatsoever. Within a few years two definite and unacceptable answers were given by these mission societies to southerners. The die was cast: separation of Baptists in the South was a foregone conclusion.

It had been rumored in Georgia that the Home Mission Society would not appoint any slaveholder as a missionary. To test this rumor, in April 1844 the Executive Committee of the Georgia Baptist Convention requested the Society to appoint James E. Reeves (some sources spell this "Reeve"), a slaveholder, as a missionary. The Georgia convention even assured the Society a salary for Reeves. The Society's executive board refused to appoint him. Then, in November 1844 the Alabama Baptist Convention asked the executive board of the General Missionary Convention if it would appoint a slaveholder as a missionary. Again, a negative answer was given.

In reaction to these two answers, on April 10, 1845, the Virginia Baptist Foreign Mission Society issued a call to "those who were aggrieved with the recent decision" to meet for a consultative convention in Augusta, Georgia, on May 8, 1845. Though William Bullein Johnson (second pastor of Savannah Baptist Church) had favored and been present at the founding in 1814 of the General Missionary Convention, he energetically supported such a convention in the South in a speech before the South Carolina Baptist Convention just one week prior to the Augusta meeting. He also urged that a centralized ecclesiology replace the loosely constructed societal pattern. The movement toward separation and the founding of a new denomination would not be denied.

Train, stagecoach, boat, private horses—all contributed to bringing 293 delegates (or, "messengers," a later more popular designation) to Augusta in early May. Eight states and the District of Columbia were represented but Georgia and South Carolina led the numbers by far—139 and 102 respectively. Only 166 of 4,126 Baptist churches in the South were represented. This was actually a regional convention with limited intentions, but with an organizational structure which allowed later expansion geographically as well as in relation to services rendered.

Surely the young twenty-seven-year-old host pastor, W. T. Brantley Jr., was a case of nerves as he called the meeting to order on May 8 and welcomed such persons as James B. Taylor from Richmond, Richard Furman from South Carolina, W. B. Johnson from South Carolina, and J. B. Jeter from Virginia. Perhaps the most forceful of the visitors to the young pastor that morning was William Bullein Johnson, now sixty-two years of age and with unparalleled experience in Baptist work. Johnson was the only one there that May day who had also been present at the organization of the General Baptist Convention in 1814. Though obviously favoring separation now, he had just recently served as president of this first national Baptist organization from 1841 to 1844. He had also led in forming the first state Baptist convention in 1821 (South Carolina) as well as serving as its president since 1825. He was a "natural" for the position of first president of the soon-to-be-founded Southern Baptist Convention. Johnson would also be the driving force behind a more centralized and comprehensive structure for this new denominational body. From the start the office of president would be a powerful one and this certainly reflected the style of W. B. Johnson, even from his young days as pastor in Savannah. For good or ill, the Southern Baptist Convention would be stuck with this principle from its founding days.

Virtually the first act of the Convention on May 8 was the election of officers. W. B. Johnson was elected as president. An organizing committee worked through the day, and in the afternoon presentation and debate over numerous issues resulted in adjournment until the next morning. After extended debate and dialogue, the delegates voted unanimously to sever all connections with the old body and to form their own separate denomination. A committee was then charged with writing a constitution for this new organization. The constitution presented on Saturday was largely the work of one man—W. B. Johnson. He had come to Augusta with virtually a draft of it in his hip pocket.

In April Johnson had traveled widely in the South visiting individuals and churches and urging his ideas. In early May he had called, as president, a special meeting of the South Carolina Convention and had shared in detail his organizational plan for a new Baptist body. The plan called for centralization and comprehensiveness. His charisma succeeded in getting the endorsement of his state convention. This same plan was presented in Augusta to the organizing committee and was presented to the general body with few revisions and additions. His ideas, then, became the basis of organizing a new convention—centralized and comprehensive. On May 10, 1845, by unanimous vote the delegates adopted the new constitution of a body to be named the Southern Baptist Convention. The once arrogant pastor of Savannah Baptist Church had left his impress on this new denomination, and the powerful office of president which he first occupied would result in major turmoil at the close of the next century.

The balance of Saturday was spent in busy elections to boards and offices as well as in planning the next year's meetings. Sunday was a day of ecumenical Baptist worship with a special communion service attended by a large number of persons. Denominational communion was a common occurrence at this time even among Baptists. This practice would later be criticized as heretical by the Landmark Movement which in its views limited communion participation to only those who were members of the church in which it was being conducted. The final session of the convention on Monday was ill-attended—more than seventy per cent of the delegates had returned home. "Busywork" was conducted, such as applying to the State of Georgia for an incorporation charter. W. B. Johnson closed the meeting with prayer and then a hymn was sung—the only reference to any music at this first meeting.

Alongside the Methodist Episcopal Church, South, founded on May 1, 1845, emerged the Southern Baptist Convention. Unfortunately, the context of these founding days and the major reason for the appearance of these two new denominations on the religious scene would never be forgotten. One of these traditions would fortunately join hands with others at a future time to form the United Methodist Church while the other would almost praise itself in its separateness. Some member churches, such as Savannah Baptist Church, would be forced to wrestle seriously with the consequences and theological implications of this separation because, from the start, this church would have ecumenical roots and commitments.

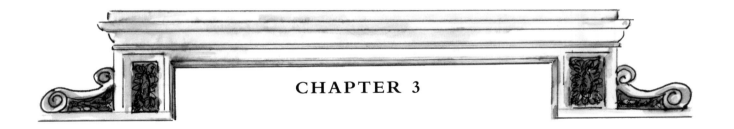

ORIGINS AND EARLY DAYS OF THE BAPTIST CHURCH IN SAVANNAH

Georgia was the last of the original thirteen colonies. English settlers had begun to hew out their kingdom in the wildernesses of New England and Virginia as early as 1607 and 1620 respectively. The charter for the Colony of Georgia was not even granted until 1732. James Edward Oglethorpe and twenty other well-to-do gentlemen petitioned King George II in mid-1730 for a tract of land "on the south-west of Carolina for settling poor persons of London." The wheels of politicians grind exceedingly slowly, however, and the charter was not granted until the passage of two years. The trustees would have control of the colony for twenty-one years and at that time it would become a royal colony. The "poor persons" original plan was scuttled and those who were eventually on board the ship *Ann* were a cross section of the English population—there was really no large debtor element. The ship sailed on November 17, 1732, with circa 120 settlers including Oglethorpe and one minister, Henry Herbert. Arriving off Charles Town on January 13, 1733, the settlers remained there while Oglethorpe scouted out a likely place to settle. His view of the Yamacraw Bluff and a friendly encounter with Tomo-Chi-Chi, the Yamacraw Indian Chief, resulted in his decision to settle at that site. After returning to Carolina with his news, Oglethorpe and all the settlers arrived at the bluff on February 12, 1733. That evening a town of four tents marked the beginning of the Georgia colony. Sources vary in their reports, but at least two Baptists were among the number and "soon afterward" at least three were in residence—William Calvert, William Slack, and Thomas Walker.

The settlers of Carolina were indeed pleased that they now had a buffer zone between themselves and the Spaniards in Florida. More settlers were definitely needed in such a wilderness context and the trustees were active in recruiting others to come—even non-British. Within thirteen months the earliest Salzburger Lutherans had arrived and had been served breakfast by a Jew from Frankfurt, Benjamin Sheftall. From the start, the few Baptists present were in an ecumenical setting where unity and cooperation were valued. In a way, the colony of Georgia was a "lively experiment" not too unlike Rhode Island and Pennsylvania. Georgia could become a refuge for religious pilgrims in search of "place" and escape from persecution. The two decades as a colony of the Crown witnessed an established church in Georgia, the Church of England. However, even during this period widespread toleration and a general acceptance of the ecumenical context existed. Following the crown period, Georgia, along with the other states of the new United States, was committed to the principles of the separation of church and state and religious liberty. This was no radical change for Georgia as it was for Virginia and Massachusetts, which eventually gave up on the idea of a state church in 1833. Baptists really never suffered religious persecution in Georgia and were better fitted for rapid growth patterns in such a frontier setting. Their presence in Savannah was simply one more part of the ecumenical spectrum.

Separate, Particular, General, Regular, Particular-Regular, Seventh Day—the variety of terms which refer to Baptist life in the New World is descriptive of fragmentation in the midst of some unity. All this is part of the background of the emergence of formal, or organized, Baptist life in Savannah. The earliest Baptist witness in Savannah was individual and these individuals expressed their religious experience certainly in ecumenical settings. One need not emphasize what divides but rather what unites in a near-mission context. Growth through conversion, charismatic leadership, and simply more persons of a particular religious persuasion moving in usually result in the birth of an organization or institution, in this case, a church. This was definitely the pattern and the warp and woof of the beginnings of the Baptist Church in Savannah (not referred to as "First" until much later).

By 1794 the population of Savannah was only circa twenty-five hundred and it was sometimes described as a "sickly hole in the woods." This "sickly hole" did pay special attention to religious organizations, however. In September 1790 an ordinance was passed by the city granting specific lots to the Episcopalians, Presbyterians, Lutherans, Baptists, and Jews. Early the next year, in January, lots were presented to the various religious bodies. Separation of church and state did not preclude such gifts in the eyes of the politicians or recipients.

In January 1791 the City of Savannah gave lot number 29, located on Washington Square, to a Baptist Society. In 1795 this lot was exchanged by the city for lot number 19 on Franklin Square and given to the trustees of the "Calvinistic Baptist Society." The named trustees were Ebenezer Hills, John Hamilton, Thomas Harrison, John H. Roberts, John Miller, Thomas Polhill, and Samuel G. Sargeant. The new lot was on the corner of Bryan and Montgomery Streets and faced Franklin Square.

By 1794 efforts had already been made in the direction of building a worship place for Baptists in Savannah even though at this

A Conjectural Picture of the Earliest Baptist Church at Savannah, drawn by Edward Vason Jones, Architect, and based on information contained in the Church Minutes of the First Baptist Church of Savannah. Built in 1795.

time there was really no formally organized and chartered church of individuals and pastor. Indeed, "church" is in essence that people of God who go everywhere during week days rather than that building to which they make tracks on weekends. Definitions notwithstanding, however, interest was afoot in getting a structure erected. Jonathan Clarke, George Mosse, Thomas Polhill, and David Adams took the lead in this project and were encouraged by the Reverend Mr. Reese, a Baptist minister from Wales who happened to be visiting the city. Contributions toward this end came from interested Baptists in South Carolina, interested citizens of Savannah, and from other denominational bodies in the city. Again, the importance of ecumenical cooperation is illustrated from the earliest beginnings. In 1795 a frame building some fifty by sixty feet began to be built on the northwest corner of Franklin Square. The handful of Baptists in Savannah now had a meeting place.

The worst enemy of frontier towns was fire. Most buildings were wooden structures and there was little, if any, fire fighting equipment. On November 29 and December 6, 1796, two especially vicious fires swept through Savannah. At least one account has judged the November 29 fire to have been the worst fire ever experienced in America. It may well have been. In only four hours 229 houses were burned to the ground. Several churches were also burned. Christ Church, the Presbyterian Church, and the Lutheran Church were all destroyed. The unfinished Baptist structure survived. The unchartered and ministerless Baptists came to the rescue and leased their structure to the Presbyterians "without a home." There was joint use of the structure by both groups—each having it half of each Sunday—until the Presbyterians completed their new church on St. James (Telfair) Square in 1800. This early pattern of "sharing" would also mark the future relationships of the Independent Presbyterian Church and the Baptist Church of Savannah.

While still using the Baptist structure, the Presbyterians succeeded in calling a "supply pastor" in 1799. Strange to the modern mind but not so strange to the frontier mind and experience, they called a Baptist minister to fill this role. One wonders whether or not the Baptists were involved in this, but no records exist to that effect. In any case, the Reverend Henry Holcombe, pastor of the Baptist church in Beaufort, South Carolina, came to serve as supply pastor for the Presbyterians. He came at a then-handsome salary of $2,000 per annum. When the Presbyterians moved to their new structure in 1800, the Baptists fortunately had a resident minister available if they so chose, and they did. Evidently during the preceding year they had been very favorably impressed with this hulk of a man, Henry Holcombe.

Henry Holcombe

This 6-foot-2-inch, 320-pound man already had a distinguished history. Born on September 22, 1762, in Prince Edward County, Virginia, Holcombe soon moved to South Carolina with his parents. As with many young children of this time, his formal education ended at age eleven. From this point on he was self-educated and became one of the finest minds as well as writers on the Baptist scene in Georgia. He entered the Revolutionary Army and rose to the rank of captain in the cavalry by the time he was twenty-two. Around 1784 Holcombe was deeply considering his own religious experience as well as his future and made a turn both denominationally and professionally. Baptized as an infant in a Presbyterian context, he decided that by belief he was a Baptist and sought adult believer's baptism. Licensed to preach upon his baptism,

Henry Holcombe
1800–1811

he was called to become the pastor at Pike Creek Baptist Church in South Carolina. Preaching for a few months as a licentiate, he was ordained on September 11, 1785, and on the same day was called upon to baptize three young men. In June 1786, among twenty-six converts, he baptized his own new wife, Frances Tanner. Within a few months he had also baptized his brother-in-law, his mother-in-law, and his own sixty-one-year-old father. Holcombe was certainly effective as an evangelist. While pastor in Pike Creek he experienced the honor of being appointed as a member of the South Carolina Convention which ratified the Constitution of the United States. In the founding days of this nation, ministers often played such political roles because they were among the brightest and best-educated minds and were widely respected by a cross section of the population. In February 1791 he was called to the Baptist church in Euhaw and in 1795 moved on to Beaufort as pastor of the Baptist church. One of his interests here was the founding of Beaufort College and he was honored by being made a trustee of this new school. In 1799 he moved yet again, this time to Savannah.

The Baptists of Savannah were indeed fortunate to have this kind of leader in 1800. The building on Franklin Square was completed and then dedicated on April 17, 1800. Doing some detective work with key words and incidents in the oldest record book of the church (the first fifty pages from 1800–1805 are for some reason missing, though there are references to those years in other materials—especially in an article in the *Savannah Morning News*, November 25, 1900, reporting the centennial celebration), a partial description of this earliest structure can be given. It was a wooden building with dimensions of fifty by sixty feet. There was a gallery, implying two stories, but probably no porch or vestibule because the record speaks of ladies sweeping sand out the door. References to fire alarms as well as members being called to worship suggest some kind of bell tower. No specific description of the tower is given. Probably it was a simple one reflecting the Baptist emphasis on simplicity. There was a lightning rod and, later, a baptistery. Oil lamps furnished light, and as with other churches of the period, the pews had doors which opened on the aisles (the pews, it must be remembered, were rented).

Henry Holcombe accepted this people's call and this humble building. The salary which was offered was a generous one for the time—$2,100 per year. The church was not formally constituted until November 26, 1800. Those original charter constituent members are worthy of being named, one of them a most recent baptizand, Mary Jones. They were as follows: Henry Holcombe (first pastor); Frances Holcombe (Henry's wife); George and Phoebe Mosse (George was the first deacon); Elias, Mary, Peter, and Elizabeth Robert; Rachael Hamilton; Eunice Hogg; Martha Stephens; Esther McKinzie; Elizabeth Stoney; Joseph and Mary Hawthorne; and the newly baptized Mary Jones (one account describes her as "the first white person who had ever received that holy rite in Savannah"). Thus, five males and eleven females became "church" in Savannah in an official way on this late day in November 1800. Oak trees do indeed eventually grow from acorns. The legal Charter of Incorporation (see appendix A) was not granted until December 10, 1801, and this time the list of applicants includes ten males: Henry Holcombe, George Mosse, William H. Mathers, John Rose, Elias Roberts [sic], Joseph Wiseman, Theodore Carlton, Joseph Davis, Isaac Sibley, and William Parker. The charter also stipulates that "George Mosse, William H. Mathers, and John Rose, and their successors in office, may be known and distinguished by the name and style of The Deacons of the Baptist Church in Savannah." Done at the State House in Louisville, it was written by the Honorable John Berrien and signed by the governor of the State of Georgia, Josiah Tattnall Sr. Holcombe would quickly become an effective leader and preacher because the membership had grown to one hundred and thirty-five by 1805. White Baptists now joined in an official way the larger Christian community of Savannah which included the First African Baptist Church, Christ Church (Episcopal), the Lutheran church, the Presbyterian church, St. John the Baptist Catholic Church and, within a few years, the Methodists, Unitarians, and Mariners' churches. There would be diversity but sensitive and important unity within that diversity. Also, these white Baptists had already been granted equal rights with other denominational bodies when in August 1801 the church was given lot number 20 in Franklin Ward by the city, bringing it to equal land given to the other groups. This allowed expansion toward the west, and a pastor's home was later built there.

This new religious community of Baptists was indeed fortunate to have such an able, intelligent, and well-rounded person as its first pastor. Initial leadership is critically important for future continuity of any religious body. Holcombe offered that kind of critical leadership which developed an early congregation with strong character.

According to Holcombe, his earliest and most dangerous problem in Savannah had to do with "stage-players." Not fifty yards from the Baptist church was a theater which Holcombe vigorously opposed. He wished to banish all theatrical performances and led the way by appealing to the city council to rid Savannah of this "Satanic force." As a result, an attempt was made by theater supporters to kill him. Delivered from this attack, Holcombe later judged that these interests "without patronage, gave ground on all hands; and virtue . . . rose into respectful notice." No other experience in Savannah would be so potentially dangerous as this one; Holcombe's life there was never physically threatened again.

Beyond the usual sermons, baptisms, marriages, funerals, and typical ministerial responsibilities, Holcombe displayed a wide range of other interests and commitments. For his time he was truly an ecumenical and progressive Baptist especially interested in education, missions, and a variety of social services.

For a self-educated man, Holcombe received unusual honors. In 1800, as reported by the *Columbian Museum and Savannah Advertiser* on December 30, he was conferred with the honorary degree of Master of Arts from Rhode Island College (now Brown University and the oldest Baptist institution of higher learning in the United States). In addition, South Carolina College (now the University of South Carolina) in 1812 conferred on him the honorary degree of Doctor of Divinity. He contributed to a number of educational interests. One of these was the publication of probably the first religious periodical in the southern United States—the *Georgia Analytical Repository*. Begun in May 1802, its stated purpose was to

> consist of religious intelligence from every part of the Christian world—a view of the origin, and present circumstances of all Religious denominations in the state—accounts of the constitution and incorporation of churches—the ordination of ministers, and opening places of worship—remarkable conversions and revivals in Religion—together with short, if judicious, essays, in prose and verse, on any Religious subject—the out-lines, or any striking parts of original and ingenious sermons—happy deaths of pious persons of all descriptions, and well-authenticated anecdotes, tending to illustrate and confirm the all-important doctrines of Divine Revelation—the Doctrines of Sovereign and free Grace.

Unfortunately only six issues appeared—four in 1802 and two in 1803. However, spade-work was thus done in ecumenical and denominational communications by use of the media of papers and periodicals.

Another educational "first" was Holcombe's role in the founding of Mount Enon Academy. Located some fifteen miles south of Augusta on one hundred and two acres of land owned by Holcombe, it finally opened in September 1807 and was the first Baptist institution of its kind in the South—surely in the background of the later Mercer University. The school was in active operation for nearly four years, declining when Holcombe left Georgia to go to Philadelphia.

Holcombe also had social and organizational interests. In a sense he was the founder of the Savannah Female Orphan Asylum, an institution committed to the care and education of orphaned females. He was also sensitive to certain errors in the penal code of Georgia. He urged revision of this code to distinguish between the seriousness of the crime and the appropriateness of the penalty. Some minor crimes were being punished with the death penalty which should have been taken care of with an incarceration system of penitentiaries. In this case he attempted to be one of the consciences of the state and urged moral and merciful legislation in relation to penalties.

Baptist cooperation through appropriate organization was another interest. In 1802 he sensed early on the need for cooperative ventures on the local as well as state levels. After numerous efforts he succeeded in bringing the Savannah church, the Newington church, and three black churches together in an organized association in southeast Georgia. The Savannah Association would shortly thereafter become the Savannah River Association and would reflect early Baptist commitment to associational affiliation with a constellation of denominational and some ecumenical goals. Holcombe was also one of the driving forces behind a series of meetings in Powelton in 1802 and 1803 resulting in the "General Committee," the seed for the later Georgia Baptist Convention of 1822.

Holcombe was widely known and appreciated in Savannah. Reflective of American civil religion, the town council of January 6, 1800, resolved on the occasion of the death of George Washington that Holcombe be requested to preach a special funeral sermon. On January 19 Holcombe preached such a sermon generously honoring the first president of the United States, and a large number of Savannah citizens attended the service. At a later time the sermon was published and sold for $.18$\frac{1}{4}$ by Seymour and Woolhopter, on the Bay (see appendix B).

A near perfect example of nineteenth-century American civil religion, the sermon's text was "Know ye not that there is a great man fallen" (2 Samuel 3:38). Praising Washington as God's "illustrious servant," Holcombe carefully traced his life, mental abilities, and educational accomplishments. The Baptist Rhode Island College (later, Brown University) was praised for conferring the LL.D. degree on Washington in 1790. Depicted as greater than Alexander the Great, Washington was also described as a supremely pious man and an excellent illustration of ideal Christianity. Holcombe then called upon his listeners and readers to imitate the virtuous and spiritual examples set by the late president. Closing with a flowery prayer, he confessed: "Though we mourn, we do not murmur; nor is our sorrow like theirs who have no hope." He finally urged that religion should permeate the new nation—"this favored land."

Holcombe evidently took literally the biblical injunction concerning "replenishing the earth"—he was the husband of one wife but the father of ten children, seven sons and three daughters. Infant mortality was high in those days and three of the sons died as infants. Holcombe was survived by his other four sons and three daughters.

For a brief time in 1805 Holcombe was privileged to have an assistant pastor, unusual for the time and situation. He was Joseph Clay Jr., a Virginia gentleman with a most prestigious background. An honor graduate of Princeton, he studied law in Georgia and became a U.S. district judge in Georgia as well as a trustee of the University of Georgia. Under the influence of Holcombe he was converted and baptized while in his thirties. At this time he resigned his judgeship and decided to pursue the Christian ministry. Licensed to preach in 1802 and ordained in 1804, it appears that he became assistant pastor of the Savannah Baptist church in early 1805. Extant records first mention him on February 10, 1805, upon the occasion of his preaching a sermon as well as announcing the excommunication (see the chapter on discipline) of a member because of public drunkenness and use of profanity. It was Clay who first suggested to the church that no one be quickly admitted and baptized—that there be a waiting period and a careful investigation of the candidate. Due to his influence, every candidate for baptism was given the choice of being baptized in the Savannah River (the usual site was Pooler's Wharf) or in the church baptistery. In May 1805 Clay resigned his position but remained in Savannah for awhile and sometimes preached as well as assisted with church ordinances. In early 1806 he requested a letter of dismissal but evidently his trip north was delayed. The letter was granted in April 1807 to the First Baptist Church of Boston where he succeeded the famous Samuel Stillman. Following such a strong pastor presented numerous problems, and in 1809, following ill health, he resigned from his position. He never regained his health and died in Boston in January 1811.

Holcombe not only took care of the spiritual needs of this steadily growing community of Baptists, but he also managed many of the business and temporal affairs of the church. Church records note, however, that in May 1807 he requested relief from all these burdens and expressed his wish that he be allowed to "give his exclusive attention to the appropriate duties of his office, as preaching the Word and administering the ordinance of Christ; the exercise of Gospel discipline, and visiting my Christian friends whenever sent for as their minister. . . . " He wished to back away from some of the busywork which had "filled my head, heart, and hands for the last twenty-two years." He deserved such relief.

Successful ministries are often foreshortened by calls to other churches. From June through July 1810 the Baptist church in Beaufort urged the Savannah church and Holcombe himself to consider making a change. This church wanted Holcombe back and Savannah had him! A long and involved letter stated the numerous reasons including "a state of Schism and innovation" and a pastor who had left them in a "destitute and widowhood situation." The letter pled with Savannah: "We request you to give up your Pastor to become our Pastor once more." In other words they needed a very strong and charismatic leader to mend their shattered congregation. Savannah answered quickly and at length: "So far is his usefulness from appearing to be at an end, we are happy to find that it continues unabated." In other words, we need him here and, have faith, God will provide your needs in due time. Regardless of Savannah's feelings, Beaufort sent a letter of unanimous call to Holcombe. Just as quickly Holcombe answered in a sensitive and experiential way:

> Sensible and from long and daily experience of my weakness and of the extreme delicacy which must attach to an attempt to restore your concerns to order and harmony, I tremble at the idea of embarking in your cause. Having escaped with no material loss the dangers of controversial seas, and highly relished for some years the security and

repose which a good harbor affords, I thought it would be risking much to launch my crazy bark again, and sail into conflicting billows.

Ill health as well as satisfaction in Savannah dictated the colorful language with which he basically declined. However, Holcombe would be willing to visit them briefly and try to help solve their major problems. This he did in late July, returning to Savannah in early August with a positive report on his accomplishments there.

In declining health for some time, in late 1810 Holcombe resigned as the first pastor of the Savannah Baptist Church to move to Mount Enon in an effort to recover from his sickness and to regain his strength. This charismatic "first" remained on very friendly terms with the church at this time and even returned on January 20, 1811, to preach and administer the Lord's Supper. The leaving was somewhat tainted, however, by a situation that began in April and was not resolved until early August. The situation involved money matters and caused friendly yet at times heated correspondence between the church and Holcombe. Holcombe had declined another invitation to become pastor in Beaufort as well as one from the Baptist church in Boston. A third invitation, however, would not be refused. A unanimous call from an eleven-hundred-member first church in Philadelphia was an offer he could not refuse! At this time, then, Holcombe requested a dismissal letter from Savannah Baptist to Philadelphia First Baptist. In late July the correspondence became rather heated because Savannah would not send such a letter until Holcombe could give "satisfactory explanations" to the church concerning some money matters involving some five hundred and seventy-five dollars. These funds related to building materials, a loan to Mount Enon Academy, and the poor funds of the church. Long letters were exchanged on this subject. In one of them Holcombe spoke of "not inconsiderable trials of my private life" and of a "cloud" of troubles. In a mid-July letter Holcombe was virtually overcome with emotion: "O Savannah! Savannah! Can I forget thee. O Individual! Dear individual of this most loved society, can I forget thee! No. No. No. No. Never can I forget thee." The church continued to refuse to give the letter of dismissal until their specific questions had been answered. Holcombe's lengthy and detailed answers came in early August with some complaints that anyone would think or insinuate that he had cheated the church out of a few hundred dollars. Concluding his detailed explanations and strong words, he left the matter to their decision and signed himself, "I remain, my Dear Brethren, I trust *immovably* yours." The church, acting quickly, completely accepted his explanations and apologized for any misunderstanding and then sent him a copy of the saccharine sweet dismissal letter to Philadelphia.

Holcombe was a great first pastor but hardly the saint as described in the letter: "*Meek and humble, benevolent and humane, fervent in prayer. . . . singular talents, gifts, and graces. . . . valuable, rare, and singula*r character." Holcombe doubtless blushed as he read this vivid equivalent of an apology for any misinterpreted accusations. Late in August Holcombe extended a cordial appreciation for their "generous" letter. Thus, a positive closure between a congregation and its first pastor was achieved. This would not be the case with the second pastor.

In early 1812 Holcombe moved to Philadelphia and served First Baptist Church there until his death in 1824. He was less active in civic affairs there but continued to be a productive writer. His positions on several issues late in his career distressed some of his friends, though one of them is certainly commendable for its idealism. For one, he became an ultra-Calvinist and opposed foreign missions. For another, he began to oppose the whole concept of war, becoming a pacifist, for he believed that war was definitely contrary to the very essence of the spirit of Christianity. Though not so public a figure in Philadelphia as he had been in Savannah, his funeral notation observed: "The whole city did honor to his memory; it is said that the concourse of people in attendance was, for numbers, such as was never before seen in Philadelphia." Though certainly no saint, Holcombe was a godsend as the first pastor of those who called themselves Baptist in the young city of Savannah.

Savannah and its population suffered numerous problems in the second decade of the nineteenth century. War, unrest, disease, and fires crisscrossed the historical land-scape. The War of 1812 disrupted commerce and personal lives. Fires, both accidental and due to arson, took their toll. Smallpox and yellow fever always lurked just around the corner, with mild as well as catastrophic effects. Life in Savannah was perennially subject to disruption—blankets of security were always in danger of being suddenly jerked away. Churches, too, were affected by all of this.

For our purposes here, "beginnings" will include attention to the second pastor of the church, especially in view of his later major role in the birth of the Southern Baptist Convention in 1845. William Bullein Johnson (1782–1862) was a native South Carolinian, born on John's Island, the son of the Reverend Joseph Johnson.

William Bullein Johnson

Following Holcombe's retreat to Mount Enon, the church came together on December 9, 1810, "fasting . . . in order to supplicate the throne of Grace for direc-tion to our procuring a Pastor." Churches then as today usually experienced interim periods between pastors using whatever persons were available to fill the pulpit, administer communion, and baptize candidates. Such periods were certainly times which developed strong lay leadership or which sometimes witnessed church decline. Calling a new pastor was not an easy or immediate matter and congregations often tried and failed. On February 17, 1811, the church unanimously agreed to call the Reverend Brantley of Augusta as pastor. Humbly, the church wrote among other things the following: "We have but little pecuniary advantage to induce your residence among us: Our Preacher has hitherto been supported from the sale of the pews and occasional voluntary contribution." Brantley was offered the flexible amount of somewhere between $1,000 and $2,000. By March 15 the church was told that Brantley had accepted a call to the Beaufort church. For several months following it appears that Charles O. Screven acted as a kind of interim pastor—preaching, communing, and baptizing.

On May 17 the church extended a call to W. B. Johnson, a young man who had been recommended by Holcombe himself. Again, the church was not sure about salary, but it promised that if the sale of pews did not bring in $1,500, "we will then use our best endeavors to collect the deficiency." At least there was not as much flexibility as in the offer to Brantley. Johnson had been converted in a revival in 1804, had served a church in Euhaw, South Carolina, from 1805 to 1809, and had been in Columbia, South Carolina, for two years preaching to college students. On August 23 Johnson wrote favorably to Savannah but requested a delay until November for his formal answer which would probably be "yes." He wanted to be sure that his Association would replace him in his ministry and that when that occurred he would come to Savannah in January 1812. Quickly the church responded positively and promised to

**William Bullein
Johnson
1811–1815**

wait on him, but also added that if his successor came in November, "it would highly gratify us if you could come to us by the first of December."

On November 9, 1811, Johnson wrote his formal letter of acceptance. A long letter of complimentary rhetoric concluded with almost a prediction of the future: "Let us endeavor to nip in the bud the risings of controversy, which are the bane of peace and brotherly love." Perhaps Johnson was speaking from secondhand experience of Baptist controversy, but he would learn soon enough of firsthand controversy—and in this case it would lead to his own angry departure from Savannah. But these late days in 1811 were the prehoneymoon days and he urged that he might "be daily renewed with might in the inner man to be valiant for the Lord of Hosts and successful in his cause."

Either Johnson's memory was dimming by 1860 in a letter reflecting his move to Savannah or later controversy garbled his memory, for he reported in 1860 that he moved to Savannah in December 1812. The church Minute Book for December 22, 1811, reports as follows: "Our Rev. and Beloved Brother Wm. B. Johnson arrived in this city with his family, but too late to preach this day." Thomas F. Williams had mainly filled the pulpit during the recent interim, but on December 8 the church heard a familiar voice in the pulpit—that of Holcombe as he "bid us an affectionate adieu." On December 29, 1811, the church clerk noted: "Our beloved Pastor preached his two first sermons to us in the fore and afternoon of this day, highly satisfactory." The *Savannah Evening Ledger* reported on April 23, 1812, that Johnson and his family were living in a "commodious dwelling house" in Oglethorpe Ward where Holcombe and family had previously lived. Even where ministers lived was a part of the lively local social scene!

Savannah had a young pastor—Johnson was only twenty-nine years of age. Although a man of tremendous vision, he would also prove himself eventually to be immature and rather arrogant in some religious views. At this time, however, he was definitely committed to education, missions, and ecumenism—at least within Baptist circles. Early on, January 19, 1812, he gave communion to "members of sister churches present." Strident Landmarkism had not yet been born with its separatistic and sheerly local view of proper communion. And in February of the same year he committed himself to beginning a missionary fund in the church after he attended the meeting of the General Committee of Baptists at Mount Enon. Within a few weeks Johnson had already implemented the passage of a motion that every three weeks every member would give $.06¼(!) to the treasurer for missions.

Aware of the threat of war, Johnson and members joined with other denominations in a day of fasting and prayer on February 12. The nation stood now on the threshold of the War of 1812 and ecumenical prayers were offered in hopes of peace. By August these same Baptists and others were complying with the government's request for a day of humiliation and prayer, asking God's blessing on the nation in this time of trial. The trappings of American civil religion are perhaps most vivid during the outside threat of war.

Before he had been there one year, Johnson, perhaps sensitive to local missions, was beginning to urge a different plan of finance than the renting of pews. He pled: "It might be more to the glory of God to have our pews free." However, pew rentals from June 1811 to December 1812 produced $2,121, a substantial percentage of the total income. Committee compromise had to be achieved. The committee successfully suggested that the three back pews be left free and that the word "free" in capital letters be painted on the entrance doors to these pews. The other pews would be rented for $30 and $40 per year. Protective finance as well as evangelistic mission were both accommodated.

Johnson often arranged for itinerant ministers to preach as well as lecture in the church. On December 16 and 19, 1813, Savannah was fortunate to have the famous Luther Rice to preach and lecture before the Baptist congregation. Sent out as a Congregationalist minister to India in 1812 along with the equally famous Adoniram Judson, Rice and Judson became convinced of Baptist views before they arrived in India. Once there, Judson remained while Rice returned home to attempt to generate Baptist interest in missions. Die-hard Calvinism had rejected foreign missions as interfering with God's plan. Now, a modified Calvinism in Rice and others agitated for creative world missions. His wide travels and charismatic enthusiasm were eminently successful in this regard and Johnson had great vision in bringing him to Savannah in 1813. In fact, in May 1814 both men were involved in the founding of the General Convention of the Baptist Denomination in the United States for Foreign Missions— more popularly named the Triennial Convention, the first national organization of Baptists in the United States. Luther Rice's missionary efforts truly composed an important turning point in Baptist history. Johnson himself would later serve as president of this Convention from 1841 to 1844. Johnson certainly must have punctuated many of Rice's statements in Savannah with decisive "amens." Church Minutes also reflect Johnson's interest in education, especially in a notation of July 1, 1814, after Johnson's return from meetings in Philadelphia. In relation to the Convention,

> He . . . briefly stated the success that resulted from the meeting . . . and the hopeful prospect of sending the Gospel into the heathen Land and of Establishing a seminary of learning in some central place in the United States for the purpose of Educating young ministers called of God to preach the Gospel.

These ideas were certainly the seeds of the later founding of schools such as Mercer University, Furman University, and The Southern Baptist Theological Seminary.

Johnson did not even complete three full years as pastor. Unfortunately, his last three months were critically marred by controversy in large part caused by his own immaturity, arrogance, and disrespect for congregational collegiality. From late July to late October 1814 the church was in turmoil and as a result would suffer its first schism. Church membership would be reduced from seventy-eight to sixty-six; however, within a few years most of the schismatic members would return home.

Johnson had become convinced "with prayer to God for right understanding," that the New Testament required doing all of God's business on Sunday. At this time, all business sessions of the church were conducted on Friday. On July 22 Johnson urged that to continue the present practice would be unscriptural. A decision on the matter was deferred. On August 5 Johnson expanded his views to include weekly communion on Sunday as well as a weekly collection for the poor and unfortunate. The church opposed all of these views. By August 26 Johnson shared a letter with the church concerning his views which he believed to be "the mind of Christ as to the constitution, order, and authority of the churches." Although this letter was to have been entered in the Minutes, it is not presently to be found there. In early September, the church clerk (Mr. Robert) read some of his own views on the subject to the congregation and reflected that Johnson's ideas really had no scriptural authority. On September 16 a letter from the Beaufort Church was read before the Savannah congregation which also argued against the scriptural validity of Johnson's views. Discussions and presentations continued through September and into October. On October 14

Henry Holcombe entered the picture in an advisory capacity disagreeing with Johnson. Johnson became indignant, stating that Holcombe had "no right to interfere with the business of this church." Things came to a conclusion on October 16 when the church officially rejected Johnson's views. At this point, "Mr. Johnson rose up and declared himself no longer our Pastor." He withdrew his and his wife's membership and volunteered to continue to preach for three more weeks if the church wished him to do so. Then he walked out of the service with a congregation still sitting there without dismissal! The church decided at first that he should preach for three more Sundays but not to dwell on his differing views. At the business meeting on Friday, October 21, John Stillwell presented twelve names including himself and his wife, Jane, as withdrawing from church membership over this controversy. On Sunday, October 23, Johnson stated his views and "made several injudicial remarks, pronouncing the church a corrupt body, etc." He then read a letter concerning the twelve schismatics with an obvious attempt to gain more followers. The church met on Wednesday and drafted a letter to Johnson suspending his services immediately. There is a hiatus in the church's Minutes of some six weeks with one notation that the clerk (Robert) was ill. There followed on Sundays a series of visiting preachers during an interim period of reflection and healing. By December 23 the church was urging conciliation with those members who had withdrawn as well as attempting to "reclaim them." After a brief stay in Savannah, Johnson returned to Columbia.

Interestingly, in late 1815 (November 18), the church addressed a letter to their association asking a question which arose out of their disagreement with Johnson. In essence the question dealt with the validity of baptism performed by Johnson after he had rejected the views of the church he served and removed himself from that church. If those members baptized by him joined another Baptist church, could they be admitted without baptism "in a due and regular manner?" No answer to the question is found in the Minutes.

On January 1, 1820, at a Saturday church conference meeting, a letter was read from Johnson as well as one from his church in Columbia asking for a closer relationship and stating that Johnson had given up his differing views. The Minutes reflect an abiding resentment and yet near total forgiveness of Johnson: "The church *almost* unanimously agreed to readmit brother Johnson to union and fellowship with themselves." Johnson had entered the realm of realistic politics and had made peace with his fellow Baptists. Savannah Baptists could forgive but they would probably never forget. In 1831 when they moved into a new building, the cornerstone document listing pastors misspelled his name—Johnston. And in 1900 at the centennial celebration no mention of his name was made in the *Morning News* account.

Johnson, of course, went on to greater glory from Savannah. He was the only Baptist who served as president of the Triennial Convention (1841–45) and the Southern Baptist Convention. In fact he was the first president of the latter convention and led in the organizing process as well as in composing the plan of organization itself. He successfully supported a more centralized plan rather than a more loosely structured societal one. One can only surmise at this point that he remained more committed to hierarchical structure and more rejecting of collegial cooperation and appreciation as he had in Savannah as a young man. Perhaps the bit of arrogance and belief in pastoral authority was a carryover to the founding days of the Southern Baptist Convention. If so, then Johnson is one of the watersheds for the late twentieth-century controversy within the Southern Baptist Convention in which the president has such critical raw power (not to say moral authority) of appointment. It is true as well that the persons at the heart of the fundamentalist political takeover of the Southern Baptist Convention also seem to be committed more to the authority of the local minister as opposed to collegiality and the principle of the priesthood of every believer.

The founding days had been extremely interesting ones for Savannah Baptists. They were indeed fortunate to have such an ecumenical and mature founding pastor committed to all those principles which would become the essence of the Baptist movement within the United States. And, then, with their second young and comparatively inexperienced and immature pastor, they enjoyed the honeymoon days only to experience the grief of divorce within a few years. The congregation refused to be blackmailed by ministerial authority even if it meant the further grief of early schism. The young congregation was finding its own maturity in its continuing commitment to those major principles which make Baptists Baptist—especially the collegiality and mutual respect of a covenanting congregation which balances the freedom of the priesthood of every believer with the spirit of a covenanting and ecumenical community. This essence of religious experience would mark its first two hundred years of historical pilgrimage.

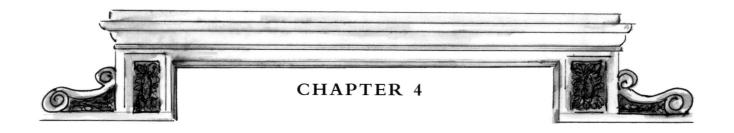

CHAPTER 4

PASTORAL LEADERSHIP AND BUILDING CHANGES

This volume attempts a chronological as well as thematic approach. The chronological history is best told, perhaps, by means of rehearsing the ministerial leadership and major contributions as well as problems of each minister. Although a church's history is certainly not dictated by its pastors, the history does nucleate around these ordained men and their unique talents. Savannah has definitely had its share of charismatic and effective ministerial leaders.

No complete list will be given here, though this will be attempted in appendix H. Baptist churches often have interim ministers between "pastors"; however, more attention will be given here to "pastors" who usually had longer tenures of office, though some of these others will be mentioned. Another difficulty, especially during the first one hundred years, is that Baptist churches, including Savannah, usually gave "annual" calls, with the beginning and ending date more often being November 1. Perhaps due to this circumstance more than to any other, more than 50 percent of the pastors who served the church are named during the first fifty-nine years of the church's history. And, at least one of them (Thomas Meredith) left when the church refused to give him more than an annual call. Perhaps this was intended to protect the church from a minister who proved in the short-term to be unwanted, but it was still a demeaning experience for the pastor as well as a practice that might result in greater political astuteness and less of gospel truth. Later, Baptists properly gave up this practice in the main.

Following Johnson's departure, a series of persons filled the pulpit and administered the ordinances, including Brantley, Sweat, Williams, and Screven. By June 2, 1815, the church was beginning to commit itself to Benjamin Screven, but obviously due to its recent experience with Johnson, wanted more information. In a letter it urged that "we wish to understand one another well." The church desired a few friendly visits and conversations on such issues as discipline, frequency of the Lord's supper, letters of dismissal, and conduct of business. Their letter expressed a church "poor in temporalities" and in "extreme need in our forlorn and embarrassed situation." An almost promise was made that no one else would be considered during the period of getting to know one another and that the call would be extended in late October. Screven was certainly already "licensed" to preach and had often done so. Now, he would be "ordained" to serve this specific church. Baptists in the colonial and frontier periods carried with them a great deal of baggage from their Congregationalist background. One part of this baggage had to do with ordination. A minister without a church was really not ordained, for one needed the reaffirmation and commitment of a congregation in order to be "ordained" to a specific task. In the records, then, there are often references to "the ordination of our pastor" when in modern times we would use the word "installation." In a real sense even today, a minister without a church is really not ordained. In any case, on October 29 Screven was "ordained" as pastor of the church in the presence of four other Baptist ministers—W. T. Brantley, James Sweat, Charles Screven, and Isaac Nichols. The clerk reported that "a very numerous congregation attended." The next month the church reported to the Savannah River Baptist Association that it had a pastor and that "we again begin to resume our health generally," and that with sixty-nine members (see appendix C).

Benjamin Screven

Early in 1816 Screven revived the practice of conducting prayer meeting once a week in homes and also urged the teaching of Baptist doctrine and practice by families at home, followed by teaching and examination of the children of the church once a week by the pastor. Thus, Baptists committed themselves to religious education through the medium of catechism. Screven also pioneered in giving special attention to music. In late January 1816 "the church agreed to employ Mr. White [as] Master of Musick, to lead in Psalmody in this Church, and for his services agreed to make him some compensation." Volunteers had helped prior to this, but now professionals would serve.

By September Screven and his wife were sick and felt the need to leave Savannah to recover. They retreated to his plantation in South Carolina (thirty miles away) and promised the church to come back and preach twice a month. For the next several months a number of persons preached, including Luther Rice on a return visit, again raising funds for missions. On December 21 the church was informed that the deacons had invited a Mr. Potter to fill the pulpit for the next six months. The next week Screven was in town, a bit miffed because he had to learn from a newspaper account that he was no longer pastor. He objected that the church had acted improperly. Duly chastised, the church agreed and apologized, though urging that its motives were pure—it wanted to save Screven from the burden of returning thirty miles twice monthly. Forgiveness was exchanged by each side and the church agreed to grant him a letter of dismissal to a church nearer his plantation. The next six months would see at least nine different preachers filling the pulpit including Jesse Mercer, the man who would become the first president of the Georgia Baptist Convention in 1822, a position he held for the next nineteen years. One preacher hailed from as far away as New York.

Until October 1817 the church was barely existing. The associational letter of October reported only forty-eight members. On October 19 Screven was recalled as minister for the next year on an "occasional" basis as his health allowed. Whenever he was not present, which was often, a Brother Armstrong preached. Quite often during

**Benjamin Screven
1815–1818**

this period the Minutes sadly note, "No service this day"—"no meeting this day." During this period, often there were not even enough itinerant ministers to fill pulpit needs. From February 6 to June 18 the church records show a gap with only the notation—"our meetings were regular with one exception."

James Sweat

On August 15, 1818, the Minutes simply note: "Brother Sweat was called by the Church to take the pastoral of the same." In September Sweat accepted and by October Savannah Baptists had their fourth full-time pastor. In his mid-fifties James Sweat had been baptized in 1785 by none other than Henry Holcombe. He had labored in the Euhaw church where he was especially successful as an evangelist in converting new members. Jesse Campbell, however, did him no great favor in describing him as a "Godly man of moderate but useful talents." As a teenager he had fought in the Revolutionary War in the second siege of Savannah and now, forty years later, returned to the city. Useful talents were also shown in siring children, for with his first wife Joanna (she died in 1798) he had four children and with his second wife Susannah (she died in 1820 of the dreaded yellow fever) he fathered seven children. At the age of fifty-six he married his third wife, Margaret, who bore no children.

Elias Robert had done an excellent job as clerk of the church and had kept full notes on all the transactions, evidently, for the Minutes are full and complete. Due to illness he was replaced by John Carr who had "moderate" talents. Even the excelling historian, Mabel LaFar, judges that, "The minutes from now on [December 25, 1818] in this book are hard to read and poorly written. Brother Carr did not record enough of the proceedings of the assemblies." The present writer certainly concurs, and, to be sure, is thankful along with LaFar for that vast majority of clerks who were so committed to recording complete and clear minutes.

The Baptist Church in Savannah had been active in associational work from the start. In 1802 the Savannah Association had been organized with five churches. Henry Holcombe served as the first moderator and Elias Robert as the first clerk. In 1806 the association changed its name to the Savannah River Association and the number of churches grew to fourteen. In 1818 yet another name change occurred when it became known as the Sunbury Association. The next year Sweat served as moderator. In 1820 the Association met in Savannah with Sweat again serving as moderator. He drafted a circular letter to all member churches and spoke of the "declining state of religion" as being "truly lamentable" and of sinners as "careless and stupid as ever." His minimal public relations skills were evidenced by the slow growth in his own church.

Pastors need homes. By April 1820 the church was looking into building such a structure. By February 1821 it was deeply in debt as a result of this venture during hard times. The church, as well as the city, experienced a "pause of three months" between August and October 1820 when the city was hard hit by yellow fever, an ever-present threat in the port city. The entire church conference of June 24, 1821, was devoted to a full discussion of the problem of the church's debt. The committee reported in detail how it had spent far more on the project than was first anticipated. The cost had been $3,262.41¼ and the unpaid debt remained at $1,212.82. In order to avoid a legal battle over this debt, the committee urged an annual subscription and an every-member canvass. The church accepted the plan and was close to owning another piece of property as well as a house for its pastor. However,

James Sweat
1819–1822

it committed itself to a three-year loan and a mortgage on the house and lot (see appendix D for a reflection on 1821).

The church conference of December 19, 1821, was solemn and tense. Sweat had evidently lost his temper on some matter. He reported that he had expressed himself "in an unguarded and unchristian manner" and though he felt God had forgiven him, there was a "dissatisfaction prevailing in the minds of a part of the church." This being the case, he decided it was best and proper to resign immediately. No other comment is found in the Minutes—not even an appreciation statement. This was one rather sad Christmas season for both church and former pastor.

Supply ministers, including W. T. Brantley of Augusta, filled the pulpit. Virtually no Minutes were kept for the first two months of 1822. By early March the church had invited the later-famous Basil Manly to be its pastor but he declined. However, the church received several letters of recommendation in relation to Thomas Meredith of New Bern, North Carolina. By early April the church had heard Meredith preach several times and was so favorably impressed that it issued a unanimous call on April 21 (see appendix E). The call extended the time beyond one year—to January 1, 1824. Interestingly, the manner of voting was that all the "yes" votes were instructed to remain seated while all the "no" votes were to stand. No one stood! Meredith responded positively on April 25.

Thomas Meredith

Born in Bucks County, Pennsylvania, in 1795, Meredith, a University of Pennsylvania graduate, had moved to North Carolina in 1819. An immature young man in his late twenties, Meredith early on experienced the negative results of rumors "being in circulation that would prove injurious to our beloved pastor's character and usefulness." These rumors continued from October 1822 until March 1823. Although the substance of these rumors is uncertain, they were serious enough for him to quit his responsibilities until action was taken. A committee appointed to deal with the problem concluded that Meredith was wrong to withdraw his services and urged him to be mature and not act so precipitously. Meredith rejected this suggestion and designated this censure as "*illegal and unjust*." A new investigation declared that both sides had misunderstood one another and that forgiveness was needed to heal the matter. By early April this healing had taken place and Meredith resumed his pastoral responsibilities. A young pastor and a young congregation showed signs of partial maturing together.

By September Meredith and the congregation were again at odds with one another. Though the church agreed to give him another yearly call, Meredith rejected it with four pages of reasons. Primarily, he declared himself against the idea of a yearly call as demeaning to the individual, and he objected to the sale of pews as the main source of income toward a pastor's salary. Meredith opined: "I cannot consent to place the subsistence of my family upon a vague and uncertain income." The church rejected his argument and even refused to grant him a dismissal letter though it did extend such an offer to his wife. On November 1 Meredith responded: "The proceedings of the church have been so ridiculous and corrupt I have no further fellowship with her and I wish to be free of all charge from the present evils. . . ." On December 6 he "renounced" his pastoral charge. An external Council from sister churches urged that pastor and people "exercise mutual forgiveness and consign all of the causes of controversy to

Thomas Meredith
1822–1824

oblivion." This was not to be, however, and in February a call was extended to Henry J. Ripley to become the new pastor.

Savannah Baptists had experienced the hard luck of growing pains with two of its first five pastors—both immature young men. Perhaps the church itself was inexperienced as well, but in essence the young pastors seemed to have a long way to go in achieving maturity as well. Interestingly, both Johnson and Meredith did achieve "greater glory." Savannah had been an early training ground for them. Johnson, of course, became the architect of the Southern Baptist Convention and Meredith became "Mr. Baptist" back in North Carolina. Among other things, he was one of the founders of the Baptist State Convention there in 1830 (drawing up its constitution), he helped to form Wake Forest Institute (later, "University"), he founded the *Baptist Interpreter* in 1832 (in 1835 it became the *Biblical Recorder*), and in 1838 he urged the founding of a "female academy." In 1909 the Baptist school for women in North Carolina was renamed Meredith College in his honor. Indeed, Johnson and Meredith had rough beginnings and so did the Baptist congregation in Savannah.

Henry Ripley declined the call as did Ben. M. Hill of New Haven, Connecticut. The church then turned to Henry O. Wyer of the Savannah Missionary Society for a six-month period to June 1825. Wyer filled this interim but spoke of the "past difficulties of the church" and "its present low conditions." Though expressing honestly these feelings, Wyer finally accepted their call. On November 6 "the Rev. Henry O. Wyer was ordained pastor of this church" (note again the use of the word "ordained" in the same sentence in which he is referred to as "reverend") with T. B. How, pastor of the Independent Presbyterian Church, delivering the charge.

Henry O. Wyer

Wyer would serve Savannah Baptists at two different times, 1825–1833 and 1843–1845. Such a two-time pastorship was unusual and perhaps spoke of his greater maturity, for he was in his forties when he first came. Educated at Columbian College (later George Washington University) in the District of Columbia, he was described as a man with a deep intellect, a "sonorous voice," and a sanctified heart. He must have been an effective pulpiteer, for within four years of his coming the membership had grown from 63 to 131. Wyer had an electric, charismatic personality. Savannah was certainly ready for a sustained and mature pastorate. Wyer agreed to the traditional one-year's call without argument.

By July 4, 1828, the congregation was encouraged by so much numerical growth under Wyer that it adopted a flowery resolution appreciative of his contributions, promised another yearly call, and granted him four months off "during the unhealthy part of the year"—the summer. In this same year the deep commitment of Josiah Penfield, deacon and treasurer, was illustrated in the generous contributions in his last will and testament. He designated $2,500 toward the erection of a new place of worship as well as for work to be done on the parsonage. He also left $2,500 for the education of young men for the ministry to the Georgia Baptist Convention on condition that the Convention would match his gift with an equal amount. It did and this became the seed money for the later foundation of Mercer University (see photo, next page).

By early 1829 the city had given assurances of new lots for a new church—lots twenty-seven and twenty-eight of Brown Ward. In April the church had its title deeds for its next location. Though called and accepted in September as pastor, in November Wyer

**Henry O. Wyer
1825–1833**

Administration Building, Mercer University—Josiah Penfield provided the seed money for Mercer University in his will of 1828. Photo courtesy of Mercer University.

shared that the Augusta Baptist Church was interested in him and that he had experienced a "cold" shoulder by some of the Savannah members, especially in relation to his absenteeism in the summer months. The church responded by literally begging him to stay with overly flowery language. Impressed, Wyer closed off discussions with Augusta.

Savannah was fortunate that Wyer decided to remain, for the congregation was headed in the direction of a building program on the new lots granted by the city on Chippewa Square. On February 2, 1831, the cornerstone of the "New Baptist Church now erecting in this city" was laid and beneath it a number of important historical materials including the names of the Building Committee, the Covenant, the Constitution, and the Bylaws of the church (see appendix F). Funds raised for the purpose of construction included Penfield's legacy, monies collected during a fair conducted by "ladies of various denominations," "subscriptions of benevolent citizens," and the sale of the former lots and church building to the First African Baptist Church.

In the midst of fund-raising and the building process itself, the Sunbury Association met in Savannah in November 1831 with extended preaching services. Savannah reported "occurrences happening among them, which tend to make the Christian's heart bleed"—evidently a reference to numerous cases of discipline in the congregation. The ecumenical nature of the extended services was illustrated in the offer by the Independent Presbyterian Church of the use of its building to accommodate the large crowds and of their minister doing some of the preaching. The association duly reported: "Our Paedo-Baptist brethren heartily united with us during this interesting season."

By April 1832 the congregation was worshiping and conducting business in its new church and Wyer was continuing efforts to raise funds toward paying off the debt and completing the finishing touches. Walter C. Hartridge, in his *Architecture of Savannah,* described the new structure:

The First Baptist Church was another characteristic building of the Greek Revival. In shape it was a simple temple with a flight of steps leading to the portico and a small lantern tower crowning the pediment. The portico was reduced to two columns, a small room being placed on either side of the entrance.

Through the years this basic building would be enlarged, remodeled, repaired, and repainted numerous times, but it would survive storms, fires, and the normal ravages of time to remain the oldest standing religious structure in Savannah. (See photograph on page 96.)

In October 1833 Wyer resigned as pastor. Prior to his resignation as well as after, the church was involved in a heated controversy with the First African Baptist Church. Associational records and the church's Minutes reflect at length on this controversy which reached its peak in 1832 and 1833. Associational records of November 1832 report: "Resolved, That the First African Church, as a member of this association, on account of its corrupt state be considered as dissolved; and that measures be adopted to constitute a new church, as a branch of the White Baptist Church." It also recommended that the Second African Church become a branch of the white Baptist church and that "we adopt measures to constitute all the African churches branches of white Baptist churches." The next year, 1833, the Association resolved:

> That this association having undoubted testimony of Andrew Marshall's holding the sentiments avowed by Alexander Campbell, now declares him and all his followers to have thrown themselves out of the fellowship of the churches of this Association and it recommends all of its faith and order to separate from them, according to the advice of the Savannah Baptist Church.

By 1837 the church as well as Marshall had been readmitted to the Association upon the assurance from Marshall that he had rejected the views of Alexander Campbell.

What had transpired?! In 1778 the First African Church had been founded by Andrew Bryan and had been among the first congregational members of the Savannah Association. His congregation had grown to over four hundred members and two daughter churches had been born. After his death, his charismatic nephew, Andrew Marshall, became pastor of the church. By 1830 the congregation had grown to over twenty-four hundred members. Within a few years evidently Marshall adopted some of the views of Alexander Campbell, who in white Baptist circles was considered as extremely heretical and certainly he had proved himself to be a threat to Baptist life and belief. For one, he believed that baptism was necessary for salvation and had caused schism in Baptist circles. Obviously, the slave issue was involved as well, with whites desiring a great deal of control over black churches. The fact that the black church was using the former white church building for "heretical" purposes poured more salt into the wound of relationships.

By January 1833 the black church on the surface agreed to place itself under the watchful eye of the white church but set down a series of conditions which actually preserved its own fundamental autonomy, a key Baptist congregational belief. It proceeded to retain Marshall and to keep its doors open for business. Offended, in August the white church tried to exert pressure by writing a letter to William T. Williams, mayor of Savannah, which was crystal clear in intent: "The individuals composing the First African Church are in part the property of our citizens, and it is for them, if they feel any interest in their everlasting or temporal welfare, to interpose and save them from the baneful influence of a designing man." There is no record of the mayor's response in the Minutes and First African Baptist Church remained open. In conclusion, the black church really did what it wanted to do and retained its self-determination. Perhaps Baptist ecclesiology was the real victor in this controversy and within this context of racial tension. In 1837 the healing process was completed when the black church was readmitted into the association. Marshall remained eminently popular, and before his death in 1856 his services had become tourist attractions, even being mentioned in the travel accounts of such European writers as Fredrika Bremer and Charles Lyell. The white Baptist Church of Savannah was forced now to deal with its own major problem in late 1833—it was once again without pastoral leadership and reported to the association that it "expressed sorrow on account of their low state of religion."

Within a few days of Wyer's resignation, the church had made contact with William T. Brantley of Philadelphia. Their offer was only half of what he was making, but he was still interested if he could supplement the salary by teaching in the Savannah Academy or privately. Correspondence continued with Brantley until late March 1834, and finally his vascillation turned negative as he recommended a Brother Malloy of Augusta to the congregation. This suggestion was not taken. On June 1 Josiah S. Law of Liberty County was finally called by a large majority on the third ballot. He assumed his duties in mid-October. Wyer's comparatively longer ministry in Savannah would be followed by a series of short tenures of office. Not until late 1859 and the coming of Sylvanus Landrum would there be a long and sustained ministry in the church.

Prior to Law's appearance, Savannah went through another siege of yellow fever. The church participated with other congregations in setting aside a day of prayer to God to "stay the Pestilence" since the mayor and his council would not do so.

Josiah S. Law

When Law arrived in October 1834 he was only twenty-five years old, but he had been well educated at the Newton Theological Seminary, a Baptist school. Later he would make a major contribution to Christian education as well as to black evangelism. At his death there were some sixty black converts of his who were awaiting baptism. His earlier contact with blacks in Savannah had not been so pleasant, for the Marshall situation was still continuing and Law urged him to withdraw or to reject his Campbellite views. News on the new church debt was positive, however, for the church owed only $1,300. Law did see to the revision of the bylaws which included the prohibitions of secular business on Sunday, dancing, and the use of "ardent spirits." Numerous discipline cases (see chapter 5) took place and in March the congregation requested Law to preach a sermon about excommunication as soon as possible. The nineteenth century would be marked by hundreds of discipline cases and numerous excommunications—a word rarely used by modern Baptists but often appearing in the nineteenth-century Minutes.

In June the Union and State Rights Society requested the use of the church building for a July 4 celebration. The church granted this one-time use but then showed great maturity in the following resolution: "Resolved, that from and after the 4th day of July, 1835, this church shall not be granted to any political party for anniversary celebrations, or for any political meetings for other purposes." One might have wished for a full presentation of the discussion concerning this motion, but the conclusion did show sensitivity to the issue of neutrality in relation to highly charged political issues. In July Law refused the call to another year of service for several reasons. First, he urged

Josiah S. Law
1834–1835

his youth and his need to do more serious study, and second, he needed a higher salary for his family's sake. Honestly, he reported: "I was told when I first came to take charge of you, that I would find you difficult to please." Continuing, he encouraged the congregation by saying he had not found this to be true. Though offering a slightly improved salary, the church could not meet his needs even though he was urged several times to remain. If needed, he would remain until the spring, but the church rejected the offer and began its balloting. Finally, on a sixth ballot it recalled Henry Wyer with the proviso that if Wyer would not accept, that "*any well educated well recommended and experienced Baptist Preacher*" be offered the same amount—$1,200. A single man would be offered $200 less. Wyer, due to his health, turned down the call and after a series of supply ministers, finally in late April 1836 Charles B. Jones was called and accepted.

Prior to Jones's call, one very interesting incident took place in relation to membership. On March 28, John Simpson, Martha Munger, and Arthur Stevens of the Third African Church applied for membership. Their stated object was "to obtain greater edefication" [*sic*]. The Membership Committee recommended that they be admitted as a "class by themselves." As might be guessed, there was long debate. As might not be guessed, they were rejected by a *small* majority.

Charles B. Jones

Jones, a more mature man in his late thirties, had been born on Wilmington Island and in early life described as having "plenty of money." After witnessing an uncle killed in a duel, he had joined the Savannah Baptist Church, was licensed, and began to preach. His tenure as pastor was only one year and following the Civil War he went to Palatka, Florida, as a missionary of the Northern Home Missionary Society. He died there in 1879.

Unusually excellent records were kept and generally preserved by the nineteenth-century white Baptists in Savannah. Some Minutes, however, were unfortunately lost or misplaced (perhaps to be rediscovered someday in some member's dusty attic trunk!). For example, there is a hiatus in the Minutes from April 1836 to April 1852. Later announcements from church clerks were evidently unsuccessful in locating the lost Minutes. They were, however, obviously available to those who planned the first centennial celebration and are reflected in the newspaper accounts of November 1900. From these reflections, the Sunbury Association Minutes, and other scattered sources, one can piece together a number of important matters concerning pastoral leadership during this time. At least one major incident took place as well—the only major schism in the history of the church.

**Charles B. Jones
1836–1837**

The associational Minutes reflect a great deal of growth in the midst of continuing turmoil concerning Pastor Marshall of the First African Baptist Church as well as over the slavery situation in general. Between 1835 and 1842 the church membership had more than doubled—from 126 to 301. Pastors Jones and Binney must have been effective evangelists during this period.

Joseph G. Binney

Following the one-year tenure of Jones, the church called Joseph Binney as pastor in 1837 and he remained in Savannah until 1843. (Interestingly, he later became a missionary and died in 1878 while on board a ship in the Indian Ocean.) Binney certainly enlarged the membership with his persuasive preaching. With stronger economics he enlarged the building itself, as reflected in the brief history given in 1900.

Joseph G. Binney
1837–1843

In 1836 the North-South issue in relation to abolitionism was certainly resulting in strong Southern objections as reflected in the Sunbury Minutes: "Resolved that Northern Abolition is Anti-Scriptural, and is regarded by the Delegates [one reads both the words "delegate" and "messenger" in these early minutes] of this Association with feelings of honest indignation." Baptists, Catholics, Anglicans, Presbyterians, and others expressed themselves strongly on this ever-sensitive issue that would lead to religious as well as civil schism in the country. Though Andrew Marshall was again censured for his heresy in 1836, he and his church were readmitted into the association in 1837 due to his stated rejection of the views of Alexander Campbell.

During the balance of Binney's tenure there was continued support of the Triennial Convention, though new winds of thought on this subject were gaining strength. In a rather liberal though truly Baptistic stance, Sunbury Association decided that in relation to the matter of accepting the baptism of a paedo-Baptist minister (one who believed in infant baptism), the decision should be left to the judgment of the individual and the local congregation. In the Savannah area this was an early precedent in relation to the acceptance of what is generally known as "alien baptism" (or, baptism not performed by a Baptist minister).

Henry O. Wyer

Henry O. Wyer, the tenth pastor, followed Binney in 1844 and remained only until November 1845. At this same time the church and the association went on official record approving and joining the newest Protestant denomination in the United States—the Southern Baptist Convention: "Resolved that this Association approve the action of the convention called in Augusta, Georgia, in May last, and which resulted in the organization of the Southern Baptist Convention." One major denominational schism would soon be followed by one major local schism in Savannah, though for very different reasons.

Henry O. Wyer
1844–1845

Albert Williams

Following Wyer's brief tenure was the ill-fated pastorate of Albert Williams who was called in 1845 and left in 1847. Reportedly a very learned man, he had not really earned a unanimous or even near-unanimous call and during his first year did not bring unity to the congregation. Having given up the "yearly call" recently, the church's new "extended call" was so opposed by a large segment of the congregation that on February 4, 1847, a major schism took place that would last for a dozen years. Approximately 40 percent of the membership left and became known and constituted as the Second Baptist Church. Though called the First Baptist Church on the street, the Savannah Baptist Church never officially changed its name, still retaining its corporate name of the Deacons of the Baptist Church in Savannah. The schismatic group bought the meeting house of the Unitarians located on the corner of Bull and York Streets.

Albert Williams
1845–1847

The schism was a painful one but the end of the story, as shall be seen, was positive in every way. There must have been extremely strained relations among these Baptists in May 1847, however, for the Georgia Baptist convention met in the Savannah Baptist Church. Relations were even more strained in November 1847 when the Second Baptist Church applied for admission into the Sunbury Association and was opposed by the Savannah Baptist Church. Withdrawing its request temporarily, the church later renewed its application and was accepted as saner and fairer minds prevailed.

In this strained context, Williams left and was replaced by **Joseph Robert**, who also had a brief tenure of ministry from 1847 to 1849. Thomas Rambaut came in 1849 and remained until late in 1855. Interestingly, meanwhile at the Second Baptist Church a former pastor of the Savannah Baptist Church, Henry O. Wyer, served twice—from 1847 to 1849 and from 1854 to 1855. These were indeed tense times!

Thomas Rambaut

**Joseph T. Robert
1847–1849**

Extant Minutes pick up the local story again in April 1852 while Rambaut was pastor. By 1852 the mood between the two churches was friendly finally. Prayer meetings were jointly conducted and they shared the baptistery of the original congregation. Sunbury Association met in that year in Savannah and the overture of the meetings was cooperation and unity. By 1854 relations warmed enough for Second Baptist Church to be invited for joint worship services during a long pastoral absence. February 1855 witnessed a flurry of communications between the two churches in favor of unity because the "cause of Zion" among Baptists in the city had been "languishing." Both sides urged that the past "be veiled in oblivion." "Let us be one" was the cry of both congregations.

Although the goal was agreed upon, how to achieve it would involve a few years of negotiations. What to do with two pastors and two buildings and be fair with everyone was a difficult problem. While it would take four years, neither group lost sight of nor commitment to the final goal of unity. Though the plan of 1855 for unifying the congregations was rejected, it was done in a fraternal spirit with a promise for cooperation and further negotiation.

**Thomas Rambaut
1849–1855**

Joseph B. Stiteler

Later in 1855 Rambaut resigned amid flowery resolutions concerning his ministry. Turned down by P. H. Mell as well as by H. O. Wyer, the congregation in April turned to Joseph B. Stiteler who accepted the call and began the briefest tenure of any pastor at the church, because a few months later in 1856 the fourteenth pastor died in office. "Destitution" was even reported that year throughout the entire Sunbury Association. Stiteler had witnessed, however, the meeting of the Georgia Baptist Convention in April in Savannah along with important cooperation with Second Baptist during this event.

**Joseph B. Stiteler
1856**

Samuel G. Daniel

In late October a few weeks following Stiteler's death, the church called Samuel G. Daniel as pastor and he accepted. Another brief tenure of three years would follow but with closing positive results, for the two congregations would finally unite on February 6, 1859, nearly twelve years from the very day of the schism.

Daniels had been pastor only a few months when a damaging rumor in Savannah and Augusta concerning his sermons had to be investigated. Some member of the church had maliciously spread a story that Daniels was guilty of preaching other men's sermons In brief, he was being accused of plagiarism. A church committee dealt with the problem, read a number of his manuscript sermons, and found no basis whatsoever for the rumor. The pastor was further vindicated when the guilty member admitted error and requested forgiveness. Certainly such a "common life" rumor could do great damage to any minister even though it is a well-known fact that even the most successful ministers have "borrowed" from other ministers at times.

In April and May 1858 joint revival meetings were held by the Baptists. This provided the perfect background for the final drive for organizational unity between the two congregations. Unitive moods and elements have often resulted from revival efforts and this was certainly the case in Savannah. Revival experiences do jog the collective memory of what is most important and what unites. On January 26, 1859, the Second Baptist Church was urged "to lose their identity as a separate and independent church and to unite and become one with us." A committee of five persons from each church was appointed to work out the details, and on February 4 it was announced that the "hour and moment of our dissolution as a separate and distinct organization has come." At worship on February 6 a unanimous vote received eighty-eight members from the dissolved Second Baptist Church and the electric moment was celebrated with the ritual of total unity—communion. Pastors and buildings were dealt with sensitively. Pastor Winston at Second Baptist had already resigned and Pastor Daniel expressed his intention in a lovely letter to leave in the fall of the same year so that a completely fresh start could be made with new pastoral leadership.

Samuel G. Daniel
1856–1859

Within a short period of time, the property of Second Baptist was sold and decisions made as to the use of the money. The funds were used for three projects: (1) all debts of Second Baptist were paid; (2) certain funds were designated toward the purchase of a parsonage for the new pastor who would be called later in the year; and (3) some monies were designated for the renovation and furnishing of the large room beneath the nave, later to be called the Lecture Hall. However tragic the twelve-year schism, the reunion's timing was excellent. The Savannah Baptist Church would meet the hard days of the Civil War with a larger congregation and enough financial strength to weather the crises of the war years. Unlike so many other churches, it would be completely solvent following the war. In addition, the church had perhaps learned important lessons about the retention of congregational unity, for there would not be another schism in its future history. Any future drainage of membership would result from establishing mission churches, for this church would become the mother of a number of other Baptist churches in Savannah. Thus, negative schism yielded to flexible unity and to greater mission efforts.

Securing a new pastor for the unified congregations would consume a number of months but the end result would be well worth the effort. After receiving Daniel's letter of intention in early March, the congregation quickly appointed a pulpit search committee. Three of the committee traveled to the Southern Baptist Convention in May in Richmond to make some contacts and reported that they "met with much more difficulty than they expected." However, upon returning the committee was unanimous in recommending P. H. Mell of Athens (later, the chancellor of the University of Georgia, 1878–1888). Upon Mell's declining the offer, in August the church called R. Jeffrey of Philadelphia. After yet another rejection, the church extended a call to Poindexter S. Henson of Virginia in September. Henson declined in November and immediately a call was finally accepted by Sylvanus Landrum of Macon. Idealists might point to matters other than economics, but it is nevertheless the case that Landrum was offered $2,500 as well as the newly purchased parsonage, a better financial package than any previous minister. Perhaps the recent healthy growth of the congregation to over three hundred members allowed this. His predecessor, S. G. Daniel, had only been paid $1,200.

Sylvanus Landrum

Educated at Mercer, Landrum already had valuable pastoral experience in Athens and Macon. Savannah was indeed fortunate to have an intelligent, experienced, and well-liked pastor who would give continuity of ministry through the harsh years of the Civil War and into the stabilizing years of Reconstruction. Landrum remained as pastor until late in 1871.

The irrepressible conflict was just around the corner for the American people, and even the associational Minutes of the Baptists reflected growing tensions by 1857. In 1858 Sunbury Association passed resolutions to reduce the representation from member black churches, and in 1859 even revised its constitution to take away the direct vote of such messengers: "But the delegates from the colored churches shall not in any case exercise the right of suffrage. The delegates from each of the colored churches shall, however, have the right of selecting a white member of the Association to represent them before the Association, in any matter which concerns them." Landrum not only came into a church situation sensitive to the continued healing that must take place after schism, but he was also a part of the local schismatic scene that was already reflecting future national schism.

Each section of the once united states was soon to draw its sword on the side of the Lord. The God of each side did indeed go to war, and though Julia Ward Howe gave a war hymn to the Union, her words could easily have been adopted by the Southern Confederacy: "Let the hero, born of woman, crush the serpent with his heel, Since God is marching on." Both sides were equally sure that they were fighting God's war and that the defense of liberty, home, life, and church was divinely inspired. Many volumes could be filled with near bloodthirsty condemnations, prayers for aid from Almighty God, and self-righteous and self-serving biblical interpretations. As the famous historian Sydney Ahlstrom has so correctly put it: "The pulpits resounded with a vehemence and absence of restraint never equaled in American history."

As an aside, the excellent penmanship of Sam B. Sweat, clerk, reported in December 1859 that Minutes were missing. He never reported that they were ever found—thus the hiatus that must be filled from other sources.

**Sylvanus Landrum
1859–1871**

Savannah's churches began early on to have union prayer services asking for the protection and blessing of Almighty God upon the Confederacy as well as to take up collections on behalf of this new government. Instead of state-supported churches it was going to be partially church-supported states! The Baptists joined the other denominations in Savannah in these efforts. Baptists and Methodists had long since separated from national bodies over the slavery issue and now other denominations followed the same schismatic pattern as well and for the same reasons. The Bible and prayer would be widely used to further the causes of the South.

Savannah Baptists were fortunate to have a leader such as Landrum to guide them through the chaotic years of the war. Due to his astute leadership and their commitment in unity, the church never closed its doors (as did so many others) and prospered financially in the midst of widespread devastation. By early 1860 Landrum saw to the publication of eight hundred copies of the church's revised Constitution, Rules, Bylaws, Covenant, Confession, and Rules of Decorum. There might be chaos in external society but there would be order and cosmos within the congregation. Extensive improvements were made in the nave, continued work would be completed on the Lecture Room, and new hymn books were planned. As well, later in the year, even in the context of imminent secession, Landrum was calling for volunteers to entertain, house messengers, meet trains, and publish programs for the meetings of the Southern Baptist Convention being planned for Savannah in May 1861. By the time of these meetings secession had occurred and the Civil War had begun. Among others, Savannah Baptists applauded numerous resolutions approving of both and referring to the "degenerated" Union. Specifically the Convention resolved in a unanimous vote, "That we most cordially approve of the Confederate States of America, and admire and applaud the noble course of that Government up to this present time." Later conventions would issue similar resolutions during the war.

The Sunbury Association met in Savannah in 1863 and reported the widespread "desolation of war" as well as the closing and disbanding of many churches. Savannah reported 332 members. As late as October 31, 1864, the Minutes report: "The Deacons take pleasure in announcing that the church is entirely free of debt and this should be a subject of gratitude in view of the severe ordeal through which we are now passing as a nation." Indeed, funds had been given to home and foreign missions, all bills had been paid, and the "Poor Fund" stood at $815. Not even Sherman's march to the sea with its widespread destruction touched the Baptist Church in Savannah. Landrum preached to Confederate soldiers one Sunday and the next to Union soldiers following Sherman's Christmas gift to President Lincoln of the Savannah jewel. By this time in late December the irrepressible conflict was approaching its last days. Though many religious and public buildings were put to secular use by Sherman, the Baptist church was spared.

The silence on Palm Sunday, April 9, 1865, at Appomattox was penetrating after the noise of the cannons' roar. By late May all Confederate armies had put aside their guns and on August 20, 1866, President Andrew Johnson proclaimed the official close of the "Rebellion." The life of the Southern nation had been short-lived and at the expense of over one million casualties. Religious citizens searched for meaning as well as for survival. An almost-chosen people must now attempt to build one nation under God. Memorial Day soon took its place on the American calendar as a day of healing and reconciliation. Reconstruction began and the churches slowly started to play their appropriate role as a stabilizing and comforting element within the culture.

Baptists in Savannah reported a "financial crisis" due to the "changes and embarrassments in our condition brought about by the war," but Landrum's yearly report in November 1865 was marked by thanksgiving and optimism. Reporting 322 members, he summarized:

> Wonderful has been the history of the past year in events affecting our church. At our last annual meeting a great army was sweeping down the state toward the sea. In fifty days from that time it surrounded and occupied the city. Since then we have been under the military government of the United States. Thus the civil government of the past four years passed away and with its failures in our city all of our available means became worthless. On the first day of January last, the church had not a dollar to meet her expenses and her congregation were all in the same impoverished condition. But our prayer has been that our House of Worship might not be desolated nor desecrated by War and that our organization as a church might not be broken nor our services suspended. My people, that prayer has been answered. Our House stands. Our organization exists, and not even for a day during all the overturnings of war has our service been suspended. In deep humility let us offer adoring gratitude to God. . . . With peace

around us and now the return of many of our members, though poor and afflicted, let us hope through the mercy of God our Savior that henceforth our labours and efforts may be crowned with increasing prosperity.

Landrum thus became part of the early healing process. The annual report of the church revealed that due to the failure of the Confederate dollar, not a single dollar remained in the treasury. The hope was that financial recovery would consume only one year. For the present, however, some adjustments had to be made such as in lieu of a salary, the organist would be granted "pew number 85 in the middle aisle" and its rental fee. Some night meetings were also suspended due to the expense of gas lights and the difficulty of many persons in going out at night. By 1867, however, the church was paying Landrum $2,800 per year, buying him an insurance policy, and even planning to open a mission church elsewhere in Savannah. Recovery had perhaps been painful but also comparatively rapid.

Due to the desolation caused by Sherman, in 1866 the Sunbury Association decided to dissolve itself and form a new association under the rubric of the New Sunbury Association. Churches from Union, Piedmont, and Sunbury Associations formed the new association and immediately made an application for membership to the Georgia Baptist State Convention. The new constitution did not insist on strict Calvinism nor on plenary verbal inspiration but did urge the principles of congregational autonomy and discipline as well as a commitment to believer's baptism by immersion. The Association rejected any kind of ecclesiastical power while committing itself to the idea of being an advisory body. By this time it was also apparent that black churches would no longer be under the supervision of white churches, and by 1874 there were no black churches which were counted as members of the New Sunbury Association. This schism was strictly sociological, not theological, and perhaps would never be completely healed.

Landrum was committed to missions, education, and social services throughout his ministry. He was the first pastor of Savannah Baptists to generate productive interest in the establishment of a Baptist mission in Savannah. A goal of such a mission, of course, was eventual full congregational status as a church. As early as 1868 the church was attempting to find a lot on the southside of town that would be a suitable location for a mission building. Turned down by the city in its request for a free lot, the church bought lot number 19 in Lloyd Ward on the corner of Barnard and Gwinnett Streets. When the church required repairs, the decision to build a mission was delayed. Painting, a new roof, window glazing, and organ repair cost the congregation far more than was anticipated. By 1870, however, the mission had been built and was flourishing. Arrangements for the examination and baptism of members there were made and by June a vast number had joined the mission. Between 1869 and 1870 the membership of the church had jumped from 421 to 506, since mission membership was always counted as a part of the mother church's total.

The meeting of the New Sunbury Association in Savannah in November 1870 continued to reflect on the vivid interest in missions, evangelism, and education. Effective preaching was noted by the Association in Baptist, Presbyterian, Methodist, and Lutheran congregations in Savannah. The war years were now yielding to successful outreach to the total population. Further Sunday School education was urged and a formal request was made of the host church to form a tract society for the spreading of the Christian gospel.

Perhaps this expansion was further evidence of Landrum's ministerial talents in Savannah and even more reason for the church's deep grief in August 1871 when the pastor announced his resignation. He had guided them through the war years and well into the period of reconstruction and expansion. In fact even in his last year he had urged social meetings of the congregation so that the glue of happy and celebratory times could offer even more binding unity of the congregation by playing together as well as praying together.

Landrum was headed to distant Memphis, Tennessee, and the Central Baptist Church. A pall fell over the congregation as it began the laborious search for a replacement, never an easy task and in this case even more difficult. In September the church called Dr. Thomas H. Pritchard of Raleigh, North Carolina, and within the same month was rejected. The church's annual letter urged that the congregation during these days of being pastorless "act honorably and be united." The second candidate to be called was I. W. Curtis of Philadelphia. He, too, declined. The church then issued a strongly unanimous call to a native of England, Dr. Timothy Harley, then living in New Brunswick, Canada. The church was becoming even more international in its outlook and leadership, for this third candidate accepted. Harley must have been enthusiastic, for his acceptance arrived by telegraph. After nine months of supply preaching, by May the enthusiastic Englishman was on the scene and already making some changes, such as observing the ordinance of communion on the first Sunday of each month. One might expect an English Baptist to be a bit more high-church in his liturgical expectations.

Timothy Harley

Harley may have been enthusiastic to come, but he found his first summer in Savannah to be stifling and unacceptable. He even published a notice in *The Christian Index* complaining of the summer heat in Savannah and praying for God's call elsewhere! That call did not come for a few years but his hot summer was moderated by a visit to England in July to escape the heat. Harley was also bothered by the hustle and bustle, even on Sunday, in the ever growing Savannah. Periodic letters to the mayor and *ad hoc* committees wrestled with the issue of Sunday street noises which disturbed the Baptists' worship. The church even requested that police be assigned to the area during Sunday worship to retain the peace and to keep the quiet. Efforts evidently were not too successful since the Minutes annually reflected this concern.

Though still practicing the rental of pews to meet budget needs, the church was led by Harley in early 1873 to adopt a new plan of giving in order to strengthen locally and develop more broadly denominational needs. Evidently blessed with more expertise in management than former pastors, Harley proposed an eight-point plan: (1) discontinue all public collection except at monthly communion unless authorized by both pastor and deacons; (2) develop an alphabetized members register book; (3) divide these names between ten or twenty persons who would visit all the members and seek pledges; (4) twelve envelopes for giving would be shared with each member; (5) these envelopes would be returned with monies on the second Sunday of each month and placed in a collection box near the door; (6) all members, it is hoped, will keep their promises; (7) if any member fails for two months to return an envelope, the committee is to send a notice; and (8) 50 percent of the income thus collected will be assigned for

Timothy Harley
1872–1879

missions and 50 percent to the church's local needs. If somewhat naive, the plan was an early effort to replace pew rental eventually and to bring emphasis upon individual responsibility in relation to the financial support of the church. On January 13, 1873, the plan was adopted *in toto*. The nation as well as Georgia was entering a five-year economic depression; therefore, every effort on the local church level to raise funds would be critically important.

Harley's organizational abilities are also to be observed in his wholistic plan for "every member participation" in the total church program. In the same month as the adoption of the new financial plan, a committee was appointed to implement the new pastor's six-point plan of activities engaging the total membership: (1) teach more serious Bible classes for everyone; (2) conduct district prayer meetings in homes; (3) continue churchwide social gatherings; (4) assign homework in Sunday School; (5) sponsor Sunday School mission work; and (6) organize the young men of the church into a Christian Union. Plans to buy a new furnace were matched by these plans to heat up the membership for committed participation in the whole *koinonia* (community of faith).

By October 1873 economic hardships were making their appearance and the plan of monthly contributions was altered to an emphasis on weekly contributions with special scriptural appeals to the membership. Finances were not too weak, however, to discourage continuing involvement in local missions. The church became interested in conducting mission work ten miles west of Savannah at Hardin's Swamp with a view toward establishing a church later. At home these Baptists remained ecumenical under Harley's leadership, allowing the Knights Templar as well as the United Synod South Lutherans to make use of their building.

In October 1874 the New Sunbury Association met yet again in Savannah noting no blacks in attendance and adopted a resolution concerning "coloreds" in absolute error at one point and at another showing virtual ignorant insensitivity. The resolution spoke of colored churches having been in the Association for fifty years prior to the Civil War with "equal representation with the white churches." If white Baptists believed this they were professing a rather different interpretation of "equal," to say the least. The resolution continued, "for reasons unknown to us, [they] have, since the war, withdrawn and formed associations of their own." The words "for reasons unknown" illustrate an unusual insensitivity, if the Baptists were being completely honest. Sent to all colored associations in the area, the resolutions must have resulted in a few laughs and head wagging. For the next three years the association decried the manufacture, sale, and use of any kind of liquor—even wine. However, at this time and for years to come Savannah Baptists retained local autonomy in relation to this matter by continuing to use wine in communion. Of course, prior to the days of prohibition in the twentieth century, most Baptists used wine in communion, and even one of their famous thinkers and seminary professors, John A. Broadus, said that if wine were not used in communion it was not true communion, just as if water were not used in baptism it was not true baptism.

Between 1874 and 1875 Savannah Baptists grew from 497 to only 500 in membership and reported to the Association: "We cannot report in our midst any great spiritual awakening, but have to acknowledge coldness and lack of those graces which characterized the followers of our Lord." Indeed, from 1875 to 1879 the church would decline in membership to 460. These were tough years economically and evangelistically.

Summers and economics were both hard on Harley. He resigned in 1876 and 1877 only to be talked out of it by the church leadership. These were unhealthy times as well. Harley must have wondered about the wisdom of his decision to remain in Savannah in 1876 when the scourge of yellow fever hit the city. Citizens had had their share of pain and suffering from this disease already but nothing like that which took place in 1876. Many persons simply left the city and many churches suspended their services. Surely the Baptists did as well, since the Minutes have a major gap between July 13 and November 27. A dark cloud hung over the city as described by the *Morning News* of September 13:

> Yesterday was probably the saddest day we have experienced since the commencement of the epidemic. The large mortuary report published in the *News* in the morning had a depressing effect, and the large number of funerals during the day seem to impress upon every one the fulness of the calamity which has befallen our city. Nevertheless, it was almost impossible to realize, amid the natural beauty of our Forest City, its grassy parks, stately trees, and shaded walks, and the clear balmy air of early morn, that a fearful pestilence was raging in our midst. Before dark the streets were deserted, and the general gloom is only relieved by the lights which here and there gleam from chamber windows of the sick.

Within only two months it is estimated that between eight hundred and two thousand persons died in Savannah. At this time, Savannah's total population was only about thirty thousand persons.

It is difficult to imagine what a psychological impact this had on the city and its citizens. Wealthy people left the city; distress among the lower class was vividly illustrated in every direction. The medical caregivers were on the verge of collapse. Each day outdid the previous one in deaths. The peak of forty-seven deaths took place on September 23. In the midst of this suffering religion was certainly a private comfort to the people, but not so much in a formal way. Most of the churches were closed and when open, attendance was low. Estimates of those left in the city range from seven thousand among the whites to fourteen thousand among the black population. It was almost a medieval day of doom.

The Minutes of November 27 and December 14 reflected on the plague. The church had lost seven members in October and though mourning their deaths, the Minutes expressed thanksgiving in God's sparing so many within the congregation. Speaking of the pestilence and its effects on "our beautiful, beloved city," the Minutes called on all members to help share the burdens and not be "pining in neglect." With decreased membership as well as financial depression, the leadership experienced high anxiety over the finances but expressed hope about their solution.

Harley's now almost yearly resignation in March 1877 was withdrawn in April and in May he was paid two months salary in advance and given leave to return to England during the stifling summer months.

In October and November 1878 an interesting dialogue and debate took place in the church. Perhaps a feminist before his time, T. J. Elmore had made the motion that the Bylaws and Constitution of the church be changed in relation to voting by striking "white male" before the numbers relating to a quorum being present. At this time only males had the vote in Baptist congregations just as they did in the civil society. When the resolution came to a vote, it was tabled indefinitely by a very large vote. Elmore should be remembered, however, for his creative and prophetic insights about a truly pure Baptist democracy in a congregational setting. During these years the Register of the church reflected the growing religious diversity in Savannah which gave numerous options to searching souls as well as dissatisfied members. Fellowship was being "withdrawn" during these years from members who were transferring to the Independent Presbyterians, the Methodists, the Christian Scientists, and even the Swedenborgians. A potpourri of possibilities was now available.

Sylvanus Landrum

In April 1879 Harley resigned yet one last time, for perhaps both sides were serious—the church accepted the resignation and Harley left. Within a few days the church had called back its beloved pastor, Sylvanus Landrum, from Memphis. Either proving that "you can't go home again" or that it was the wrong time in his career to be in Savannah, Landrum's second tenure at the church was less than two years. Perhaps the recall itself was his greatest compliment. Two significant moments in the life of the church took place during this brief period, however. First, West Baptist Church dissolved and Savannah Baptist profited both numerically and economically. Church membership jumped from 460 to 499 and hundreds of dollars were transferred from West Church's treasury to Savannah Baptist. Second, the Georgia Baptist Convention met in Savannah in the spring of 1880 with the congregation as well as Baptists in general receiving a great deal of visibility in the city. So strong was the congregation's assistance in entertaining the messengers in attendance that enough money was left over to purchase new communion plates and to contribute a significant amount to the poor fund. Associational notations also reflect that the church continued its commitment to missions and Baptist expansion: "The Church owns a very eligible lot on Barnard St., W. of Forsythe Place Park for another church edifice."

Sylvanus Landrum
1879–1881

In February 1881 Landrum resigned to become Financial Secretary and Lecturer in Theology at Mercer University. He would remain for a short period in Savannah, however, and the church did another honorific deed in his direction—it made him chair of the search committee for a new pastor! Held in high esteem by the community, his memory was honored in the naming of Landrum Masonic Lodge. As an aside, though Landrum was well known among Baptists, his son, William Warren Landrum, was baptized in Savannah and became even better known, serving major churches in the South, declining offers of at least three presidencies at Baptist educational institutions, and authoring a number of books, including *Our Baptist Message: Its Use and Abuse*.

Again, the church would be without a permanent pastor for a number of months and would endure the frustration of rejection. In May 1881 the church extended a near unanimous call to Dr. Thomas Pritchard of Wake Forest College in North Carolina. The word "near" is used advisedly. The first vote to call was 80 to 7. The motion to make the call unanimous, as was customary, was opposed by two persons who evidently took very seriously the idea of a Baptist democracy. So far as we know, that minor matter had no effect on Pritchard. He declined, citing the fact that he had only been in his present position for two years and it was too soon to leave. The committee then turned a bit north of Carolina—to Danville, Virginia, and J. E. L. Holmes. For a portion of the interim period, W. Stokes Walker, a student at the Southern Baptist Theological

Seminary, served the church. Holmes accepted but would not arrive in Savannah until October. Unsolicited, the Danville Baptist Church wrote a glowing commendation of Holmes to Savannah. The church was primed for a ten-year pastorate by a well-liked young man who would leave a grieving congregation in 1891, for he would die suddenly while still pastor.

J. E. L. Holmes

Holmes suffered grief early on in his pastorate when in 1883 his young wife died. The annual conference of the church reported that this was "the saddest event of the year." Holmes buried himself in his work and ministry. One of his baptizands was a criminal in jail—reflecting Holmes's jail ministry. Rules change in the context of unusual situations and Savannah Baptists were perennially open to such change. Earlier, they had refused taking communion into homes. In this case, an incarcerated person requested communion and after "considerable discussion" in the church's business meeting, and after a committee's interview of the jailed Mr. McLean, the pastor celebrated communion for him. In late November 1884 the weary pastor was urged by his doctor to rest himself from the pulpit for awhile, and the church granted a month of sick leave. Very soon he would face an earthquake, the founding of a mission and then a church, and repairs on the church. Within a few years he would himself enter that bourne from which no traveler returns.

By early 1885 the congregation was considering building a mission on the lot owned by the church on Gwinnett and Barnard Streets. By October the church had accumulated $4,000 toward this project. The church itself had also been repainted and repaired while the opposition to removing the horseshoe gallery was successful. Continued discussion about the need for Baptist expansion on the southside of the city resulted in the purchase by the church of a lot on the southeast corner of Duffy Street bounded on the east by Abercorn. This lot was purchased in late 1885, and within two months the church had sold its lot on Gwinnett and Barnard Streets for more than the purchase price of the Duffy Street lot. By November 1887 the mission building was nearly completed, and by October of the following year it had been dedicated. The Minutes reflect that Holmes had worked overtime on this mission project. In the midst of all this, Holmes experienced his first and only earthquake on August 31, 1886. Not until November 1888 were the walls of the church, cracked by the earthquake, repaired due to danger to the congregation!

The pastor must have smiled on August 1, 1888, when another feminist before his time, A. B. Goodwin, made a motion and read a paper showing deep sensitivity toward the rights and responsibilities of religious females. He urged: "It is the sense of this church that our female members should be encouraged to labor more directly and constantly in special devotional meetings of their own for the conversion and edification of their own sex." Goodwin found this to be consistent with scripture and further suggested that women "should labor in public meetings and otherwise for the special welfare of women." Another male moved that the motion be tabled—and it was—permanently!

Early in 1888 the church was searching for an associate pastor to help the overextended and weary Holmes as well as to assist with the new mission on Duffy Street. Turned down by A. G. Wilkins, the church called W. S. Royal of Virginia, who agreed to come in April. Appearing none too soon, Royal became very busy. The mission was

**J. E. L. Holmes
1881–1891**

dedicated in October, and in May 1889 Holmes was granted a three-month leave of absence due to his complete exhaustion.

One year later W. S. Royal returned to Virginia and E. Pendleton Jones of Atlanta was called in October with main responsibilities at Duffy Street Mission, which was on the threshold of being constituted as a church. Healthy in numbers and economics, Duffy Street Mission was constituted as Duffy Street Church on April 5, 1891, with eighty-two charter members, a much larger number than those few who constituted the Savannah Baptist Church in 1800. Since Savannah Baptist's first mission to become a church (West Baptist Church) had dissolved, this was the first permanent mission-church to be founded in the city by Savannah Baptist. A healthy church, by 1899 it reported 417 members and in 1900 New Sunbury Association held its yearly meeting at Duffy Street. An historical footnote should be added. Hurricane damage to the church in 1896 led to major rebuilding and by 1911 brick veneer had been added. Due to its name on the streets being "Second Baptist," the congregation followed popular talk and renamed itself in 1913. Yet another change took place in 1927 when it moved to a new location and assumed yet another name, the Bull Street Baptist Church. The original building on Duffy and Abercorn Streets is now the Asbury United Methodist Church.

In relation to missions, it should also be noted that Holmes encouraged and commended William D. King for the ministry. With the church's support, King entered The Southern Baptist Theological Seminary. In 1891, upon the recommendation of Holmes, he was ordained by the church and shortly was appointed by the Southern Baptist Convention as a missionary to China.

This rare photograph of the church interior shows the decorations for the anniversary celebration of the Sabbath School, April 30, 1893. Before 1921 there was no choir loft and the congregation sat in boxed pews. Notice the floor heating grate in the center and the elaborate wall decoration above the wainscoting and in the central niche.

Holmes had been near exhaustion for several years and evidently his heart could take no more. On December 5, 1891, at the age of forty-two and while preparing his sermon for the next day, Holmes quietly left this life. He had just celebrated ten years of pastoral ministry in Savannah in October. The next day of worship must have been especially memorable as the chair of the deacons read the sermon from the pulpit—the sermon Holmes had prepared for that day! It was a time of loss and deep grief, so sudden was his departure. Within a few days, glowing resolutions had come from many other churches in Savannah—Duffy Street, First African, Christ Episcopal Church, and the Independent Presbyterian. Duffy Street spoke of having lost "our father." Savannah Baptist named him as personal friend and brother—"an irreparable loss." He was characterized as "being neither an extremist in combating error nor yielding an iota in the firm convictions of his mind." Among Baptists as well as numerous others he was valued as simply a very good man.

S. A. Goodwin

After one rejection by George D. Eager, the Baptists were successful in their invitation to S. A. Goodwin in May 1892. Baptists in Savannah had once again raided the Baptist Church in Danville, Virginia, of its pastor. Goodwin had moved about a great deal (in a twenty-four year period he had been in nine different churches) and would remain in Savannah for only five years.

Goodwin first appointed a committee to look into placing memorial tablets somewhere in the church in honor of Holmes and Landrum. By December the honorific tablets were in place, executed by A. J. Wray of Richmond, Virginia. In 1893 the legal deed of ownership was officially given to Duffy Street, and for the first time in the Minutes, the term "the First Church" is used of Savannah Baptist.

The Minutes reflecting Goodwin's ministry in Savannah are rather sparse. He was often given several months of vacation and in 1894 was given a leave of absence between four and six weeks to accompany his son on a trip concerning his son's health. At other times he was off in other churches conducting revivals. His leaving would surely not be as grievous as that of Holmes.

The Baptists did participate in presence and funds in February 1896 in a union service involving one of the most famous evangelists of the nineteenth century—Dwight L. Moody came to Savannah! Goodwin, himself being evangelistically oriented, must have been extremely pleased with this visit.

Word had also come from W. D. King in 1894, still in China, that he had severed his relations with the Foreign Mission Board of the Southern Baptist Convention. He virtually begged the church to support him as an independent missionary. The pastor led the church to turn down this request and informed King: (1) the church is unwilling to be in "antagonism to the Southern Baptist Convention"; and (2) within the convention is the place to adjust differences instead of withdrawing from it. Goodwin seemed to be an organization man at this time and loyal to denominational organizations.

Four hurricanes blew ashore along the Georgia coast during the 1890s. One of those occurred in September 1896. Though the tin roofing of the church was damaged, this did not compare at all to the extensive damage done to the Duffy Street Church. In fact, Savannah Baptist offered to conduct union services or for them to "use our house for services" while theirs was being repaired.

S. A. Goodwin
1892–1897

Apparently some kind of turmoil must have developed in the church in 1896 in relation to Goodwin, for in October five deacons resigned only to withdraw their resignations in November. In December, Goodwin resigned as pastor and expressed himself rather curtly: "My ministry in your midst has not met with that success for which I hoped." The church accepted his resignation as of three months hence and praised him as an effective preacher. However, a motion in the Board of Deacons which asked him to give his specific reason for leaving and urged him to reconsider his decision lost by a twelve-to-five vote. As one reads between the lines, there was trouble in Zion but there are no specific hints as to what the problem really was. Needless to say, however, no tears were shed over his leaving and he was certainly not made chair of the search committee as Landrum had been.

Savannah in the 1890s experienced a number of unusual weather phenomena. In addition to four hurricanes that hit the coast during this decade, on January 8, 1893, snow fell. Another snow storm hit February 15, 1895. During one of these storms people enjoyed the rare accumulation on Chippewa Square. The church cupola rises above the trees in the background. Photo courtesy of the Georgia Historical Society.

John D. Jordan

By April 25, 1897, the church had called John D. Jordan and in May his letter of acceptance was in hand in Savannah. Jordan was coming from Birmingham, Alabama, and a position with the Baptist Young People's Union, an intradenominational organization founded in 1891 to help Baptist young people in biblical knowledge and spiritual development. Savannah now had its centennial pastor in Jordan—the twenty-first permanent in-residence pastor who would guide the church into the twentieth century. He would also be eminently successful in building membership. The greatest rise in membership occurred during his ministry—more than a 50 percent increase. The membership numbers reported to the New Sunbury Association grew from 614 in 1897 to 974 in 1906, the year of his resignation.

The first year of Jordan's ministry included a most damaging hurricane, a change in tenure for deacons, and a successful evangelistic year which commenced with revival services. In February J. W. White of Macon came to lead in revival services and evidently good beginnings had even better continuings. Church membership in Jordan's first year leaped from 614 to 716. By April the Constitution of the church had been changed to limit the single term of a deacon to three years. Prior to this the term was completely open-ended with the colorful phrase, "shall be during their good behavior." The change was certainly sensitive to church growth since those early founding days and to the need of developing more wide-ranging leadership as well as sharing membership responsibilities. August 30 witnessed a far more damaging hurricane than the one of 1896 which had done minor damage to the roof. The lecture room was so badly damaged that it was unfit for any kind of meeting. (Water

John D. Jordan
1897–1906

damage on the lower level remained a major problem throughout the next century as well.) The roof suffered major damage and needed immediate attention. The deacons were empowered to procure a large loan to take care of a wide range of repairs which, by the end of the year, included new pews and the "necessary apparatus for heating water in the baptistry." In the interim, the Baptists were generously offered a wide range of possibilities for their place of worship during repairs. They were extended invitations by Independent Presbyterian, Trinity Methodist, Wesley Monumental Methodist, and the YMCA. With these ecumenical offers the Baptists chose the most ecumenical invitation. They would meet for a number of months in the main hall of the YMCA.

The year 1899 opened with revival services again with "the London Evangelist," Reverend Varley, leading the services. That year, unlike the previous one under Jordan, showed very little increase in total membership—only six. Jordan had been spoiled by his first year and at the associational meeting in October expressed his disappointment: "Very few saved souls [have been] added to the churches and very little done for the advancement of the Kingdom of God." Under Jordan's ministry no other year would be this low in increased membership. In April, however, Baptists from all over the state were hosted in Savannah at the meetings of the Georgia Baptist Convention. The final session of the Convention in the nineteenth century reported 1,758 churches, sixty-six associations, and 167,559 members. Baptists had grown from rather obscure beginnings to become a major force in religious life in the state of Georgia. The outlook for the twentieth century was laced with optimism.

The hurricane of 1898 seriously damaged the church building, ripping off a large section of the roof and causing water damage to the sanctuary. Across Whitaker Street townhouses stand where the Sunday School building would later be constructed.

Due to the hurricane as well as a conscious awareness of the approaching centennial celebration of the congregation, the church itself was taking on new features both internally and externally. The needed external repairs combined with newness elsewhere as well: cleaned carpets; new pews and cushions; new organ; heated baptistery; new Minutes book; new pulpit desk, chairs, and flower stand; new communion table, chairs, and four silver collection plates; repaired shutters; and a beautiful electric chandelier for the entrance door enhanced the church. One thousand copies of the church covenant were printed for distribution. Appropriately, toward the close of the year the Minutes reflected deep appreciation for the women in the church "whose efforts in all good work are the leaven which active properly energizes all with which it comes in contact." The women of the church had done yeowomen's work in relation to all these

The damage from the hurricane of 1898 was largely limited to the western end of the church. Contrary to popular belief, the cupola was not affected by the storm. It was removed during the renovation of 1921–1922.

changes. The pastor also spoke of the deep fraternal relations between pastor and people, and that unmarred by discord. In November the membership was being urged to observe the one hundredth birthday "fittingly." It was so "fittingly" done that the *Morning News* gave a full coverage for three days along with photographs. The church has never since received such full coverage from the press as in those days. The celebration lasted over a three-day period, November 25–27, and the end of the first year of the twentieth century for the Savannah Baptist Church would be remembered for years to come. Baptists in Savannah had definitely come of age and were a major force in their beautiful city. (For a detailed description of the centennial celebration, see "Interlude: Celebrating the First One Hundred Years.")

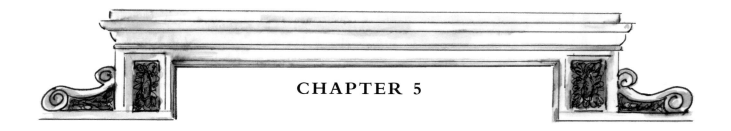

<h1 style="text-align:center">CHAPTER 5</h1>

<h1 style="text-align:center">CHURCH DISCIPLINE</h1>

Since the early days of Christian expansion and growth, discipline has existed in churches. The goal of such discipline was not the legalistic establishment of a list of petty moralisms with numerous "don'ts" concerning life and living. Instead, the major goal was to build spiritual health and strength by means of a democratically disciplined community that would also be capable of spiritual warfare against the forces of evil. The principle of original sin was taken seriously as well as the need for pastoral care by the entire congregation along the way.

Once Christianity became the state religion of the Roman Empire after 380, hordes of persons were admitted to the institutional church with the name "Christian" but with little else. Discipline was institutionalized and placed within the hands of the ordained clergy. Congregational discipline virtually disappeared and was replaced by the confessional and the sacrament of penance. Unfortunately there was a dark underside of discipline as well, witnessed in the attitude toward "heretics"—those who disagreed in any major way with the establishment. Theological monopoly was the order of the day and discipline as being redemptive yielded to discipline as being punitive—sometimes horribly punitive. The "search and destroy" missions in the Middle Ages as the Inquisition rooted out heresy are well-known and well-rehearsed. Moral discipline was replaced by the raw power of physical and sometimes horrible force. Granted, on the grassroots level there were numerous instances of genuine redemptively oriented discipline, but the orientation of the organization at the top was generally otherwise.

The magisterial reformers of the sixteenth century, such as Luther and Calvin, certainly were interested in the practice of moral discipline but they, too, still thought in terms of one church in one state. This, to a large degree, politicized the practice of discipline especially in relation to theological matters. The radical phase of the Reformation brought new insight to the historical discussion table, however, in its new emphases on the practices of the separation of church and state and religious liberty. The "free church" tradition was thus planted and would see its greatest contribution to political and theological thought made in the founding of the United States which incorporated these principles into its founding documents.

The "free church tradition" (free from state interference) once again committed itself to the genuinely redemptive discipline of the early Christian churches. From the seventeenth through the nineteenth centuries in America, the free churches struggled with the meaning and application of discipline toward the goal of spiritual health and happiness. True, sometimes certain disciplinary features were used in a strictly denominational way, but the main thrust was toward establishing and maintaining a true people of God. By the twentieth century, however, there was a growing interest in simply reflecting the values of the community in the congregational mirror. At this point, the fine scholar Franklin Littell has posed an important question in his *The Free Church*. There he states: "The question arises whether, although legally 'free,' institutions with a promiscuous view of church membership are really Free Churches." Perhaps his question is best explored in relation to the discussions about "American religion in general" and civil religion. Among Baptists more recently, the question of denominational totalitarianism in relation to discipline merits extensive exploration and discussion. Discipline is definitely prostituted in the free church Baptist tradition in situations in which democracy and congregationalism are negated by the external exercise of raw power (definitely not to say moral authority).

From the start, Savannah Baptist Church inscribed itself in the larger free church tradition and more specifically within the Baptistic segment of that tradition. One rarely hears of the discipline issue in Baptist circles anymore, but in the nineteenth century it was widely practiced and definitely among Savannah Baptists. With the page limitations of this book, it would be impossible to tell the myriad of stories from Savannah Baptist Minutes. A selection of accounts will be given here to illustrate the wide range of cases and issues. Pastors and deacons, men and women, clergy and laity, and sometimes even outsiders were involved in the cross section of issues.

Discipline procedures in Savannah were simple on the surface but terribly complicated and "sticky" in administration (see appendix G). Loyalty to the description of church discipline in chapter 18 of Matthew was the ideal, but not so easily attained. To be placed on the discipline committee was a tough assignment and rarely considered a pleasant experience. Even in cases of restoration there were painful moments in the process. Church conference and discipline meetings were regularly held and attendance was virtually mandatory. To be sure, one had to hold membership in order to qualify for being a candidate for discipline. For this reason there were always numerous "hearers" in Baptist churches, for they could not be disciplined. Baptists were democratic but authoritarian with their members, and those on the "outside" might even be critical of their exclusivism and separatism in their discipline. Early on, a citizen of Savannah described the whole process as "a relic of barbarism, of which only puritanism could be guilty." Nevertheless, these Baptists expected loyalty and commitment to their local congregation's belief and practice. In *Democratic Religion*, Gregory Wills estimates that in Georgia alone there had been forty thousand excommunicated Baptists prior to the Civil War.

Discipline committees were usually "standing" of two or three members but at times were ad hoc to deal with special cases. Their investigations sometimes consumed several months with numerous meetings and dozens of interviews. Sometimes private and more often public discipline involved several levels. Of course the accused members could be declared innocent and some were. If found guilty, there were several levels of dealing with the subject. The least severe decision was rebuke. The next level was suspension from the Lord's Supper, the supreme illustration of unity and brotherly love.

The most severe decision was excommunication. It is true that Baptists used this term usually associated with Roman Catholic discipline. Later in the nineteenth century, as anti-Catholicism grew by leaps and bounds in the United States, the term was replaced by words such as "exclusion" and "expulsion." Of course at any time the individual could publicly express his/her guilt, remorse, and repentance and be restored to full membership status, though sometimes after an interval of time which generally proved sincerity.

Voting on discipline matters seems to have a zigzag history. For the bulk of the nineteenth century Savannah Baptist women did not officially have a vote in any matters—management or discipline. The Manual of the church in 1860 stipulated that all business of the church "shall be conducted exclusively by the regular white male communicants over eighteen years of age." Obviously, no blacks had votes even though they might be baptized members. Both these facts certainly belie the claim to pure democracy. As did most others, Baptists in this regard reflected the times rather than the theological truth of equality and complete collegiality. Women and blacks were generally discriminated against although sixty to sixty-five percent of Baptist members was female! It is correct to note that the church Manual in the twentieth century changed the voting stipulation to read "exclusively by the regular communicants." In other words, women were given full voting rights.

The word "zigzag" is used above, however, because in the nineteenth century there are times reflected in the church's Minutes that women not only had a vote in discipline cases but also in church government. In wider Baptist circles women were often allowed a vote on discipline matters but not on church governing matters. In Savannah the Minutes reflect a "sometime" vote in both areas. In 1809 Pastor Holcombe insisted that women be given the vote on discipline matters and this vote was retained later as well. The Minutes also indicate that women often had the vote on other matters as well, even though the general practice was quite the contrary. Savannah Baptists were in many matters more liberal and ahead of their time than other Baptists. There is some indication that in the 1850s the women of Savannah Baptist gave up any vote whatever, however temporary, toward the goal of ending the decade-long schism, because the Second Baptist Church did not believe in a female vote and would not reunify as one church unless this principle was adopted. Freedom yielded to unity, though within a few years the zigzag pattern resurfaced. Patience and understanding are often the preface to progress.

"Firsts" are often valued for historical reasons. The Register of the church lists William Parker as the first male member to be excommunicated, on September 30, 1804. The Minutes of these early years are extinct, however. Extant records reveal that on February 10, 1805, "Brother William Swain was excommunicated for drunkenness and profanity" and, interestingly, that "Brother Clay, assistant pastor, preached a sermon suitable to the occasion." Often, pastors used the tragedy of excommunication as an opportunity to educate, moralize, and encourage congregations toward greater commitment. The church Register lists Ann Sibley as the first female member to be excommunicated on October 18, 1816. This is incorrect, however, since the Minutes of that date speak of at least six other females, including "Ann Sibley now Albritton," who were excommunicated as "members long absent." Discipline was often used to update the membership rolls and probably many of these members never even knew they had been excommunicated!

A high plateau of excommunication was reached in 1835 when thirteen baptized members were excommunicated while all-time lows were enjoyed in 1857 with only one excommunication, and in 1871 the yearly letter of the church claimed virtually no discipline cases and thanked God for such "goodness" in the congregation. Eva Marlow seems to have been the last member, in August 1887, to be described as "excommunicated." After this there are multiple preferred terms such as "dropped," "expelled," or "fellowship withdrawn." The Register also reflects other colorful words and phrases in relation to the loss of members such as "erasure" and "not heard of for many years." In every case the result was the same—no longer a covenanting member of this particular Baptist congregation. Indeed, in 1888 Mary Trowell and thirty others were purely and simply "erased."

One case early on touches upon all the major aspects of Savannah discipline and merits presentation for illustrative reasons. It took place on May 13, 1808, and involved John Maclin:

> Brother John Maclin who had been considered for some time since as in a state of suspension, and who has been perpetually absent from our meetings both before and since, tho cited to attend, being charged with great impropriety of conduct as a Christian, who was this day considered as living in a direct state of opposition to the rules of the Gospel and the discipline of this church. On the Question being put, the Church unanimously agreed to expel him by the public act of Excommunication, and the Pastor was desired to pronounce said sentence in the open congregation on the third Lord's day in June next except he should manifest signs of repentance, meeting the approbation of this Church previous to that day, and the Clerk is requested to write a letter to him, of the church's act, and request his attendance at or previous to that day.

This case also reflects thorough examination, patience, and interest in redemption and restoration, for the public excommunication did not take place until January 22, 1809. This was two days after the following incident:

> Mr. John Maclin present, on stating the charges brought against him by this church, he equivocated and refused to comply with the reasonable request they made of him to perform, and finally charged them with intention to injure his reputation as a member and then rose saying he would not stay longer to hear the church, and went out in great disorder.

Obviously, there was no possibility of restoration in this case and on the Lord's Day, Pastor Holcombe excommunicated Maclin "from all the special union and privileges of this Church."

The Savannah church Manual dealt with discipline in Article IX of the Rules and Bylaws. The process which has been described consumed most of the article. Since the sky was almost the limit in relation to types of offenses and cases, the article was flexible in its description—"the minute rules to govern the exercise of discipline are too numerous to allow, and too obvious to require mention. . . . " Specifics were sometimes added to the understanding of discipline as the sensitivity of the congregation was heightened in relation to certain issues. Two examples are vivid enough to illustrate. Strong drink always posed a problem for both males and females. On October 8, 1832, in conference the congregation adopted specific resolutions in relation to "ardent spirits" and recognized these rules as part of the discipline of the church. The resolutions ran the gamut from educating against "ardent spirits" to not using, offering, producing, or selling hard alcohol. The only exception was the use of alcohol in the preparation of medicine as "prescribed by a regular bred Physician." Since the church used wine at this time to celebrate communion, one resolution is not surprising at all: "As wine is not prohibited in Scripture, but recommended in certain cases, we will where cases require, only use it with extreme moderation." Not until Prohibition would wine be included among "ardent spirits." Societal changes resulted in disciplinary changes.

A second illustration of church conference meetings dealing with specific disciplinary resolutions occurred on February 24, 1835. During that conference nine resolutions were adopted and the final one was as follows: "A violation of any of the foregoing rules shall subject the individual transgressing to the discipline of the Church." The briefer resolutions dealt with not "attending to secular business on the Lord's day," with "dancing and other discipation" [sic], and a reaffirmation of the prohibition of "ardent spirits." The bulk of the resolutions, however, dealt with expectations concerning membership as matters of discipline. Baptists were beginning to have denominational awareness as well as deeper sensitivity concerning denominational commitment. If desiring membership on experience without supporting letters, the applicant had to have been known by another member for at least six months. Members were enjoined to attend meetings regularly—worship, conference, and discipline. In fact, deacons were urged to divide the city into four divisions and be alert to all the members in their assigned division. Members were informed that if they left the city for less than a year, they were to be active in a Baptist church and bring back a letter of good conduct. If absent for more than a year, they were expected to request a letter of dismission and join another Baptist church. Any Baptist coming to Savannah and wishing to associate with the church was also required to bring a "letter of dismission or recommendation." Baptists intended on having order, commitment, and denominational loyalty and participation.

Specific cases of discipline among Savannah Baptists in the nineteenth century were far-ranging and included clergy as well as laity, women as well as men, and blacks in addition to whites. Though impossible to list the hundreds of cases, a catalogue of issues and a selected number of illustrations will be useful and informative. The catalogue of issues is as follows: ministerial heresy, ministerial as well as members' "withdrawal," cruel treatment of slaves, disagreements over disciplinary decisions, nonattendance, desire to join and actually joining other denominational churches, gossip, sexual harassment, spousal abuse, use of liquor, public drunkenness, violations of the sanctity of Sunday, doctrinal error, improper out-of-town conduct, stealing, card playing, betting on horse racing or entering a horse in a race, fornication and adultery, remarriage, irreconciliation between members, profane language, dancing, attending the theater, public quarreling and fighting, and rejecting the authority of the congregation. With such a long list of possible infractions, it is amazing that the church could report in October 1871 that there were virtually no discipline cases during the year! Baptists were indeed attempting to build their kingdom of God on earth and to be the conscience of the community.

Humanness, poignancy, humor, colorfulness, sensitivity, intolerance, and more are illustrated in the numerous cases. A limited number of incidents will be surveyed as a cross section of disciplinary action within the Savannah Baptist Church.

Ministers were not immune to discipline. As early as 1806 the Savannah River Association announced that it was indeed an error to listen to a minister who had been excommunicated. This implies that there were Baptist ministers itinerating the countryside who were excommunicated from some congregation. Thus the practice of "ordaining" a minister to a church in the presence of other ministers who had questioned him makes clear sense. In 1814 the congregation came very close to excommunicating their own pastor and later founder of the Southern Baptist Convention, W. B. Johnson. After his terribly harsh condemnation of the congregation and his statement of "withdrawal," the church questioned his right to "withdraw" under the circumstances of his causing schism and using condemnatory words. Under normal circumstances, such a withdrawal would not have been allowed—excommunication would have been the result. Young pastor Johnson was fortunate that justice was tempered by mercy in this case. In late 1821 pastor Sweat resigned under a cloud of controversy after he admitted that he had expressed himself "in an unguarded and unchristian manner." Again, Sweat could have been subjected to public censure at least, but instead his resignation was accepted by the congregation. Between March and April 1823, Pastor Meredith walked very close to the line of excommunication in a case involving his interpreted insensitivity to a widow who lived in a house on one of the church lots. He suspended his own services to the church until the matter was resolved but those were two tense months. Meredith's cantankerous pattern reemerged in November and December 1823 when he rejected the idea of an annual call and eventually resigned. At first the church agreed to give his wife a letter of dismission but refused to do so for Meredith himself until better feelings and communication were experienced. Eventually Meredith was granted his letter, but once again the congregation showed amazing patience and understanding, perhaps because he was, after all, their pastor.

Nonattendance was a perennial problem. On October 16, 1812, the clerk announced in conference that "Sister Sibley had been more than five years absent from this church, Sister Mary Fox was enjoined to confer with her and to bring in reasons why she does not appear among us." Sibley was finally excommunicated four years later along with a number of other nonattenders. On December 31, 1834, the church adopted a resolution stipulating that if a person lapsed in attendance for a period of two months that he/she would be a proper subject for discipline.

Incidents involving slaves as well as white supervision of the First African Baptist Church illustrate certain disciplinary tensions between the races as well as among the whites themselves. In 1832 the New Sunbury Association resolved that the First African Church was to be considered dissolved and urged that all African churches be considered branches of white Baptist churches. As reflected in chapter four of this section, discussions continued in 1833 and 1834 as Savannah Baptist Church advised the black Baptist church in relation to what it considered to be the Campbellite heresy of the pastor, Andrew Marshall. The heresy of a black minister in this case was a matter of discipline. The white church kept urging that Marshall be suspended as minister, but he was retained by the black congregation and finally, in 1837, he rejected the views of Campbell. At this time he and his church were restored as members of the Association. In this situation, the disciplinary process lasted long enough for restoration.

Cruelty and violence to slaves did not go unnoticed, though when there were self-economic interests due to ownership involved, even whites could disagree with one another. A most interesting case involved Thomas F. Williams, a licensed minister who often preached with "good effect" at times in the white church; Aaron Shave, Williams's slave driver (yes, even ministers owned slaves); and one of Williams's slaves. Shave had struck and killed the slave and pled self-defense. The discipline case began in December 1815 but was not completed until July 1816. Williams brought the case before the congregation desiring a stiff punishment for Shave. Williams requested that the testimony of two black witnesses to the incident be allowed. The testimony was allowed. Neither saw the slave strike Shave as Shave alleged. Williams believed Shave's report to be a lie, though Shave expressed regret and even humility before the church. Pastor Screven urged mercy and suspension from the communion table for a period of time rather than excommunication. The congregation so voted in January. In February Williams and his wife requested withdrawal from the church by letter due to the "dishonorable" act of such a minor punishment for Shave. The church opposed such a withdrawal as irregular. In mid-February the Williamses attended the church conference and declared their right to withdraw due to the offensive act of the church. Pastor Screven disagreed saying that "members who rent themselves from the Church for a supposed grievance were true breakers and meritted [sic] the censure of the church." Both the Williamses remained firm in their opinion. The decision of their "unpleasant business" was postponed. In early June the Williamses and Shave were urged to attend the conference meeting later in the month. Shave appeared, was restored, and "given the right hand of fellowship by our Pastor." The Williamses chose not to attend and the vote to excommunicate both was unanimous. On July 5, 1816, seven months after the affair began, Thomas and Sarah Williams were declared from the pulpit as excommunicated. The church also suspended Williams's license to preach and rejected the idea that any member could simply "withdraw" due to a difference of opinion. The same principle was involved here as that concerning W. B. Johnson. The church was not nearly as liberal with Williams as it had been with Johnson.

In 1827 Harriet King was not dealt with as mercifully as Shave had been, though there may have been other considerations as well. On December 1, 1827, "the committee reported Sister Harriet King as having been cruel to her servants and to a young woman in her house and that her life had not been such as Christians should live and that she refused to hear the church." She was summarily excommunicated. Though accepting slavery as a legitimate institution, the church could be lenient as well as strict in its interpretation of administering this institution. Kate Wall, a slave member, in June 1805 was not dealt with so redemptively. Pregnant and without a husband, she was excommunicated from the "union and communion" of the church. Indeed, these white pilgrims were sometimes wayfarers when it came to dealing with issues involving blacks.

Numerous disciplinary cases dealt with members leaving the Baptist church in order to join churches of other denominations. For a long while this was considered as a just cause for excommunication. By the close of the century, however, the more popular phrase was "withdrawing the hand of fellowship" even though at the same time a letter might be sent to the other church commending the character of the member who was leaving. Though Savannah Baptist was ecumenical in some ways, there were early separatistic views and loyalty to denominational standards. There was also unevenness resulting from ecumenical relations with some denominations such as the Methodists and Presbyterians. With these the Baptists were more prone to friendly separation and avoided such terms as "heresy" or "heretical." This was certainly not the case with such groups as the Swedenborgians ("New Church," so-called), Christian Scientists, Catholics, Mormons, Disciples, and Christians. All these were designated as heretical and considered as sects and cults at times.

The list of illustrations of switching denominations is too lengthy to rehearse completely but a few are worthy of being told. Early on one case of this type illustrated the Baptist commitment to "close" or "closed" communion. It was deemed that one needed the proper kind of baptism to qualify one for the communion table as well as a proper symbolic interpretation of the ordinance. Baptists, in the main, though from different congregations would share a common communion table. In the nineteenth century, however, Baptists in the South would not have intercommunion with other denominations. Their communion table was "closed" to all but fellow Baptists. Savannah Baptists at this time practiced closed communion. At the church conference meeting of January 19, 1810, Mary Holmes was questioned as to whether she had requested membership with a Methodist Church and it was implied that she perhaps had taken communion with Methodists. Though she answered in the negative, she was told not to attend communion the next Sunday and that her case would be investigated. In April Holmes was invited to attend a discipline meeting. She did not attend, was found guilty of lying concerning the matter, and was unanimously excommunicated.

Not all such matters ended in excommunication. On May 10, 1811, Sister O'Connor was accused of a number of matters which she denied. One item she did not deny but said that she had done this only to satisfy her husband. The act of which she was accused was as follows: "For attending the Roman Catholic worship and taking a blessing, as they called it, by taking the water and crossing herself and bowing to the images. . . . " She was barred from communion until she "saw her error." Her meek spirit and expression of regret were accepted and on June 7 she was "restored to the fellowship of this Church." Other similar cases often led to switching denominations—especially if other critical beliefs were adopted. Denominational pluralism offered a variety of choices. On March 18, 1814, it was reported that Sister Houver had worshiped with the Methodists and "thought that if she had an infant child, it would be her duty to have it sprinkled." Present at the meeting, Houver agreed that this was the truth and that she still was committed to this belief. A committee was appointed to speak and pray with her and "to instill in her correct principles." The committee was unsuccessful and within the month Houver "was suffered to withdraw." Under pressure and perhaps due to changed beliefs, she joined a different Protestant fellowship. Another such case concerning the Methodists took place in August 1831 and involved a Mrs. Dean who had actually joined the Methodist Church as encouragement to her husband and also because she was "not having fellowship with some of the members" of the Baptist church. However worthy her motives, Dean had not informed the Baptists and had broken her covenant with the congregation. She was summarily "cut off" as a part of discipline. In the next century switching denominations would be an easier and much friendlier matter.

Baptists seemed perennially to be losing members to the Methodist Church. An especially poignant case took place in August 1832. Sisters Middleton and McClean were reported as having joined the Methodist Church and a discipline committee investigated. Middleton reported that in her sick condition she had been completely neglected by Baptist members and joined the Methodists. McClean's account was especially moving. Yes, she reported, she had joined the Methodists, for as a stranger in the city and the Baptist church, "from the coldness and the distance which the members of the Church manifested towards her, she felt herself agrieved [sic], that on one ocasion [sic] she was made sport of by some of the members of the church, and she presumed for no other cause than that they were finer dressed than what she was." The committee sympathized and "mourned over the circumstance" but decided in line with disciplinary expectations—both women were censured and of course lost to the congregation.

Alexander Campbell's ideas not only affected the First African Baptist Church, but the white church's membership also experienced his "Herrisey." At least the Methodists were not considered as heretical, but the tradition coming to be known as the Churches of Christ was already a direct threat to many Baptist congregations in the South. In April and May 1833 it was determined that Sarah Brook and Rebekah Stillwell had associated themselves with a "body who profess the Doctrine of Alexr. Campbell which we believe to be Herrisey." Both women were "cut off and excluded" from the Baptist Church. There would never be peace or reconciliation of Baptists with Churches of Christ in the nineteenth century.

In late 1859 and early 1860 an interesting discipline case occurred involving one who wished to become an Episcopalian with a view to entering the ministry. Brother Falligant reported such an interest to the church and obviously hoped for a friendly leaving. This would not be the case, however. Though correspondence, often heated, occurred over a period of months, the congregation finally declared Falligant's relationship with the church dissolved, for he had "departed from the faith and practice of the Baptist denomination." In 1875 and 1880 some members joined the Catholic Church and one became a member of the "New Church"—the Swedenborgian. All of them were "cut off." Pluralism in American Christianity had not yet achieved too much ecumenism on the grassroots level, especially in relation to switching denominational membership. By the end of the century, however, though the "hand of fellowship" was generally withdrawn, a letter affirming positive moral character was often sent to other denominational churches which were receiving members who had formerly been Baptist. On September 2, 1896, Mrs. E. D. Miltier received such a letter as she left the Baptist Church and united with the Independent Presbyterian Church.

Doctrine was sometimes directly a component in discipline cases. Baptists were not "creedal" but they were definitely "confessional." Individual churches certainly retained their congregational rights relative to the interpretation of doctrine and confessions, but Baptists did subscribe to a particular, more popular confession. In 1742 the Philadelphia Baptist Association, the oldest in the country, adopted the first major Baptist confession in America, and it became regularly used in the South. Based on the 1677 Second London Confession of English Baptists, the confession reflected strong Calvinistic beliefs. In 1833 the New Hampshire Baptist Confession of Faith appeared, reflecting a much milder form of Calvinism that attempted to retain both the sovereignty of God as well as individual freedom and salvation as a possibility for anyone who responded in faith to the Christ-act. Savannah Baptist Church reflected what was popularly happening in Baptist circles regarding confessions and their Manuals illustrated this confessional commitment.

Early on in relation to doctrine, a blatant case was resolved quickly. On February 22, 1811, Brother Justis Starr was quoted in conference by an investigating committee member as having said that "he did not believe the Scripture to be the word of God, and that, if in his power, he would destroy the Bible." Nevertheless, "he begged the indulgence of the Church for a time." The "for a time" was extremely brief, for Baptists were outraged by such blatant language. One week later Starr was unanimously excommunicated.

An unusual doctrinal case took place a bit later in 1811. At the discipline meeting on April 5, 1811, it was reported that Brother Sheldon Dunning "does not hold us in fellowship, but that he says we are acting contrary to the rules of the Gospel." Here was a reverse situation. A member was accusing the church first, and that of serious doctrinal error. Dunning was invited to the discipline meeting one week distant, appeared, and proceeded to read a statement for an hour and a half! In brief he accused the church of the unscriptural act of prohibiting voluntary withdrawal of membership, of not conducting the business of the church on Sunday, and of not celebrating communion on a weekly basis. Interestingly, three years later Pastor Johnson would condemn the church for these very same reasons. Dunning then affirmed that he had "excommunicated us from his fellowship"—this was discipline in reverse and a reflection of extreme congregational individualism. A former deacon, Dunning also claimed that the church owed him a great deal of money. Some of this was paid but Dunning refused to be reconciled or to admit error. Because of this, on April 21 he was unanimously "suspended" from the church.

Two years later there was an intriguing footnote aftermath to this painful incident. For several months Dunning's sister, Mary, had been investigated as to her own withdrawal and her attitude toward her brother's case. On April 30, 1813, Mary stated, "that this church acted contrary to scripture and affirmed that she had a right to withdraw from us as she had done and that the church had no right to exercise discipline towards her nor would she abide by our discipline as a church, for that the Lord alone had the dominion over her conscience." She also declared that the church had no right to dismiss her brother. Her case was delayed for a full year. During this time, associational advice was sought by the church, and in 1813 the association sided with "liberty of conscience"—this ruled out disciplinary action in Mary's case as interpreted by the Association. Late the next year, however, the Association reversed its decision and ruled such individual withdrawal as subject to congregational discipline. Prior to this reversal, the church dealt with Mary in a way which was contrary to the associational advice of 1813. Pastor Johnson actually disagreed with the final church decision—he urged that she had a right to withdraw and not be disciplined. The vote on March 4, 1814, was a large majority vote to excommunicate her. Only four voted against the motion. Both Dunnings were excommunicated. Within the year, Pastor Johnson would claim his own right to "withdraw." No excommunication procedures were imposed on him, however. One must observe that he received preferential treatment even though he caused the first schism, however minor, in the church. The Dunnings and Johnson had accused the church of serious doctrinal error. Only the Dunnings were disciplined.

Two excommunications took place in 1816 and 1822 involving several key Baptist doctrines at the time. On July 12, 1816, Brother Rawson was excommunicated for believing in and practicing "mixed communion." Baptists at this time generally accepted only "closed communion"—that is, a Baptist was only to take communion in a Baptist church. On June 1, 1822, Sister Ball was excommunicated not only because she had joined the Methodist Church but also because she now believed in infant baptism and rejected the Calvinistic doctrine of the perseverance of the saints. Thoughts on these matters would change or at least be modified in the next century.

Numerous cases dealing with morality are found in the Minutes. By far the act most often calling for discipline concerned liquor and public drunkenness. Both males and females suffered serious censure for this act, especially if they seemed unable to reform. A very moving case with Elizabeth Jones took place in May and June 1812. Prior to Alcoholics Anonymous and the availability of professional help, based on cases cited herein it appears that alcoholism was not considered a disease but a serious lapse in morality. On May 10 Elizabeth was called before the congregation for "having been too frequently intoxicated by liquor." She showed public remorse and promised not to be guilty of this act again. The church delayed its decision to see if her repentance was genuine. By June 19 it was reported that "she had again drunk to intoxication so that she fell down once in the public street and again at her mother-in-law's door." On June 21 she was excommunicated. It was noted that she could be "very penitent when brought before the church, and then she would go back to the same habit, so the Church thought it best to expel her." Obviously an alcoholic, Elizabeth did not receive the kind of redemptive help that she needed. Moreover, she was only one of many such persons. The cases of William Eaton and Amelia White had lingered for several months in 1822 and in September both were excommunicated. Of Sister White the Minutes recorded: "It is well known she is waxing worse and worse." Several members had "seen her in a state of inebriation, and while in this state associating with very improper company." Redemption did sometimes take place—in August 1824 "Bro Eaton was restored to full fellowship in the Church." The church could be understanding in unusual circumstances as is illustrated of Brother White on Christmas Eve 1832. The Minutes report:

> Brother White who was charged with having been intoxicated acknowledged the fact, and says it did not proceed from a desire to indulge in drinking, but he was tempted by Satan, through the disturbed State of his mind on account of circumstances beyond his control, and he farther states that he has not tasted a drop since the period to which we have reference. He feels truly penitent for his conduct, constantly praying that the Lord will have mercy upon him and not cast him away on account of his transgressions.

He was then admonished and restored to full fellowship. As late as 1907 the New Sunbury Association was urging the use of strict discipline on those who persisted in drinking liquor.

The nineteenth century saw a number of Sabbath Societies founded across the country to urge worship and quiet on the day of resurrection. Savannah Baptists did not have a society, but in their discipline they were most sensitive to a proper keeping of the Lord's Day. In February 1825 Ann Lillibridge was invited to give an account of herself at the discipline meeting. She was described as being "in the habit of disposing of goods on the Sabbath day." She appeared and expressed sorrow for selling goods on Sunday. She was forgiven. An unusual Sabbath case involving George Ash occurred between August 1831 and January 1832. In August it was reported that Ash went "on a maruning [sic] excursion, to be absent some days, thereby violating the Holy Sabbath" with a number of persons "some of whom is known to be unfriendly to Religion, which conduct is calculated, to bring disgrace upon the cause of our Master, and shame upon the church." Ash then later asked for a dismission letter—he would simply become a "hearer" not subject to discipline. The church finally declared this to be against all the doctrine and procedures of the church and then censured him. Economy often played a role in Sabbath keeping. In March 1835 Brother Dellamotta was called on by the discipline committee due to his keeping his barber shop open on Sunday. Dellamotta told the committee that to do this was "indispensable for the support of his family, and the accommodation of his customers." He also judged that he was being too harshly dealt with and "would rather be free from Membership than continue under the restrictions." By June the barber had been socialized, converted, or felt the pressure of a potential boycott, for he agreed to close his shop on the Sabbath. He added, however, that he was doing this "not for fear of what the church can do but after mature deliberation." Part of his "mature deliberation" had to have included a fear of the loss of patronage, sometimes worse than excommunication.

A wide variety of other cases illustrates the broad application of discipline, some very logical and moral and others bordering on a rather strict legalism. Watchfulness even included out-of-town trips. In September 1856 Brother William Phillips was suspended and later excommunicated for intoxication, gambling, and visiting "improper places" during a visit to New Orleans in earlier April. In September 1832 Thomas Williams was excommunicated for being "guilty of taking a few articles from the Store of Mr. A. Champion." Stealing was certainly frowned upon by the people of God. There seemed to be flexibility in relation to card playing. Of course if a person were gambling with cards, that was a serious disciplinary matter. In November 1820 Brother Tupper reflected on some benefits: "Mr. Tupper owned that he took a game at cards, without betting, sometimes; to keep young men from worse employment; but was willing to relinquish it, provided, that it offended the brethren in the church." Profanity was also frowned upon, especially if in the presence of other offenses. Brother Fennel in March 1853 was excommunicated for profanity and neglect of duty. From June to September 1806 Brother William B. Barnes was reduced from "Brother" to "Mr." by excommunication and certainly did not help his case by his explosive profanity. He had fallen out of fellowship with some members, had requested dismission to join another church, and was invited to a discipline meeting. There it was reported that when the invitation letter was delivered, Barnes "appeared very angry, expressed dissatisfaction with some of the Brethren, and at length swore profanely that he would not appear at any Ecclesiastical court, for that he hated them, and always had hated them." For contempt and "the horrid sin of profane swearing" he was suspended and later excommunicated. Though the Minutes reported in mid-September that Holcombe pronounced the excommunication in a "very moderate and delicate manner," there was no doubt that there would ever be restoration for Mr. Barnes.

Dancing was considered offensive and worldly. In May 1822 reports had circulated that "Brother and Sister Postill and Sister Sweet" had committed "unworthy conduct in attending recently a public ball." "Admonition" was the discipline imposed since they expressed regret for their actions. As late as October 1877 two pages of Minutes were used to give a judgmental report on "modern" dancing with a conclusion that the church needed a baptism of the Holy Spirit and members were urged not to conform themselves to the world with its worldly amusements such as dancing.

Attending the theatre was certainly considered to be a component of worldly amusements. In April 1832 Sister Trespar was censured for attending the theater, and one year later Sister Banks was excommunicated for the same offense, but with a different twist. This free-thinking woman saw nothing wrong with it! The Minutes in June 1833 reflected the committee's report on Banks: "She conceives that no evil can be attached to her visiting the Theatre, manifests no disposition of penitence, and upon further conversation stated, that if an opportunity offered would again commit the same Sin." Banks was a Baptist who was culturally ahead of her religious age and context.

Horse racing and betting mixed with card playing proved to be sufficient grievances for the excommunication of Brother John Gill in December 1834: "The charge against Brother John Gill was that he was engaged not long since in a horse race (the horse being his own) and betting, also engaged at playing at cards." Multiple offenses perennially earned being cut off from the church completely. Fornication, adultery, and intense quarreling invariably merited excommunication. The church did show sensitivity in relation to wife abuse, however, in October 1810 with Sister Jourdan and in April 1836 with Sister Huchison, who had been slapped numerous times by her husband. In November 1807 Sister McMullen seemed to have experienced sexual harassment and pressure was brought upon the male to state his guilt in public and to request forgiveness. Sometimes legalism could definitely be on the right side of situations.

Bringing civil suit against another member of the church was also frowned upon and dealt with by the use of discipline. In February 1833 a special committee was appointed to draw up guidelines concerning this matter. Within two months the committee submitted a lengthy report (adopted) which in brief said that the scripture did forbid such practice. The biblical reference used was Matthew, chapter 18:15–18, whose ideal is that the congregation is the final tribunal. The report's key paragraph read as follows:

> The church then is the tribunal, in the last resort, if the parties cannot settle the difficulty among themselves, to which all brethren who are unhappily at variance, must appeal for a removal of the cause of their differences and disaffection. And that this is the only tribunal is evident, among others, from this consideration. The differences which arise among Christians, should be settled on the principles of the Gospel, and everyone should be willing as indeed he is duty bound to act according to them, for they are based on strict justice and equity.

Obviously a simplistic idealism is reflected here which, one must say, is winsome within the Christian context. However, the full report also showed realism as well. If the person against whom the offended brother brought charges refused to accept the decision of the congregation, then he became, to the church and the offended brother, "a heathen man and a publican." The report then offered another avenue of justice. The offended brother was allowed to "adopt those means for the redress of his grievance and the maintenance of his rights which the civil and judicial institutions of the community in which he dwells secure to him." Suits especially concerning financial debts were perennially possible. The congregation had acted, however, and these guidelines were its expectations. Otherwise, discipline would be applied.

Cases involving multiple and continuous infractions were quickly handled by the judgment of excommunication. In September 1858 Brother Mulhyne was cut off quickly for playing cards, using profane language, and being a member of a thespian group. In January 1868 George Ulmer and Isaac Crawford were excommunicated "for a long continued course of unchristian conduct." Fellowship was also withdrawn from William Cole in August 1892 for an "unchristian manner of living and a recent act unworthy of a man and church member." We are left in the dark concerning the latter act but it must have been public and with contextually moral implications.

By the close of the nineteenth century even Baptists were becoming socialized in relation to certain social and amusement practices. For example, dancing offenses simply disappeared from the discipline cases. Even though associations as well as the Southern Baptist Convention continued to oppose certain "worldly amusements," local congregations such as Savannah Baptist did not show much interest in disciplining over these matters. Pastoral counseling in its own way began to deal with the more serious cases such as public drunkenness.

Though the Baptist theologian John L. Dagg in mid-nineteenth century had declared that "when discipline leaves a church, Christ goes with it," Savannah Baptists had found other ways to deal with discipline in the main by the twentieth century. Discipline was redefined as the socialization process took place. Urban Baptist churches especially changed and did not retain old forms of discipline. Teaching, education, and pastoral care and counseling replaced the old ways of doing things. The theology as well as the economy of the retention of members replaced the "lopping-off" philosophy. The vision of a pure church of committed pilgrims yielded to the idea of an efficient church redeeming the "sometimes" wayfaring pilgrims through counseling, religious education, and congregational nurturing. As early as October 1871 Savannah Baptists, without a pastor, in its yearly letter reported: "Our membership as a whole is orderly in Christian walk and conversation, and but little occasion has existed, and does exist, for arraignments of our memberships for misconduct." The yearly letter of 1871 was prophetic of the next century.

Part of the dynamics for the decline of discipline was the growth of the idea of individual freedom, of the concept of tolerance, and perhaps of the hesitancy to judge others lest one be judged! Congregational responsibility for keeping the purity of the church yielded to the stress on individual responsibility.

So, a constellation of reasons led to the decline and redefinition of discipline. The brave new fact of the twentieth century, ecumenism, also led to new understandings about church membership on the pluralistic American scene. For good or ill, there was always another church around the block to fit the beliefs and life styles of the individual—sometimes within the very same denomination. And, it would be rare indeed today if someone were excommunicated for merely "withdrawing" and aligning oneself with a different church, whether of the same denomination or otherwise.

Gregory Wills is correct, however, in his recent book, *Democratic Religion* when he observes of discipline:

> A significant residue remains. In the Southern Baptist denomination, churches occasionally exclude an adulterer, but usually prefer to sentence offenders of different kinds to private therapy rather than communal discipline. More commonly, perhaps, Baptist associations agitate to disfellowship churches that ordain women, tolerate homosexuality, or recognize alien immersions as valid baptisms.

Wills's list could correctly be expanded to include persons and churches that accept female pastors, believe in the freedom of choice in relation to abortion, and do not accept a plenary verbal theory about the inspiration of the Bible. The new Southern Baptist Convention is politically dominated and run by neofundamentalists who have reversed the process of discipline on these and other matters on their agenda. Discipline in this denomination presently is a matter of power imposed from the top rather than authority percolating from the bottom. Individual responsibility and congregational autonomy have been replaced by the raw power of those at the top who issue papal pronouncements. In this respect, Baptist history has been "broken" and replaced by nonhistorical Baptist principles. In other words, there has been a prostitution of the principle of discipline which aimed at establishing the Kingdom of God among us to a principle determined to produce people and churches that sing and play the very same tune of faith and practice as a select group of fundamentalist leaders have composed. Baptist history gives the lie to this approach as does the history of discipline in the nineteenth century in Savannah Baptist Church.

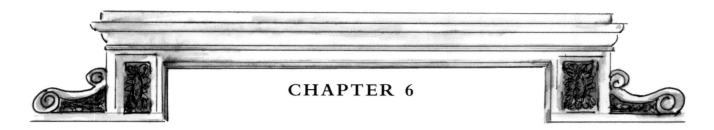

CHAPTER 6

DOCTRINE, LITURGY, WORSHIP, EDUCATION

The four prongs of this chapter overlap greatly with one another—if you please, they are interdisciplinary—doctrine, liturgy, worship, and education. Each is of great importance on the local congregational level and each has its own history within the larger story of the Savannah Baptist Church in the nineteenth century.

DOCTRINE

The denominational complexity of the Baptist movement as well as the Baptist commitment to the priesthood of every believer and to the autonomy of the local church have resulted in a confused and often confusing pattern in the search for doctrine and then orthodoxy. Instead of one orthodox position there have been numerous orthodoxies and thus many conflicts and controversies. Baptists have not been a silent people in this respect. Baptist history has included dozens of major controversies and heresies ranging from problems of order to problems of doctrine and including sociological, psychological, personal, and economic motifs. Religious controversy is never *simply* religious. General Baptist history as well as that of the Southern Baptist Convention give numerous illustrations. There is not only denominational pluralism in relation to doctrine; there is also Southern Baptist pluralism. The question "What do Baptists believe?" is a terribly complex question to answer. And, the answer changes with the moving years.

It has already been noted that Baptists have been a confessional people but not a creedal people. Being honest, however, sometimes confessions are interpreted creedally and used in the same way as creeds have been used in high church traditions such as the Roman Catholic. No doubt about it, the fine line which separates creeds and confessions is often redrawn by the times and the interpretations. The *intent* of Baptist confessions, to be sure, was not creedal, but the use and interpretations have often moved in that direction.

More specifically, Baptists in America and in the South were especially influenced by two major confessions, one of which was more strictly Calvinistic, the other more softly Calvinistic and moderated by Arminian ideas. These two, which have been mentioned earlier, are the Philadelphia Confession of 1742, more strictly Calvinistic, and the New Hampshire Confession of 1833, softly Calvinistic. The Manual of 1860 of the Savannah Baptist Church follows very carefully the wording of the New Hampshire confession though certainly influenced in earlier years by the very popular Philadelphia Confession. Many of the articles found in the Savannah Manual would be acceptable in a number of different denominational contexts, but a few are distinctly related to the Baptist tradition. It must also be noted that individual members were usually less likely to be so legalistic about doctrinal statements than some ministers, associations, and national bodies. Grassroots members are far more likely to be ecumenical in any generation on these matters.

Certain articles of the Savannah Declaration of Faith (1860) should be pointedly discussed as they reflect on specifically Baptist belief and practice. The article "The Scriptures" is flexible and lends itself to widely diverse interpretations. It is an umbrella which allows a variety of acceptable interpretations—from plenary verbal to a historical and critical view of the scriptures. The genius here is an acceptance of Christian experience which takes the scriptures seriously regarding religious truth. The "theory" of inspiration is not that important—the commitment and experience are. In the Savannah Baptist Church of the nineteenth century no debates or arguments over theories of inspiration occurred.

Strict Calvinism among Baptists, Presbyterians, and other denominations resulted in numerous controversies, especially in the face of moderating or softening attempts by Calvinistic Arminianism. Baptist thought was opened to Arminianism due to widespread revivalism as well as a developing interest in missions through the likes of Luther Rice, who had visited Savannah on several occasions, and others. Revivalism and missions simply did not get along experientially with theological predestinarianism promoted by a strict Calvinistic view. In fact the strict Calvinists among Baptists often entered the antimission ranks; one of the results was schism. Savannah's Declaration of Faith of 1860 followed the softened position of the New Hampshire Confession. The article "The Freeness of Salvation" proclaimed "that nothing prevents the salvation of the greatest sinner on earth." Articles "Repentance and Faith" and "Sanctification" are found in the Savannah statement, topics which usually were signs of the New Hampshire tradition. Double-edged predestinarianism, which left no room for the concept of the freedom of the will, was rejected. Savannah had been and would be positively inclined toward missions and that kind of evangelicalism which expressed itself often in revivalism. The kind of "election" to which Savannah Baptists subscribed was "perfectly consistent with the free agency of man." God acts and human beings react. Legalistic predestinarianism was rejected out of hand.

It is true that both the New Hampshire Confession and the Savannah Declaration stressed the church as being a visible congregation of baptized believers. From the start, Baptists had urged local autonomy but most of them would not be extremists like the schismatic Landmark tradition with their absolute lack of a theology of the universal church. Savannah urged local autonomy but was also committed to the associational principle both with Baptists as well as other denominations (and through the years would progress to an even more complete ecumenism).

Article xiv dealt forthrightly with the only two ordinances (the preferred word among Baptists) accepted by Savannah Baptists—Baptism and the Lord's Supper. Baptism is of course described as "immersion in water of a believer," a badge of honor and scriptural correctness among Baptists. They also rejected infant baptism as an improper form though they certainly did not reject the later lives lived as committed Christians. The brief statement describing Baptism left numerous questions to be answered through the years of the church's pilgrimage and growth. Early on in 1804 an example of this was observed on the Savannah Association level. The question arose as to whether or not baptism performed by an unbaptized person was "valid." The association's answer was "not ordinarily." This certainly left the door open for those extraordinary situations involving life-threatening contexts when an individual requested baptism and no one was present who had received any kind of baptism. The implication was that the "human thing" would be done and the person would be baptized by the unbaptized. In such a case, then, if the newly baptized person survived, there would be no rebaptism because Baptists did not believe in such. In 1842 the New Sunbury Association was thrown another sticky question.

This time the issue was whether baptism by a paedo-Baptist minister should be accepted. The Association's answer moved in the direction of a negative answer but finally left the matter to the judgment of the local church and the individual involved. This really raised the question of "alien baptism" or baptism by someone other than a Baptist. Different practices were to be and still are found among different Baptist churches. Savannah Baptists set an early precedent toward a more liberal and ecumenical attitude. The Minutes of May 6, 1866, report that G. F. Fowke became a member of the church and was not rebaptized. He had been immersed in the name of the Trinity as an adult in the Campbellite or Christian tradition, and his baptism was received as valid. Many other Baptist churches at the time would have rebaptized the gentleman.

In the first and second buildings there were baptisteries. It is recorded that in the first church Holcombe baptized the first person in the Savannah Baptist Church in late 1800—Elizabeth Ladson Godfrey, only child of Anthony and Elizabeth. Candidates sometimes waited for a week or more before baptism was performed, though occasionally it was almost immediate. In October 1817 it is recorded that James Roe professed his faith during the morning worship service and was baptized on the same date at 2:30 in the afternoon. Candidates were also given the choice as to whether they would be immersed in the baptistery or in the Savannah River. In the river they were more often baptized at Pooler's Wharf or at Wayne's Wharf. Times were sometimes changed due to accidents. In August 1805 the Minutes inform us: "This was the day set for Mrs. Stackhouse to be baptized, but for lack of water, some having leaked out of the font [an unlikely use of this term in Baptist circles], baptism was necessarily deferred until the next Lord's Day." The tides also determined times for those who chose the river. In May 1809, "Mrs. Jordan was notified that the tide would suit for the administration next Lord's Day immediately after the morning service." Rather odd hours were sometimes used for baptism. In April 1811 an unusual time and a very brief waiting period are noted in a descriptive Minute of an evening service:

> Mr. Aaron Shave . . . came forward and related a satisfactory work of grace wrought on his soul, and desiring to be baptized . . ., Brother Screven agreed to Baptize him this night tho' the moon did not shine. . . . He with the Candidate followed by the Church, repaired to the river at Wayne's Wharf . . . he solemnly Baptized him at 11 o'clock p.m. After singing a doxology the members retired to their homes, blessing and praising God for all his goodness manifested to them on this happy day.

An early morning baptism with its resurrection symbolism nicely reflects Christian theology. Such a one was held in July 1812: "At a little after sunrise this morning the church assembled at their place of worship from whence they proceeded to the waterside in company with the [two] candidates for baptism who were immersed in the presence of a large concourse of people notwithstanding the early hour of the day." The number of persons being baptized varied. On one Sunday we read of ten and then on another Sunday of eleven persons who "went down together." The baptistery in the first church was probably under the pulpit platform. The first baptistery in the Chippewa Square church was definitely beneath the pulpit platform and was made ready for use by lifting two large trap doors from the floor. Candidates after December 1898 must have appreciated the physical circumstances of the ceremony because by then the church had installed "the necessary apparatus for heating water in the baptistery." Upon acceptance in the membership each person signed the church covenant (making him/her subject to discipline), received a copy of the church's declaration of faith, and upon being baptized was able to receive the Lord's Supper. In fact, communion was often celebrated after baptism, thereby continuing an important ancient church tradition.

The Lord's Supper, or Communion, was the second ordinance accepted by Baptists and only through baptism could one sit at this common table. As baptism symbolized the resurrection and the new life, communion celebrated the unity of the covenant people of God as well as the gift of Jesus the Christ. At this time Baptists practiced "close" or "closed" communion, however. Although Baptists from other churches were invited to participate, members of other denominations were not. The communion table was "closed" to them in the nineteenth century. The common cup was used—a large goblet. No individual cups were passed around the congregation. Wine was also appropriately used by the congregation until very late in the century. As early as 1833 the Association was calling for "total abstinence." By 1876 the Association was urging that no Baptist should buy or sell any liquor—even wine. As late as 1878, however, the records of Savannah Baptist specifically refer to the purchase of wine for use in communion, perhaps as late as 1892. Some Baptist churches even in the next century would use wine and some still do. Most of these churches stopped using wine during Prohibition, but later many religious leaders no longer urged total abstinence. The common cup was also given up in December 1906 when the church switched to its newly purchased "individual communion service." The Declaration of Faith of 1860 described the ordinance as one "in which the members of the church, by the sacred use of bread and wine, are to commemorate together the dying love of Christ; preceded always by solemn self-examination." As well, the Covenant reminded all members that they were "to walk together in Him with brotherly love."

All the other articles of the Declaration of Faith placed the Baptists essentially in the Protestant camp of evangelicals with little if any difference. Even the article "Civil Government" presented a fairly mild statement, for the Baptist emphases on religious liberty and the separation of church and state had already been achieved by virtue of the founding documents of the comparatively new United States.

LITURGY AND WORSHIP

Baptists have not generally been considered to be a liturgical community. Actually, though, liturgy simply refers to the "work of the people." Perhaps it is more helpful to refer to high and low liturgies and/or to uniform and spontaneous or flexible liturgies. Liturgy is simply the way Christians go about their worship, and sometimes the lowest of liturgies are the most highly predictable—even to voice inflections.

As already observed, the topics of this chapter more often overlap than not. Part of the liturgical worship pattern to be described among Baptists has to do with their celebration of the ordinances which has been discussed above. There are other, numerous parts of their total liturgy, however.

Savannah Baptists conducted three main types of congregational services, and their Manual called for a regular participation in all of these. There were services of worship, church conferences or business meetings, and discipline meetings. Worship was mainly conducted on Sunday, of course, but days for the other services varied from Friday to Saturday to Monday, usually.

Services of worship on Sunday are more reflective of those major moments in the religious affection of Baptists in Savannah. Worship services were conducted primarily in the morning, afternoon, and early evening. Funerals, yellow fever, lack of a minister, and other reasons sometimes caused cancellations. An average Sunday, however, was a terribly busy worship day. Baptists in Savannah staggered home refreshed on an average Sunday evening. February 7, 1808, touched all bases with even an ecumenical flair: "Brother Lugg preached an acceptable sermon in forenoon after which Mr. Mallard preached in afternoon and in the evening Mr. Capel, another Methodist preacher, preached a sermon highly satisfactory. We hope their united labors may be blest of God for good to the hearers this day."

It is difficult if not impossible to describe a typical worship service in the early years of the nineteenth century. It is correct to say, however, that the preacher's sermon was central and consumed most of the time. Beyond that, the liturgy or "work of the people" was flexible. For example, worship on February 14, 1808, is described as follows: "Our pastor [Holcombe] preached in the fore and afternoon of this day with an unusual degree of animation and zeal, and in the Evening Brother Dunning went forward in Reading, singing, and prayer, and Brother Williams closed the duties of the evening by expounding and exhorting to a very numerous Congregation." Sermons, scripture, prayer, music, and emotion were all parts of the liturgy. Even the building lent itself to simplicity—like a meeting hall. Most early Baptist churches were simply large rectangular rooms with a centrally located pulpit. Savannah Baptists' first church building was a large, simple rectangular room; even the second building was described as "a simple temple with a flight of steps leading to the portico." Both buildings were first and foremost meeting and preaching rooms.

Music certainly played a major role in all Baptist services. There was probably no organ in the first church of the Baptists. At least there is no mention of such in the Minutes. There was a great deal of music, however, and often some kind of instrumental music. Henry Holcombe, first pastor, supported classes in singing as well as instrumental music. In December 1804 the *Columbian Museum and Savannah Advertiser* announced: "Mr. Horace Bull respectfully informs the inhabitants of Savannah that he intended to commence teaching psalmody in the Baptist church . . . and instrumental music at the home of Mr. Holcombe in the evening."

Far more is recorded concerning music in the church after 1856, though some items are mentioned earlier. There are gaps in the record, of course, including the first five years, 1800–1805, and during the schism, 1847–1859. Certainly there was music in the early years, but the congregation was small and struggling. Soon enough, however, specific attention was given to leadership in this aspect of worship. In January 1816 the Minutes report:

> The church agreed to employ Mr. White master of Musick, to lead in Psalmody in this Church, and for his services agreed to make him some compensation. Sister Ann Williams was desired to acquaint Mr. White herewith,—also Sister Shick was desired to say to Mr. Blockwood that the Church feels grateful for his proferred services in aiding us in Psalmody and requests the favor of him to acquire as much knowledge as he can of sacred musick during the stay of Mr. White among us, after which time the Church will gladly accept of his services in that line, should the views of the Church meet his approbation.

Reading between the lines, the church planned to pay a professional for awhile and then, hopefully, the novice Blockwood could continue as an informed volunteer. The first mention of an instrument used in worship occurs a bit later in the same year, July, but unfortunately on a negative note. The clerk of the church in conference "professed his grief at the introduction of a Bass Viol in the Church, at the time of Divine worship, in singing as being unwarranted by the worshipers of Christ under the New Testament dispensation, which he stated was repugnant to the feelings of him and other members in this Church." He further urged that any other instrumental music would not be used. The pastor followed this up by thanking the "Gentlemen singers" (leaders) for their services to the congregation and hoped they would continue to sing but without the accompaniment of the Bass Viol. These music leaders were culturally ahead of their times, of course, although some Baptists even in the twentieth century do not accept any musical instruments, not even a piano or organ, to be used in their services. Savannah Baptists were not so conservative later, but Pastor Screven backed away from this problem in 1816 with his request, which was honored.

Scattered notations also inform us that Thomas Y. Lee directed music between 1829–1831 and was paid $25 each quarter of the year for this service. During this time it is also recorded that a dozen music books were purchased for $10. On February 4, 1831, the Minutes observe: "Thomas Y. Lee resigned from the choir as leader of the singing department in this church." Lee apparently returned for a number of years, however, for his name appears in the budget as late as 1835 as having received payment for his services. Nothing special is noted in the Minutes, though. During some years the Minutes were very skimpy, some virtually unreadable.

Savannah Baptists, at least some of them, were surely influenced and taught about music from the various activities of Lowell Mason in Savannah between 1812 and 1827. This man who eventually would be nationally famous due to his contributions in the field of sacred music, was not only organist at the Independent Presbyterian Church but he also conducted singing schools for sacred music in Savannah. Surely a few Baptists attended some of his classes conducted in Chatham Academy and heard some of his organ concerts. As shall be observed shortly, Mason also made groundbreaking contributions to the beginning of Sunday Schools in Savannah. Some of his most famous hymns are even today found in virtually all Christian hymn books. Three of many famous ones were written in Savannah and must have been sung by Baptists early on—"When I Survey the Wondrous Cross," "From Greenland's Icy Mountains," and "Safely through Another Week." (For an excellent presentation of Mason, see Margaret F. LaFar, "Lowell Mason's Varied Activities in Savannah," *Georgia Historical Quarterly*, September 1944).

By July 1856 a series of numerous entries begins in the Minutes implying that a piano had been used for a long while in the services and that it would be sold to the First African Baptist Church and money raised to purchase an organ. By the end of the summer of 1856 the organ was in place in the rear gallery, and Sister Falligant was the organist. By October 1856 the church had adopted rules and regulations for the choir. It would be under the supervision of the congregation and not independent; it would elect its own officers and add to itself by election; the choirmaster would be appointed by the pastor subject to church approval; and the organist would be selected by the choir without committing the church in money matters without a congregational vote. These rules fluctuated and were flexible through the following years.

Salaries, titles, and personnel changed, sometimes yearly. In 1860 the organist was paid $150; by 1861 this was reduced by $50 while the leader of music, or choir leader, was paid $100. In 1860 Brother W. H. Farrell, appointed as leader of music, requested a screen in the gallery to separate the choir from some "rude boys who sit in the gallery." The church not only granted the screen but carpet and more chairs as well; however, it did not find the funds to extend the gallery as requested by Farrell. The congregation evidently valued the organist, for in 1862 the salary was doubled and again in 1864. In 1865, however, the financial crunch reduced the salary to zero. Mrs. E. S. Gustin, then organist, was given pew number 81 in the middle aisle and whatever rents were forthcoming as her salary.

In 1868 the organ was repaired and the next year G. O. Robinson was offered the position of "leader of music" at the then handsome salary of $1,000. He was urged to recruit children for the music program as well as to "sing such tunes as that the congregation may join in." Soon thereafter he was again requested to select "music adapted to congregational singing." Professor Robinson may have been using music over the heads of the people, for in 1871 the church raised Gustin's salary to $400 and then stipulated that a member should be appointed to lead music *voluntarily*. Brother Bacon was at that point appointed as "leader of singing" and told to "make singing congregational."

By 1875 the Minutes state that Sister Gustin was raising funds by various means (surely by some concerts) in order to keep the organ in repair. The church did not seem to be as sensitive to the instrument as the artist. Still desirous of congregational participation in the music, in March 1875 the church appointed a committee to look into changing the hymnbook and to investigating the "propriety of introducing congregational singing." In April *The Baptist Hymn and Tune Book* was adopted. At the same time Bacon reported to the church that he believed he could fill a voluntary choir except for a good soprano and would raise funds himself to pay a soprano. A precedent was now being set for a paid choir—even among Baptists.

Early in 1876 Bacon resigned and Gustin added to her duties by becoming "leader of psalmody" in addition to being organist. The church conference in May was still pleading for "suitable church music." Exhausted, in June 1877 Gustin requested six weeks of leave and received it. Shortly after her return, Gustin requested a higher salary but was gently refused. The church virtually said, "We would if we could," but finances prohibited a raise. This rejection led in 1880 to the church's granting Gustin permission to give concerts and charge admission to improve her income. The budget of November 1882 included $850 for the organist and a choir of soprano, tenor, alto, and bass. Baptists had their paid choir, but Gustin resigned the next month to leave the city for a season. A glowing letter of appreciation was sent to the long-suffering organist by the church with the final compliment: "Our social life has been adorned by her womanly graces and virtues."

In October 1885 Pastor Holmes led the church to yet another hymnbook change. He wanted *The Baptist Hymnal* published by the American Baptist Publication Society, basically the Northern Baptist publication house. He also had the perfect financial plan—individual members would help pay for these books. By late 1888 Gustin was back in the city and once again serving as organist. Mrs. G. B. Whatley was the leader of music. They became the first all-female team in the history of the church. The quartet choir system was abolished at this time in favor of a chorus choir which, it was believed, would more greatly encourage full congregational singing. These Baptists were still convinced that they were not getting enough music out of the congregation.

By January 1889 there were two organs in the church as reflected in the insurance bills. The records indicate the pipe organ being insured for $1,800 and a reed organ for $200. The reed organ was evidently in the lower lecture room. A 100 percent volunteer choir did not work, evidently, for by November 1889 the budget included a soprano, alto, and bass who were being paid. The volunteer system was retained, however. They reasoned that having these paid singers would assure that there would always be a choir while the volunteers would sometimes add multiple voices to the various parts. In 1891 there was a motion in the church conference to move the organ from the gallery to the main floor. As usual for such motions, a committee was appointed, and it would be several years before action was taken.

Congregational participation in music seemed to be a lingering problem as numerous solutions were attempted. On November 9, 1893, the church conference voted to discontinue the choir and to depend on Sister Gustin, organist, and Professor R. E. Cobb, cornetist, to lead singing. It was believed that this move would be more economical and would improve the quality and quantity of congregational participation. One senses some tensions on this issue in late December when Gustin requested that she have "full control" of the music program in the church for one month. She wanted to see if alone she could improve congregational singing. One wonders if she was behind the request to move the organ, for on January 31, 1894, the organ was moved from the gallery down to the north side of the pulpit on an elevation. Gustin and her organ were now down among the people instead of far away in a gallery. The logic of the move made sense. In addition, the organ was overhauled, revoiced, and tuned. The cost of doing all this was covered by the income from "musical entertainment" on February 18, 1894. The budget in October reflected that the organist had been paid $400 and the cornetist $240. The budget of 1896 reflected that the choir was back and that some funds were being used to pay singers. Obviously, a paid choir was being phased out, however, and members would be educated toward the commitment of volunteering their services in the music program, at least in the choir. In February and March 1897 the Minutes tell of the purchase of a "grand piano" for $150. The funds were received from several sources. Fifty dollars credit was given for a "cabinet organ" (the reed organ in the lecture room), $26 was given by the Choral Association, and the balance of $74 was paid by the church. The Choral Association was a bit ahead of its time in Georgia—on the cutting edge. Early in the next century in Georgia there would be a growth in the encouragement of formal music. The Georgia Federation of Music Clubs would be founded in 1918, and by the 1920s music departments would begin to appear in the universities of Georgia. For decades Savannah Baptists had played their role in the encouragement of formal music in their city.

The terrible storm of August 30, 1898, wrought havoc in Savannah and the Savannah First Baptist Church (the term "First" was being used by May 1893 at the founding of Duffy Street, later Bull Street Baptist Church) was so terribly damaged that the church temporarily held its meetings in the Y.M.C.A. The organ was critically damaged and plans were made to replace it with a new organ and soon with a new organist. The Minutes stipulate that the organ was to be placed behind the pulpit, but one picture of the interior of the church in the *Morning News*, November 25, 1900, shows an organ in the center of the rear balcony. This was an old file picture. The organ had definitely been moved in 1894 to the main level of the sanctuary. In the twentieth century the new Skinner organ would be placed in the center of the choir loft high above the pulpit in the remodeled church of 1922. It would appear that the *Morning News* had used an old file picture. Though this minor matter is a bit uncertain, there is no uncertainty about the change in organists. Gustin was paid through March 1899. Samuel P. Snow came from Nashville, Tennessee, as the new organist and director of music and was paid $1,000 per year as salary. He could solicit a volunteer choir! Water-damaged hymnals were replaced by new ones made possible by the church's matching the gift of $100 made by Mrs. Carey A. Moore. At the annual conference meeting some restructuring was also completed. The Music Committee was dissolved and the Finance Committee assumed its responsibilities. Fittingly, in early March an organ recital celebrated the restoration of the church as well as presented the abilities of the new organ to the public. On the first Sunday in March Pastor Jordan yielded the pulpit to Dr. J. B. Hawthorne of Nashville, Tennessee, in the special celebratory worship service. Things were in place for the next year's celebration of the first one hundred years of history of this Baptist congregation.

EDUCATION

Savannah Baptists have from the beginning of their church been interested in education. Their Baptist ministers themselves, if not exposed to formal higher education, were self-educated. Never again in the American religious experience would ministers be better educated than in the colonial and early national periods. Baptist ministers in Savannah were well-educated from the beginning and the expectations of the congregation in relation to the education of its ministry remained high. Throughout the nineteenth century numerous interests in various kinds of education are illustrated in the life of the congregation. These will be observed after a survey of Sunday School, the single most important aspect of education in the local congregation.

The roots of the Sunday School movement in America extend to Germany and England and to traditions other than the Baptist. In the late seventeenth century the Lutheran pietist, A. H. Francke, had founded a Sunday School at Halle as one part of a constellation of new Christian institutions aimed at thorough conversion and education. A century later, Robert Raikes in England began his famous labor with the founding of Sunday Schools. Under pietistic influences, John Wesley established a Sunday School at Christ Church in Savannah. Local Sunday Schools began to appear in the Middle Colonies as well as in New England by the late eighteenth century. By 1824 the American Sunday School Union had been founded, and one of the early concerns of the union was the publication of educational materials. It became a kind of nondenominational educational tract society. The beginnings of a more formal Sunday School movement in the churches of Savannah are inscribed in this larger context.

A famous church musician is the one most responsible for the start of a Sunday School movement in the city of Savannah. Perhaps now best remembered as the author, composer, or arranger of a vast number of popular Christian hymns, Lowell Mason was the driving force behind the beginnings of the Sunday School movement in Savannah. It is perhaps appropriate that a hymn writer of such ecumenical Christian treasures as "When I Survey the Wondrous Cross" would also be interested in interdenominational Christian education.

As a young man of twenty, Mason came to Savannah in 1812 to pursue a vocation in banking as well as to develop his serious interests in music. He remained until 1827, when he returned to Boston. He was the paid organist ($300 yearly) of the Independent Presbyterian Church and had the honor of playing before President James Monroe in 1819 on his visit to see the launch of the steamship *Savannah* for its initial trip across the Atlantic. In 1827 he was also a charter member and one of the first three elders of the First Presbyterian Church, he and others declaring that "independency" was not really a part of Presbyterianism.

Mason made a major contribution to religious education in Savannah in addition to numerous other contributions. In the winter of 1815–1816 the first Sunday School was founded in Savannah by the following persons: Lowell Mason, Josiah Penfield, S. C. Schenk, Edward Coffee, T. H. Condy, and Mr. Rowson. This was a truly interdenominational group. Mason served as superintendent, remaining in this office until his departure from Savannah. This Savannah Sabbath School opened with seven male "scholars" and met in a building belonging to Solomon's Lodge. This was a union school with several denominations participating, including the Baptists. By November 1816 the school moved to the Chatham Academy, included males and females, and the Savannah Sunday School Union Society was formed. On January 21, 1817, a long letter from Mason appeared in the *Savannah Gazette* and served as a perfect public relations piece. It urged parents to support the children at home who were attending as well as in their school attendance. The moving first report of Mason is on record for February 3, 1817, and is an excellent summary of early goals as he begged for the earnest support of parents. School sessions were held twice on Sunday except for the months of August through October. Times varied—from 8:30 A.M., 9:00 A.M., 12:00 noon, to 5:00 P.M. For disciplinary purposes the *Black Book* was introduced on March 8, 1818. Various offenses such as numerous absences, swearing, fighting, and lying resulted in the student's name being placed in the book with graduated penalties, the last of which was "to expel a scholar from the school with shame and disgrace." The teachers met weekly on Saturday evenings for prayer as well as discussing and planning the work of the school. Rules were also adopted at these meetings. One of the earliest rules stipulated that the "scholars shall attend public worship." The education was religious and church attendance was a major goal. By 1818 there were 165 members with an average attendance of 140. The original seven members had been multiplied many times.

Records of Mason's Sunday School go into great detail on the rules and regulations and also report a number of interesting features and scenes. By 1818 the library already included 110 volumes, and in November it is noted that 106 boys and 110 girls attended sessions one Sunday. On May 8, 1819, there was no school due to President Monroe's visit. The big fire of 1820 and the scourge of yellow fever later in the year took their toll on attendance. The poignant note of October 22, 1820, reads: "Present: Lowell Mason and one little girl. She repeated a good lesson from memory, read a lesson from the scriptures, and received a punctual attendance ticket, another for good behavior, and an extra ticket. She was then dismissed."

Soon, the different denominations became interested in establishing Sunday Schools within their own churches. In a way, this was an expected and desired part of the expansion and success of the movement. In July 1822 the Methodists took the first step by establishing the Wesleyan Sunday School. By November 1822 the Baptists and Episcopalians were making plans to establish their own Sunday Schools. The Yamacraw Sunday School for Baptists was founded in September 1823 and by January 1824 Holmes Tupper, a deacon in the Baptist Church, became a teacher. The next step for the church was a Sunday School in its own building. On April 22, 1827, the initial meeting was held in the gallery of the church. One week later, April 29, the Savannah Baptist Sunday School Society was founded with Robert Brown as the first superintendent and Holmes Tupper as the vice-superintendent. The superintendents for the first twenty years of the Sunday School were Brown, Tupper, Thomas Dowell, Henry Furman, James Hogg, and George Davis.

No records are extant from September 1827 to 1841, but by 1842 the school had grown to 182 "scholars." During the schism there were two separate Sunday Schools, both successful, but with few records. When the two churches reunited, the record of Sunday School reads: "The record is imperfect,—very imperfect! All human records are necessarily imperfect. But God's record is complete."

From the records which are available, however, some facts emerge. There were male and female teachers just as there were scholars both male and female; there were rules similar to Mason's; there were different times for meetings (a new time of 3:00 P.M. is mentioned), the teachers met monthly for discussion and planning; and an annual report was given at the annual church conference meeting. November 10, 1861, was a red-letter day with few attending due to the fear of a Union attack on the city. Many members had left with their families and some property due to the danger. Those present heard a historical lesson concerning the founding of the Sunday School as on this date there was a dedication of their new school room—the lecture hall beneath the main nave of the church. By 1868 materials were being ordered from the Baptist Publication Society of America, and there was an excellent ratio of teachers to scholars, 19 to 154. Teachers were also urged to limit their sessions to one hour; furthermore, the need for uniform lessons was being discussed. In June 1868 the Minutes reflect that the Young Men's Effort Association had founded a Sunday School in the suburbs to the south. This was perhaps the first move to establish a mission on the southside. In November it was decided that the annual meeting of the Sunday School should take place during the A.M. worship service so that the school would be "brought before the congregation and a deeper interest awakened."

Numerous entries are found in 1869 concerning the rowdiness of scholars and the need for teachers to take more disciplinary measures with the students—"very bad order prevailed in some classes," reports the Record Book. Even Pastor Landrum reported that there was too much noise during Sunday School. Uniform lesson plans were adopted and teachers were also reminded of one of the most important goals of religious education—conversion. Late in the year books began to be awarded as prizes to excelling scholars and a high enrollment of 262 was reached. By late 1870 the uniform lessons from the American Baptist Publication Society in Philadelphia were being used and praised. Since Southern Baptists did not begin publishing Sunday School materials until after 1891, prior to this Savannah Baptists were dependent on other publishing houses.

In 1872 Superintendent Berrien Zettler was urging teachers to put the lessons in their own words rather than depending completely on the published materials as a crutch. In the midst of growing Baptist self-consciousness he also began to push for more Baptist doctrine and principles to be taught. On April 28, 1872, at the annual Sunday School meeting, a special forty-fifth anniversary celebration took place as teachers were reminded of "gallery beginnings" in 1827. It was also reported that the Sunday School library had the finest collection in Savannah—750 volumes! Eighteen seventy-three saw plans put in motion to assign "homework" to scholars and to expand the program to include more serious studies for everyone in the church. Prior to this, Sunday School was definitely limited to the youth of the church, first and foremost as a conversion tool. This new step would

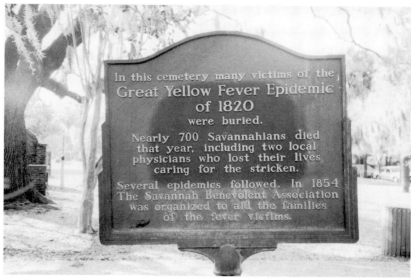

This plaque is in Colonial Cemetery at the corner of Oglethorpe Avenue and Habersham Street. There were often more patients than medical help. Many citizens and ministers offered aid and became victims themselves.

enlarge the educational goals of the church to produce well-educated priests of God (the priesthood of every believer) equipped to the total ministry of the church. Conversion remained a central concern, however, and by 1879 it was noted that two-thirds of the professions of faith that year were enrolled in the Sunday School program.

Superintendent A. P. Abell presided over the fiftieth anniversary celebration on April 29, 1877. The broader history of Sunday Schools in Savannah was rehearsed as well as a poignant reflection on the sad news of the previous year, when due to the scourge of yellow fever there had been no classes between August 25 and November 26, and there had been losses of one teacher and seven students by death.

The yearly report of 1886 numbered teachers as 32 and scholars as 289—still an excellent student/teacher ratio. Volumes in the library had been reduced to 350 by weeding out many of the outdated and dilapidated volumes. Even Sunday School scholars should receive honors, or so thought Louis Falligant in 1890. He donated funds in that year whose interest was to be used each year thereafter to award a gold medal to the "most proficient" Sunday School scholar. Also, the medal was to be named in honor of his wife. It would be called the Elizabeth Falligant Medal. The committee appointed to administer the award had one interesting concern. They wanted to describe it in such a way as to avoid any system of competition in the Sunday School. Perhaps naive, but ever so idealistic, the committee hoped to avoid what it considered to be secular values in a religious setting.

James R. Cain was the transition superintendent between centuries as was pastor Jordan as minister. Cain served from 1895 to 1906. The educational agency of the local church was the Sunday School—the church at study was ready for the twentieth century.

Baptists in Savannah were interested in, and committed to, many other phases of education as well, however. Some of the educational points of contact are worthy of mention, especially to illustrate that the religious educational enterprise is multifaceted.

For example, through the years numerous printings and editions of the Manual of the church were made available to the membership. This tool informed the reader of the church covenant, the charter of incorporation, a historical sketch of the church, the declaration of faith, the rules and bylaws, and the current roll of members. The Manual was regularly used in formal and informal ways and the church was sensitive to its availability. In 1860, eight hundred copies were printed; in 1881, one thousand copies were printed; and in 1900, another one thousand.

Savannah Baptists had always insisted on a well-educated ministry for itself. Though the call of God was certainly a priority, the commitment to being educated was virtually a corollary to that call. When without a minister in late 1835, the church described its needs in a not unusual way—"any well educated well recommended and experienced Baptist preacher." The leader of the congregation must educate weekly; therefore, he himself must be well-educated. No uneducated man ever took the permanent pulpit of Baptists in Savannah. These men perennially brought others in to educate the congregation on some aspect of Christian service. For example, as has been noted, Luther Rice made two visits to Savannah to educate the congregation about a new-found service among Baptists—Christian missions. As well, almost yearly the congregation was sensitized to the need of ministerial education with a peak moment being experienced in Josiah Penfield's contribution which was at the very roots of the founding of Mercer University. His will stipulated a substantial amount to "Rev. H. O. Wyer, in trust to create a fund for education of young men for the Gospel Ministry." By 1833 Mercer Institute was opened in Penfield, became a university in 1839, and moved to Macon in 1871. Through the century, Savannah was a supporter of the school both financially and otherwise. In the summer of 1886 a ministerial student at Mercer, B. D. Ragsdale, filled the pulpit during the long vacation of Pastor Holmes. The next century would continue and deepen these relationships. Once The Southern Baptist Theological Seminary got underway in Greenville, South Carolina, in 1859 (it moved to Louisville, Kentucky in 1877), the church sent numerous contributions and corresponded with such great Baptist scholars there as John A. Broadus and Crawford Toy.

Although there may have been some suspicions about religious education among some Baptists, this was not the case in Savannah. The cause of education was advanced and nurtured by the Savannah Baptist congregation. Any disagreements basically exhibited the growing pains of a people striving for maturity and excellence in the educational work of the church—"that God's people may be mature, fully equipped for every kind of noble work."

CHAPTER 7

ECUMENICAL ROOTS—
UNITY WITHIN DIVERSITY

*And now I am no more in the world, but they are in the
world, and I am coming to the Holy Father, keep them in
thy name, which thou hast given me, that they may be one,
even as we are one.*

—John 17:11

*The age of nations is past. The task before us now, if we
would not perish, is to shake off our ancient prejudices and
to build the earth.*

—Pierre Teilhard de Chardin

Since the earliest days of the Christian faith there have been divisions as well as unity. No one has ever particularly wanted the fractures, but they have existed from the start, nevertheless, like existential signposts indicating the humanness of Christians who have a dream but are unable to achieve it completely. Living within this situation from the beginning, then, resulted finally in the plea of Christianity for the ideal: unity within diversity. From the first there was obviously diversity in leadership styles, charisma, types of churches, interpretations of Jesus, et al. But there was also the unity of a love-community searching for that kind of oneness of which Jesus had prayed—"that they may be one." The story of the ideal of the prayer and that of the search itself, the real, the actual have been quite different. One expects discrepancy between confession and practice to a certain extent, but at times the gap is so great as to lead to depression for idealists. Then again, moments of vision and slight foretastes of unity give succor to those most actively seeking the ideal. Sometimes they live only through partial sustenance by heritage and most certainly by hope.

Christianity in its institutional forms has sometimes been identified with western civilization, especially the democratic segment of this civilization. But it is actually a world religion, and some of its oldest and most genuinely productive churches are located in cultures and places other than the West. It has sought unity in its own midst, and at the same time it has had ambitions and dreams of world community in its evangelization and institutionalization. Sometimes in certain denominational forms it has exhibited a high level of intolerance toward other world religious confessions and has idolized its own denominational forms. Belief in its own uniqueness has often resulted in demonic activities. Christianity's exclusivity and separateness have at times led to arrogance, misunderstanding, violent controversy, and even bloodshed.

But there have been moments in Christian history when individuals and churches have tried to tug denominational institutions in a different direction—toward being at the heart of that search for Christian unity in community. They have been possessed by a dream, a vision, a near passion for unity. They have discovered the essence of reality to be in that experience of unity wherever that experience is to be had. Finding that the essential points of Christianity are not owned exclusively by any one denomination, they have been committed to their own institutional expression of Christianity, though not with arrogance or a closed mind. They have been pilgrims in process, en route, on the road. They have been committed to the principle of "detached attachment" in relation to their chosen denomination—"detached" enough from their "attachment" to be aware of other truths and values within denominations other than their own. In earlier centuries these Christian geniuses were men and women before their time, not seriously heard except in their own inner circles. But the twentieth century with its "great new religious fact," the ecumenical movement, has been more prone to take seriously what these prophets with a vision of unity have said. Doubtless, "world shrinkage" as well as the real possibility of world catastrophe have played major roles in this change of attitude. One would also like to hope, however, that Christians have finally come to distinguish between the essentials and the nonessentials in Christianity.

All Baptist denominations, whether they admit it or not, are rooted in the larger movement which obviously fractured the religious unity of western Europe in the sixteenth century. In addition to this, their ecclesiology from the start limited their horizons in relation to unitive efforts, for Baptists have always insisted upon the autonomy of the local church under God. This ecclesiology with its rather loose connectionalism (perhaps seen first in associationalism) accounts in large part for the many Baptist denominations in the United States, for in the last analysis there have been no institutional ties strong enough to bind all of them together. So the Baptist movement has been marked by numerous fractures and divisions generally emphasizing Christian unity but actually giving little attention to Church unity. Most Baptist bodies have not formally related to major institutional illustrations of the ecumenical movement and have sometimes even opposed such efforts. They have had hard enough problems in relation to intra-denominational unity. In fact the Southern Baptist Convention, the largest Baptist as well as Protestant denomination in the United States, has been a kind of small ecumenical movement all by itself—trying to hold together for cooperative purposes a wide variety of local churches which are often radically different from one another in style and content. Great is the variety of churches in this mammoth convention, largely kept together by cooperation in its missionary and evangelistic efforts. Indeed, the associational principle of cooperative efforts for the sake of ministry to the world has been present from the start of Baptist history.

Though each Baptist denomination has its own mini-ecumenical movement within itself, in 1905 Baptists around the world founded an international body reflective of Baptist witness and named it the Baptist World Alliance. Even such a conservative body as the Southern Baptist Convention joined (though it has always rejected joining the World Council of Churches), but the Baptist World Alliance in its preamble had to make perfectly clear that it would never be a threat to the independence of the churches or member bodies. Baptists have usually (though not in the last two decades of the twentieth century) been more service oriented and less theologically expressive in their unitive efforts. As observed in earlier chapters, the first national body to be organized among Baptists in the United States was due to an interest in missions—first abroad and then at home. In May 1814 the General Missionary Convention of the Baptist Denomination in the United States for Foreign Missions was founded in Philadelphia. This was the first national organization among Baptists in the United States. Unity was thereby given expression in an intradenominational way toward the goals of mission and service.

Unitive efforts among Baptists are perhaps best seen in the symbol of three concentric circles. Within the smallest circle are the intradenominational efforts such as those which resulted in the founding of the Triennial Convention in 1814. The next circle includes activities of an ecumenical nature whose goal was some kind of organizational structure giving evidence of unity among numerous Baptist bodies in the United States and/or over the entire world. On this level the founding of the Baptist World Alliance in 1905 would be the finest example. The last circle of unitive efforts involves interdenominational activities giving witness of the whole Christian community and the unity in its midst. On a worldwide level, the World Council of Churches would be the finest illustration. The roots, however, of the activities of all three circles are to be found on the local church level. This is grassroots ecumenism, if you please. From the start, Baptist life in Savannah was grounded in ecumenism growing out of a healthy denominationalism. Though a growing and maturing process was taking place, Savannah Baptists experienced in numerous ways the truth of the concept of "detached attachment."

The earliest Baptists in Savannah worshiped in interdenominational settings and their first building was given over to the Presbyterians for their worship. Indeed, their first pastor, Henry Holcombe, had preached for the Presbyterians with surely some Baptists present prior to the organizing and chartering of the Baptist Church in 1800. Early roots of Baptist life in Savannah are perfect illustrations of grassroots ecumenism. Holcombe was definitely ecumenically popular in Savannah or else he would never have been invited by the town council to preach the sermon for the city to honor George Washington on the occasion of his death. Surely on that occasion the Baptist church was filled with persons of various denominational backgrounds. Much evidence also exists to the presence of multidenominational hearers in many worship services. Savannah was virtually a frontier town for a long while with a minimum of churches as well as preachers. The Minutes contain numerous examples of the pulpit being filled by whatever minister was available. Methodists and Presbyterians often filled the pulpit and the pews. In "mission" or "almost mission" situations, ecumenism is generally the order of the day as grassroots folk get back to the basics of Christianity and beyond denominational separatism. On February 5, 1808, the Minutes state that "Mr. Mallard a Methodist preacher exhorted." Several days later, Mr. Mallard preached again and "Mr. Capel another Methodist preacher preached a sermon highly satisfactory." Especially at revivals joint services were experienced. In February 1808 Holcombe also led the church to participate with the Church of Christ in Beaufort in their revival efforts. On April 16, 1815, it is recorded that Brother Brantley, Baptist preacher, "preached in the Presbyterian meeting house." Visiting preachers often participated in this "exchange of pulpits" as well as giving special lectures during the week. On Tuesday, February 13, 1816, such a situation is illustrated: "Lecture

This fountain facing First Baptist Church was the effort of individuals and committees of First Baptist Church and Independent Presbyterian Church and was installed in 1871. Photo courtesy of Georgia Historical Society.

this evening at Candle light by Mr. Flint a licensed preacher of the independent Church from the state of Massachusetts Bay." Even socials with other denominations were planned and enjoyed. In conference on April 23, 1832, it was resolved: "That this church join in a social or union meeting, with other denominations of Christians which will take place in this city." Worshiping, praying, playing, and eating contexts mingled the denominations in Savannah.

Baptists were perennially cooperating with other denominations in Savannah in various kinds of union services. One lapse occurred in August 1827 when the church turned down an invitation from the Presbyterians to join in a united prayer service. Led in January 1828 to negate this action by more ecumenical maturity, the church committed itself in the future "to meet at the Presbyterian Church and unite there with all Christians who choose to assemble with us for that purpose." Prior to the New Sunbury Association meeting in Savannah in November 1831, Savannah Baptists appointed a committee to "invite Brethren of other denominations in this city to meet with us in the Association." This associational meeting was flanked by preaching at both ends and during these seven days ecumenical attendance and preaching were observed. On one of the days the crowd was too large for the Baptist Church and so it was invited and met at the Independent Presbyterian Church; in the afternoon the Presbyterian minister filled the pulpit which had been filled the same morning by a Baptist. The associational minutes recorded: "Our Paedo-Baptist brethren heartily united with us during this interesting season." Special prayer days throughout the nineteenth century bound denominations together. The "pestilence" of yellow fever provided one of the major reasons for such reunion prayer days. In September 1834 the Baptists resolved to participate in union prayer with other denominations to the end that God "would stay the Pestilence that is now visiting our community."

Other denominations in Savannah were themselves experiencing denominational self-consciousness as well as ecumenical growth, and at such times there were additional denominational overlaps. In May 1874 the Lutherans hosted the United Synod South which itself would take giant ecumenical steps forward within Lutheranism. It appointed a consultation committee which would meet with other Lutheran bodies in the planning of a time and place for "holding a general colloquium of all Lutheran bodies in North America." Baptists actually made their own small contribution to this meeting by giving up their church and pulpit on the first Sunday in May for Lutheran use. Surely many Baptists were in attendance at this momentous gathering.

The chapter "Pastoral Leadership" illustrates during the tenure of virtually every pastor many ecumenical moments within and beyond the various Baptist denominations. From the founding days of Holcombe to those of the last pastor of the century, Jordan, Savannah Baptists were led by men who were first Christian and second Baptist. One need only cull out the numerous illustrations from their careers. Some were founders of the associational principle, such as Holcombe, while others were participants. Savannah Baptists especially through their leadership were active in the local association, in the Triennial Convention, and in the Southern Baptist Convention. These commitments did not prohibit them, however, from being active ecumenically with other denominations on the grassroots level. The Baptists' own leadership had taken an international turn when Timothy Harley came—a man nurtured in the English Baptist tradition who came to Savannah by way of Canada. The next century would certainly build upon the strong ecumenical roots being unconsciously planted in the nineteenth century.

Savannah Baptists had rejected the more radical beliefs of Landmarkism, a rather severe denominational interpretation that did not even allow Baptists to take communion together unless they were members of the local church administering it. Early on in Savannah, Baptists from numerous churches mingled with one another at the communion table—that basic symbol of Christian unity. In July 1808 the Minutes describe such a moment: "In the afternoon the Ordinance of the Lord's Supper was most solemnly administered to the members of this and other churches in union with us who were in fellowship with each other." Members of "sister churches" were often in attendance at communion and they definitely participated in the ordinance. It is true that Savannah Baptists, with all other Baptists, did not allow members of other denominations at their communion table, nor did they normally participate in communion in churches of other denominations. The next century would see a change in this practice as they matured even more in their ecumenical sensitivity.

In relation to the ordinance which allowed persons to sit together around the communion table, namely, the Lord's Supper, Savannah Baptists faced in ecumenical directions. Since they did believe in believer's baptism by immersion, in the nineteenth century this was the only kind of baptism received. However, the precedent was set for receiving those who had been immersed as adult believers by paedo-Baptist ministers or in cases of emergency even by someone who was not a believer. Unusual situations were considered as worthy of unusual responses. Again, these Baptists rejected in spirit and fact the "meanness" and anti-ecumenical stance of Landmarkism. There were already numerous points of contact with other denominations even in relation to the ordinances which would continue to mature in the twentieth century.

The ecumenical stance of nineteenth-century Savannah Baptists displayed the same spirit which had been expressed in 1790 in England by the famous John Rippon. In the preface to his first volume of the Baptist *Annual Register* he wrote:

> Though I feel it an honour to rank with the Calvinists, whose system, commonly called orthodox, is peculiarly dear to me; yet conceiving that all who hate sin, and love our Lord Jesus Christ in sincerity, are good men, if they do not think of Baptism as I do, nor embrace half my Creed, I delight in such as my brethren, and embrace them, by thousands, in the bosom of warm affection—and, with my views, it would be criminal not to do so. . . .

Clergy and laity in Savannah Baptist Church subscribed in spirit to this warmly ecumenical statement. Savannah Baptists were not isolationists nor were they ultracritical of other Protestant bodies. Anti-Catholicism lingered in the New Sunbury Association as late as 1892 when at the yearly meeting Roman Catholics were deemed lost souls. No mention of this is noted in the Savannah Minutes, however, and it probably was reflective of rural attitudes more than the urban center of Savannah. Isolationism and extreme judgmentalism existed among some Baptists in relation to other denominations, but they existed mainly in those sections of the country most influenced by Landmark attitudes. The spirit of Landmarkism was definitely rejected in Savannah from the beginning.

In the nineteenth as well as the twentieth centuries, there is no Baptist body or person who speaks for all Baptists, for the autonomy of the local church and the priesthood of every believer forbid such. Nowhere is this better illustrated than in relation to the ecumenical movement. Brooks Hays and John E. Steely in 1981 perceptively made this point clear in their fine *The Baptist Way of Life*:

> Nowhere is the inability of one Baptist to speak for all Baptists more obvious than in this area [ecumenical]. Our attitudes toward the life and work of fellow-Christians range all the way from utter indifference, or even unseemly competition, to passionate involvement and eager desire for unity and union. For most of our people, both in theory and practice, the Baptist position is somewhere between these extremes. Without attempting to foretell the course of future events, it may be fair for us as individual Baptists to express the hope that, as we come more clearly to see that all Christians worship and serve the same Lord, we may also see more clearly that we belong to each other.

The spirit of this statement was being spelled out among Baptists in Savannah from as early as 1800. Baptists in Savannah had certainly sung the famous hymn "O For a World," which had been arranged by Lowell Mason. Its poignant words are even prophetic in the twentieth century: "O for a world where everyone / Respects each other's ways, / Where love is lived and all is done with justice and praise. / We welcome one world family. / A world where goods are shared, misery relieved, truth spoken, equality achieved."

The great nineteenth-century church historian, Philip Schaff, had a keen interest in religious music and at one point in his career even edited a hymnbook. He affirmed: "The church-hymn is one of the most powerful means for promoting the unity of the faith and the *communion* of saints." The most ecumenical moments (sometimes unconscious ones) for all Christians, including Baptists, are to be experienced at hymn time. Experience, emotion, and sheer delight in the music supersede any judgmental interest in hard-line doctrine. As Savannah Baptists sang such hymns as Lowell Mason and others had written, composed, and arranged, their ecumenical sensitivities could only have been enhanced. Ecumenical hymns have always been an important part of the liturgical worship of Savannah Baptist Church.

Ecumenical commitments generally lead to a rejection of proselytism with a retention of healthy evangelism. Granted, only a fine line divides the two, and this line is marked by sensitive toleration and acceptance of the commitments of other world religions. Savannah Baptist displayed this attitude toward the Jewish faith in the nineteenth century, and this is a major reason why the twentieth would witness such close relationships between First Baptist Church and Mickve Israel Synagogue. One is safe in saying that no member of this Baptist Church would ever say or believe what one of the twentieth-century fundamentalist presidents of the Southern Baptist Convention, Bailey Smith, said publicly: "God does not hear the prayer of a Jew." This kind of arrogant anti-Semitism was never a part of Savannah Baptist's experience. Until 1878 Baptists and Jews in Savannah had neighboring sanctuaries—most of the time being only two half blocks away from one another. Christians and Jews in Savannah had a deep respect for one another. By the close of the century, Savannah had its only Jewish mayor for the century—Herman Myers, who served 1895–97 and 1899–1907. When the Jewish congregation moved to its beautiful sanctuary on Monterey Square, Timothy Harley was present on April 11, 1878, for the consecration of the synagogue. He sat on the right front pew alongside the Methodist and Episcopal ministers. On June 30, 1904, Pastor Jordan was an honorary pallbearer at the funeral of the venerated Rabbi Isaac Mendes. Later in the twentieth century there would be numerous and even deeper illustrations of the good will that existed between First Baptist Church and Mickve Israel Synagogue. Savannah Baptists were well aware that 50 percent of the Judeo-Christian tradition is Jewish!

Toward the close of the century Baptists were also more sensitive to the possibility of friendly changes of denominational affiliation in an ever growing pluralistic society. Though earlier this was a matter for the Discipline Committee, increasingly the church moved to a position of being willing to write a "good character" letter to the receiving denomination and church. In August 1887 Marie Hopkins joined the Independent Presbyterian Church and a letter concerning her positive moral character was sent to the church. In September 1896 Mrs. E. D. Miltier took a similar letter with her as she joined that same church and denomination.

The religious liberty for which early Baptists in America had fought so bravely had resulted in widespread religious pluralism. Baptists in Savannah awoke early to the implications of all this change and began to act more appropriately and maturely in line with their initial commitment to religious liberty. No one could possibly deny the concept of the freedom of conscience and be true to any authentic understanding of religious liberty. Both ideas to which Savannah Baptists subscribed led them to ecumenical involvements within their own denomination, in relation to other denominations, and at least to even one other world religion. And all this took place during their first one hundred years of history. Their ground was fertile for the seeds sown by the great new fact of the twentieth century—the ecumenical movement.

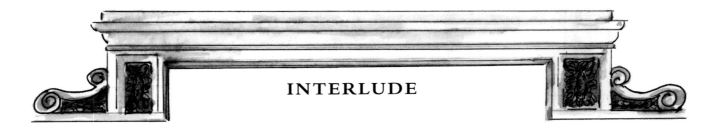

CELEBRATING THE
FIRST ONE HUNDRED YEARS

For three days, November 25–27, 1900, the *Morning News* of Savannah gave full page and more coverage (including photographs) of the celebration by Baptists of one hundred years of ministry in Savannah Baptist Church. Luminaries from the state and national convention agencies were in attendance along with other local denominational ministers. To a filled sanctuary, F. H. Kerfoot, secretary of the Home Mission Board (HMB) of the Southern Baptist Convention, preached a sermon in the morning of the 25th based on the text of Romans 8:28: "And we know that all things work together for good to them that love God, to them who are the called according to his purpose" (KJV). In the evening S. Y. Jameson, secretary of State Missions for Georgia Baptists, gave an extended address on the history of the church as well as the first pastor and first deacon. The next day various speeches were given by Dr. R. J. Willingham, secretary of the Foreign Mission Board of the Southern Baptist Convention, and by pastors in Savannah—John D. Jordan, R. Vandeventer, and S. Edenfield. The benediction was offered by E. Cork, pastor of Wesley Monumental Methodist Church. On Tuesday, November 27, the celebration was completed with speeches by J. B. Taylor, general manager of the Georgia Baptist Orphan's Home, who outlined the work of the Home; and by P. D. Pollock, president of Mercer University, who explored the subject of Christian education.

The news accounts went into great detail. One picture correctly showed a nave with the organ behind the pulpit (no choir loft there), semicircular pews, a horseshoe gallery, and only two columns guarding the entrance to the church. The news writer then gave major moments in the history of the congregation which had grown from a mere handful of persons to a congregation of more than seven hundred, the largest white Protestant church in the city. The circumstances of the founding, the call to Henry Holcombe, the move to Chippewa Square, and the major changes in the structure were well-rehearsed. Holcombe was virtually beatified by the writer as he summarized the pastor's numerous contributions to education, religious newspaper publication, reform of the Georgia penitentiary system, and organized Baptist life in the state. The article presented as well a summary of pastors and their unique contributions—Wyer was a pulpit orator; Robert was a linguist who at one time filled a professorial chair at Iowa State University and was later the president of a seminary in Atlanta; Rambaut was a great preacher educated in law who later was president of William Jewell College and then a pastor in Brooklyn and later Newark, New Jersey; Harley was an excellent writer who published an article entitled "Southward Ho! A Tour through Georgia" with numerous references to Savannah and especially the epidemic of yellow fever in 1876; Landrum was a most beloved pastor guiding the church through the Civil War which "was probably the only white church from Baltimore to Galveston that did not close during the entire war"; Holmes was a scholarly trustee of Mercer University who died while still pastor; Goodwin was one of the greatest orators ever to live in Savannah; and Jordan was a young man who brought unity and rapid growth to the church. Interestingly, no mention whatsoever appeared in the newspaper columns of the second pastor, W. B. Johnson. Savannah Baptists forgave but never forgot what this pastor did, and the newspaper writer evidently did, too, for Johnson received "no press."

Jameson, Kerfoot (one of Jordan's former professors at Southern Seminary), and Willingham all received full coverage of their addresses. W. W. Landrum, famous son of Sylvanus, was supposed to have given an address but never arrived in the city. Both Jameson and Kerfoot summarized the rapid growth of Baptists in the nation and more especially in the South. Jameson ascribed this growth to the principles of the separation of church and state and religious liberty. He seemed to take some delight in referring to the "hardshell" division among Baptists in its statistical decline after the schism. Kerfoot gave a briefer address because he had a train schedule to keep. He, too, emphasized Baptist growth statistics, paid special tribute to home missions, and expressed the need for expansion in the southwestern United States. Willingham also surveyed Baptist mission work and especially made note of the fact that the first foreign missionary society in Georgia was organized in 1814 (other sources, 1813) in the Savannah Baptist Church.

The last speakers during the three days, Taylor and Pollock, did not receive equal attention in the press. Pollock was spotlighted and he did give an excellent survey of religious and secular education in the nineteenth century, tying in Savannah Baptist history with this theme. After briefly surveying Thomas Jefferson's views on education and politics, Pollock named Furman, Mercer, and Holcombe as representing the same kind of statesmanship in religious education as Jefferson and others had in politics. They all involved themselves in founding denominational colleges with a major goal of educating ministers. Just as state universities (after the 1862 Morrell Land Grant Act) stood for the ideals of a liberal culture and an educated citizenry, so did the religiously oriented colleges and universities. Pollock emphasized the fact that thousands of graduates of these religiously oriented educational centers had taken their places in every area of life and had participated in redeeming the culture to higher values. He pictured state and denominational universities as working side by side in relation to this redemptive goal. Pollock then wisely praised Holcombe and Josiah Penfield for their vision and contributions which led to the eventual founding of Mercer University.

Pastor Jordan and dozens of others surely breathed a sigh of relief on the evening of Tuesday, November 27. The celebration was a major coup—all had gone smoothly and newspaper coverage had been indeed generous. Citizens all over Savannah were now aware of many up-to-their time unknown or forgotten parts of the Baptist picture in Savannah and beyond. Savannah Baptists could indeed be proud of such moments to remember.

Even glowing newspaper accounts get back down to earth eventually; it was mundanely reported that all the speakers had been guests of the De Soto Hotel. The next evening at their weekly conference on November 28, the deacons tabled a resolution about building a reception room and a pastor's study on the lower floor entrance to the church. Later the resolution was withdrawn when it was discovered that in order to do such, a formal application had to be made to the city council. All visits to the mountaintop are followed by returning to day-to-day life on the plain where the time being must ever be redeemed from insignificance.

A CHURCH BETWEEN TWO SQUARES

"First Baptist faces Chippewa Square. In the center stands a statue of General James Edward Oglethorpe who established the Colony of Georgia in 1733. The statue was created by two American artists. Henry Bacon, architect, designed the base and Daniel Chester French was the sculptor. These two created the Lincoln Memorial Washington, D.C." (Margaret La Far)

Facing the Educational building is Orleans Square. In the center is a fountain given by the German Historical Society, German Friendly Society, and Georgia Salzburger Society. "This fountain commemorates the religious, agricultural, economic, and political contributions of early German immigrants to the establishment and growth of the colony of Georgia." (erected and dedicated, 1989)

SERVICES OF COMMITMENT

Parent-Child Dedication.

Baptism.

Deacon Ordination.

HOLY NIGHT

Christmas Eve Communion Service.

Sharing the Good News with the World.

HOLY WEEK

Youth and Children's Choirs on Palm Sunday.

Maundy Thursday Communion Service.

Proclaiming the Resurrection.

Ministers and members of the Diaconate, 1999.

ROW 1 (left to right): Joseph E. Becton; Elizabeth Hodges; Milton Newton; Dottie Adams; Catherine Scholl; Alsie B. Rabun; Susan Sutton; Janis Lewis; Richard Lewis; Harry Skinner; Fenwick T. Nichols Jr.; Leander K. Powers Jr.; Nancy Sutton; Kristin M. Andreason, Assistant Minister; James C. Richardson, Associate Minister

ROW 2 (left to right): Philip G. Morgan III; Lamar W. Davis Jr.; William E. Hodges; Hudson Harrison; Bays Anderson; Sarah Davis; Joe Adams; Allen Davidson; Patricia Craig; Douglas Craig; William C. Sutton Jr.; Molly Wright; Florrie Kirkley; William C. Sutton III; John M. Finley, Senior Minister

ROW 3 (left to right): Henry C. Frech III; Lynne Davis; Betty Yonke; John Dekle; Carol Anne Richardson; Ellen Davis; Jeryl Davis; Raymond Keebler; Fran Arnsdorff; Bridget Browne; Donna Plunkett; Earl Kirkley; Nancy Lazard

ROW 4 (left to right): Jack H. Usher; Ann Frech; Shirley Allen; Joseph T. Stubbs; Arthur Hay; John S. Tyson III; Michael Schroeder; William C. Burgstiner; David T. Lock; Rance Pusser; William O. Plunkett Jr.; Robert K. Mills

ROW 5 (left to right): Barbara Creaser; Reed G. Creaser; George E. Worthy; Randy Murray; F. Vreeland George Jr.; Harrell Roberts; Mitch Palles; Lem Brawner; Chris Cooper; Jim Cooper

Deacons not pictured: John Anchors; James Anstine; Edith Bennett; Darnell Brawner; Mebane Bristow; Charles C. Brooks; Jord Claiborne; Christopher Hendricks; Helen Cooper; Lamar W. Davis Sr.; J. Harry Duncan; Jake Fulcher; Emily Garrard; John Glenn; Tom C. Graham; Steve Hamlin; Margaret Hardy; Jane Jennings; John Jennings; Earl Lawhorne; Greg Lawhorne; Randy Lazard; J. Curtis Lewis Jr.; J. Curtis Lewis III; Joseph McNellage; James Miles; Evalyn Miles; Win Morgan; Jack Murphy; George Pruden; Marie Cowart; Doris Thomas; Charlie Waldrop; Jack Williams; Jerold Woods; Bill Wright; George Yonke

Current Chairman—Diaconate, Richard Lewis
Current Secretary/Treasurer—Diaconate, John Dekle

Life Deacons: Mary Louise Claiborne; F. Vreeland George; J. Curtis Lewis Jr.; Paul E. Robbins; William C. Sutton Jr.

Ministerial Staff:
John M. Finley, Senior Minister
James C. Richardson, Associate Minister
Kristin M. Andreason, Assistant Minister
C. Lee Canipe, Pastoral Assistant

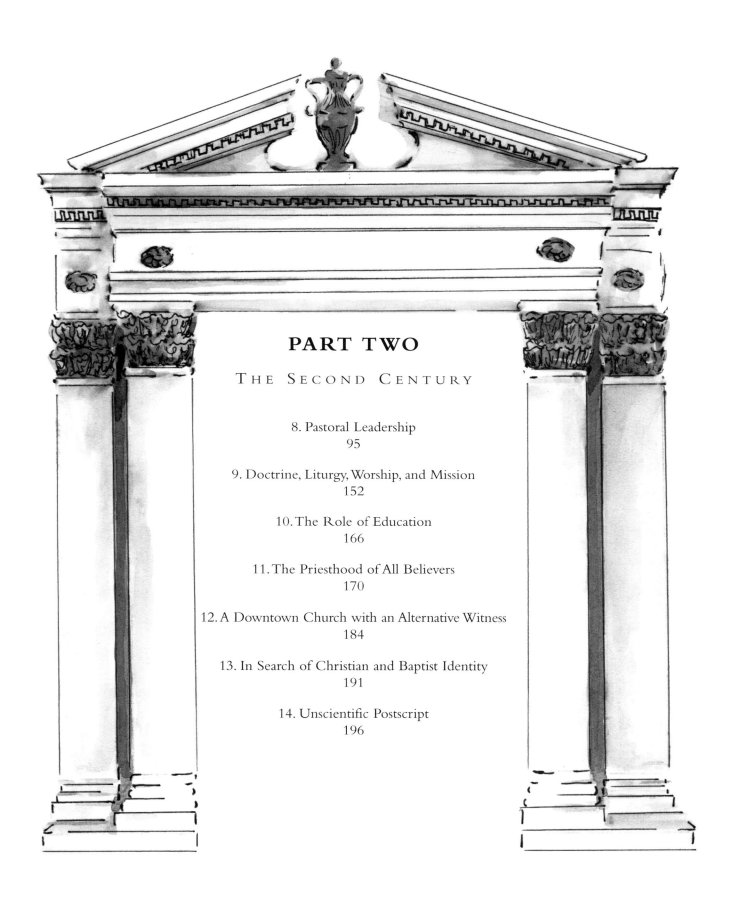

PART TWO

THE SECOND CENTURY

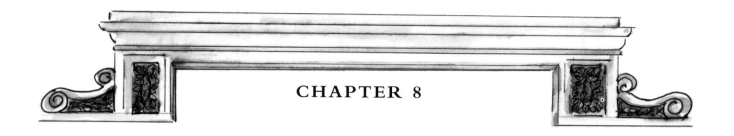

CHAPTER 8

PASTORAL LEADERSHIP

In one hundred years, Georgia's population had jumped from 162,686 to 2,216,331 persons. Savannah's population had grown from 6,226 to 54,244. The Savannah Baptist Church had increased from sixteen to somewhere between 769 and 773 (associational minutes differ from those of the church). In numbers it was the largest white congregation in the city. The average pastorate for the first one hundred years lasted less than five years. The twentieth-century pastorate would average more than eight years with the two longest ones being seventeen and nineteen years. Longer tenures allowed deeper pastoral imprints left by Leroy G. Cleverdon and Thomas D. Austin. Pastor Jordan had seen the church through a "fitting" celebration of its first one hundred years, but in January 1901 he had to descend from the mountaintop of this peak experience to the daily problems of the plain. On January 2, the Finance Committee brought a resolution to the church on behalf of borrowing $4,500, for the bills had to be paid. Nothing can bring one back down to earth like financial matters.

The famous Methodist evangelist, Sam (Samuel Porter) Jones, called the "Moody of the South," came to town in May 1901 on his revival tour and loudly preached to Savannahians about the sins of alcohol consumption, profanity, and gambling. He was considered by some to be irreverent and crude in his use of blunt language and slang. Nevertheless, the Baptists along with other denominations closed up shop on the Wednesday and Sunday evenings during his campaign. Their own attendance and membership took a big jump in 1901, in part due to Jones's evangelistic efforts.

In May 1901 the committee appointed to nominate a Board of Deacons requested that their committee be dissolved, claiming their committee was neither scriptural nor historical. The whole church in its "collective capacity" would henceforth elect deacons. The three-year term was retained, and by the next year the number of deacons had grown to the needed number of fourteen.

By the close of 1902, debts, especially those resulting from storm damage, had been completely paid and the Finance Committee submitted a clean balance sheet. Pew rents were still bringing in the bulk of funds and the congregation even felt that its rents were extremely low "for the large number of very desirable pews we have." Committees were also formed for the various needs of 1903 since the Southern Baptist Convention would meet in Savannah only for the second time. The first time was in 1861, but due to the war only 177 messengers came to represent some 650,000 Baptists and 8,000 churches. In 1903, 1,136 Baptists would flood into the city to represent the 1,805,889 Baptists in 20,431 churches. Perhaps the meeting caused Savannah Baptists to be more historically conscious, because in conference they moved to purchase a large safe for the keeping of "valuable church books."

Savannah Baptists greeted 1904 in the best financial condition they had experienced in "many, many years." All the debts had been paid and there were still funds in the treasury! So, they began to save toward some specific and needed projects—to remove the iron fence in front of the building (the fence had been there to protect the steps and porch from being dirtied by wandering animals), to pour a concrete pavement completely around the building, to hang electric lamps in the front of the church, to paint the exterior, and to tend to other repairs in relation to total beautification. January 13 was set aside as thanksgiving day and all mortgage notes were burned.

Pastor Jordan was highly praised in each annual report but especially so in January 1905. The first *typed* annual report affirmed: "We have worked harmoniously together for the saving of souls, the worship of God, and the betterment of those with whom we came in contact in this world of ours." The praise for Jordan remembered his "anxiety for the moral condition of the city" and urged members to help him clean it of the "barnacles of sin fast accumulating." Pew rental was on its way out—the envelope system of giving finally resulted in bringing in more funds than did pew rental. The report praised it as scriptural and best for the church.

Population and growth in Savannah were moving southward; sensitive to this fact the church started a mission on Jefferson and Green Streets and by 1906 had completed a worship structure there. By June and July of 1908 the mission officially became the Green Street Baptist Church. Plans were also made to conduct quarterly social gatherings of the congregation.

Through the years Savannah Baptist had either licensed or ordained a number of men for the ministry. The church had always taken this responsibility seriously. Just how seriously was illustrated in August 1905. B. A. Hurley, a member, had been

Elias Carter's original design for the church consisted of Savannah's gray brick walls covered with stucco, a recessed portico, and a cupola. Iron fencing was added in front of the church to prevent stray animals from gaining access. In the renovation of 1921–1922, architect Henrik Wallin's design called for more of a Greek temple form. The cupola was removed, the portico enclosed for a narthex, the front extended to create a new portico, and the entire building clad in limestone.

called by the Springfield Baptist Church to come as pastor. An investigating presbytery or council in the church met with him and afterward postponed his ordination when "it was found that he had not studied systematically so as to fit him to look after a charge." In other words, he needed some systematic course of theological study. Hurley was licensed in June 1906 but was not ordained until July 1908. As a part of Jordan's own continuing education, in December 1905 he was granted a three-month leave from February to May to visit Europe, Palestine, and Egypt. Every minister had dreams of going to the Holy Land someday—Jordan's were realized. Dr. Theodore N. Compton would serve as pastor pro tem.

By mid-May 1906 Jordan was back and running but evidently sitting at times for the portrait painter, Oscar Durham. Durham's oil of Jordan was given to the church with Jordan's expressed hope that the church would from that point on have a painting of each pastor.

In October 1906 the New Sunbury Association chided church members for their "commercialism" and urged them in relation to liquor to "quit drinking it, quit buying it, and quit voting for it." Agitation on behalf of prohibition was already well underway. Certainly with no connection to this act, Jordan announced his resignation within two weeks, effective on December 31. The well-liked centennial pastor was highly praised by the congregation for his excellent preaching and superior fund-raising abilities but also especially for his being a "genial companion ever ready to enter the hearts of the people"—a compliment greatly to be treasured by any pastor. One of Jordan's last acts was to inaugurate the evermore popular individual communion service which had recently been purchased. The "common cup" was going out of style with urban Baptists.

W. Lowndes Pickard

The annual report of 1907 was the first one to report over one thousand members. Under Jordan the church had experienced more than 40 percent growth, and in his last year, ninety-two persons were added by baptism. Carter T. Willingham served as interim pastor until W. Lowndes Pickard came later in the year as pastor-in-residence. The Jordans' church letters with glowing comments were sent to the Jackson Hill Baptist Church in Atlanta. Slightly over one year later, April 1908, the sad news of Jordan's death came to the church by telegram.

Pickard's ministry early on showed a cultivation of the up-and-coming women's ministry in the church. The association reflected a strong and active Women's Missionary Union (WMU) with the leadership of the likes of Mrs. H. W. Way, Mrs. Courtney Thorpe, Mrs. F. C. Wallis, and Miss Leila Gilliard. Pickard also saw to the creation of female committees to assist the deacons in visitation of the sick and benevolence matters. He also appointed a committee of women to look after the interior of the church as well as one to keep an updated list of members and their addresses. He even expressed sensitivity for the homeless in his urging the finding of a house or location for those in "distress" in Savannah. Additionally, he began to meet certain evenings with comparatively small groups of members—a kind of "evening with your pastor" format. The deacons also had an opportunity to fill a kind of "wish box" of ideas which included the following: a chorus choir now, a sermon on the Trinity, an assistant pastor to help with pastoral burdens (surely welcomed by Pickard), concrete pavement around the church to be replaced by grass and flowers (early ecologists?), and a signboard in the rear as well as the front of the building.

**W. Lowndes Pickard
1907–1914**

Although other pastors had called for the elimination of pew rental and designated it as the scriptural thing to do, not until October 1908 were pew rentals voted out as of the new year. On the first Sunday of 1909 members and "hearers" sat as they chose. Stewardship now depended entirely on individual giving by means of the envelope system. Never again would any member be billed for a particular pew; never again would any pew be off-limits to any member or visitor!

In the annual report of 1909 Pickard reported that he had made eleven hundred visits as well as delivering 152 sermons and addresses. He was a busy pastor—especially, by his own word, as assisted by the "sisters" of the church. Due to his superior speaking and preaching abilities, Pickard was much sought after and attended. He was the type of preacher people of all denominations might travel miles to hear.

By early 1909, two thousand copies of a new church Manual were being planned and ordered for midyear. By then the bylaws were updated, and the Manual also contained an historical sketch of the church, the covenant, declaration of faith, and a current membership listing. To defray some of the expenses, a number of advertisements were also found. Within not too many years, later editions of the Manual carried ads for J. C. Lewis Motor Co., Merry Widow Self-Rising Flour, Dixie Crystals, Clary Drug Co., Philip Levy and Co., and the Savannah Georgia Laundry, whose motto appeared as "Cleanliness is next to Godliness"!

Several important changes in the Rules and Bylaws were made:

1. Before a letter of dismission to another church would be granted the person must have completed his/her financial obligation to the church.
2. The Music Committee would be composed of five persons and would be in charge of the music program, the employment of the organist and managing the choir, and would with congregational approval set salaries.
3. Voting on business matters would be done by "the regular communicants." Females were now *officially* voters though they had actually voted on most matters from the beginning. However, some chauvinism was retained in the stipulation that for business to be conducted, seven *male* members had to be present as a quorum.
4. The pastor was now "pastor for life" (no yearly call), but dissolution could take place with three months' notice being given. The pastor was described as one who "shall always be of the Baptist denomination, of orthodox principles, and unblamable character and deportment."
5. Discipline rules were kept though they were rarely applied—only in extreme cases.
6. The Declaration of Faith retained its soft Calvinism with the phrase stipulating that election was completely consistent with the belief in the free agency of humankind.

The republication of the Manual was in the context of growing denominational self-consciousness and the necessity of unity. For several years the association had to counter the controversial antimissionary movement, especially in rural Baptist churches. It warned member churches of "an anti-missionary spirit in some churches due to not understanding the Bible and due to some anti-missionary literature." Primitive Baptists, strong in Georgia, were antimissionary and strict Calvinists. Savannah Baptists had already gone on record as approving mission work and as being Arminian Calvinists.

In 1910 the question of "alien baptism" or "alien immersion" was discussed once again. A precedent had been set in 1866 in the church favoring "alien baptism" but perhaps the pilgrims of 1910 were unaware of it. Once again in conference, the church dealt with the issue. Pastor Pickard favored the practice, reflected that Baptists were divided on the issue, and correctly concluded that it was up to the local congregation itself to determine its own practice—for there really was no "Baptist" doctrine on this question except that of local church autonomy. Though the motion passed with a near unanimous vote, James R. Cain, a former Sunday School superintendent for ten years, vigorously opposed it. Within a few years Cain would face major problems himself with his unbending attitude and cantankerous spirit. Mrs. W. O. Benton was received as a member from the Christian Church and was not required to be rebaptized due to her previous adult believer's baptism in another denomination.

Properties and special funds are often willed to churches by committed members. In June 1910 the Elizabeth E. Reynolds Fund came into being as she left $5,000 to the church. One-third of the fund was to be used by the church at its discretion, but two-thirds of the income from the fund was to be used to attend to the structure of her vault and the surrounding ground in the Laurel Grove Cemetery. The fund was accepted. The next year Robert Groves left property at 508 Tattnall Street to the church—lots 34 and 35 of Charleton Ward. Penfield had set an early precedent in the nineteenth century and a number of wills in the twentieth would continue to supplement the budget of the church.

Discipline cases were few and far between in the twentieth century, but two in 1911 are worthy of note, with a positive footnote to one as late as 1917. In March the Discipline Committee preferred charges of "unchristian conduct" against John E. All. He was called before the church to give an account concerning a financial matter. He had received money from the National Bank of Savannah for unmerchantable cotton, and civil charges had been brought. All never appeared, but he sent a long letter of explanation stating that he did not drink, smoke, chew, or curse! He claimed to be misunderstood, with a broken heart, and not guilty. "My Lord's people, the Jews, misunderstood me," he cried. The church did not accept his emotional explanation and since he showed no sorrow for his act, the "hand of fellowship was removed" (the word "excommunication" was no longer used). Several months later, in August, W. F. McCauley resigned as a member and his name was erased from the roll. He had evidently divorced and remarried, which was not accepted by the church. He resigned before the hand of fellowship was removed. However, in March 1917, the matter was reconsidered and he was restored to fellowship. The church was forsaking yet another judgmental stance—one having to do with divorce and remarriage.

Pickard was a strong pulpiteer and believed in having revivals. In March 1911 the church participated for three weeks in revival with other Baptist churches. There were 260 more Baptists in Savannah at the conclusion of these union services, sixty of them at Savannah Baptist. In March and April 1912 Pickard did yeoman's service. For five weeks he preached a revival every night but Saturday—"strong and convincing sermons." Forty-five persons were added to the church, most of them by baptism. By the time Pickard left, the church membership had grown by over 40 percent. Jordan and Pickard had led in greater church growth in numbers than any other pastors in the history of the church.

In March 1912 property belonging to the Baptist Church Extension Society of Savannah Baptist was sold for $1,882.46. The church accepted the committee's recommendation to apply this money to its debt of $2,350. An interesting and perceptive minority report was written by Charles W. West opposing the action: "I cannot conscientiously subscribe to the appropriation of a City Mission fund, contributed for that definite purpose, to the church debt, and am therefore opposed to this." West posed a legitimate question for later consideration, namely, the misappropriation of funds. Does the congregation really have the moral right, even in a vote, to change the original intent of certain funds and to use them elsewhere? Perhaps this is a contextual question, but it was and is one for major concern and discussion.

Building a semi-basement in low-lying Savannah was perhaps foolish, for flooding was a yearly possibility. In July 1912 the first reference in the Minutes to building a retaining wall is found. This was an architectural problem that would not be finally solved in either century.

Pickard reported 1912 as one of the busiest years of his life. In addition to responsibilities at the church, he had preached in numerous other churches, had preached the baccalaureate sermon at the University of Georgia, and had attended the trustee meetings of five different colleges. He was becoming even better known in the state. The church must have experienced some difficulties sharing their pastor with the rest of the state and the broader Baptist world.

All the bills had been paid by the end of 1913 and there was money in the treasury. Unfortunately, the hard working sexton, Mack Tyson, who had repeatedly asked for a raise, was turned down once again. No reason was given.

Sharing Pastor Pickard with others reached its conclusion in July 1914 when he was invited to become the president of Mercer University. His evergrowing popularity was no boon for Savannah Baptist for he accepted the offer and left in late September. Glowing letters were written on both sides. The last section of Pickard's letter read as follows:

> I brought to you, my friends, a life of integrity and have tried to preserve such a life during every minute of the years through which I have been your under-shepherd. In life and teachings I have tried at all times to be true to the Word of God and the great principles of our Baptist fathers. Of my work I shall say nothing further. The record is written on your churchbook, in your hearts, in the history of your city, and in God's book on high. There I shall meet all the record in his presence whose I am and whom I have tried faithfully to serve. I trust I shall meet that record with joy when the "leaves of the book are unfolded." Faithfully yours, W. Lowndes Pickard

J. Judson Taylor
1915–1918

The leaving was full of tears and sadness. Pickard had been one of the most effective pastors in the church's history. Although ministers often make excellent university presidents, some find that they critically miss the local pastorate. Pickard stayed at Mercer only four years and left to become a pastor once again. In later years he returned to Savannah, and the church showed its special appreciation of him by naming him as its first pastor emeritus. The close of the career of the next pastor at Savannah Baptist would not be so tender and touching.

J. Judson Taylor

W. D. Hubbard had to serve as interim pastor for only three months. A few of the Search Committee stayed in Knoxville, Tennessee, for three days hearing and interviewing Joseph Judson Taylor at First Baptist Church. With the winds of war blowing and the probability of the United States being drawn into the war, one question which the committee did not ask was the one concerning Taylor's pacifism. He was a pacifist and had so expressed himself in writings on the subject. It is surprising that this matter was not broached by anyone on the committee. The committee, chaired by D. B. Morgan, in its recommendation of Taylor to the congregation stated:

> He stands among the foremost of our preachers in a Southern pulpit. In doctrine he is sound, clear, and conservative. As a man he is scholarly, yet genial; aggressive, but prudent; commanding the respect of the world as he wins the hearts of all. As pastor he is active, loyal, and acceptable, looking for the welfare and interest of his own flock first, then seeking to lead into the fold, lost men and women.

What a glowing report! However, Taylor had two strikes against him before he ever arrived in Savannah—he was succeeding the best pulpiteer the church had ever had, and he was a pacifist at a time of the outside threat of war. In his acceptance letter of December 1914 Taylor spoke of the "pang" of leaving Knoxville and also observed that "a new pastorate always has some elements of uncertainty." Though a prophet, little did he know of the pain that would come in three years. The New Sunbury Association was also rather prophetic itself in 1915 when it reported that some churches want to "boss" their pastor and when he shows some "spunk" they cease their financial support and the minister has to move elsewhere. Financial strings have often been like puppet strings, to lift up and to allow to fall. The minister's role to comfort and to challenge often results in tension if there is too much "challenge."

The first two years were rather quiet ones for Taylor. He presided over the sexton's still not receiving a raise, even with pitiful requests concerning the price of meat and groceries and a family to support. Tyson requested even a "little raise" and promised "to remain your obedient servant." A stray sheet of paper in the historical records simply noted, "History repeats itself." Indeed it did—both in the request and the denial. Taylor also witnessed one of the ever fewer cases of discipline in 1916 as the reader is simply told of Barney E. Jones, William G. Macon, and Mattie Douglass: "After careful examination we find the following members are unworthy of Christian fellowship and recommend that the hand of fellowship be withdrawn."

Taylor was invited to do the honors of the baccalaureate at Alabama Polytechnical Institute (Auburn University) in 1916, and he presided over the "largest assembly ever gathered in conference" at the church in January 1917. An excellent year of service was reported and plans were begun to make major repairs on the church. Later in the year, after raising $20,000 toward this goal, further efforts were discontinued—the country was at war and the congregation was in turmoil over its pastor.

Taylor came to Savannah a pacifist. He was even on record as one in his writings. The committee and church should have known this; it was no well-kept secret. Being a self-proclaimed literalist, for one, Taylor could not interpret the commandment "Thou shalt not kill" in any other way except the pacifist. In 1917 at the Southern Baptist Convention in New Orleans, Taylor, as a messenger of the congregation, opposed a resolution on the floor of the Convention which endorsed the nation's participation in the war. Taylor even introduced a counter resolution which received only twelve votes. The Convention did the "civil religion" thing and supported its nation in relation to war. Saddened by this action, Taylor returned to Savannah and preached a sermon on the situation, elaborating on his views for the entire congregation.

Turmoil erupted and continued in the church until November and December 1917. The associational statement of 1915 was graphically illustrated—there appeared a deficit of funds with "poor prospects of recuperating under the present spiritual condition of the church." The church's overwhelming support of the war effort had at this point resulted in weakening financial support of a church with a pacifist pastor.

Relations within the church were extremely tense for a number of months, and finally in a deacons' meeting of November 3, the following motion was made and passed:

> Whereas the Pacifist views expressed recently by our pastor . . . at the Southern Baptist Convention at New Orleans and the expression of views of a similar nature, both in private to the members of the congregation, and in the pulpit of our church, have in the opinion of the Board of Deacons, greatly weakened his influence, now therefore be it resolved that . . . he tender his resignation to the church, believing that by so doing he will save both himself and the church further embarrassment and will strengthen the work of the church in this community.

The longer motion went on to affirm love for the pastor and denied that the motion had anything to do with his character or ability.

Two days later, Taylor answered his deacons in a moving and poignant statement:

> The disquieting affairs of the First Baptist Church [officially, not yet] were submitted to a full meeting of the official Board of the church July 8th, last, with the assurance that I would cheerfully conform to any course the brethren might agree upon. Since then the whole question has been in the Board's hands. Many individuals have expressed their opinions pro and con, and many rumors have been afloat. Only recently has the Board reached an agreement and it is the first authoritative statement that has been made. This preamble states my position fairly and fraternally. I am a pacifist both for church and state. I regret that what seems to be my best interests in a secular way does not meet my convictions of duty in this case. But I in no wise admit that a pacifist is not a patriot. As our country is in war, I am absolutely loyal to the country's interest in every fibre of my being; and I am confident that the pacifist will be more popular later than he is today.

To save a formal vote and perhaps even more division in the church, Taylor submitted his immediate resignation. The deacons did adopt a resolution to pay him three months of salary and had to take a loan with the Savannah Bank and Trust company in order to do so. Taylor was requested to vacate his study in the church, a rather sad footnote to the affair.

Taylor left to go to Leaksville, North Carolina, as pastor of the Baptist church there. As a scholar, he had numerous contacts, for he had served earlier as the president of Georgetown College in Kentucky, and his brother was the president of Stevens College in Missouri. From Leaksville he moved to the Baptist Church in Jasper, Alabama. While there he introduced another resolution concerning peace to the Southern Baptist Convention in 1922 meeting in Jacksonville, Florida, and presided over by the famous Baptist scholar from The Southern Baptist Theological Seminary, E. Y. Mullins. The Convention was so impressed by him *and* his resolution that it passed the resolution and elected him vice-president! Taylor had been prophetic in his words to Savannah Baptist—this was "later" and the pacifist was "more popular." The "war to end all wars" was over and the mood of the nation was now oriented toward peace. Peace movement statements were both respected and appreciated. Taylor's scholarship and commitment in this direction were so respected that he was put on a committee to draft a platform on peace that is to be found in the Southern Baptist Faith and Message statement of 1925. Perhaps contextually understandable, but the Baptist pilgrims of Savannah were obviously wayfarers in their handling of this situation. The price of unity was pain for both sides. Taylor was far more "Christian" than those who opposed him, though, for it is a truism that the earliest Christians were pacifists during their "minority" days.

Luther Rice Christie

Taylor's middle name was Judson—he had been named after the first Baptist foreign missionary from the United States. The next pastor would appropriately be named not only for the founder of the Protestant movement but also for the itinerating colleague of Judson who had come to Savannah on several occasions to raise funds for foreign missions. In February 1918 the church called Luther Rice Christie to become its pastor (the Search Committee of fifteen included five women). Christie quickly accepted and was in the pulpit by March 10. His first year was spent in mending bridges and restoring unity within the hurt congregation. Christie even showed his clear patriotism as he led the church to make a patriotic as well as a good investment by investing its building funds in liberty bonds. The "unsettled condition of the church" put building plans temporarily on the table.

As has been noted, discipline cases were beginning to be few and far between. Christie's year of 1919, however, opened in January with fellowship being withdrawn from two members—R. R. Oakman and Ida Perkins. Very soon, however, a most notable discipline case would disturb the pastor and the congregation and would involve James R. Cain, a former Sunday School superintendent, and his wife. Though this family had been a "storm center" for a number of years, matters came to an unfortunate conclusion in April and May 1919.

In the Church Conference of April 2, Mrs. Cain had expressed herself with such rude opposition to the pastor that he had left the meeting with the stipulation that he would resign if the church could not solve the problem. He reported that it was evident that the two of them could not live peaceably in the same church together—one must withdraw. With the pastor gone, a committee found it impossible to work out anything with her and finally the Conference withdrew fellowship from her. The pastor returned and withdrew his resignation. Her husband, James, was of course terribly offended by this act. Conversations and letters exchanged sides over the next two months. Christie reported to the deacons that "he was being annoyed by the unsympathetic and hostile attitude of Bro. J. R. Cain to his work as pastor, and the matter would have to be cleared up." Over a two-month period the deacons "exhausted their resources without any shadow of success" in relation to reconciliation. Because Cain had thus violated the spirit and letter of the Church Covenant, the board recommended that the fellowship of the church be withdrawn from Cain and the church accepted the recommendation.

The saga was not over yet, unfortunately. It was extended to the associational level. The Cains had evidently been accepted as members by Calvary Baptist Temple without

**Luther Rice Christie
1918–1921**

Circles have long provided a focal point for mission and social activities for women in the church. A group of ladies gather for a meeting of the Sarah Dixon Circle c. 1920.

letters from Savannah Baptist. This was in opposition to associational principles. In October Cain came as one of the messengers of Calvary to the yearly associational meeting at Olive Branch Church. Christie protested Cain's being there as a messenger, for this was not in harmony with Baptist practice. Christie then proceeded to preach the introductory sermon and that afternoon a motion was made to seat everyone but Cain. When the motion passed, Pastor John S. Wilder and his delegation walked out with Cain. The next year, 1920, Cain was back with the Calvary delegation but Christie was not present and no one else objected. The saga closed and once again denominational church pluralism offered other options for solving cantankerous membership problems. It is much simpler to find a church and pastor with whom one feels rapport than continuously to be involved in controversy and even risk schism.

In the meantime the church decided to move ahead with its major repair and building program. Christie's first two years had been consumed with the search for healing and unity in the congregation. His last two years were then taken up with the problems of raising funds for the major renovation project and coping with the disturbances caused by such building. In addition, the country was in an economic slump in this postwar period. Margaret LaFar estimated in her research that the total cost of this building venture was $233,375. This was an absolutely amazing undertaking given the total circumstances. It required charismatic leadership and committed membership. LaFar in her *Historical Sketch* observes the deep commitment of the women of the church:

> During this time the women of the church worked many long hours to finance the purchase of new pews for the new church. They opened a cafeteria on the southwest corner of Bay Lane and Bull Street, which gained a fine reputation for its fine food. The job required dedication, stamina, and senses of humor. Such a team made their goal and the church got its pews.

At the same time of this building project, the Southern Baptist Convention was putting pressure on its member churches to participate in the Seventy-Five Million Campaign. Between 1919 and 1924 the Convention had committed itself to raising this amount of money. Times were hard and a minor depression prior to the Great Depression of 1929 was going on. The timing of the Convention could not have been worse—the subscriptions were over ninety-two million, but by 1924 the contributions were only fifty-eight and one-half million. That Baptists in Savannah could participate in this campaign as well as complete its building project by 1922 is a huge tribute to the commitment of the members and the pastoral leadership. Business efficiency in the Convention became a priority as it also did at Savannah Baptist. At the close of 1920 the church had its first financial secretary, Miss Elizabeth Medlock. By then the church had reached the critical point of either ceasing or continuing work on the church—

the members had been extended to the limits of sacrifice. More members stepped forward in this crisis and the work continued.

The rains of July 1921 caused even other problems—the semi-basement flooded badly yet again and an appeal was sent to the mayor and city council to give some "relief" in relation to this problem. The plea resulted in twenty-four-inch sewer pipes being laid under Whitaker Street. The city engineer believed that this would solve the problem. Mayor Murray M. Steward received a most thankful letter from the church, which in a few months would finally have to change its stationery letterhead.

Though often during the years the church was referred to on the streets and even in its own Minutes as "First Baptist," its name had never been officially changed from "Savannah Baptist." In conference on November 30, 1921, a committee was appointed to take care of the legal details to change the corporate name of the congregation to First Baptist Church. One person favored keeping tradition—W. A. Johnson went on record as opposing the change. It is completely correct, then, after this date to refer to the First Baptist Church of Savannah, Georgia, never forgetting the first full official corporate name of December 10, 1801—"The Deacons of the Baptist Church in Savannah."

A few weeks prior to the name change came the low point in the year, for on November 13 the resignation letter of Pastor Christie was read to the congregation. He would leave by the end of the year to become pastor of the First Baptist Church of Meridian, Mississippi. In his letter he reflected on the fact that the church was now ready to move into a building "for architectural design and construction unsurpassed in the South." He urged that they needed a new man for the new house and assured them that their hardest days were behind them. After the letter was read, eloquent tributes were made to Christie although pleas that he remain were rejected.

Christie was not present at the October associational meeting of the New Sunbury Association. He had not been present in 1920, either. Perhaps the fact that J. R. Cain and the Calvary Baptist group were back had something to do with this. If the association seated such messengers, Christie would not attend on principle. Nevertheless, there were messengers from Savannah Baptist to witness an interesting development. Women had been seated as messengers on the first day and on the second day John Parker resolved: "That we reconsider our action in yesterday in seating certain lady delegates as members of the New Sunbury Association, in view of the fact that it is contrary to our Baptist policy and practices, also to the plain pointed teachings of God's word." All this was the rhetoric of a fundamentalist male chauvinist. A "spirited discussion" followed and the motion lost by one vote. This momentous vote was witnessed by four female voters from First Baptist—Mrs. J. Read Sweat, Mrs. D. T. Furse, Mrs. James Brown, and Miss Elizabeth Medlock. Women had gained the vote in the United States; Baptist women now had the vote in all matters in their own church as well as in the more conservative association!

First Baptist Church met the new year of 1922 without a pastor. The January annual report stated: "We refer to it [the year] with hesitancy but with a sigh of relief." The year of building and renovation had taken its toll. Mrs. F. V. George gave a report from the Cafeteria Committee which had given $4,600 to the building fund. A special motion was adopted praising all the many women of the church who had worked so hard in heat and cold to make this contribution possible. They, too, must have breathed a "sigh of relief."

**Norman W. Cox
1922–1927**

Norman W. Cox

Meanwhile, the church was having difficulty in getting a new pastor. Attempting to get Dr. G. L. Yates of McKinney, Texas, to come after a call was extended consumed a number of months. The church even volunteered to pay Yates's moving expenses but he never came. By midyear the committee had successfully recommended that Norman W. Cox be called. Shortly after midyear Cox was in residence.

Services in the beautiful new church were held without a pastor in residence. On March 19, 1922, the first service took place, a two-week revival conducted by Pastor J. J. Wicker of Richmond, Virginia. Prior to the opening of the revival, the new building was dedicated in formal services. Dr. Tillman Bowden Johnson of New Rochelle, New York, presided, and Pastor Neal Anderson of the Independent Presbyterian Church preached the dedicatory sermon. There must have been numerous "ohs" and "ahs" over the beauty of the completely redone exterior and interior. It was really like a new church building. The revival was very successful with 103 additions. On April 3 J. J. Wicker used the new baptistery for the first time, immersing Sara Sheftall and Carl Helfrich into the full membership of the church. Ruth Harrell coming from the Methodist Church of New Smyrna Beach, Florida, did not need immersion since she had been immersed as an adult there. She and her "alien immersion" were received on her experiential Christian statement.

Margaret LaFar in her *Historical Sketch* nicely summarizes the numerous changes and additions in relation to this building program. The lengthy description is worth repeating. Mr. Henrik Wallin had been the architect and Mr. Farquhar McRae the contractor and builder. One major problem was the raising of the roof. But by 1922 the herculean task had been completed. LaFar summarizes:

The church was enlarged by converting the old portico into the narthex. Compare pictures and you'll see the three openings and a small room at either end. The city granted permission for a new wide, more open portico and wide steps to be built in front of the old building.

In shape, the church is a simple Greek temple form, crowned with a handsome pediment. It is fronted with a wide flight of steps leading to the lofty portico with its six tall, non-fluted columns, topped with adaptations of Corinthian capitals. Notice that the bottom leaves are carved in detail while the upper rows show only curved

Although a poor photograph, this image, which appeared in the Savannah Morning News, *November 25, 1900, is the only known picture showing the galleries before they were removed in the 1921–1922 renovations. The balconies were located on three sides of the sanctuary and were supported by cast iron columns.*

These photographs reveal the architectural detail of the extensive 1921–1922 renovations, including the exterior columns and the last major interior revisions made to the sanctuary.

Shuttered Palladian windows and walnut pews.

These photographs show Greek and Roman architectural influences.

suggestions of leaves. The Roman influence is seen in the square plinths of the Roman shaft columns and the tall arched windows down the side of the building. These complete columns were created in the Savannah plant of Mr. Kleinsteuber's Cut Art Stone Company. The building has 18 inch walls of brick, now covered with cast stone masonry blocks, also manufactured by Mr. Kleinsteuber.

Interior remodeling called for the removing of the horseshoe shaped balcony and the construction of a new chancel. A chancel in a Baptist church usually consists of the pulpit, baptistery, organ, and choir loft which were placed in front of the sanctuary. The First Baptist Church will be ever grateful to Mrs. Carl Moltz, the widow of George F. Armstrong, for her most generous and gracious gift of the Camp Memorial organ in honor of her parents. The superb Skinner organ was built by Mr. Ernest M. Skinner himself and was valued at $25,200. At that time it was one of the largest church organs in the southeast. The gift was made in 1919 and was installed in the new choir loft at the front of the remodeled church in 1922. New hanging lamps and smaller side wall lights were installed. A small balcony was in the center rear of the church with an office at the southern end. Lofty pilasters were added between the tall windows and they were topped with wooden capitals, hand carved by the world-famous wood carvers of the Black Forest district of Germany.

The interior of the sanctuary would undergo other changes through the years, but never again would such major changes be executed. Soon after Pastor Cox arrived in Savannah, he wrote of the finished product in these words: "We now have what is pronounced by many competent critics, the most beautiful church auditorium in America. One of our friends of discernment recently said of it: 'Its exterior is a dream in stone, and its interior a sublime poem in its chaste simplicity.'"

There is a hiatus in the church Minutes from May 1922 through 1927. Fortunately, *The Messenger* began to be published in October 1922, for four months as a large two-page monthly and by February 1923 as a large four-page weekly—including advertisements to defray the cost of publication. Far more is told in these over one thousand pages of the ministry of Norman Cox than can even be summarized. Major matters, however, merit presentation.

In late February 1923 the Evans Business-Baracca Class made possible the radio broadcast of Sunday morning services and later broadcasts of other special services. These were the first radio broadcasts of any church in Savannah.

Pastor Cox was such a popular preacher that he was often in demand outside Savannah. Within the first half of 1923 he had preached revivals in Glasgow, Kentucky; Madison, Georgia; and Pearson, Georgia. On April 15 he had also exchanged pulpits with Pastor W. A. Taliaferro of Second Baptist Church. The church was generous in accepting his absences and during his first year he was even granted a sixty-day leave from June 25 until early September in order to attend the Baptist World Alliance in Stockholm, Sweden (July 21–28) and to tour western Europe.

Thanksgiving was mixed with sadness upon the death of longtime Deacon J. J. Cummings in May. Thanksgiving was due to his generosity in giving the property behind the sanctuary, bounded by Whitaker, Hull, and McDonough Streets. On it was an older building that could be used for Sunday School purposes until a new one could be constructed in a few years. Plans for this project would be in the works for a few years.

For many years, the largest men's Sunday School class was the Evans Business-Baracca Class, its members shown here in 1923.

Sensitive to theological winds blowing in religious circles, Cox announced in early June that he would be preaching a series of sermons titled "What is Fundamentalism?" The fundamentalist-liberal movement was now well underway in the nation, resulting in a kind of two-party system within numerous denominations. Cox, though committed to certain "fundamental" principles, was more of a conservative evangelical—as were most Baptists.

With the pastor back in the fall, church life was flourishing. A. Leslie Jacobs, organist, was joined on the staff in October by Luther J. Williams, a native of Wales who had been in the United States for sixteen years. He would have the title of musical director and had expansive plans for music in the church including a male chorus or glee club, a children's choral society of one hundred, and a quartet joined by a chorus of twelve for regular Sundays. Over three hundred members had been added to the church and Sunday School average attendance had jumped from 355 to 539. Cumming's gift was already paying off. More efficiency was also needed in budgetary matters; therefore, Cox added the first business manager to the staff in the person of Mrs. E. L. Jarrell.

On February 24, 1924, a high-water mark was achieved in Sunday School—1,361 in attendance. On this date Savannah topped the entire state among Baptists and by March its financial giving was third in the state. Cox, a trustee at Shorter College, Southern Seminary, and Southwestern Seminary was achieving prominence in the city, state, and nation among Baptists. He was also ecumenical in his conservative evangelical orientation. On June 1 he announced a series of sermons called "What Baptists Could Learn From." The phrase was completed by sermons on Episcopalians, Presbyterians, Methodists, Christian Science, and Catholics. His series concluded with "What the World Could Learn from Baptists." Cox was superior in public relations as well—he promised that each sermon

Social activities were an important part in the life of the church. First Baptist dominated city basketball leagues for several years. The 1923 women's team poses for its championship photo.

would be no longer than twenty minutes. In August Cox must have smiled as the church adopted resolutions praising his first two years and what he had done in additions (554 members), financial funds, and Sunday School attendance. The church admitted that when he had come it was "staggering under a load of debt that threatened to break our spirit." He had brought great relief.

In late August Sumner Thorpe, one of "Savannah's own," replaced A. Leslie Jacobs as organist, and in September a new position of educational director was created and Mr. W. J. Stribbling became the new director. The church also received a taste of a future pastor, as in September Arthur Jackson filled the pulpit as "one of the most eloquent preachers" the church had ever heard.

During his tenure of office, Cox made valuable use of his many contacts by bringing national figures in Baptist circles to Savannah. The New Sunbury Association was coming back to Savannah on October 22–23, 1924, after a very long absence (1900 was the last visit to Savannah). That same week Cox was instrumental in bringing the presidents of Tift and Mercer as major speakers to Savannah as well as the nationally famous Baptist scholar, A. T. Robertson. Robertson spoke daily at the YWCA as well as each evening in the municipal auditorium. His winsome topic was the Sermon on the Mount and its appeal to modern life. A few weeks prior to this Cox had been able to bring E. McNeil Poteat Jr., missionary to China, to the pulpit. Savannah Baptists within a few weeks of one another had heard national and international Baptist figures—one, an ecumenical missionary, and the other perhaps the most famous New Testament scholar eventually produced by Southern Baptists.

A footnote concerning the 1924 association is in order. The incident of 1919 with J. R. Cain was evidently now history. John S. Wilder, Calvary's pastor (Calvary was by then the largest white congregation in Savannah), was moderator and the cantankerous J. R. Cain gave the report from the Education Committee. The country was only one year away (1925) from the famous "monkey trial" of Dayton, Tennessee, and Baptists, among others, were nervous over the issue of evolution. Cain reported for his committee that it was an "encouraging sign" that "one of the learned teachers, brilliant, efficient, scholarly, has been requested to resign. Because his expressed views of God's word did not coincide with that held by the masses of our Baptist folk." The reference was to Professor Henry Fox of Mercer, a biology professor and evolutionist. Officially he was dismissed for theological, not scientific, beliefs. He was an agnostic in relation to the divinity of Jesus and the virgin birth of Jesus, and did not accept the concept of the inspiration of the Bible as particularly important. He refused to leave and threatened a lawsuit. Offered one year of salary, Fox dropped the suit and left Mercer. President Rufus Weaver in this case sought the advice of the Administrative Committee of the Georgia Baptist Convention as well as that of the trustees. This serves as an illustration of the monitoring of Mercer by the sponsoring denomination. In later years such monitoring would be a continuing concern for both sides, especially the issue of the boundaries of academic freedom in a denominationally related institution of higher learning. In any case, Cain and certainly Wilder and others agreed with this decision in 1924. In May 1925 Pastor Cox used *The Messenger* to present the New Hampshire Baptist Confession on "The Creation and Fall of Man" as well as a lengthy statement from the famous Baptist theologian, E. Y. Mullins, in which he affirmed the supernatural beginnings of humankind. The issue of evolution was tabled for later and a more mature and precise discussion.

The church was delighted to have the year of 1924 close with a thrilling presentation of Handel's *Messiah*. Luther Williams, director of this musical high moment, retired the next August and was replaced in December by Mrs. Sara McCandless. The congregation seemed divided over what it really wanted at this time in relation to certain aspects of the musical programs, and for awhile a quartet sang in the morning and was joined in the evening by a chorus choir.

November and December were red-letter months. The 125th anniversary celebration would be followed by the Georgia Baptist Convention meeting in Savannah. The celebration took place between November 22 and 29—one full week. Originally, W. W. Landrum, more famous son of one of Savannah's former pastors, was to give the anniversary sermon on the 26th. His illness resulted in the substitution on that day of former Pastor Pickard. Other special speakers during the week included B. D. Gray, corresponding secretary of the Home Mission Board; A. C. Cree, executive secretary of the Georgia Baptist Convention; and J. F. Love, corresponding secretary of the Foreign Mission Board. Former pastors Taylor and Christie joined Pickard on the program. Among local lay members, Mrs. F. V. George reflected on the role of women in "The Ministry of Its Women in the Work of the Church." Pastor Cox in one of his sermons on the first Sunday gave historical sketches and reflections of seven distinguished ministers of the church with his greatest attention being given to Holcombe. W. B. Johnson was briefly mentioned among less famous pastors. On November 23 and during the week the *Savannah Morning News* gave full coverage to the celebration. The membership of 1,526 could be truly proud of the celebration of 125 years of service.

Nineteen twenty-six would probably be the most significant year in the ministry of Pastor Cox, especially in relation to finances and building projects. For years the Sunday School had met in the semi-basement with makeshift folding partitions dividing rooms. Since 1923 the old building on the lots behind the sanctuary given by Deacon J. J. Cummings had provided additional meeting space, while some classes even met in the YWCA. But by early 1926 plans were underway to change all this.

With a keen business mind, Cox led the church to consolidate all its loans in a large $100,000 loan from Penn Mutual Life Insurance Company at less interest than it had been paying. Part of this loan could also be used to construct a new building for Sunday School on the large lot across Whitaker Street.

On January 3, 1926, the church formally approved of these plans and the process commenced. The jump start for the building was possible due to the generosity of two widows. J. J.'s widow, Bertha Cummings, gave $22,500 toward a new building in memory of her husband, and Lucy Armstrong Moltz gave $10,000 in memory of her husband, George F. Armstrong (after whom Armstrong College would later be named). The church would soon own property and buildings worth over $400,000 and would owe only $100,000 at an excellent interest rate. The architects would be Levy, Clark, and Bergen; the builder awarded the bid would be T. R. Worrell; and the hardworking Building Committee was A. M. Dixon, A. F. King, J. C. Lewis, D. T. Furse, and F. B. Vincent (the Sunday School superintendent).

On April 1 the old building on the lot was torn down and wise plans were made to sell the lumber to help defray expenses. In May 70,000 bricks went up for sale for $.20 each. This plan would raise $14,000 and would hopefully involve the entire membership of the Sunday School. By June $7,000 had been raised. On July 4 at high noon, with streets closed by the police and to great fanfare, the cornerstone of the building was laid. The exterior of the stone read "A.D. 1926" and was planted on the northeast corner. In the hollow interior a small copper box was placed containing the one-hundred-year history of the Sunday School (as of April 27, 1927). A few unidentified additional documents were also put there. The fanfare ceremony was led by the Grand Lodge of Masons, Soloman's Lodge #1. Pastor Cox was the chaplain of this lodge. A. F. King gave a brief speech and Frank Vincent presided over the ceremony. The building would be called the First Baptist Bible School—the Bible being the central educational feature of every Christian Sunday School. Soon these Baptists would have a beautiful new building large enough to accommodate an estimated 1,800 persons. About this time Cox started a tradition of having the congregation vote for "preach it again" sermons. Appropriately for such a building season, there was a tie between "A Seat in the Balcony" and "Needed: A Generation of Altar Builders."

In late July, Cox's fourth anniversary in Savannah was celebrated. He had been a builder and shaker. One virtually new building was in place and another actually new

Educational Building built in 1926, remodeled in 1975.

one would soon be completed, and during these years there had been 942 additions. In his celebration sermon Cox called for a religious awakening and named its two enemies: "The forces of rationalistic unbelief and materialism, like a twin octopus, crushing and sucking the spiritual life of our churches to death." Internal changes must match all the beautiful external changes.

Builder Worrell must have used a large work force because the building was ready for occupancy on October 31. The October 17 edition of *The Messenger* was a mammoth ten pages with numerous ads—one simply labeled "Cox" and another by the builder himself. Though ready for noise and persons, the building remained silent on October 31 as the pastor used excellent psychology—until more funds were raised "our songs are silenced," he said. The plan worked and on November 7 the building was used for the first time with only one more thing needed—more chairs for the larger attendance of 667. For excellence in teaching, Cox began three months of lectures for Sunday School teachers who would take an examination at the close of this period and be awarded a "Normal Course Diploma" upon successful completion.

Cornerstone of Educational Building located on corner of Hull and Drayton Street.

The week of April 24–May 1, 1927, was devoted to special services to celebrate the one hundred years of Sunday School at the church—one of the oldest in the Southern Baptist Convention. On Sunday special sermons were preached by I. J. Van Ness, executive secretary of the Baptist Sunday School Board, and George Andrews, Sunday School secretary of Georgia. On May 1 the week of celebration closed with the production of a pageant written by Cox—"The Passing of a Century in Review." Present at Sunday School on April 24 were 829 "scholars" but "yet there was room" in the attractive new building.

Perhaps two major building programs had drained the energies of Norman Cox, for on May 22 he announced his resignation effective June 12 to become pastor of the First Church in Meridian, Mississippi, the very church Pastor Christie had left Savannah to serve. Rarely does this circumstance take place. Cox, a young man in his late thirties, was destined to make a major contribution to Baptists. Keenly interested in local church history while in Savannah, he later began to urge Southern Baptists to establish a historical commission. In 1951 the commission was finally created and Norman Cox was appointed as the first directing executive secretary of this agency. In this capacity Cox made major contributions not only to historical awareness on the part of Baptists but also to the preservation of numerous church records from the local level. Grassroots history was given a distinctive boost by this former Savannah pastor who had "made" so much history there.

Reflections on Cox's five years praised him for leading the church to such greater days. He had had to make constant pleas for funds, he was "a great preacher wasting his eloquence in a low ceilinged basement" (while the sanctuary was being redone), he had to endure a "superior choir" trying to sing accompanied by a "Tinpan piano," and he constantly dealt with low morale in the congregation. In relation to Sunday School it was remembered that when Cox came "we were a group[-]meeting Sunday School"— meeting in a basement, no graded classes, few trained teachers, and bad attendance. Cox made stupendous contributions during his five-year tenure and, amazingly in such predepression years, he was leaving the church in comparatively excellent financial shape just prior to the crash of 1929.

John E. White
1927–1931

John E. White

Thirty persons were placed on the pastoral Search Committee. The search's executive committee had Albert M. Dixon as chair who presided over six other members, including one female, Mrs. F. V. George. In the interim, C. L. McGinty, dean of the WMU Training School in Kentucky, would preach in July and W. L. Pickard would return for the month of August. On July 24 *The Messenger* carried a picture and a write-up of the new pastor who would begin in the fall—John Ellington White from Anderson, South Carolina. Former pastor Christie wrote White of what a wonderful experience he would soon have: "There are fewer complications and less littleness about them than any bunch I know. They will give you the best time you ever had in your ministerial life."

Savannah had just experienced the boundless energy of a young man; now it was perhaps ready for a seasoned older man who had already made his reputation among Southern Baptists. Unfortunately, his ministry would be brief, but it would be deeply meaningful. A later pastor, Thomas Austin, in one of his historical sermons would name him as "one of my favorite pastors" at First Church. He was already known as the "social conscience of Southern Baptists," and at the time of his death in 1931 he was serving as president of the Georgia Baptist Convention and first vice president of the Southern Baptist Convention. If he had lived longer, First Church of Savannah would doubtless have had its only president of the Southern Baptist Convention—he was that popular and revered among Baptists.

White, a native of North Carolina and fifty-eight years of age, had just completed eleven years in a double role. He had been pastor of the First Church in Anderson, South Carolina, and also served as president of Anderson College. Quite a scholar, he had given special lectures at the University of Virginia as well as at the University of Chicago. His publishing record was also lengthy, including *The Silent Southerners* and *The Christian Pacifist*. Ironically, First Church had forced J. J. Taylor to leave because of his pacifism and now, a few years later, it had called a known pacifist to be its minister.

Under the leadership of ministers Norman W. Cox and John E. White, the church saw unprecedented growth. A number of young families posed in front of the sanctuary c. 1926.

Times had changed; these were days of peace emphases, and the personalities of the two men were different. White was more flexible and his manner of communicating did not seem to alienate people. He shared his pacifistic views openly but did not offend the membership. It is true, of course, that there was no world war going on.

About the same time as White came from South Carolina, the organist, Sumner Thorpe, left for Spartanburg, South Carolina. Miss Thorpe was soon replaced by Mrs. George Dutton. White met the year of 1928 by preaching a revival in his own church and many new members were added. But now the church would have to share this well-known pastor with others. In September White attended an important meeting in Nashville, Tennessee. A member of the Executive Committee of the Convention, he was called for an emergency meeting. The treasurer of the Home Mission Board had absconded and disappeared. In October White traveled to Pensacola, Florida, to preach revival services. He was not the mover and shaker Cox had been at home, and by early 1929 Sunday School attendance was down considerably, in the three hundreds. In February White was again off—to speak at Religious Emphasis Week at Mercer. President Darrell praised him for his "intellectual and spiritual scholarship and power." With White back "in pocket," Sunday School attendance rose in March to over seven hundred "scholars." The revival in March resulted in ninety-four new members, so the church was humming statistically once again and meeting its bills during the year of the crash on Wall Street.

Mrs. Dutton became seriously ill by summertime, and Dwight Bruce supplied as organist. Within one week Bruce was listed in *The Messenger* as the new permanent organist. He was immediately given most of the summer off for organ study in New Haven, Connecticut. On his return in the fall he planned and executed a number of organ recitals and the quality of music took a rapid turn up in classical quality. Mrs. Sidney McCandless was still music director, but by 1932 she no longer held that position. Bruce was both organist and choir director.

In November 1929 White was the popular choice for the presidency of the Georgia Baptist Convention and was elected to the prestigious office. By May 1930, the month of the meeting of the Southern Baptist Convention in New Orleans, a number of state Baptist papers were suggesting White for the presidency of the Convention to replace the famous George W. Truett, who had held that office for three years. The Convention actually elected W. J. McGlothlin of South Carolina as president and White as the first vice president. In all likelihood he was destined for the presidency if his unfortunate death had not occurred.

The associational meeting of October 1930 met in Pooler and a great deal of attention was given to the history of the Association dating back to 1801–1802. Savannah Baptist figured prominently in this history, of course. Interestingly, J. R. Cain wrote the report. His denominational pride was apparent in his following remark: "We tell all this in part to show that we are the equals of other denominations—intellectually, socially, and financially." Baptists had widespread inferiority complexes—Cain gave a boost to Savannah Baptists' abilities. Symptomatic of the times, Cain revealed his racial prejudice in referring to the "*New* Sunbury" name change with the observation that if a black church had had membership, then logically the delegation would be entitled to "*entertainment* in the *homes*" where the association met and that this would have been "a situation *absolutely intolerable.*" In a rather condescending way he then stated that the "leaders of the denomination have striven to discharge their duty to their colored brethren." He showed even more insensitivity in never mentioning anywhere in the history the circumstances of women receiving votes as delegates to the associational meetings.

In January 1931 the congregation affirmed its good relations with White and stated: "We face the future with confidence." By the news of July 21 some of this confidence was dashed, for word came of White's sudden death. He was the third pastor to die while in office, but this time the congregation was in unusual grief. It had lost perhaps its most famous pastor and friend after such a comparatively short tenure of ministry. Except for ads, the entire issue of *The Messenger*, July 26, 1931, was devoted to John Ellington White (see Appendix I). Messages of sympathy flooded the congregation, one from none other than George W. Truett of Dallas, Texas. The Minutes of the associational meeting of 1931 grieved the loss of this "friend of God, friend of the brethren, friend of a lost world." The church's memorial statement reflected that "at the funeral there was no hint of doubt, no note of despondency, no wail of gloom." On July 26 a memorial service for him was conducted on the Capitol grounds in Atlanta. Participating were many Baptist leaders, the president of Georgia Tech, a professor from the University of the South, and the pastor of the Second Presbyterian Church. White was well-known in wider circles than simply the Baptist. The congregation would not soon forget this truly great Christian Baptist who was also a pacifist.

Arthur M. Jackson

By late July the new Search Committee was already at work and on October 19 a unanimous vote of the congregation extended the call to Arthur Jackson, pastor of the First Baptist Church in beautiful Hendersonville, North Carolina. He gave a positive answer and he would soon leave the Blue Ridge Mountains and beautiful apple country to move to the flatlands of Georgia. *The Messenger* of December 6, 1931, carried a picture of the new pastor as well as a notation that Pastor Pickard had been named pastor emeritus by recommendation of the Board of Deacons.

An interim word should be said at this point about the church's weekly publication. The aftershocks of the Great Depression resulted in a number of cutbacks, even salaries. Publishing a large *Messenger* was expensive, even with advertisements (and they were diminishing as well). *The Messenger* for years had been four pages, measuring eight by eleven inches. On December 20, 1931, a smaller one of four pages appeared measuring six by nine inches. There were fewer ads, and basically it contained the order of worship and a few announcements of church activities. Still called "*The Messenger*," this was reduced to two small mimeographed pages in January 1934, mainly with the order of worship. As late as November 1941 this format remained and it was still named "*The Messenger*." The contemporary *The Calendar* of 1998 carries the designation of being volume 64. A bit of subtraction gives the birthdate of *The Calendar* as 1934. This is technically incorrect, though by 1934 the main item in *The Messenger* was the order of worship, a few announcements, and no advertisements. In other words, eventually the longer and more involved *The Messenger* became the efficient and smaller *The Calendar* and no specific date can be given. It was a normal evolutionary process.

Arthur Jackson came at a time when he would need to lead the church out of the doldrums of the Depression, and at one point his commitment to do this would result in his own salary cut. He was a short man with a commanding, booming voice and an evangelistic style to his preaching. During his tenure over one thousand members would be added to the church. If the debt of over $96,000 which he inherited was to be taken care of, more giving members were needed and he was indeed the man of the hour.

Arthur M. Jackson, D.D.
1931–1941

Reducing the remaining building debt was a priority for Jackson, but times were hard and this would take a number of years. The budget of 1933 had to reduce the salaries of the pastor, organist, and secretary. Aftershocks of 1929 were still being felt—these were still the Depression days of cutbacks. Between October 1, 1933, and the same day of 1934, two hundred new members had been added. Jackson's evangelism was effective, but even with so many new members the church was still not reducing the building debt as rapidly as it wanted. By 1934 the church was even suggesting a program to remove the debt in from eight to ten years.

Meanwhile on the associational level, more female messengers from the church were attending than males, and the leadership of the association was concerned with education and morality. In 1933 the New Sunbury

Children of the church studied mission activities through the Royal Ambassadors and Girls Auxilary. A group of R.A.s pose with their teachers c. 1937.

urged that Baptist schools must be Christian and Baptist, or "there is no other justification for staying in the educational field." The next year messengers were told that the repeal of the Eighteenth Amendment (having to do with liquor) was a wicked backward step, and the association also urged the churches to agitate for "cleaner moving pictures" and not to patronize "picture houses of questionable character." Every Sunday, Jackson, while greeting members at the door of the sanctuary, could see the theater just across the square. If he had read carefully about Henry Holcombe, first pastor, he would have been reminded of Holcombe's condemnation of actors as "his Satanic Majesty's forces"!

Mercer was remembered in the budget of 1935 with $1,000, and later in the year Mercer reciprocated by awarding Jackson the honorary Doctorate in Divinity. The newly "doctored" pastor was indeed honored but still preoccupied with fund-raising and debt reduction—urging committed members to become genuine 10 percent tithers. Even with the debt, however, the church was ever sensitive to missions, and in 1936 he led the church to start a mission in Twickenham Terrace. The ever-giving Women's Missionary Union made a large gift for this project in addition to that of the regular church budget. By October 1937 the Twickenham Mission had been organized into the Morningside Baptist Church. First Baptist had yet another daughter church.

Jackson opened 1938 with a plea that a deep and genuine revival was needed in the congregation. Perhaps to jump-start this goal he supported the attendance of the congregation at an ecumenical religious service—the John Wesley Memorial Services of two hundred years of history at the church and the city auditorium. Wesley's experience of a "strangely warmed" heart was just what Baptists needed, mused Jackson. Jackson himself must have warmed hearts with his loud and energetic style. Julian Quattlebaum, contemporary member, remembers hearing Jackson while a boy, Jackson dressed in his morning clothes: "He was an energetic, loud preacher, punctuating his sermons with hatchet-like banging on the pulpit. There was a standing joke between the Presbyterians and Baptists. In the summertime before air conditioning when the windows were open, the Presbyterians got two sermons—one from their preacher and one from Dr. Jackson!"

October 12, 1938, marked a momentous deacon's meeting. Perhaps prophetically, the meeting opened with the singing of "On Jordan's Stormy Banks I Stand." During the course of the meeting, Frank Oliver suggested that women should be added to the Board of Deacons. Unfortunately, no detailed records exist that summarize the discussion. The pastor did admit that the Bible provided for deaconesses. He, of course, did not have the benefit of contemporary scholarship which points out that the word "deacon" used of the first seven in Jerusalem was the same word used of Phoebe in Rome and other women in early Christian churches. The 1938 board in Savannah was not yet ready to accept this change, however. Oliver's motion was tabled and died a quick death. He must be commended, however, as a prophet and a deacon ahead of his time, though at this time he was unsuccessful in his efforts, for there were no females on the list of nominees for the deacon's board in 1939. This was the momentary negative comment by the board on this forward-thinking and sensitive suggestion.

In 1939 Jackson was president of the Georgia Baptist Sunday School Convention and was honored in April as the Convention met in Savannah at the site of one of the oldest Baptist Sunday Schools in the state. Jackson and the deacons also exchanged in April some interesting correspondence concerning junior deacons with the Vineville Baptist Church. Savannah's side of the correspondence said that Pastor Cox had instituted the practice fifteen years earlier and that presently there were twenty-four senior deacons and equally as many junior deacons. In giving the idea, Cox was complimented: "He needed these Junior deacons to do some of his special hustling where some of the Senior deacons were too old to go fast!" The letter also said that fifteen or so years earlier the church tried a rotating system briefly but dropped it when it was judged not working. In fact a few months earlier than the correspondence, the church had rejected the motion that a deacon had to sit out even one year after serving a full term. It was determined that any deacon could be reelected to another term. Perhaps with some humor, the advising letter also said: "Our church is possibly the oldest church in Georgia [actually one of the oldest] and old bodies are hard to move, not that we are in a rut by any means but we do not like changes." In fact, changes had taken place perennially at First Church.

Ecumenism and Christian education were given boosts in July and October. In July forty members of the congregation attended the Baptist World Alliance meetings in Atlanta and broadened their vision of the different kinds of Baptists around the world as well as deepened their understanding of the common history and spirituality binding Christian Baptists together from across international borders and languages. No one attending such meetings could ever walk away from such experiences without a heightened ecumenical awareness. In October the congregation was made more greatly aware of opportunities in relation to Christian witness and education as Miss Daniel from the Sunday School Board in Nashville addressed the church concerning the role of the Baptist Student Union among college and university students. She called for initiating participation in such an organization at Armstrong Junior College as well as in the business schools in the city.

The year 1939 closed on a slightly negative note in relation to the abiding building debt. In December the church corresponded with J. B. Lawrence, executive secretary of the Home Mission Board in Atlanta, inquiring about any loan funds which might be available to churches in relation to past (in this case) building projects. Their present loan was down from their original $100,000 to $66,500. The letter gave the history of thirty men in the church having to endorse the loan and that this had "created quite some feeling in our church." In other words, there was discontent after over a decade of a heavy debt. If the church could only get a $25,000 loan at less interest from the HMB it would greatly ease the situation not to say the "endorsers." The negative answer from Williams came within days: No church could be given a loan for prior indebtedness. Times were on the threshold of change for the better, however. The war years would bring lower unemployment and higher salaries. First Baptist would soon be free of a debt dating back to the major building program of 1921–1922. By the end of 1943 the church would already have reduced the debt by 50 percent.

For awhile, J. B. Johnson's idea of communion every Sunday began to be the practice in 1940. Women were in the majority on the committees having to do with music, flowers, and communion, but still no females were nominated for the Diaconate. In July a promotional secretary was employed and would be given a complimentary car by J. C. Lewis Ford Company (Lewis was a stalwart in the church). The church was joining the organizational age and would make strides in debt reduction with new pledge cards and a dotted line on which to sign. Missions and denominationalism were not forgotten, however. The church was alerted to the fact that in relation to the growth of Savannah in Industrial City Gardens, "at least two other denominations had churches there now." First Church would contribute to a mission church being founded there, since it was estimated that over 250 Baptists presently lived there. Toward the close of the year, Pastor Jackson also was successful in having the deacons pass a plan for a complete departmentalization of the church and the setting aside of Wednesday evening as Church Night with a complete meal and then group meetings of the various departments and interest groups. The church was learning lessons from secular business organizations and was gearing up for mid-twentieth century.

Although the church was inspired by the famous Westminster Choir (Princeton, New Jersey) in concert in February 1941, it was nervously aware of world conditions. At the start of the year in his annual report, Jackson as a good civil religionist reminded the congregation that "democracy in all its relationships is threatened throughout the world" and that "Christianity is the foundation stone of all our liberties." He knew that the universal draft in the United States was imminent, and he was using every effort at his fingertips to draft more members for the church—setting a goal of one thousand in church on Sunday morning.

On October 5, 1941, Pastor Jackson, during a Sunday Church Conference, announced his resignation to become the pastor of Morningside Baptist Church in Atlanta. He would not leave until the last day of November, just before the Japanese strike on Pearl Harbor on December 7. The church urged him to revisit his decision to no avail, and as his last days there drew near, the church praised him for his decade of leadership in inspiring united activity on the part of the members and in adding more than one thousand members to the church during his tenure of office. He was also highly commended for his active contributions within broader Baptist life as well as to the city of Savannah.

Jackson's abilities as an organizer and fund-raiser did not go unnoticed. His tenure at Morningside was brief, for on August 26, 1943, he was elected as the first executive secretary of the Georgia Baptist Foundation and Endowment Committee and assumed office on September 15. He served in this office until his retirement at the close of 1954. From the start his office was responsible for raising funds for all Baptist colleges and universities in Georgia. As in Savannah, his talents for fund-raising and effective organization were utilized and the committee's work was eminently successful.

The church was without a resident pastor on Sunday, Pearl Harbor Day. This was indeed a time for a realization of the doctrine of the priesthood of every believer. The church was a congregation of ministers to one another and to outsiders during these dreadful days of the United States entering the most dreadful war in the history of humanity.

Citizens of Savannah as well as all other Georgians responded in true patriotism to this outside threat to democracy and civilization itself. Hunter Field had already been established as a training center for Army Air Corps crewmen. Fort Stewart Army Base was also close to Savannah. Shipbuilding and port facilities began to boom. Savannah was experiencing a financial success story in its numerous expansions during the war years. In Georgia about one of every ten persons in the state would serve in the armed forces and of those who served, some seven thousand would fail to return. Savannah and other coastal areas were more immediately aware of the war than others due to the oil spills and wreckage that washed up on the beaches resulting from German submarine sinkings in the Atlantic. The flip side of the pain and grief of such a war for Savannah as well as the state and nation was that World War II did what the New Deal had been unable to do—through payrolls and production it spelled the end of the Great Depression and started a period of great prosperity and expansion. From 1940 to 1950 the per capita personal income in Georgia had trebled. First Baptist Church would no longer be in debt and would be financially secure. The population influx would also lead to numerical growth.

The church was without a resident pastor for six months, but had the able leadership of W. C. Allen as interim pastor.

Leroy G. Cleverdon

By the first Sunday in June 1942 the twenty-eighth pastor of First Baptist Church, Leroy G. Cleverdon, was in residence and in the pulpit. Though not even mentioned in the index of J. A. Lester's *A History of the Georgia Baptist Convention*, he would have the longest tenure of office of any pastor in the church thus far, nineteen years, and would certainly be the best-educated pastor ever claimed by the church in Savannah. He came to Savannah from Marion, Alabama, where he had been president of Judson College for thirteen years.

Cleverdon actually had grown up in the Methodist Episcopal Church, South, and intended to enter the Methodist ministry. Married at nineteen, he needed a scholarship in order to attend seminary but for some reason was unable to get one from a Methodist school. Perhaps in jest he gave his daughter, Shirley, the reason: "I think it's because I didn't love to sing and every Methodist minister loves to sing." In any case, the Baptist Bible Institute (in 1946 the name was changed to the New Orleans Baptist Theological Seminary) offered him a work scholarship in these words as remembered by his daughter, Shirley: "If you are willing to stoke furnaces at 4:30 in the morning, are willing to sweep classrooms, and also to grade papers, willing to do anything we ask you to do, we will give you a small apartment right at the edge of the campus." By then Cleverdon was married with three children. He accepted the offer and studied there for a number of years and earned the doctor of theology degree. Some nights he studied until 1:00 A.M. and then had to be about his chores by 4:30 A.M. After completing this degree he earned the bachelor of arts and the master of science degrees at Tulane University. Supplying numerous pulpits during this time, following Tulane he went to

Leroy G. Cleverdon,
Ph.D.
1942–1961

the Calvary Baptist Church in Alexandria, Louisiana, as pastor. A church in heavy debt, Calvary was led to solvency by Cleverdon in three years. Next, Cleverdon's insatiable desire for knowledge led him to Yale University and a doctorate in world missions under the greatest missiologist in the nation at that time, Kenneth Scott Latourette, a Baptist. All this education would certainly be to his benefit during the remainder of his career in a college and in a large urban church with a highly educated congregation. From Yale he immediately went to Judson College and from Judson to Savannah where he would retire. To his credit, at Judson he was sensitive enough to his young students to allow dances. For this he was accused by fundamentalist ministers of sending the girls (it was a women's college) "straight to hell" and forced to resign. Judson's loss was Savannah's gain.

During the war years, Cleverdon's greatest strength, as well as enjoyment, was in the field of pastoral counseling. He made unusual and successful contributions in counseling alcoholics and unwed mothers. His ministry touched many service personnel during the war, and he and his wife showed unusual sensitivity to the needs of unwed pregnant women. On several occasions the Cleverdons arranged for pregnant young women to live in their home during the pregnancy and then involved themselves in adoption procedures. At least two of these served briefly as secretaries in the church. Due to the morality of the times, all this was rather secretively done but it vividly illustrates the love and concern which the Cleverdons had for their fellow human beings. They took risks because they cared. During the war years especially, Pastor Cleverdon's "greatest job and pleasure," according to his daughter, Shirley, was in counseling both men and women who came to him with serious problems.

In August 1943 the church began to publish the *Service Flag News*, a four-page news quarterly. It was to be sent to the men and women of the church who were serving in the armed forces. This first issue reported that the church had "171 representatives serving in all branches of the armed forces." By the war's end, 255 men and women from First Baptist had served. Five had given their lives in the defense of their country: Tom Cook Cheney, Ernest Samuel Hatcher, Ramson Hiott, Francis McDonald Oliver Jr., and William Malcolm Ross. Cleverdon himself had a son and a daughter serving. Annie Beth, lieutenant, at that time served with the Medical Corps at the Station Hospital, Maxwell Field, Dothan, Alabama. The son, Leroy C., was then a cadet in the Air Corps stationed in Miami Beach. Pastor Cleverdon was touched by grief along with so many other families. Later his son was a prisoner of war and when released weighed only eighty-five pounds. Soon after his release he died of amoebic dysentery. No one could claim that Cleverdon was an outsider to war grief. Shirley, the second daughter, was honored by her father performing her wedding

During World War II the church opened up the Lecture Room under the sanctuary (site of Memorial Chapel) as a canteen for soldiers stationed in the area, holding parties, such as this Christmas party in 1943, dances, concerts, and other social events.

ceremony on July 1, 1943. She married a serviceman—Major John Gray Anderson, and her sister, Annie Beth, was her only attendant. The Cleverdon family was intertwined with the war effort. Throughout the war the church continued publishing this paper with news from back home for those so far away from those they loved so dearly.

As noted, though the war years were tear-stained, they brought financial success to the church. The year following the close of the war witnessed the burning of the church's mortgage and the elimination of a debt dating back to 1921–1922. The last three years of the war saw the congregation paying off the final $65,000. Before an overflow crowd on January 18, 1946, former Pastor Jackson preached, and then Julian K. Quattlebaum, chairman of deacons; S. B. LaFar, church treasurer; and Otis Stubbs, chair of the Finance Committee, burned the mortgage while Cleverdon witnessed the joyous occasion. For the first time in twenty-four years the church was debt free!

The church began aiming for its next red-letter year, 1950, with some renovation of the educational building and slight improvement and redecoration of the sanctuary. The year 1950 would be marked by an elaborate sesquicentennial celebration. The

Leroy Cleverdon burned the church mortgage during a Sunday morning service in 1946. The choir loft above him was extended in 1967.

preface to the special day of November 26 took place on November 14–16 as the 129th session of the Georgia Baptist Convention was held in the church with the famous R. G. Lee of Belleview Baptist Church in Memphis, Tennessee, preaching the final sermon.

The committee of preparation had worked long and hard, and the only glitch on November 26 was providential—it was a bitingly cold day and one scheduled outside address had to be done indoors. Other than that, the church could not have wished for smoother sailing. *The Calendar* for the day was twelve pages in length and included an excellent thumbnail historical sketch of the church by Cleverdon. It also gave the full text of the bronze tablet that was to be placed that day on the outside wall at the right of the center door of the sanctuary (see appendix J).

Scores of greetings and messages prior to the day were received from Savannah and elsewhere. Dr. R. G. Lee, recently there and also president of the Southern Baptist Convention, wrote: "On this notable occasion, I rejoice with you in every worthy achievement and in every act of faith throughout these fast-flying years." The most ecumenical greeting came from Savannah's Temple Mickve Israel's Congregation: "This 217-year-old congregation holds your congregation in affectionate regard and welcomes this opportunity to give its expression." The *Savannah Morning News* of November 26 gave full coverage to the day's events.

Among luminaries from the state and convention was Henry J. Stokes, one of First Church's native sons and pastor of the First Baptist Church, Knoxville, Tennessee. The distinguished list of other speakers included John Wilder, pastor of Calvary Baptist Temple; Searcy Garrison, pastor of Bull Street; Raymond Wood, pastor of the Lutheran Church of the Ascension; T. L. Holcomb, executive secretary of the Sunday School Board in Nashville; and former pastor Arthur Jackson, executive secretary of the Georgia Baptist Foundation. Dwight Bruce enhanced the services with appropriate hymns including How's "For All the Saints, Who from Their Labors Rest." The highlight of the afternoon service was the unveiling and dedication of the bronze memorial plaque, recently arrived from New York, and its mounting on the front outside wall. Native son Stokes preached an evening sermon, "The Baptist Witness in Savannah." The high moment of the service, however, involved Mabel Freeman LaFar, historian of the church *par excellence*. Flowers in her memory were placed in the sanctuary by her family and copies of her *The Baptist Church in Savannah, Georgia: A History of Its Early Days (1800–1836)* in two volumes were presented to the church. LaFar had culled the essence of the church from the Minutes of these years into 1,044 pages. To summarize all this rich material of only the first thirty-six years of the history of the church would be a challenge to any historian. Mabel LaFar's contribution was actually the most important moment of the day insofar as the actual sesquicentennial celebration was concerned. Her role in "historic keeping" at First Baptist Church cannot be over-estimated. Three cheers for Mabel LaFar.

By September 1953 many new plans were set in motion. Missions was given special attention on September 13 when the Riverside Mission was incorporated as a church and numerous gifts were made by First Baptist including a pulpit Bible and a piano, not to mention the scores of members who now officially changed their membership. Also in February a special planning committee of thirty-five (including ten females) began to look at long-range needs. Their study was to include the following potential projects: air-conditioning both buildings, renovation of the lecture room in the semi-basement, installation of a modern kitchen, installation of an elevator in the Sunday School building, and giving special attention to the needs of young people in the church. The committee was also to consider seriously one final item: "The disposition of present church property and building a new church with adequate parking facilities in the south or southeastern section of the city." Every downtown church in urban centers has faced the decision about relocation. First Church would reject this possibility and continue to wrestle with its mission in a downtown setting. It decided not to escape to the suburbs.

The recommendations of the committee were approved by the congregation in early January 1954. No mention in the report was made of relocating. All of the other items were planned and a building fund would be initiated soon toward the goal. The church would use the Department of Church Architecture in the Convention, hoping their advice would be less expensive.

While plans moved ahead to do renovation and building in phases as monies were raised, the church voted to buy the Trinity Methodist Church parsonage and lot adjacent to and west of the Sunday School building. There was some disagreement about this decision especially since the fire chief of Savannah, D. P. Dawson, said that the building was so hazardous that it should be torn down. It was bought, however, and soon torn down. In the interim, though, it had been used by the Sunday School as a kitchen and dining room and for choir practice. The controversy caused Cleverdon to go on record as follows: (1) Baptists agree that the majority always rules in a democracy, and (2) when funds are designated, they must be used that way unless the donor agrees otherwise. There had been some questions about redesignating funds in relation to the purchase of this property. After the motion to purchase passed, Cleverdon spoke on the need for love and understanding in community and stipulated that "any member could cancel or amend his or her pledge by giving written notice to the church or to the treasurer." And the church moved on from this minor controversy to attend to more important business.

Dwight Bruce was the center of attention in June 1954 as he celebrated twenty-five years as minister of music. *The Calendar* praised his "magnetic personality, superior judgment, diplomatic technique, and outstanding choirs." The church treasured its association with him.

In 1955 two women were named on the five-person Nominating Committee but still there were no female deacons. Oliver's motion of the 1930s was still tabled and he was now deceased. The Recreation Committee was especially active planning moonlight boat rides, sweetheart banquets, fish fries, and harvest banquets. After some controversy, socializing was part of the healing process. In March Cleverdon showed that he still believed in revivals as he led the church to participate in the Baptist Southwide Evangelistic Crusade by bringing James P. Wesberry from Morningside in Atlanta to preach for a week. There were twenty-one additions. In that same month the church again illustrated its sensitivity to its own history. Margaret LaFar, James Wells, and C. D. Ellis were appointed as a committee to review and preserve church Minutes and other records, note any omissions, and preserve them in a bank vault.

Priorities in relation to construction were set: (1) semi-basement work, (2) educational building work, and (3) any construction on the newly purchased property. Carl E. Helfrich was the architect for the basement work and reported that with a new system of heating and air-conditioning, the air would be "cleaner, healthier, and more comfortable." No one could argue that point and so the work commenced on the basement. Additional problems emerged; one was termite damage, but the work continued apace and within the year was completed. As Margaret LaFar describes it, in 1956 "the lovely small intimate Memorial Chapel was dedicated." Many other things were done to improve the entire area, but the spotlight was perhaps focused on the lovely chapel.

Ever conscious of missions, in 1956 Cleverdon played a major role in the founding and opening of the Savannah Baptist Center as a goodwill mission. The Center opened on August 1 with Evelyn Stanford as the first director, and the activities of the Center were located in the facilities of the First Baptist Church. In 1958 the Center moved to the former facilities of the Taliaferro Baptist Church at Harris and Habersham Streets and worship services began there on August 10. First Baptist extended its church membership to those who joined and gave authority to the pastor of the Center, John W. Beam, to administer the ordinances of baptism and the Lord's Supper. Its activities would expand through the years eventually to

Leroy Cleverdon at the dedication of Memorial Chapel in 1956. The chapel replaced the Lecture Room and its folding walls which could be extended to create Sunday School rooms. The furnishings and fixtures for the chapel were donated in memory of family and friends of the church.

have a clothes closet, food pantry, and financial emergency aid as well as all the usual worship and educational offerings of an average church. Cleverdon would have been duly proud of the evolving ministry of the Center to downtown Savannah.

Cleverdon had been perennially active in ecumenical endeavors throughout his ministry in Savannah and two of those moments merit mention. The 1943 National Brotherhood Week witnessed a series of panels planned by a special ecumenical committee composed of Cleverdon, Rabbi Soloman of Mickve Israel, and Msgr. McNamara of the Cathedral of St. John the Baptist (an appropriate name!). According to Saul Rubin, "this was the first interfaith endeavor involving clergy of the three major faiths" in Savannah. In March 1946 Rabbi Louis Youngerman of Mickve Israel (active in Christian-Jewish dialogue) preached from First Baptist's pulpit and Cleverdon preached from Mickve Israel's pulpit. This was the first pulpit exchange like this in the history of Savannah and the *Savannah Morning News* praised it as "an inspiring manifestation of brotherhood in America at its best." Cleverdon was continuing to spell out the pilgrim meaning of those earliest ecumenical commitments of the congregation in 1800. Cleverdon had an absolutely amazing record as well in relation to broader ecumenical meetings. He had been an accredited visitor at the First Assembly of the World Council of Churches in Amsterdam in 1948 and a delegate to the third World Conference on Faith and Order in Lund, Sweden, in 1952. In Baptist world circles he had been a delegate to the Baptist World Congress in London in 1955.

Before Cleverdon's retirement he had pointed out the need for a "trained worker in education and in promotional visitation." In the context of its building projects there was never the flexibility of budgetary funds for such a new position in the church. Cleverdon's excellent idea was tabled until a later time. Cleverdon was perhaps weary of long well-doing, as well as the effects of a heart attack, and in September 1961 he announced his retirement. Within four years the church honored him by declaring him pastor emeritus. Margaret LaFar later described him as a "brilliant and gentle" man but also a doer. Indeed he was. Of all the thirty-two pastors of two centuries of existence of First Baptist Church, he had the longest tenure of office and would not soon be forgotten. From war years to debt retirement to new building projects, Cleverdon had been their friend and leader. Only minor normal controversies appeared during these two decades—nothing major interrupted the understanding and tolerant pastoral ministry of this man. As T. S. Eliot said of Thomas Becket, so may be said of Leroy Cleverdon—he was, after all, truly a great man.

William Forrest Lanier

The Search Committee was soon successful in bringing William Forrest Lanier as pastor to the church. In the brief interim, Rufus D. Hodges had served from the pulpit. Lanier was in the pulpit on Palm Sunday, 1962. He had been a kind of tumbleweed and, as a matter of fact, the Committee had requested Ralph Crutcher on a business trip to Scotland to go to Edinburgh and interview Lanier who was there studying at the university. Lanier had earlier completed degrees at Mercer and The Southern Baptist Theological Seminary and from there had served the First Baptist Church of Rome, Georgia, for about ten years. Sensing the need for more education, he had resigned that church to go and study theology in Heidelberg and Edinburgh. While on the continent he was able to hear one of the greatest theologians of the age, Karl Barth. High German was terribly difficult, however, and after one year he went to Edinburgh. While there, Crutcher came by on an announced visit and Lanier's wife, Gene, baked a coconut cake for high tea. Gene recalls that later Crutcher often said that "the coconut cake was what called Forrest to Savannah." In any case, the call was extended and Lanier accepted.

Early on, in January 1963, Lanier urged the need of a revival in the church. He grieved over the fact that a 1,500 plus member church had baptized only fourteen persons in the preceding year and located the basic mission of the church in saving those who are lost. He immediately began an emphasis in his ministry on the theme of love in the called community of pilgrims as well as expressed toward all those outside this community. It is not surprising that his favorite passage of scripture was I Corinthians 13—the most famous love passage in the entire Bible.

The Supreme Court Decision of 1954 having to do with racial equality and integration had made no major impact yet on First Baptist Church. Surely there was negative street talk about all the social implications but no official action had been taken. In 1963 the Supreme Court had taken on another touchy issue in its ruling to prohibit mandatory Bible reading and recitation of a prescribed prayer in public schools. In June 1963 the new pastor tried to educate his congregation. Though being very careful in his language, he finally concluded that "legally the court did what it had to do." Lanier showed that on a controversial issue he would indeed commit himself but would try to be sensitive and attentive to all sides of the debate. Having lived in Europe for two years, Lanier was aware of that kind of pluralism in societies that necessitates tolerance as well as of the essence of the Baptist commitment to the principle of the separation of church and state.

Lanier soon faced two more controversial topics—Viet Nam and the Civil Rights Movement. Gene Lanier gives insight on the latter subject in relation to the first deacons' meeting which her husband had attended. When he came home he told her, "I

William Forrest Lanier
1962–1969

don't know if I'm in the right place or not." Someone in that meeting had proposed that an immediate decision be made that blacks were not going to be admitted to the church as members. Lanier did not agree with this; he wanted a church "open" to all comers.

Prior to May 2, 1965, blacks had been in the worship service with no particular problem. W. W. Law, head of the NAACP in Savannah, had visited the church somewhat regularly and at times some young black Girl Scouts had been brought to the church in groups and no one had objected. However, on May 2, a large group of blacks appeared at the church door with a single intent of desegregating the service. Such actions were going on all over Georgia, including many other churches. Two men at the doors closed them and did not want to let the group in. The church was without an official policy, but Lanier insisted that two men could not decide this matter for the whole congregation, and the doors were opened. The deacons met the next evening and the "integration attempts" were discussed. The deacons decided that until the congregation officially developed a policy, the doors would be open to all. Lanier was relieved and gratified. It was not until March 1968, however, that the congregation officially voted on an open-door policy. Lanier opined that he was "saddle sore from carrying such a deep feeling" about this. He believed that the church had "come of age" on the matter. Careful plans for the congregational vote had been made.

In February 1967 at a deacons' meeting, Lanier had said: "There is a growing realization in the church for the need to retain a downtown ministry in order to meet the challenge of modern living. It will require a growing feeling of redirection in the congregation to turn the church over to the Holy Spirit. We must stay abreast of developments and build our church in prayer, love, and sacrifice." One year later in March, Lanier told the deacons that it was long past time to face the issue and clearly to define the church's policy. He then went on record as saying that he could not in good conscience deny anyone access to worship. Privately, Lanier had grieved deeply about this issue. After "an at-length" discussion, Deacon Layton moved that resolutions be presented to the church without endorsement, that voting be secret, and that the church would vote on the resolutions on March 17. The materials to go before the entire congregation were as follows:

1. Be it resolved that all people be admitted to public worship services in the First Baptist Church.

2. That this resolution be presented to a called meeting of the church after properly instructing them of the intent of this resolution.

3. That all future candidates for membership in the First Baptist Church, not previously so cleared, be referred to a committee composed of the Chairman of the Board of Deacons, the Vice-Chairman of the Board of Deacons, and three (3) members to be appointed by the Chairman of the Board of Deacons. This committee will make recommendation to the Church before membership is granted and this must be approved by a vote of the congregation.

The vote of the congregation was decisively positive. The doors of the church were now open to all persons by an official congregational vote, however late it came. Lanier told his wife that if the vote had been negative, he would have respected the congregational decision and remained with the church. He did not tell her how long he would have remained. Observing the "whole Lanier," however, it is very doubtful that he would have stayed very long. His feelings were too strong to be pastor of any church that closed its doors to blacks. Baptists in Georgia had made a long and tortuous pilgrimage in relation to race since those days in 1845 when the average Georgia delegate to the founding of the Southern Baptist Convention owned between twelve and twenty-eight slaves!

On another controversial issue of the sixties, the Viet Nam War, there was no doubt about Lanier's opposition. He did not take to the streets with the protesters, but he spoke and wrote in obvious disagreement with U.S. foreign policy. As early as the summer of 1967 he called it a "seemingly senseless war." In the same summer he spoke of the "loss of the American conscience." In January and February 1969 he wrote in *The Calendar* his most judgmental words. As the war was ending in January he wrote of "the orgy of the past few years" and of the nation with a "hangover." The next month he virtually cried—"most wars are stupid—especially this one." The church had matured a great deal since it had fired Pastor Taylor during the First World War. It now carefully and attentively listened to prophetic words about a war later judged by scholars everywhere as useless and actually stupid.

Cleverdon had led the church into a debt-free period, but by 1966 the church led by Lanier sensed a number of changes needed in the sanctuary and the church voted to allow the Board of Deacons to borrow up to $70,352, the estimated cost for this renovation program. The architectural firm of Gunn and Meyerhoff had made a thorough study of the major needs of the main sanctuary building and cut the final estimate by $25,600 when it advised that the church did not really need any addition of side balconies. Edward Braun Jr. would be the contractor and work would begin on June 20, 1966. Ironically (especially in view of the history of the church's attitude), the church first planned during the period of building to have morning worship services in the Savannah Theater, just across the square. Evening service would be in the chapel and the work was to be completed within one hundred days. Due to disagreements over financial arrangements, the theater was not used and the Independent Presbyterian Church offered its own facilities for the church's use in the early hours of Sunday morning. Lanier believed that this experience truly nurtured the bonding of the two congregations. Afterward, the Baptists expressed their deep appreciation by giving a fountain for the pool in the courtyard of the nearby church. In addition to repairs being made on the organ, Margaret LaFar summarized the changes made in the sanctuary:

> He [Braun] painted those pilaster capitals and the medallions with gold leaf. Off-white and gold are the main colors used in this beautification project. Gold carpeting and pew cushions were installed and long graceful gold lamps were hung. The small side wall lights were removed. Because of the TV ministry it was necessary to install electronic sound equipment, improved acoustical materials, and a controlled lighting system. The choir loft was extended across the entire width of the sanctuary to provide more adequate space for musicians in the church services.

LaFar's final value judgment of the work reads as follows: "One receives the impression of simplicity, beauty and dignity of light and of soaring curved shuttered windows and pilasters—truly a sanctuary conducive to worship, to soul-searching, and dedication." Pastor Lanier himself perhaps expressed the most moving summary of the venture:

> In the worst of times, we have wrought the best of buildings. In the most casual and profane climate in our long history, we have furnished a sanctuary for men to come and listen to the Voice of God. This building speaks in its brightness of a God who cares and is very near. And in its elegance this sanctuary speaks of a God who is worthy of

worship and adoration. In an age of shifting values and changing priorities, this House of God will give quiet and elegant testimony to the fact that God is still God. The gold is for royalty, and this is where the King of Kings shares his spirit as in no other place. And with the open Bible this love is preached to all men and nations on the face of the Earth. For if man, made in God's image, is to love his fellow man it will not begin in the Congress or in the nation, nor will it be enforced by the courts, it is here around this common altar that it is either true or false. Now let us live up to the commitment that made this beautiful offering to our God possible.

No finer tribute as to the raison d'etre of the sanctuary could be given even in the contemporary year of 2000.

Lanier and the church came down to earth quickly from the peak experience of being back in such a beautiful and holy sanctuary. Secularism was rapidly encroaching in Savannah. First, a neighborhood bar was too close to such a holy place, so the church petitioned the city that The Dungeon not be allowed to open. The church also went on record as approving the mayor and aldermen's appointment of a committee to review movies being shown in the city and forbidding the showing of the most obscene ones. The church had not completely forgotten the subject of discipline from the nineteenth century. It also didn't hurt that congregational member Curtis Lewis had recently been elected as mayor of Savannah on the Republican ticket. During all this surely Lanier remembered his favorite sermon preached years earlier in Rome on the thesis of what if everybody went to the same place when they died. It would indeed be heaven for some and hell for others. Lanier was certainly aware of Jean Paul Sartre's famous line, "People is hell."

January 1, 1967, opened with the only ordination of a "home boy" during Lanier's tenure—John Rabun Jr., one who would make unusual contributions at a later time and will be discussed elsewhere. Lanier made the cover of *The Calendar* on April 13, 1967, as the church celebrated his having been there for five years. The statement of appreciation certainly illustrated the humanness of this man who could relate to people on so many levels—even to his love of fast cars, much to the chagrin of his wife. The church paid tribute to this humanness in the following words:

> His radiant personality has reached far beyond the sphere of our own church. His messages of hope, love, and understanding, his comfort and counsel, his patience, his being our friend with whom we could hunt, fish, laugh and play, have all inspired us to greater heights and bound us closer together by cords of love.

Lanier had been successful in these five years of redeeming the time being from insignificance. This was deeply appreciated.

June of 1968 was a month of honors for both Lanier and long-time organist Bruce. On June 2 Lanier was given the honorary Doctor of Divinity by Mercer University, which meant so much to him. Yet in genuine humility he said that it truly belonged to all the folk who had encouraged him through the years—but especially the members of the two churches he had served, in Rome and Savannah. June 9 was Dwight Bruce Day in the church. The man who had brought inspiring music to the congregation for thirty-nine years was retiring. For all these years he had provided the church with a truly outstanding musical program in both formal and informal church music. Savannah had earlier honored him by placing him on the cover of the *Savannah Morning News Magazine* on February 27, 1966, with his most famous student, Earnest W. Murphy Jr., one of

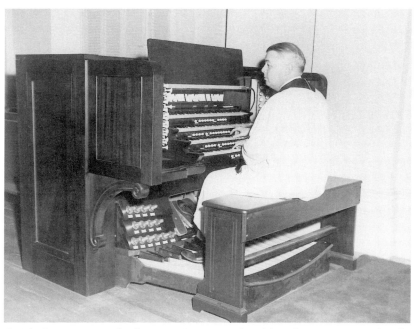

Dwight Bruce was a man for all seasons. He was not only a dedicated part-time organist but also enjoyed a successful career in broadcasting.

possibly only four countertenors in the world who made their living in that role. Murphy had been encouraged, taught, and mentored by Bruce and later sang with the famous Robert Shaw Chorale as well as with Pro Musica of New York. Special services honored Bruce, and as he played the organ for the last time as official organist, all the beautiful memories brought tears to many eyes. Thomas E. Carswell replaced Bruce as the organist and choir director.

The church closed 1968 having declared itself officially as an "open" church, but Lanier recognized that "these have been difficult times." In the same breath, however, he "expressed the belief that we have taken the right course." Early in 1969 he established several goals which would have to be revised later: (1) to purchase a bus, (2) to appoint a minister of education, and (3) to make plans for a new Sunday School building and social hall. The matter of the bus was later tabled; the building plans were revised into renovation plans and were not completed until 1974; and by July Eugene W. Baker had been invited to come as the minister of education.

In June 1969 a brief civil rights issue had to be faced by the deacons. A racially mixed a capella choir had been founded and directed by Carswell and, though not affiliated officially with the church, had used the facilities for practice and social gatherings. Deacons Bland and Skinner believed that if this continued it would "aggravate an already tense situation among some members." These two deacons made a motion that the choir not be allowed to use church facilities. After a strong statement by Carswell the motion lost. At the close of the meeting, Lanier praised the ministry of Carswell, yet called for better communication and prior dialogue in the future. Race relations under such strong leadership could only continue to improve from the early tense moments.

Ecumenical Holy Week in April 1969 illustrated the continuing ecumenical commitments of the church and, in this instance, of Lanier. For one, Msgr. Andrew McDonald spoke to Baptists concerning the devotional aspect of the Christian life. Lanier had spoken in numerous other Christian churches and had invited ministers of other denominations and faith (Jewish) to speak from the pulpit of First Baptist. Lanier's widow, Gene, remembered one humorous ecumenical context when her husband spoke before the Hibernian Society and with a twinkle in his eye, rose and said, "I'm going to give special dispensation to all Baptists. They can drink tonight." With a twinkle in her own eye, Gene Lanier remembered Training Union manuals which began to have quarterly temperance lessons. In "wet" Savannah she judged that these lessons were hard for many of the people to take seriously and felt that this was the beginning of the end of Training Union at First Baptist.

Lanier also received wide visibility through the radio ministry. The famous writer Eugenia Price came for a special visit with him after being impressed by his radio message. Another listener from South Carolina came to compliment Lanier on his message but criticized the idea of a split lectern and a central cross in a Baptist church. Lanier, again with a twinkle, responded, "If it would make one person worship any better, I wouldn't care if we had a ten-foot cross in this church!"

In the summer of 1969 Lanier decided to celebrate his and Gene's twenty-fifth wedding anniversary by going to Europe. She had had a rather miserable experience during their two-year stay nearly a decade earlier, and now he promised her "warm hotels with hot baths and clean sheets." One of their most memorable, though sad, moments was spent in visiting the site of the infamous concentration camp at Dachau. From this experience, the Laniers would come back even more ecumenically committed than ever.

Only a few months following their return, Lanier submitted his resignation in October in order to become the pastor of Northside Drive in Atlanta. His most famous member in Atlanta would be Governor Jimmy Carter, destined to be elected president of the United States in 1976. Later Lanier went to Shorter College as vice president in charge of development—interestingly enough, the same position Pastor Christie had occupied prior to coming to Savannah.

Kelsey McCall, church clerk, wrote of Lanier: "He was an eloquent preacher and possessed a magnetic personality. He was a fearless advocate of policies he considered it his duty to propound and exerted an affinity of magnitude with the youth of this church." Surely no one had ever forgotten his dramatic first sermon in the church, "I am Zaccheus." It was one of Lanier's favorites and he repeated it at an evening service while filling in at the Isle of Hope Baptist Church. Later, Lanier's widow made a value judgment of his years in Savannah: "I think that First Baptist was the apex of his ministry as far as how he was involved in the community and his relationship with the church."

The torch was being passed as Dwight Bruce, back as interim minister of music, became chair of the Search Committee. Dr. Pope A. Duncan of Georgia Southern College supplied the pulpit several times, and in March 1970 Dr. A. Warren Huyck was appointed as interim pastor. He would serve for nearly nine months in this role. In August while the church was without a resident pastor, the morning worship service began to be televised on WJCL—the first live remote church service to appear in Savannah. The station's owner was J. Curtis Lewis Jr., an active member of First Baptist.

Thomas D. Austin

Thomas David Austin was a young minister in his midthirties in Richmond, Virginia. He was of the new breed of minister committed not only to *comfort* his flock but also to *challenge* his people. Initially hearing of First Church when Dwight Bruce called him from a pay phone on Interstate 95 through Richmond, Austin eventually agreed to converse with the Search Committee. Tom sensed tension on the committee and was not really convinced they were even agreeable concerning his candidacy. On visiting the church he found a beautiful sanctuary and a dilapidated Sunday School building. His wife Edna was also not too enthusiastic about leaving Richmond. God works in mysterious ways, however, and Tom agreed to make the move. He would be in the pulpit on December 27, 1970. He hit the ground running and for awhile the church was breathless in Savannah just trying to keep up the pace with him. His tenure of office would be second only to Cleverdon in length.

The first month on the job he requested and received permission to give communion to Christians in the hospitals and nursing homes and announced that there would

Thomas D. Austin
1970–1988

soon be more congregational participation in the services. Jack Usher was elected chair of the Board of Deacons and was challenged to keep up with Tom. From the start Austin had multiple plans. He would style a participatory worship service with sermons that would challenge both intellectually and spiritually. From the start he wore a formal robe in the pulpit. Excellence in music (he would soon have James Richardson by his side) would be stressed as well as a strong youth ministry and varied social ministries. Ecumenism would also mark his ministry, and within three months he was already announcing that in July and August the church would have evening union services with the Independent Presbyterian Church.

By July 1 James Richardson was in residence as the new organist-choirmaster, fresh from his degree at Southern Seminary. He would be responsible to Austin, and the Music Committee would be an advisory unit. Again, Austin would be a strong "take-charge" leader. Richardson also from the start stated his goals, which included increasing the understanding and appreciation of church music by the congregation as well as urging members to take a more active part in the church's worship. Repairs on the Sunday School building were delayed while a thorough evaluation of the building was made.

By September Austin had led the church to eliminate the office of director or minister of education and to replace it with an assistant pastor with responsibilities in developing an imaginative youth program (40 percent), developing a day program of outreach and visitation (30 percent), and designing, developing, and supervising a "meaningful educational program for all ages below youth." By the end of the year, T. Floyd Irby ("Skip") had been employed to fill this position. Irby was also a "comfort and challenge" minister—a recent graduate of Andover-Newton Theological School, young (twenty-five) and full of energy and fresh ideas.

Austin was not one to avoid controversial issues when committed to principles. A number of progressive Baptist churches had adopted an "open membership" policy in relation to the ordinance of baptism. That is, these churches began to accept members transferring from other denominations and their "meaningful baptism," whether it had been by immersion or not. These churches, then, refused to rebaptize by immersion those transferring their membership who were satisfied with their baptism. Normative baptism for new converts would remain as immersion of believing adults. This position recognized baptism first and foremost as a Christian ordinance and not strictly a Baptist denominational ordinance. It was not only an ecumenical gesture recognizing the legitimacy of other forms of baptism, but it also removed a disadvantage in receiving persons from another denomination. It did not, however, remove the witness of the Baptist tradition that believed that normative believer's baptism was by immersion. Local church autonomy certainly allowed such a position as well as the pilgrimage mentality which has marked the Baptist way of life from the beginning. In any case, in early 1972 Austin began to discuss "meaningful baptism" membership and was given permission immediately to waive baptism altogether when in his judgment health reasons dictated that being baptized would be dangerous for the individual. In this case, baptism would truly be a "spiritual" experience. Austin had also recommended that the bylaws be revised to make it official that the pastor would be given six weeks of study leave every two years, and this was approved.

Austin's organizational strengths would be apparent in these early years of his ministry. A Long Range Planning Committee had already been appointed in 1971 and made a lengthy report and recommendations in January 1972. One of Austin's priorities was to do something about the dilapidated Bible School building. This Committee had determined that for about $300,000 the building could be renovated in such a way as to meet the needs of the church. Their report recommended that their Committee be renamed as the Renovation and Building Committee. The report also urged that plans move forward and architectural services be secured for the project. Evidently there was some opposition to such an expensive project, for by March, Austin was asking the deacons not to speak out openly in opposition to it and also to help in clearing up any misunderstandings. The architectural firm of Gunn and Meyerhoff was finally hired again to draw up functional as well as aesthetic plans for the work. The Braun Construction Company would also be rehired to do the actual construction and the church would borrow up to $350,000 for the work.

This early in his ministry, Austin, by the close of 1972, requested two months educational leave during the summers of 1973 and 1974, without losing vacation time, in order to pursue the Doctorate in Ministry at Southeastern Baptist Theological Seminary where he had received his basic Master of Divinity and then Master of Theology degrees. The church was most generous and understanding in granting this request to its new, young pastor.

July 1972 saw a special recognition of the Lewis Broadcasting Company for providing during the past number of years the facilities for a radio-television ministry. WJCL-TV had brought the church into the modern age of television in black and white and soon in color, and WJCL-FM had begun in June to send the service out on the airwaves to as far as Tallahassee, Florida. Words of thanks to those responsible made the cover of *The Calendar*.

The new year of 1973 saw plans moving forward for the 175th anniversary of the church. Alsie Rabun was chair of this Planning Committee and Mabel LaFar's daughter, Margaret, was hard at work on the brief history of the church (it would be a thirty-six–page pamphlet with careful use of the sources, especially her mother's volumes).

For months the church engaged itself in a "Together We Build" campaign, even using the assistance of the Stewardship Commission of the Southern Baptist Convention. By October 1973 the church membership pledges totaled $304,502.80— in excess of the goal of $300,000. Austin did not want the church saddled with a heavy debt. These pledges assured him that that would not happen, and so plans for building moved forward. By March 1974 the contract to build was given to the Braun Construction Company and work began.

Pastor Austin had real reason to give thanks in the ecumenical Thanksgiving Service of November 22, 1973. He preached the sermon in the nearby Lutheran Church of the Ascension for most of the downtown churches. Throughout his ministry he had excellent relations with all the many downtown churches which had stayed and not moved to the suburbs. Cleverdon's death in May 1974 prompted ecumenical musings and compliments from Austin. He praised the pastor emeritus for his "healthy denominationalism" and his leading the church to a healthy ecumenism. Austin concluded: "He recognized the distinctives of Baptists, but also that God's gifts to others were just as numerous. To wit, he was a participant in the World Council of Churches meeting in Amsterdam, and the World Conference on Faith and Order in Lund, Sweden. He saw very clearly that to affirm the unity of the Church is not to deny the denominational branches of the Church." Pastor Austin definitely assumed Cleverdon's ecumenical mantle in every way. He, too, had a strong dose of healthy denomination-alism as well as ecumenism.

By mid-1974 Austin felt secure enough in his role as minister to tackle two more congregational matters which were and still are controversial among Baptists. He took the discussion of "open membership" in relation to baptism off the table where it had remained since 1972. The motion put before the diaconate on June 3, 1974, read as follows: "That the pastor be authorized to waive immersion for those candidates for membership who have been previously baptized when he is satisfied that said prior baptism was a meaningful Christian experience." There was precedent for this motion reaching back to the nineteenth century and specific ministerial practice. The motion passed, but in July there was further discussion about Baptists and orthodoxy (what is it?) as well as a broader discussion of the real meaning of baptism. The motion was not reconsidered and remains the policy of the congregation.

The second matter had to do with bringing females onto the diaconate. Fundamentalists who were Baptists certainly opposed this in Southern Baptist circles but there were already a number of Baptist churches with female deacons. On October 16 the bylaws of the church were changed by vote of the congregation to allow females as deacons, and on November 4 the nominations for deacons of the church included the names of Mrs. Mary Louise Claiborne and Mrs. Rose Usher. On November 17 they were elected and the church continued its pilgrim's progress. Austin had grappled with two of his own commitments and led the church to follow. Both women were later honored by being voted Life Deacons by the church. The skies didn't fall nor was the church dismissed from the association for unorthodox practices.

A practice started in December 1974 which then became traditional, adding beauty and insight into the meaning of the season. First Baptist Church had not one but two beautiful Chrismon trees in the sanctuary. Hours of planning and even workshops in relation to this were conducted. Numerous Chrismons were created for the trees and Eleanor Blood did yeoman's labor.

In the background, work continued on the educational building and by April 1975 had been finally completed. The dedication of the completed building took place on April 20. The formerly dilapidated brick building looked sparklingly new both inside and outside. The numerous changes left one with the impression that it was a completely new structure. Stucco overlay all the bricks and multiples of windows had been reduced to a minimum, thus saving interior space. For example, on the first floor of the south side, eleven windows had been reduced to one and on the east side three had replaced nine. It was completely remodeled and newly equipped to meet the educational, spiritual, and social needs of the entire church.

In May Austin was officially awarded the Doctor of Ministry degree by Southeastern Baptist Theological Seminary and was honored by the church for this accomplishment with academic regalia, an unabridged dictionary, and a dictionary stand. Tom was humbled and said to the congregation: "Without your understanding, encouragement, support and interest, I would not have entered upon the program, and certainly would not have completed it." His goal of some twenty years was now achieved.

In June and July, Austin further educated the diaconate, especially for newcomers, in relation to his discretionary authority having to do with baptism. He explained his efforts to try to "destroy the stereotype of Baptist." He urged the deacons to be "pace-setters" and to involve themselves in positive community public relations as well as taking completely seriously their denominational affiliation.

The 175th celebration of the founding of the church was the peak experience of the year. Alsie Rabun and her committee had done an excellent job and on

October 26 the sterling payoff began. The five "Great Sundays" would reach its climax on November 23, the final celebration day. The themes of the first four Sundays would be as follows: (1) the great men who have headed the diaconate (and now, women also); (2) the men who have headed the Brotherhood (founded on February 11, 1932); (3) the women who have headed the Women's Missionary Union (various dates given were 1874, 1879, 1902); (4) the persons who served as Superintendents of the Sunday School, those who headed the board of ushers (formerly called junior deacons), and those who served as Directors of the Training Union (which had been discontinued in 1968); and (5) the final celebration of the founding of the congregation. Congregational members were encouraged to wear period costumes on the final Sunday. The only living former pastor, W. Forrest Lanier, was invited back to be the presiding minister and to preach. Special music was planned with soloists Edith Bennett and Earnest Murphy and an original composition for the occasion by James Richardson that would be heard for the first time. In addition to the morning worship service, at high noon a bronze memorial plaque was dedicated to the ministers of the church during the previous twenty-five years and "to the saints of this faithful and dedicated congregation who supported our spiritual leaders so affectionately throughout that period." At 3:00 James Richardson gave an organ recital of early American music and at 3:30 an in-costume 1818 Discipline Session was staged in the church. The memorable day closed with a reception and a display of historic memorabilia in the new Educational Building. Margaret LaFar's excellent brief *Historical Sketch of the First Baptist Church* was also completed and made available. There were echos into the night of numerous "thank you's" in the direction of those who had planned, executed, and seen to completion such a wonderful day of celebration and remembrance. There must have been a few proud tears as well.

Back-to-earth matters included the replacement of Skip Irby, who had resigned to take a church of his own, with John Strange. Austin, before year's end, had also done away with the membership committee, stating that it was no longer needed. It had been created during the civil rights crisis and Tom felt that the church had outgrown and matured beyond its need.

A historical interlude took place in August 1976. For a number of years Dr. D. L. Brawner had been doing research as well as restoring the earliest building used by Baptists in Georgia, at Tuckasee King near Clyo. Baptists had established a church there about 1771. At the completion of the restoration Brawner deeded the small building and property to First Baptist and the diaconate accepted the gift. On August 1, the dedication service was held and a "dinner on the grounds" was enjoyed by many members of First Baptist who had driven out to the site. History had been made and also was in the making. Austin during this time was also "reminding" the church of its former ministers in a series of biographical sketches which appeared about every two weeks in *The Calendar*. His research for these articles formed the background for a later series of historical sermons in 1986 as he surveyed the history of the church. Austin himself was an excellent historian and had done his homework on the many pastors. Perhaps this personal research gave him even deeper insight concerning his own ministry in Savannah.

Austin was as ecumenical, maybe even more, as any pastor of the church had been. In January 1977 he led the church to found the Inter-denominational Committee and to begin a "People to People" continuing program that would include experiences with the Jewish as well as Catholic traditions. The first experience was with Mickve Israel Synagogue as the two congregations shared worship and social time with one another.

Hands across faiths touched and an unusual bonding took place. Perhaps Tom's closest clerical friend during his tenure was Rabbi Saul Rubin, and through the years facilities, worship, and social moments would be shared. On April 14, 1978, Austin sat on the platform of Mickve Israel to bring greetings and salutations from the church on the occasion of the one hundredth anniversary of the consecration of the synagogue. Rubin and Austin also collaborated on a series of educational religious programs on television. On one occasion the present writer was a guest to be questioned about sects and cults in American religious history. In June 1978, due to Rubin's contacts, Austin visited Israel for two weeks as a guest of the American Jewish Committee. During this time he traveled with a group visiting with political, religious, and cultural leaders in Israel. Austin was by now well-versed in, as well as committed to, Jewish-Christian relations. Austin also used Wednesday evenings in 1977 to bring in pastors of other denominational churches in the city to speak on the general topic, "The Mission of the Church as I See It." Methodists, Presbyterians, Episcopalians, Catholics, and Baptists shared their common Christian mind on this topic.

Effective January 1, 1978, James C. Richardson assumed his new title of associate minister. In December 1977 James had been ordained and had earlier presented a beautiful and moving theological statement concerning the office and calling of minister of music: "When he uses musical language and ideas to illustrate and illuminate theological concepts, the church musician becomes a minister in the finest sense." Richardson confessed, "Ordination will be for me a time of recommitment to my high calling as a Christian, my choice of the music ministry as a profession, and my acceptance of the call of the church to serve as its minister." Austin and the church were enriched and fulfilled by this ordination act.

A long overdue commitment to bring the bylaws up to date by rewriting them began in 1978. The People to People program continued as Catholics entered the dialogue and shared experiences. An unusual "first" happened for Richardson—for the first and only time in his career he was guest organist for a day at the Southern Baptist Convention. One change for him in that setting was certainly the circus-like atmosphere, not generally conducive to inspirational organ ministry. Reminiscent of earlier years, 1978 closed on the note of Chair of Deacons Ashmore and Austin talking with the owners of the theater across the square about the inappropriateness of showing X-rated films. Baptists and this theater had experienced tension since the nineteenth century.

Noise in the sanctuary is never appreciated by musicians or preachers and little communion cups can be noisy. Early in 1979 the deacons decided that they were causing too much noise and rubber rings were needed for the communion cup pew holders. Bill Sutton, an Eagle Scout in the church-sponsored Boy Scout Troop 35, remembers that for his required service project prior to attaining Eagle rank, he installed the rubber silencers in the sanctuary. Going beyond the call of duty, he recalls: "In addition to the Silencers in the pew racks, my Uncle Wallace Winn made communion cup holders for the choir loft. We installed those racks, including cup silencers as an additional part of my Eagle Scout project." Common life incidents such as this enrich the collective memory of the congregation, and certainly the ministers appreciated the result—less noise.

In late June the church was led to strengthen its staff by calling Peggy Stout as assistant minister with special responsibilities in relation to the educational program. A recent Master of Divinity graduate of Southeastern Seminary, Austin's alma mater for three degrees, Stout had specialized in religious education. Within two years, in May 1981, the church would take yet another new step and ordain Stout. It was the first Baptist ordination of a woman as a minister in Savannah. First Baptist had broken new ground about eight years earlier by ordaining women as deacons, and Austin led the congregation to see that nothing in the Bible nor the Baptist tradition forbade the ordination of women as ministers. Indeed, Stout had decided to come to Savannah in part due to the church's "more open, supporting role for women in the ministry." Though ultraconservatives in the Southern Baptist Convention vigorously opposed such ordination, moderate positions had already by this time approved of the ordination of women. Stout was the first Baptist ordination of a female in Chatham County but not the first in Georgia nor in the Convention. Storm clouds were gathering, however, and as early as late 1979, Austin began to warn the church of criticism that would be leveled at the church over the issues of open membership and open communion. The ordination of women as deacons and now as a minister would also be opposed by ultraconservatives bordering on neofundamentalism. The neofundamentalist takeover of the Southern Baptist Convention was already being planned in secret meetings of neofundamentalist leaders, and Austin was well aware of this. Part of the agenda of these people would be the opposition of female ordination as well as any other ecumenical practices such as had been the tradition in First Baptist for many years. In September 1980 Austin had a letter published in the *Savannah Morning News* decrying Bailey Smith's (new president of the SBC) remark that "God almighty does not hear the prayer of a Jew." The Diaconate approved of this and Tom's attempt to educate the public about the wide diversity among Baptists. Prophetically, he alerted the diaconate to the fact that "we are in for some very hectic times" and increasing challenges from the neofundamentalists of the SBC.

Earlier in the year 1981 a special reception celebrated Austin's first decade as minister and he presented a positive evaluation of the ten years. As icing on the cake, in April all debt notes were burned and Tom noted: "The splendid record that you have compiled in liquidating this church's indebtedness in these inflammatory times is worthy of commendation. In the worst of times we did the best of things," he asserted.

Tom Austin was ever sensitive to social work needs in the downtown area. After church facilities had been improved, Tom led the church in discussion about social issues—of the homeless, hungry, and destitute in the downtown squares. In 1980 he led in the formation of a religious coalition to meet some of these needs. In July the *Savannah Morning News* reported: "Some two dozen Savannah churches and synagogues are joining to meet the weekend and holiday emergency needs of transients and poor for whom no service agency help is available." Austin was identified by the paper as the coalition organizer. Named CRY—Congregations Responding to You—it was an interfaith, interracial effort to meet some critical downtown needs. CRY was a "golden opportunity" for religious groups to cooperate in relation to a community need "without any compromise of beliefs or convictions."

One day Austin came back to the church from a delicious luncheon and saw two ragged men foraging and eating food found in a dumpster outside the church. This haunting experience moved him deeply and he determined that he would do something about this situation. This was the beginning of his many social ministries. At this time he and interested church members began to offer a noon meal on a take-out basis and soon were serving seventy-five to eighty-five persons. Before his untimely death, Tom remembered as follows: "We were going to use what restaurants would give us left over from the night before. Consequently we made a run early each morning, usually picking up baked potatoes and salad from the night before. This was recycled and passed through the window of the kitchen on a daily basis." Recognizing that this was somewhat of a stopgap, Austin galvanized four downtown churches to work together (with a few other churches cooperating, such as at the Landings) to provide lunch on a daily basis from the parish hall of Christ Episcopal Church. Thus, Emmaus House came into existence with what was called the "3S" or "4S" lunch—soup, salad, sandwich, sweet. Soon, from 125 to 135 persons were being served.

At the same time interest was developing in establishing an overnight shelter, and Tom was fortunate that Curtis Lewis with his political influence became sincerely interested in finding a place for a night shelter. No one seemed to want such a shelter in their neighborhood, but finally the city council became cooperative and joined in searching for a suitable location. Tom reflected that during this time he was on TV far more than he wanted to be, but the appearances generated a great deal of support for the project from average citizens. A place was finally found on Fahm Street, and Curtis Lewis was and still is generous with funding the renovation of a dilapidated building in order to make it suitable for serving men, women, and families on an overnight basis. All this transpired toward the close of Austin's tenure at First Baptist, and he remembered that one of the last things he did was to help secure the services of Micheal Elliott as the director of the newly founded Union Mission. Austin recalled: "I am proud not only of what we accomplished but the fact that we could develop consensus on the type of ministry needed in the downtown area." By 1988 the Mission was in full swing. In later years, after his death in 1997, Tom Austin received a well-deserved posthumous honor when a transitional shelter for needy families was named for him. The Union Mission and the Thomas D. Austin House, operated by the Economic Opportunity Authority, at the time of this writing are the only local shelters for families with long-term residency. To Tom Austin, a constellation of interests and factors composed true ministry in a downtown setting. He would not soon be forgotten in Savannah for his numerous social service contributions.

Meanwhile, life went on in the business of internal church life. In June 1981 shortly after her ordination, Peggy Stout resigned to return to North Carolina and was replaced in two months by Robert H. Ballard Jr. Of thirty-three on the Diaconate, eight were now female as the church entered 1982. In view of the state of Georgia soon celebrating 250 years of history (from February 1983 to January 1984), Austin promised a series of sermons on Baptist history as well as furnishing and equipping an archives room for the church. During the summer months, Austin's earlier brief biographies of former pastors were republished in *The Calendar*.

Georgia's 250th anniversary year was to bring a plethora of special services to the church. On February 13, 1983, an interfaith service at First Baptist inaugurated the year of celebration with a variety of ministers and rabbis expressing "gratitude for the providence of God, for vision and foresight of those who established this colony, and for the individuals who gave of themselves in establishing and maintaining the many vital downtown congregations that Savannah possesses." Symbolic of the times in Baptist circles, however, the next evening during the deacon's meeting, Chris Wilburn became the chair of a new committee to explore dual alignment of the church with American Baptists, a basically northern denomination but much more theologically moderate than the increasingly neofundamentalist leaders of the Southern Baptist Convention. By April Austin was describing First Baptist as an "alternative" Baptist congregation. The ecumenical mood of the leadership of the church was now carefully responding to the evergrowing changed climate in the denomination of which they had long been a part. By June Wilburn was further informing the Diaconate about the American Baptist tradition with its doctrines of open communion, commitment to ecumenism, racial liberality, and openness to the ordination of women. Perhaps due to later developments among Baptists in the South, this matter was never officially acted upon—First Baptist would not at this time be dually aligned with American Baptists. While the interior of the sanctuary was being painted, the congregation in ecumenical fashion held its services at Mickve Israel.

The SBC meeting in June 1984 was a disappointment to the church and its leadership. It was again continuing its "broken" history (veering away from, in this case, the congregational principle of local autonomy) by stipulating that it was "unscriptural" to ordain women and by electing a president, Charles Stanley, who had done more for Amway than for Southern Baptists, never having held elective office in the SBC or the Georgia Baptist Convention. In addition, his church, First Baptist in Atlanta, only contributed the meager amount of 2 percent of its budget to the Cooperative Program. All this must have certainly raised eyebrows in the congregation in Savannah, especially female eyebrows.

Ballard resigned late in 1984 and was replaced in June 1985 by Jody Wright, a recent graduate of Southern Seminary. Austin also began to try to educate the congregation more thoroughly about the neofundamentalist takeover of the SBC now well underway. Randall Lolley, president of Southeastern Seminary, came in mid-April to inform the congregation of the numerous changes taking place in the SBC which would be a threat to the Baptist way of life. A group of "concerned Baptists" also met in the church to reflect on what was happening in the convention.

During the Advent season, music took everyone's minds off denominational problems and, according to Dwight Bruce, musical history was made. In Bruce's words of gratitude to James Richardson and the choir, he stated: "I am positive that never in the past century has any church choir presented Handel's *Messiah* in its entirety and uncut." James, the choir, and soloists carried the congregation to multiple spiritual peak experiences in this presentation.

In the wake of another troubled meeting of the SBC, Austin published in the June 26 issue of *The Calendar* an excellent summary statement of the commitments of First Baptist in the context of swirling controversy:

> We shall continue to be a Baptist congregation which affirms our missionary and educational institutions and the Cooperative Program as thoroughly trustworthy vehicles for support. Secondly, we shall be a Baptist congregation maintaining our traditional support of the separation of church and state. Thirdly, we shall be a Baptist congregation which champions the priesthood of every believer, the autonomy of every congregation, and the equality of all in God's kingdom. Fourthly, we shall be a Baptist congregation that refuses to see learning as an enemy of faith, and one which will not close its mind and spirit to the God who leads always into new and larger truth. Finally, we shall be a congregation capturing the best of our past; in our life and work we will demonstrate the marks of an authentic Baptist congregation: freedom, the pursuit of truth, and undiluted integrity.

These commitments would serve any congregation well in the midst of unbaptistic changes in the denomination.

The question of discipline had not arisen for decades, but in October 1985 this issue resurfaced in relation to the Baptist Center, whose members were technically members of First Baptist. Albert Bullock, a member of the Center, had been disruptive at a number of services. The Center voted to withdraw his membership for three months and requested permission to enforce this discipline. The matter was approved and a lone disciplinary case entered the records of the late twentieth century.

In November a special presentation of Habitat for Humanity was made by James Miles to the church. Another ecumenical ministry was now available for any member of the church. Soon, this organization would be world famous for providing low-payment housing, and its most famous contributor would be former President Jimmy Carter. At the same time a special committee of nine persons, a Committee of the Future, made its report concerning needs which ranged everywhere from the elderly to youth and from singles to divorced, widowed, and retired persons. The Diaconate was urged to study the report carefully. Also announced late in the year was a counseling center to open in January 1986 with Chris Wilburn augmenting the counseling done by the full-time staff.

In June 1986 just before Austin left for four weeks of study at Southeastern Seminary, he gave a full report to the Diaconate of the recent SBC meetings. Six oversize typed pages in the Minutes present one of the finest analyses of what was happening in the convention that is even now available. Adrian Rogers, an ultra-neofundamentalist, had been elected president in Atlanta, the site of the meetings. His agenda was obviously already political and he promised to appoint only those persons to the important boards and committees who agreed with him on issues such as the plenary verbal theory of biblical dictation and opposition to any form of the ordination of women. The die was cast. Austin already knew of the hard days ahead as a denomination was changing course in midstream and rejecting so much of the genius of its prior history. These takeover folk were exclusivistic and separatistic; no moral or doctrinal diversity would be allowed. The large SBC umbrella covering a diversity of views was closed. "Ecumenical" was a dirty word to these neofundamentalists and this could only cause pain for a congregation that had been continuously ecumenical since 1800. In fact, the irony of the situation was sharply illustrated by a letter enclosed in those Minutes of June 16 from Rabbi Saul Rubin thanking Tom for his gift of the Lenox Elijah's Cup on the occasion of Rubin's retirement. In the letter Saul called First Baptist "a remarkable congregation" (see appendix K).

Austin was also concerned that the controversy in the Convention would make its way to the state level and was incensed over the attack on Jack Harwell, editor of the *Christian Index*, for being too moderate and not committed to the neofundamentalist agenda. The Diaconate, following his lead, passed a resolution affirming the ministry of women as well as sending a letter to the Home Mission Board decrying its rejection of support for any church with a female pastor. Nine of those thirty-two deacons who signed were female.

The church at this time was in a financial campaign to raise funds for remodeling and for major organ repair. It hoped to raise $400,000, and pastoral continuity was important. It was common knowledge that Austin had been considered by a number of churches and at least one university. To give some sense of assurance and security, Austin penned a letter to the Diaconate in February 1987 assuring them that except for some major occurrence he would remain for the project—and perhaps even longer. He honestly said, "I hope this kind of candor does not furnish you discomfort . . . I believe that we have a golden opportunity to demonstrate how a downtown church that offers an alternative voice cannot only survive but thrive. One of the reasons that we have done both is that our relationship has been marked by mutual trust, acceptance, understanding, and integrity." This seemed to put to rest some of the rumors about the pastor perhaps leaving soon.

By May 1987 Austin was reminding the church that the bylaws allowed affiliation with other Baptist bodies from time to time and in the same month he was off to Meredith College for the convocation of a new moderate Baptist organization—the Southern Baptist Alliance (the name was changed in 1992 to the Alliance of Baptists). The founding document read: "The Southern Baptist Alliance is an alliance of individuals and churches dedicated to the preservation of historic Baptist principles, freedoms and traditions, and the continuance of our ministry and mission within the Southern Baptist Convention." The downtown church with an alternative voice was now beginning to struggle for some Baptist alternatives. The SBC was slowly but surely cutting itself off from such moderate churches. By September the church van was made available to any members who wished to attend the SBA meetings at Mercer University.

A major occurrence did take place—even Tom did not completely understand what was happening—but in December 1987 he announced that he had accepted the call from Knollwood Baptist Church in Winston-Salem, North Carolina (near the Wake Forest University campus), and that his last Sunday in the pulpit would be January 17, 1988. He later wrote in appreciation of all the happy memories, yet was sad to think that "some may not yet understand our decision." He had thought that he would be in Savannah "forever," but "Knollwood knocked on my door."

Even Austin's last month was full of developments and activities. In January, led by Austin and the Denominational Relations Committee, the church related itself to the SBA and was pleased to have another outlet in order to support its interests, such as female ministry. Angry over the firing of Jack Harwell and finding the action of the Executive Committee of the Georgia Baptist Convention to be "arrogant and appalling," Austin and the church had placed their Cooperative Program contributions for October to December in escrow until certain state matters were settled. Austin also urged the new Search Committee to offer the final candidate the commitments of parity of women, ecumenism, a diverse theological posture, superiority in pulpit and worship, and freedom in the pulpit. Austin admitted that the last item had been one of the most attractive features for him, and he heartily thanked the church for his seventeen-year freedom! Appropriately, Dr. Jane Jennings was the new chair of the Diaconate as of January and Tom's leaving.

Austin's tenure of office was second only to Cleverdon's. Cleverdon had served during a World War and Austin had served during a denominational war which was continuing. He had made numerous changes and had successfully seen the debt retired on the virtually new educational building which had also been renovated during his tenure. Tom had shown excellent managerial skills if at times he had been a micromanager. No pastor had made the major social and ecumenical contributions of Austin's leadership. The church had far broader visibility as a downtown Baptist church with an alternative witness; however, he and the church were struggling painfully to find their place in a newly constructed Baptist context. All the changes he had led the church to make were in line with the essence of the tradition of the church, but very quickly he and it found themselves marching to the drumbeat other than that of the neofundamentalists who now controlled the denomination of which First Baptist had been an important part since 1845. Martin Luther in the sixteenth century had said that he never had left the Roman Catholic Church—it had left him! Austin and the church faced much the same situation and had struggled to make the right decisions. Austin's impress on the church and broader community would never be forgotten by his fellow pilgrims. They and others would grieve deeply as word came on June 24, 1997, of Tom's untimely death from cancer in the North Carolina Baptist Hospital in Winston-Salem. Mike Elliott, executive director of Union Mission and member of First Baptist, summarized in a nutshell: "Savannah continues to benefit from Tom Austin's presence here and it will continue to benefit. The breadth of stuff Tom was involved in included social services, ministries, and ways for people to help the poor. His social activism never forgot social compassion."

The pastoral Search Committee chaired by Jeryl Davis was soon hard at work, and the fund-raising campaign for major changes continued apace. James Richardson would be "chief of staff" during the interim and the church was fortunate enough to secure the services of Dr. Walter Shurden of Mercer University as interim pastor. Shurden was a moderate and would be one of the major interpreters in the nation of what had been and was happening in the Southern Baptist denomination. Actually he was committed to the same principles in this regard as had been Austin.

Due to the misunderstanding of some members concerning the church's joining the Southern Baptist Alliance (SBA), major efforts were made to communicate what was happening and to assure the membership that the church had definitely not withdrawn from the SBC. Member Evalyn Miles, board member of the SBA, was active in this educational project. By April the funds which had been held in escrow from the Cooperative Program were released but accompanied by a letter expressing the church's unhappiness over the actions of the Executive Committee of the GBC. By May Shurden was invited to address the Diaconate on the question of "how can we be loyal Southern Baptists without supporting things we cannot support?" For their own education, the deacons were urged to read the recent book, *Being Baptist Means Freedom*. In addition, the church began to receive multiple copies of *SBC Today* (later changed to *Baptists Today*), a publication of moderates appropriately edited by Jack Harwell, who had been fired from the *Christian Index*.

On May 3, 1988, the Baptist Women's meeting was in celebration of the one hundredth birthday of the Women's Missionary Union. A mission society had actually existed in First Baptist as early as 1813 and by 1874 (other source, 1879) there was a WMU in the church. Actually, then, the women's organization at First Baptist was prior to that of the SBC organized in 1888. By 1969 the women's group became known as Baptist Women and in 1996 changed yet again to Women on Mission. These groups had been the heart of missions in the church for all these years and the list of accomplishments is long indeed. They supported everything from education among black women, the Baptist Center, Union Mission, jail ministries, youth ministries, to hospital ministries. The list of mission accomplishments is unending. Prior to his leaving, Austin congratulated the women on their nearly two centuries of contributions and summarized correctly: "In the various missionary projects of the community, you have been important leaders and supporters. Much of what this church has done in this community would never have been accomplished without the unflagging support of Baptist Women."

The Minutes of the Diaconate for 1988 and 1989 throb with painful materials dealing with the search for denominational identity and all reflect a moderate stance leaning heavily in the direction of supporting the new SBA though retaining a partial relationship with the SBC. Richardson had attended the SBC meetings in June 1988 and had returned home disappointed as well as mentally and spiritually exhausted. Jerry Vines, an arch neofundamentalist in Jacksonville, Florida, had barely won the presidency over another neofundamentalist. The moderates had given up on elections; most were simply not attending the national meetings anymore. James reported that Vines would not appoint anyone to committees who did not share his complete viewpoints, that no women appeared on the program during the three days, and that most of the musicians used were from evangelical groups other than Baptist. Further, the Convention had rejected the concept of the priesthood of every believer in favor of complete authority in local congregations being given to the pastor. As Catholics were becoming more modern, Baptists were becoming more medieval! Richardson called for the Diaconate to reconsider fund distribution in light of what had happened to the SBC.

Richardson as well as Wright made the points that the neofundamentalist inerrantists were "scary," that the SBA was not a "liberal" organization, and that the SBA was simply struggling to find ways to support Baptist traditions consistent with Baptist history and heritage. Wright was also being alert for optional educational materials since the SBC materials increasingly would simply reflect the views of those who controlled the Convention. The Diaconate Minutes of this period reflect a slightly divided congregation trying to map out an honest route through this chaotic period in denominational history. Positive news had come that the SBA would sponsor the founding of a new and moderate Baptist seminary in Richmond, Virginia, as an alternative in theological education to the increasingly single-toned education in the six SBC seminaries. Richmond would basically carry on the tradition of Southeastern Seminary, since that school was now dominated by neofundamentalists. Richardson and Wright approved of this development.

Fred W. Andrea III

The Search Committee had narrowed its search to Fred W. Andrea III, pastor for six years of the Augusta Heights Baptist Church in Greenville, South Carolina, and recipient of the Ph.D. in 1982 from The Southern Baptist Theological Seminary. His dissertation grappled with J. Milton Yinger, a famous sociologist of religion, and he was certainly in the moderate camp of the SBC. Though taller even than Tom Austin, he was not nearly as heavy as Henry Holcombe. On May 1, 1989, he met with the Diaconate for an interview which went smoothly. On May 7 the church formally extended its call and Andrea responded positively. His first Sunday in the pulpit would be July 2. The church had been without a senior minister for eighteen months, but the staff under Richardson's direction had given superior leadership. The church was fortunate, as well, to have the services of Walter Shurden from Mercer. He had not only provided a strong pulpit presence but also wise counsel. Milton Newton would be the only messenger from the church attending the SBC in June 1989.

In 1997 Andrea reflected that during his tenure of office he had offered "a balanced model of proclamation, care, and pastoral leadership." Elaborating further, he said that he had highlighted his "attention to and concern for pastoral care, strategic visioning of the future, and warmly liturgical worship." His memory is basically correct, as from the start he illustrated nurturing pastoral care in a pietistic mode. Andrea's warmth and interest in nurturing were apparent from the start. He was following an activist who had made numerous changes over a long tenure of office. Andrea perhaps correctly sensed the need for nurturing. His first Diaconate meeting was used to compliment the deacons as "partners, colleagues, associates." He projected plans to use the deacons as well as other laypersons in a participatory way in the Sunday services. Specifically, he also wanted to "redream the dream" of the church by employing an outside consultant to study the congregation, especially its mission and future. At the next meeting he recommended that George Bullard, an outside church consultant, do this study. The cost would be $3,000. This was later approved and would consume six months. As well, in September the church voted to host the Georgia convocation of the SBA in October 1990. It was definitely associating itself with the moderate movement in the SBC.

Andrea kept the Diaconate and church informed of the continuing and upsetting developments in the SBC and urged everyone to educate themselves further by carefully reading the moderate publication, *The SBC Today*. On October 18 Andrea brought the

**Fred W. Andrea III
1989–1993**

congregation up-to-date with dismal happenings in the Convention and urged the church to retain unity with diversity within itself regardless of what the SBC did.

The year 1990 opened with vivid historical reminders. First, the special history room was open with pictures, historical documents, and memorabilia from years back. The entire congregation and visitors now had a special room for viewing materials from the church's near two-hundred-year history. It had been busy making history; now it could contemplate history with the aid of documents and other materials. Second, the Diaconate sent on behalf of the congregation a congratulatory letter to the Lutheran Church of the Ascension upon the occasion of its celebration of 250 years of history. This was also a reminder to First Baptist to be more self-consciously aware of its own celebration in ten years of two hundred years of history.

Andrea himself became distracted in 1990 with turmoil in the SBC. This nurturing pastor was grief-stricken over the "broken" history going on in the Convention and desperately hoped that a moderate candidate would be elected president in June and bring healing to a reeling Convention. His choice was Daniel Vestal, an evangelical, conservative moderate—not a neofundamentalist. He brought Vestal to the church to speak on April 23 and value-judged that if he were not elected in June as president that that would "be the end of equal representation within the SBC and the end of a 'cooperative' SBC." Andrea also told the church that if Vestal were not elected that it would need to work out "new directions"—for, he correctly noted, "We are our own headquarters!" Unfortunately, Vestal was soundly defeated, and Andrea and the church continued to struggle to find those "new directions." In view of increasing attacks on his alma mater, The Southern Baptist Theological Seminary, Andrea led the Diaconate in sending a letter of support for the seminary and its present administration and teaching stance to its Board of Trustees (see appendix L). The handwriting was on the wall, however, and Andrea was in Atlanta in September for yet another moderate direction in addition to the SBA. Plans were being made for the founding of the Cooperative Baptist Fellowship (CBF) which would establish a central distribution center to which the moderates could direct their funds as well as bypass the neofundamentalist-dominated denominational structures. This alternative funding program was called the Baptist Cooperative Missions Program, Inc. At the second annual meeting in Atlanta in 1991, the name Cooperative Baptist Fellowship was officially adopted. It has since evolved into an agency that sends and supports missionaries and a resource center for causes supported by Southern Baptist moderates who had been completely disenfranchised by the SBC, as well as slurred by names such as "heretics" and "liberals." Cecil Sherman was named the first executive director, succeeded by Daniel Vestal in 1997. Whether it will become another Baptist denomination is an open possibility at the time of this writing.

In reaction to this new missions option, in September the church voted to send 50 percent of its mission offerings in 1991 to this new organization, while funds to be sent to the Cooperative Program were designated for the Baptist Joint Committee, the New Baptist Press, and the seminaries. Further, it was announced that the SBA would meet at First Baptist in October. The moderate and ecumenical commitments of the church were also illustrated on the evening of October 28, as the First African Baptist Church met jointly with the First Baptist congregation.

By the fall of 1990 the refurbished organ was in place and Richardson gave a series of concerts in which, it was said, he really "showed off" the capabilities of the virtually new instrument. The Skinner organ of 1922 had been repaired a number of times and in 1952 the M. P. Moller Company had made additions. In 1990 the work of restoration and enlargement had been done by the Charleston firm of Ontko and Young. Most of the original Skinner pipework remained and great care had been taken to match the sound of the new additions with the old. James's series of eight recitals made full use of fifty-seven ranks of pipes, a total of 3,448 pipes, and a new four-manual console. This major restoration project had cost $162,195 but had resulted in sheer quality as well as beauty.

Meanwhile, the Bullard survey had been completed and the Mission and Purpose Committee had submitted its report to the congregation. The church was also richer by one organ. The Rodgers organ which had been used during the restoration period was now given to the church in memory of Mrs. Frances Wilkie by Allene and Vreeland George and their children and placed in the chapel.

James Richardson and the Skinner organ.

The Church Strategic Spiritual Directions Plan, thirty-eight pages in length, was the product of the Bullard study and the work of the Mission and Purpose Committee. The objectives of the report were very general in nature as well as all-inclusive. The general goals seemed to be more meaningful Christian fellowship, deeper commitment, and broader participation by the members. Plans in these directions extended through 1993 and involved numerous committees.

In 1991 Andrea began to spotlight some of his own social and ecumenical concerns. Early in the year he began to develop a sister-church relationship with First African Baptist Church and worked with Pastor Thurmond Tillman to plan occasional joint worship services. Andrea hoped to build better bridges between the black and white faith communities by sharing worship and the essence of pietism. He also planned a series of special lectures/sermons on homelessness in which he participated along with Rabbi Saul Rubin and Mike Elliott. He also began to be active in his sensitivity to a most touchy subject—AIDS. He was able to lead the church in hosting an ecumenical service sponsored by the Phoenix Project on May 19, International AIDS Memorial Sunday. The thrust of the service was toward the survivors and families touched by the disease. At the deacon's meeting which approved the hosting of the service, Andrea closed with "deep appreciation of the spirit of the discussions held and of the respect shown by everyone for the differing opinions of others on the emotional issues discussed." Out of this service Andrea was successful in creating a support group for AIDS patients and their families. There also emerged an alliance of area clergy called the AIDS Interfaith Network and Andrea was the director. His sensitivity and compassion dictated that he would be active in such efforts as this.

The History Committee, gearing up with plans for the bicentennial celebration, began to collect material and to furnish the special history room. An *ad hoc* History Book Committee was also appointed with George Pruden as chair (later co-chair, along with Joan Usher) and began to discuss the route to take in producing the two-hundred-year history of the church. The old, dusty multivolume Minutes were taken to a safe place where deterioration would cease and the public interested in research would have access—the Georgia Historical Society. No longer would the dampness and mold in the vault affect these precious documents. While this Committee was contemplating history, Andrea and the congregation were searching for their own contemporary pilgrim's way. In June, after reporting on the SBC and CBF meetings recently held in Atlanta, Andrea admitted that "he did not feel that he could make any accurate predictions of the course which our denomination will follow." The church continued its pattern of giving to both bodies as 1992 opened. In April Andrea attended meetings of the CBF but decided that he would not attend the SBC meetings in Minneapolis. Increasingly, moderate Baptist ministers were avoiding attending these meetings, for all the outcomes were foregone conclusions. Neofundamentalists now ruled the Convention with an iron hand and *their* agenda was the *only* agenda.

In August some personnel tensions related to a staff resignation surfaced and the deacons wrestled with the issue. The result was a reaffirmation of the senior minister's full authority for day-to-day operations including "direction, supervision, and evaluation of the staff." The Personnel Committee had worked in excess of twenty hours on the problems and itself affirmed Andrea as "chief of staff" as well as determining that some strife and friction had caused the staff not to be functioning at its highest level. One staff person resigned, one was transferred, and plans were made to employ a new senior minister's secretary and a fresh job description of that position was composed. Soon, Karen Kelly filled that position. At the same time the senior minister urged members to build bridges of relationships with others and to look for things to celebrate.

Much earlier in the year the church had lost one of its long-term Life Deacons, Dr. John B. Rabun, who had served as a physician for forty-three years. In November his name was honored for perpetuity as the new history room was dedicated and named for him. An appropriate and beautiful resolution on this occasion was entered in the permanent records of the church.

The church was saddened in December by the announcement by the assistant minister, Jody Wright, that he would be leaving at the end of January 1993 to become senior minister at the Warrenton Baptist Church in North Carolina. Jody had experienced a long tenure as an assistant—seven and one-half years. He would carry with him numerous friendships and meaningful experiences from First Baptist. The novice of former years was well prepared now to be a senior minister.

In early May the Search Committee for an assistant minister was disbanded due to a changed situation. On April 5, 1993, Andrea announced his resignation to become effective on June 6. He had accepted a call to the First Baptist Church of Aiken, South Carolina. Diaconate Minutes during this period and as late as October reflect some turmoil over the reasons for the senior minister's resignation. In the Diaconate meeting of May 10, a discussion took place "to explore the reasons for Rev. Andrea's departure. Sorrow was expressed over losing him. The need for self-examination was also identified to ensure that we provide our next minister with adequate support, an appropriate staff structure, and reasonable financial compensation." As Andrea left, he said that he had made his decision after much prayer and with no anger or duress. He was leaving for "a fresh and different challenge in ministry." The Diaconate meeting of June 14 continued the long and involved discussion of Andrea's departure and "any factors that may have added to his leaving." The Personnel Committee made a special report to the Diaconate concerning its involved work over the past fifteen months with much of that involving confidential matters. The report stated that "Dr. Andrea has made no statement which is inconsistent with his statements from the pulpit or his letter of resignation." It continued, "We believe continued speculation that Dr. Andrea's departure is due to any other circumstances is pointless. To persist is to question the credibility of his statements to the church and can only serve to damage his professional reputation in his new ministry. Moreover, such speculation is potentially divisive to this church." The Committee urged fellow deacons to cease any discussion that would be "counter-productive to the tough tasks of the near future." As late as the meeting of October 11 some tensions and rumors persisted: "Milton [Newton] addressed some rumors that have circulated since Fred's departure in an attempt to stop them from further circulation." Afterward, this discussion was out of sight if not out of mind.

Whatever the constellation of reasons for the senior pastor's leaving, institutions and individuals must continue on in their pilgrimages. In both cases, these few months of wayfaring would be followed by years of sensitive and genuine pilgrimage. Andrea's ministry at First Church was, in a way, a kind of interim ministry. He had been there for less than four years and had followed the very long tenure of a beloved pastor who had made numerous changes. Andrea did not challenge these changes; he lived within them as a moderate Baptist with social concerns of his own and was a genuine pietist in his spirituality. These same commitments were continued in his new charge in Aiken. Later, in answering the question, "What was your most rewarding memory of your time spent at First Baptist?" he affirmed: "Mutually supportive, loving relationships with the people." The selective memory of both pastor and people had many positive possibilities. Of the rest, "this, too, shall pass."

During this time between the times, it was the only contemporary period when a three-ministers staff had been reduced to one. Janis Lewis and Wes Monfalcone were employed for the summer as part-time interim assistants and Richardson called for a new greening of the total membership in relation to participation and commitment.

August 9 proved to be a hot Sunday in the church. For the first time in the history of the sanctuary, there was a fire (quickly extinguished) in the furnace room which led the congregation to evacuate the room and make its way to Lewis Hall, where the supply minister, Dick Ferrell, preached his providentially appropriate sermon, "Reassuring the Assured!" In the same month, Dr. Ted Dougherty agreed to be the interim minister for four months. In September Cathy Cole joined the staff as an interim minister and became the first female to preach from the pulpit of First Baptist.

Founder's Day was celebrated this year (1993) on November 14 and the famous Millard Fuller preached from the pulpit and also spoke in the afternoon at the dedication of the Habitat House. Fuller had in 1976 founded Habitat for Humanity International when he left Koinonia Partners, an ecumenical Christian commune southwest of Americus, Georgia. Since then, numerous chapters of this organization had been founded, as in Savannah, and thousands of houses around the world have been built for low-income persons.

John M. Finley

The Search Committee for a senior minister was kept busy by Chair Vreeland George and had arrived at a profile of the desired person. He must have eight-to-ten years' experience, be between the ages of forty and sixty, ecumenical in spirit, a strong leader and administrator, staff-oriented, innovative in leading worship, a good pulpiteer, and possess an appreciation of liturgical worship. He must have a good sense of humor

**John M. Finley
1994–present**

and be a good listener. Finally, the profile stipulated, "We desire a minister with vision for the future and respect for our past." Newspaper releases described First Baptist as a church committed to "contemporary Christianity in an historic setting." This must also be the description of their thirty-second senior minister.

By April the Committee believed it had found the man who met their description. It recommended that the church call Dr. John Finley of the Scott Boulevard Baptist Church in Decatur, Georgia—another tall man built for the high pulpit of First Baptist Church. An interlude of sadness and yet joyous memory temporarily interrupted the recommendation. Dwight Bruce had died—a man and a musician who was one of a kind. Richardson paid high tribute to him in *The Calendar* and closed by calling him "always my friend, my colleague, and my mentor." Special memories of him and his forty-plus years of service to the church bathed the memories of members with pleasant delight. And yet, he would be deeply missed.

In May the church received the recommendation of the Search Committee and voted unanimously to call John M. Finley. *The Calendar* of May 15 carried Finley's acceptance letter. He would be in residence by July 1. Until then, Dr. Paul Craven, former pastor of First Baptist Church of Charleston, South Carolina, would fill the pulpit. Craven's words of praise during his final week noted the unique "theology of worship and discipling," the "warm dignity," and the commitment to the downtown location of First Baptist. Within a month, Cathy Cole had also submitted her final letter to *The Calendar*—she would move as of September 1 to South Carolina to become the first chaplain of the Aiken Regional Medical Center.

Early on Finley became immersed in a historical problem inherited from the last century—heavy flooding of the semi-basement. Heavy rains in early September and October took their toll of the chapel, history room, and elevator shaft. Serious damage was done. But also, early on Finley witnessed the collegiality of the congregation as many members showed up to help remove hundreds of gallons of water from the elevator shaft, vacuum water from the history room, shovel mud from the chapel foyer, and remove debris from the pumps at the chapel entrance ramp. Here were people not afraid to get their hands dirty when necessary.

In early October John Finley was formally installed as the thirty-second senior minister in the church. Of that service John had special picture memories. For the occasion Carol Anne Richardson had written a special anthem, "Psalm 146." Finley was moved by this beautiful piece of music and at the same time amused by Walter Shurden's sermon title—"On Being a Charismatic." He and the congregation were a bit on edge as to the content of such a sermon, but of course were delighted with its presentation and content. Surely as hands were placed on Finley's head and encouragement whispered in his ears, he felt affirmed. And then, good food and good drink for all. Finally, the snapshot of God watching smilingly on the whole transaction. Finley felt accepted and "in place" and now the ministry must formally and officially begin.

The church was continuing to wrestle with finding itself denominationally. Finley from the start stressed the priesthood of every believer with the deacons' taking the lead as lay ministers. He looked forward to a deacons' retreat during which this might be explored. In 1995 two committees would also join hands and heads over finances and denominational relations. The Denominational Relations and the Missions and Social Ministries Committees would work hand-in-glove on this matter. In March Finley attended the national meeting of the Alliance of Baptists in Washington, D.C., and in May admitted to the deacons that at present it was "complicated and difficult" to express oneself as a Baptist. On May 13 the Georgia CBF met in the church as this relationship continued. Finley also shared a recent two-page document produced by the Alliance of Baptists on Jewish-Christian relations. It aimed at dialogue and education as well as opposing anti-Semitism and a theology of conversion. First Church had solid and dialogical relations with the Jewish community in Savannah and the document actually reflected this church's views developed years earlier.

By July all the formal ministerial slots had been filled. Finley, an M.Div. and Ph.D. graduate of The Southern Baptist Theological Seminary, was joined by another Southern graduate, Kristin Andreason. Filling the slot of assistant minister, she hit the sidewalk running in youth activities and religious education. Her enthusiasm, energy, and commitment to the task were deeply appreciated and "catching." She began from the start to make an immediate and positive impact.

Founder's Day in November 1995 reminded the congregation of the future as well as the past. In five years the church would celebrate two hundred years of history, and planning for special events to take place between November 1999 and November 2000 must begin soon. The past was relived in the present by a special gift of $2,500 made to the Mercer University School of Theology which would open in Atlanta in the fall of 1996. Harking to the past, the amount given was the same amount Josiah Penfield left in his 1828 will to the Georgia Baptist Convention as a challenge to "create a fund for the education of pious young men for the gospel ministry." These funds were eventually used to found Mercer Institute which later became Mercer University. In a symbolic replay of history, R. Kirby Godsey, president of Mercer, was presented with a check for this most recent effort in Georgia toward the "education of pious young men for the gospel ministry." The Penfield legacy thus lived on as well as the moderate commitments of the congregation, for the new school was one of many in several states being founded for Baptists who did not want the delimited education now offered by the six SBC seminaries dominated by the neofundamentalists.

Finley himself had two ecumenical peak experiences in November. First, he went to Cuba in a program sponsored by the Alliance of Baptists to establish sister-church relationships, promising the church that he would have a round-trip ticket! Also in November the church hosted the community Thanksgiving Service for eleven congregations—a genuine grassroots ecumenical experience for all.

By 1996 the fully replenished ministry of the church began to find itself and to map out plans for the future, especially in light of the coming year-long bicentennial celebration. At midyear, Finley described most of what had been going on during the year as "reclaiming our identity as a church in mission." Finley was correct in his observation that missions and ministry had been at the heart of the church since its founding, and he was continuing that legacy in his own leadership, following in the more recent footsteps of Austin, Wright, and Andrea. The senior minister had been reflecting on this heritage in the context of the youth mission trips to Arkansas in the summer and the emerging partnership with Cuban Baptists. His sensitivity was heightened, however, in August as he participated in the relocation of the Savannah Baptist Center to new quarters on Wheaton Street. The J. C. Lewis Foundation had made this move possible. Born during the ministry of Pastor Cleverdon in 1956 as a "mission" of First Baptist, it continued in 1996 as a mission and a reminder during the five-year historical interlude of the tasks of mission and ministry in the downtown area. Amnesia in this case was replaced by anamnesis—an energizing recollection of historical events.

In the spring of 1997 friendships with Mickve Israel were again renewed. While the sanctuary was receiving minor construction and painting, the congregation met for three Sundays in the historic synagogue of Reform Judaism in the city. Sunday School for a large group of adults was also held there prior to worship and genuine Jewish-Christian dialogue took place with Rabbi Arnold Belzer.

Fund-raising is always a difficult job, to say the least. In view of the bicentennial celebration, a long-range three-year fund-raising campaign was initiated in early 1997 with the kickoff luncheon held on May 18 at the Hyatt Regency Hotel. Veteran contributive member Vreeland George was chair of the Facilities Planning Committee which launched the Heritage and Hope Capital Stewardship Campaign. The Committee determined that major repairs, updating, and some additions were needed in both the sanctuary and educational building. An estimated $600,000 would be required to meet all these needs, and it was hoped that the work would be completed prior to the celebration of the bicentennial in the year 2000. Once again the church committed itself to a mammoth task and believed in itself strongly enough to know that it would be done. As an early indication of success, by early July 52 percent of the goal had already been pledged by the congregation.

Sadness enveloped the congregation on June 25 as word came of Tom Austin's death the day before in Winston-Salem. He had struggled with cancer for a long while, preaching his last sermons from a wheelchair at Knollwood. It was an untimely death of a truly great person. James Richardson, writing in *The Calendar* perhaps the greatest tribute to Tom, reflected: "Tom was to me a pastor, a brother, a mentor, and a friend." Continuing in his last paragraph, James captured Tom's humanness:

> But one of the great lessons Tom taught me was that one could take life seriously without taking himself too seriously. He dedicated and baptized our two children, but he also loved to sing silly songs to them. He worked long hours and was remarkably patient with difficult persons, but he enjoyed going to ball games and yelling at the referees. He expected hard work from all those on the church staff, but we had a great deal of fun as we worked together. With the death of Tom Austin early this morning, the Church has lost an outstanding pastor, preacher, and prophet. Edna, Julie, and Bryan have lost a loving and devoted husband and father. And you and I have lost a good friend who touched our lives in ways that have made us better persons. Thanks be to God for a remarkable life well lived.

Indeed, *Requiescat in pace*, Tom.

In July Richardson was pleased that for the first time the Annual Conference of the Hymn Society in the United States and Canada would meet in Savannah—this year for its seventy-fifth annual conference. First Baptist was host for many of the events over a five-day period. The conference would begin on July 13, the very day when a hymnbook change would be made in the church. The new hymnbook, donated by the Bruce family in memory of Dwight, would be introduced and the former hymnbook retired to the archives and individual homes. As *Hymns, Psalms, and Spiritual Songs* was dedicated to use, several persons whose texts and tunes appear in the book were present in the congregation. The former *Hymnbook for Christian Worship* was actually retired a week earlier on July 6 and, appropriately, a part of worship included a Litany of Gratitude for a book that had served the church well for nearly two decades. Richardson received numerous congratulatory letters concerning the Conference and even he praised it as having topped all the others.

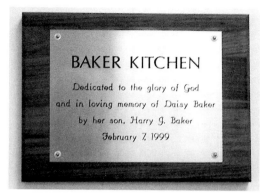

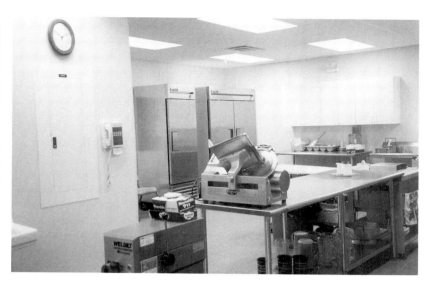

The plaque (above) is in honor of Mrs. Daisy Baker, and the kitchen (right) was funded by the generosity of her son, Harry Baker, in memory of his mother.

On October 12 the congregation said its last farewells to Tom Austin. Finley had been away at a CBF meeting in Louisville, Kentucky, when news of the death came, and on his return became aware that the church needed its own final closure. Edna, Julie, and Bryan Austin came, and Tom's closest ministerial friend, Rabbi Saul Rubin, offered the eulogy. Austin's legacy and influence had lived on in this community of faith and would continue to do so, but now grief was replaced by Christian thanksgiving and joy.

A sense of thanksgiving, joy, and community is always present when meals at First Baptist have been shared. In mid-1998 a generous bequest was received from member Harry Baker's estate for a long-needed renovation of the church's kitchen. It was stipulated that this new kitchen facility be built in the memory of his mother, Mrs. Daisy Baker. She had been an active and faithful member and was vividly remembered for cooking meals at the church on Wednesday nights. The generosity of the son and the wonderful meals of the mother would not soon be forgotten by the congregation as it enjoyed the products of this sparklingly new kitchen. As with Jesus the Christ during the final supper of his life, fresh revelations and creative religious insights often come as Christians sit at a common table and share food and drink.

Toward the close of 1997 *the* famous book about Savannah had made its way to the silver screen, for good or ill, and the premiere of *Midnight in the Garden of Good and Evil* had brought tourists and celebrities from far and near. It was the greatest public relations for Savannah since Forrest Gump had sat on a bench in Chippewa Square! It certainly benefitted the Lucas Theater renovation and the Frank Callen Center for Boys and Girls but probably not religious life in the city. Finley, in this context, recalled a superior line about midnight in Philipp Nicolai's stirring Advent hymn in relation to the coming of the Bridegroom for his Church—"Midnight's peace their cry has broken."

The year of 1997 closed with a church conference which Finley judged to be "one of the finest church conferences I have attended in nearly twenty years as a pastor." All reports were positive and all bills had been paid. The Heritage and Hope campaign was moving in a positive direction and there was stability and yet creativity in the congregation. The next two years would be prelude to the numerous special events of the bicentennial year which would begin on Founder's Day, November 1999, with the presentation of the selective two-hundred-year history of the pilgrims of First Baptist Church of Savannah, Georgia.

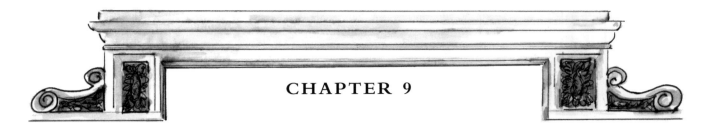

CHAPTER 9

DOCTRINE, LITURGY, WORSHIP, AND MISSION

DOCTRINE

The last published Manual of the First Baptist Church appeared sometime between 1922 and 1927. The booklet is not dated but internal matters would dictate these circa dates. The 1860 Manual was repeated in its Declaration of Faith and the Covenant was expanded slightly but with no damage done to the essence of the 1860 Covenant. The Rules and Bylaws also showed little change and the items on discipline were identical. Interestingly, the Covenant still carried no injunction against alcohol as so many later Baptist covenants did. It stressed brotherly love, prayer, setting worthy examples, supporting a "faithful Evangelical Ministry," and doing "good to all men, especially in helping to extend the Gospel in its purity and power to the whole human family" (see appendix M). The Covenant was less denominationally oriented and more illustrative of pietistic evangelical ecumenism. It would appear that since the last Manual appeared, there have been no other confessions or covenants *officially* adopted by the church. There were in practice, however, evolutionary changes which took place through the second century of Christian experiences.

Though the paragraphs on church discipline remained the same in the twentieth century, the practice dwindled to very few cases, usually without detailed description as in the nineteenth century. The hand of fellowship continued to be "withdrawn" for awhile but this was soon replaced by letters of commendation when a member joined a church of another denomination. Discipline was employed in 1903, 1916, 1919 (the J. R. Cain case), and in 1985 (the Baptist Center case). The descriptions of these cases are brief and the last two cases seemed to be exceptions to the general rule of the disappearance of the practice of discipline. American individualism was the order of the day as well as the idea of equality before the throne of God that ruled out judgment lest one be judged. Communal love and private piety in relation to morality replaced communal judgement and imposed morality. "Judge not that ye be not judged" remains even at the close of the twentieth century a rule of thumb in secular as well as religious society. Even more severe breaches of common morality are handled with extreme care.

152

Public discipline in First Baptist Church disappeared and increasingly was replaced by redemptive pastoral counseling. It was considered far better and even pragmatic to redeem errant members to efficient service and more wholesome and fulfilled lives.

Strictly doctrinal matters also experienced change as well as changed attitudes. Major doctrinal positions in the church remained Baptistic and evangelically conservative, though within an ecumenical context. The pastoral leadership remained highly educated as well as the membership, and both increasingly sought not only Christian ecumenical expressions but also continued their Christian-Jewish fellowship, especially with the Reform wing of Judaism. Early in the century the church and the Association opposed "alien baptism" and the antimission movement so vividly witnessed among such groups as Primitive Baptists. Savannah First Baptist again was loyal to its past history in missions and kept supporting this part of the essence of Baptist Christianity as it interpreted it. Though small-town and rural churches would continue to oppose "alien baptism" and "open communion," many urban churches would adopt more ecumenical attitudes. To be a downtown church and to have good relationships with other denominations, as First Baptist always had, almost dictated a changed position on these two issues. The twentieth-century ecumenical movement has often been called the "great new fact" in religious circles and was bound to have an effect on First Baptist. Its pastoral leaders and members began to attend worldwide Baptist gatherings such as the Baptist World Alliance as well as more broadly ecumenical meetings such as the World Council of Churches and the Faith and Order movement. From 1800 forward the church had been ecumenical in its outlook and practice and would remain so in the twentieth century. Communion was very early open to all Christians who wished to participate, and later in the century "open membership" began to be practiced in relation to baptism. These Baptists continued to make their witness that they believed that normative baptism was believer's baptism by immersion, but they would not claim the two basic ordinances as merely Baptist but first as Christian.

Samuel S. Hill Jr., in his *Southern Churches in Crisis*, has insightfully suggested that "the final 'way out' of provinciality for a sectarian body which has been cast in a church-type role is ecumenical involvement." First Baptist accomplished this in relation to the two major Christian and also Baptist ordinances—communion and baptism. Hill adds, "By means of thoroughgoing participation in the larger body of Christians, it could, in addition to flavoring the larger body with its contribution, realize a greater balance, depth, and richness in its own life." This suggestion was taken seriously by First Baptist as it slowly adopted positions of "open communion" and "open membership." Retaining believer's baptism by immersion in relation to new converts continued *one* of the distinct features of Baptist history, and yet recognizing other forms of baptism also committed the church to a "more thoroughgoing participation in the larger body of Christians." In making these evolving changes, First Baptist retained and valued the principles of local autonomy and freedom out of which Baptists had seen their own rise and growth. As well, the principles of versatility, flexibility, and adaptability in local church order were followed as Baptist history continued in Savannah.

One particular doctrine or belief is not what makes a Baptist church Baptist—it is a constellation of factors, one of which is simply the history of that particular congregation. One of the major strengths of First Baptist Church has been its pilgrimage mentality and its understanding that the institution itself is of necessity provisional and subject to evolutionary change. No one confessional affirmation suffices to describe First Baptist in the twentieth century; perhaps that is the major reason that no new covenant or doctrinal statement has been written. In relation to doctrine, the church has come to prefer the umbrella approach rather than the prison-cell avenue. It is not surprising then, that Sunday-to-Sunday affirmations of faith read variously. One read on a Sunday in late 1997, however, illustrates a healthy doctrinal stance that leaves many doors open for numerous interpretations:

> The First Baptist Church confesses Jesus Christ as Lord on the basis of who he was and is, and what he did and does. Who is he? We confess him to be God's unique Son, the Messiah of Israel, the Lord of Life. What did he do? He gave his life even unto death— by God's will and for our sake—on the cross. He comes again and again by the Holy Spirit, to communicate himself to his people. His people are the Church.

> We seek simply to be one visible congregation of Christ's Church. We hold Baptist views about the Christian faith. However, we also rejoice in our Lord's gracious gifts to our fellow believers, who are called by names other than Baptist. Happily, we count them as our brothers and our sisters.

> We live out our discipleship by taking seriously our commitment to each other and to the world. We share not only our words, but our money, our time, and our talents, with our friends here, and with all God's people everywhere.

This confession is a beautiful illustration of ecumenical Baptist doctrine. It is Christological, trinitarian, and ecumenically phrased, containing a Baptist commitment. Rather than separatistic, it is inclusive; rather than denominationally dominated, it is ecumenically open; rather than doctrinally preoccupied, it is mission oriented; and rather than judgmental, it stresses love and acceptance. Indeed, in doctrine and history, First Baptist Church is Baptistic as well as ecumenical and therein lies its probably unique witness in the city of Savannah—a city where downtown Catholics, Episcopalians, Lutherans, Methodists, Presbyterians, Baptists and others rub shoulders daily in social, political, and religious settings and accept one another in love and grace.

LITURGY AND WORSHIP

In non-Baptist circles, First Baptist would usually be described as low-church and non-liturgical. In Baptist circles, it would be designated as high-church and definitely liturgical. This is simply one more illustration of the contextuality of the use of terms in religious circles. Congregational autonomy among Baptists has happily allowed each congregation to develop its own worship format and style.

Liturgy, or the work of the people, is both teaching and celebration. As well, worship and ordinance are meant to develop both personal and social holiness. Christians come to life as Christians in a worshiping community. First Baptist in its worship has rediscovered the corporate conception of Christian life. This conception is engendered in the worshiping community, is nourished in that community, and expresses itself in the perpetuation and extension of such a community. Without doubt the liturgical and worship experiences of First Baptist have led to internal bonding; however, they have additionally been major causal factors toward the development of ecumenical attitudes as well as producing a people of God who go everywhere during

Music has been an integral part of the church's mission since its inception. The several choirs gathered together for a group photo on the steps of the church in 1963.

weekdays on mission. In other words, the constructive leadership produced by this church "out there" in large part is the product of what has happened "in here"—the sanctuary.

Major factors in liturgy and worship, beyond pastoral leadership and encouragement as well as congregational participation, have been two persons and one instrument. The instrument since 1922 has of course been the majestic Skinner organ through all its repairs and additions as late as 1990. Its capabilities have already been discussed and its masters introduced, Dwight Bruce and James Richardson. Bruce served as organist and choirmaster for nearly forty years and at the time of this writing Richardson has served for twenty-seven years and is the ordained associate minister who, among other tasks, serves as organist and choirmaster. Both these persons merit special presentation.

In 1929 Bruce had driven up to the church in an old Chevrolet to do a temporary "fill-in" job at the organ and in the year of the market crash he stayed on as organist as well as becoming a staff member of radio station WTOC. Bruce brought the "best" in organ performance and classical music to the church as well as replacing a paid quartet with a chorus choir which performed both formal and informal music. A "man for all seasons," he became "Happy Dan the Story Man" on radio and when WTOC entered the television age in the fifties he commenced a long-time program, the "Happy Dan and Popeye Show." It was at this time that he gave the popular anchorman Doug Weathers his first chance in television—as a film splicer. Happy Dan often shared that off-camera personality on Sunday mornings, visiting the children's department, always receiving screams of delight. Bruce rose all the way to vice president in charge of programming for WTOC radio and TV. Music in the larger community benefitted greatly from his presence. He started the Savannah Symphony Society and served as chair of its board. On numerous occasions Bruce was featured in various articles in the *Savannah Morning News* due to his widespread contributions to the larger community. In June 1968 Bruce retired and on June 9 the church celebrated Dwight Bruce Day, carefully planned by John Rabun. In the morning almost fifty present and former choir members honored their director, singing among other selections, Steffe-Ringwald's "Battle Hymn of the Republic." Pastor Lanier preached an appropriate sermon entitled "A Reward for Excellence." That evening Bruce played a wide-ranging number of works in his recital including "Clair de Lune," "Londonderry Air," and Handel's majestic "Hallelujah." The day was a complete success; Bruce had been appropriately honored and a congregation experienced in part its very raison d'etre through great music. After retirement Bruce remained active in the church, even serving as chair of the Pastoral Search Committee which brought Tom Austin to First Baptist. After numerous health problems, Bruce died at the age of 84 in April 1994. Nearly one year later, in May 1995, a sacred music concert was given in his honor on a Sunday afternoon. It was a tribute to the man who had brought the classical style of church music to First Baptist. Pastor Lanier perhaps paid Bruce one of the highest compliments he received at the time of his retirement. Lanier, smiling, reflected that "we'll miss that gray mop bobbing up and down before the organ." He continued:

> Many a Sunday has the weather been bad or the mood of the congregation sullen—the people would come in with an "I-dare-you-to-get-to-me-today" attitude. Then the music starts and the cords of resistance are one-by-one broken. Until at last Dwight hands over the congregation of hostile-become-worshipers and says in effect, "Here they are now—if you can't preach to them you just can't preach." It's sad to think of his leaving.

The present hymn book of the church, *Hymns, Psalms, and Spiritual Songs,* assures the congregation that Bruce has not completely left—for the church's copies were given in his memory.

After the brief tenure of Rick Carswell, James C. Richardson inherited the Bruce mantle and wore it proudly and with his own unique success. Richardson recalls: "He [Bruce] was instrumental in my coming to the church in 1971. The kind of programs, the kind of music he had done, interested me in following in that tradition. He had a program of the finest of classical church music."

James was not involved in a secular business like Bruce and could give more time to organization, development, and outreach. As has been noted, he also became ordained and assumed the title of associate minister with the bulk of that ministry but by no means all of it in the area of music, worship, and liturgy. Along with Tom Austin, Richardson hit the sidewalk running. Austin and Richardson were a good "mesh" insofar as their ideas of true congregational worship were concerned. They were a true worship team.

One of Richardson's early goals was the establishment of a fully graded choir program with a coordinated curriculum and an organized method of teaching music reading and vocal production. That goal was achieved and continues to maintain a high level of quality music education. He also began to lead the choirs to participate in district, state, and national festivals in Baptist and other circles. As the youth choir matured, it made performance trips as far away as Virginia, North Carolina, and New York. Specialist youth groups were also developed and numerous performance opportunities were given. Young members whose choral education came virtually exclusively from the church's graded choir program have gone on to sing with the Harvard Glee Club, the Mars Hill College Choir, the University of Georgia Glee Club, the Sewanee University Choir, and many others. Both the youth and children's choirs also began to sing a wide range of cantatas. The Handbell Choir often joined them in various performances.

The strong adult choir program developed by Bruce was continued by Richardson. In addition to a broad repertoire for regular worship services, on a regular basis the adult choir presented major presentations of cantatas and oratorios. Magnificats by Bach, Pergolesi, and Vivaldi and cantatas by Bach and Buxtehude have been performed. As has been noted already, on the occasion of the three-hundredth anniversary of the year of Handel's birth, his *Messiah* was performed in its entirety in the church, a unique musical feat. The adult choir has also joined forces with other denominational choirs in ecumenical performances. The choir was also the featured choir for both the twenty-fifth and fiftieth anniversary celebrations of the Savannah chapter of the American Guild of Organists.

Committed to the education of its associate minister, the church, on his twentieth anniversary, gave Richardson a trip to Germany and Austria. The special "Mozart package" included concerts, lectures, and museums. It was his first European trip and opened up new musical vistas. Five years later, he was given a period of time for more study in Europe. He and his wife went to Oxford University as part of the International Church Music Workshop, which gave further musical education in a fully ecumenical context. Those weeks in England and travels in Scotland would never be forgotten by this husband-wife musical team.

Richardson and Austin were sensitive to the seasons of the church year in their planning, especially to Advent and Lent. Churchwide programs began to have a music ministry sponsorship. New traditions were implemented: the Chrismon trees, the Advent wreath, and the Advent devotional booklet. Numerous congregational members participated in this broad liturgical program as writers, artists, and performers. More recently an *ad hoc* Committee on Music and Other Liturgical Arts has been established to be active through the celebration of the church's two hundred years and give special attention to drama, banners, and arts and crafts in efforts to engage persons within the church whose artistic talents might be other than in music.

When Richardson arrived the church was using the 1956 edition of the *Baptist Hymnal*, a work found in most Southern Baptist Churches and published by the denominational house, Broadman Press. With Richardson's more ecumenical knowledge and commitment, the decision was made to make a change. A study of hymnals was made and the *Hymnbook for Christian Worship*, jointly published by the American Baptist Churches and the Disciples of Christ, was selected and dedicated in 1978, the gift of J. Curtis Lewis Jr. in memory of J. Marcus Stubbs. This hymnal was far more sensitive to the church year than the Southern Baptist product. Staying abreast of religious musical developments, in the mid-nineties another hymnal search was conducted and the very ecumenical work, *Hymns, Psalms, and Spiritual Songs* (Westminster-John Knox Press) was chosen. This work

Hand Bells on Palm Sunday. L to R: Charlene Keebler, Betty Hodges, Margaret Hardy, Ginger Pruden, Edith Bennet, Hillary Canipe, Sara Davis, Ellen Davis, Barbara Creaser, George Pruden. Director, Carol Anne Richardson.

is even more sensitive to the Christian year as well as to ethnic hymns and other "spiritual songs." As has been noted, copies were dedicated in 1997 in memory of Dwight Bruce and funded by the Bruce family.

Original compositions have also marked Richardson's tenure. The Handbell Choir, for example, has often performed arrangements written by one of the players. Richardson himself has composed numerous pieces of music for special occasions such as church anniversaries and special worship themes. He has also composed liturgies for infant dedications, baptisms, ordinations, and memorial services. Original hymn texts have also been written, such as that by his wife, Carol Anne, "Faithful Christians, Arise." This was done for Founder's Day 1990 and has been sung at each such day since. James Richardson has written the text and music of a new hymn for the church's two-hundredth anniversary (see appendix N).

James C. Richardson was ordained to the gospel ministry in December 1977. As stated in an earlier chapter, he wrote an excellent theological statement prior to the ordination summarizing his calling as a minister of music. His conclusion, as noted elsewhere, is worthy of repetition: "Ordination will be for me a time of recommitment to my high calling as a Christian, my choice of the music ministry as a profession, and my acceptance of the call of this church to serve as its minister." Richardson had been a minister in the church since 1971, only now he was formally ordained by the congregation. Bravo for James!

Leading worship is a team effort when it is done effectively. The team of Austin, Richardson, and Wright was most effective. This team was invited to collaborate on an article for the *Review and Expositor*, a scholarly publication of The Southern Baptist Theological Seminary. The article was successfully completed and appeared in volume 85 (1988) of the journal under the title, "Worship Planning at First Baptist Church, Savannah, Georgia." It was an excellent presentation of worship and liturgy at the church and is herein summarized with some interpretations.

For First Baptist and others, these three ministers defined worship as follows:

> Christian worship is believing confession and believing proclamation of God's saving act. If in glad recognition of this "act" one's primal duty is to witness, one's first impulse is to worship. The aim of worship is the establishment of perfect communion between the Creator and the creature.

Continuing, they wrote the following:

> Thus to worship is to bring one's whole being into line with the will and purpose of God and to be open in every part of one's being to his impact: mind, heart, soul, will, and neighbor.

These three then attempted to plan every part of corporate worship in the direction of this divine end.

This upper-middle class, extremely well-educated congregation has never sought to be a suburban congregation in a downtown setting. Its major components have been corporate worship, social ministries which have been ecumenically based and organized, uniquely creative and innovative educational programs, a well-rounded ministry of music that places an emphasis on the classics, and some traditional Southern Baptist organizations.

For a time, each printed order of worship reminded the congregation: "The worship of God is so important that it must not be engaged in haphazardly or entered into casually." Toward this end announcements are generally not oral but written, and visitors are not welcomed until the close of the service. Hymns, prayers, ordinances, faith statements, sermons, and scripture lessons all include those special moments and themes of adoration, penitence, thanksgiving, intercession, forgiveness, and dedication. Worship services often possess a single theme emerging from a constellation of elements such as the Christian Year and contemporary issues. Sometimes a theme is kaleidoscopically explored in a series of services. The weekly Monday meeting of the ministers offers moments for theme development and discussion. Multiple readings from the Bible reflect the theme as well as avoid a proof-text approach of only a verse or two. Doxological praise takes place in both choral music and congregational hymns. The music ministry utilizes graded choirs, handbell choirs, instrumental ensembles, the majestic organ, and congregational singing. Hymn time is probably the most ecumenical moment of the hour as the congregation is linked to writers and composers of numerous other traditions and communions. Hymns of praise, petition, and commitment generally make their way into the order.

Baptists are historically noncreedal people, but they have produced numerous confessions and affirmations which are often used in worship as well as utilizing some of the more historic creeds and using them confessionally. It should be mentioned that noncreedal simply refers to the fact that Baptists have never committed themselves to binding and enforceable literalistic creeds. They have, however, favored edifying, affirming confessions. First Baptist from its foundation is Baptist at this point. Statements of faith are often used, then, in the order of worship, and they come from various sources, including at times the historic creeds of the Christian Church. Three constants in the order of worship are the Lord's Prayer, the Doxology, and the Gloria Patri. These offer familiarity and warmth for the adults and educational opportunities for the children.

The sermon sits as a diamond within the appropriate and beautiful setting. Protestant worship since the sixteenth century makes the sermon central. Baptists follow that same pattern. If done ideally, however, the sermon is not freestanding but is simply the focal point of the whole constellation of matters that make up the worship experience. This necessitates careful

Joy Shop, a week-long summer program of music, crafts, and fun! L to R: Cole Harrison, Gus Morgan, and Mary Crane Palles.

planning and creative ministerial teamwork. Probably most of the sermons preached at First Baptist are "situation-in-life" sermons which address any aspect of the human experience and at the same time are addressed themselves by appropriate parts of the written word, the scripture. There is no substitute in the life and work of the congregation for the proclamation of the good news. The minister must be both prophet and priest, however. He/she must challenge as well as comfort. One of the most appealing features at First Baptist in the twentieth century, with only a few exceptions, has been freedom in the pulpit to touch on all issues that are or should be important to the congregation. Some sermons should result in dialogue within the congregation, which is healthy, but if the prophet-challenger is muffled, the gospel ceases to speak. Pastor Austin perhaps spoke for virtually all the ministerial leaders of the twentieth century at his leaving when he made a point of thanking the congregation for freedom in the pulpit which he had experienced throughout his long tenure.

Music in worship at First Baptist is a rich heritage. Choirs, hymn books, and even an organ facilitated worship from the earliest days. In 1922 the Skinner organ which was installed was certainly one of the finest in the Southeast. Bruce and Richardson brought a higher standard with their wide-ranging classical music bringing attention to a God-experience and minimizing "showiness." Both these organists in their performances and use of choirs and special soloists weave a seamless service of worship as they also proclaim the gospel. The organ music and the hymn books have offered an ample supply of worship materials from the whole history of the Christian Church. In the worship service there can never be a more intensely ecumenical moment than when music is being performed or sung by both choir and congregation—for the resources come from the numerous rich traditions within the whole Church. Even ultraconservative Baptists experience perhaps an unconscious ecumenical moment on such occasions.

Prayer is always a part of worship. These prayers bear the imprint of both spontaneity and careful preparation. One who leads such prayers draws from the total experience of the whole congregation as well as from the vast store of prayers prayed throughout Christian history. Of necessity, then, the prayer must be inclusive and must draw the congregation into a firsthand experience with the words themselves. In this case, one does not pray for or on behalf of others; one prays with others. Ministerial and lay prayers at First Baptist resonate with these principles.

The invitation to discipleship at First Baptist has always been given. This involves a public action of confession of faith that seals a decision that has already been privately made, either lately or much earlier. Manipulative means to secure this public act have been shunned. On any given Sunday, however, the sermon, prayers, music, and scripture offer the complete potential for any individual to act upon his/her prior decision and to confess Jesus as the Christ within this worshiping congregation.

The room in which all this takes place is appropriate to the goal. The beauty of the sanctuary is simple; at the same time it is majestic. It is a house of God which, when entered, calls the worshiper to prayer almost automatically. The large hanging brass cross focalizes the prayer of the worshiper and the central furniture reminds of the two ordinances of the Baptist tradition—baptism and communion. Flanking the altar table are pulpit and lectern, themselves displaying the ancient symbol of Christianity, the cross. From one the scripture of the day is read and prayers prayed. From the other, the written word of God is meshed with the spoken and contemporary word of God. Candles speak of Jesus as the light of the world and remind the worshiper of mission opportunities. Ministerial stoles tell of the period of the church year and clerical black

Wesleyan gowns adorned with Christian symbols take the focus off whatever the ministers are wearing for the day.

Worship at First Baptist Church of Savannah has from the start followed this Charleston tradition. Order, unity, and dignity are meshed with acceptance, affection, and spontaneity. Worship informs and energizes all else that is done in the church and by the church, for this people of God who come here on weekends go everywhere on weekdays, and their worship experience becomes a vital part of their lives "out there." Christian worship provides memory and identity. Attempts to live the good life which are abstracted from a deep understanding of the worshiping community and its traditions produce only self-serving individuals perhaps only bound together by ties of convenient egoism. With proper Christian memory and identity, however, Christian pilgrims "are the kind of people who are not only obligated but can happily embrace the commission to go forth in peace in the name of Christ, to love and serve the Lord, all the while rejoicing in the power of the Spirit" (Harmon L. Smith, *Where Two or Three Are Gathered*, p. 230).

MISSION

Mission for the Christian church involves all of God's creation—it is the whole work of the whole church in the whole world. The basis and goal of mission is the whole creation as this body of Christ attempts to be the vehicle of the fullness of God. With this thorough-goingly wholistic view, mission, so often referred to as "missions," is not limited at all to an evangelistic witness either at home or abroad. Mission exists wherever and whenever the church attempts to bring Christ's fullness of whatever kind to the world in which it finds itself. From its very beginnings until the present time, then, First Baptist Church of Savannah, Georgia, has illustrated and lived mission in a variety of ways referred to throughout this volume.

Perhaps, however, some of these specifics should be summarized as well as several of the more contemporary illustrations of mission given special attention and description.

Home missions and foreign missions have often focalized interest and galvanized support of Baptists for missions. It has been noted that the famous Luther Rice visited and was heard in Savannah in 1813 and 1816. One result of this visit was the establishment of a Mission Fund in 1813 in the Savannah Baptist Church, and the founding of a Missionary Society in 1813–1814. This was prior to the national missions organization among Baptists founded in 1814. From this time on Savannah Baptists contributed on a local, associational, national, and international level to the interest of missions. Mission funds were even continued by the church in dire times such as during the Civil War. Long after leaving Savannah, Pastor Binney himself became a foreign missionary, and in 1891 the church ordained one of its own, William D. King, who was shortly appointed by the Foreign Mission Board as a missionary to China. Another baptized (1877) member of the church, J. H. Devotie, later became the first secretary of the Georgia State Mission Board for Baptists and served from 1924 to 1934. In 1924 the famous Baptist missionary to China, E. McNeill Poteat Jr., visited Savannah and made a number of addresses. More recently, the women of the church in 1965 and 1966 brought two female Baptist missionaries to speak. Lucy Wright, former missionary to China, and Minnie Lou Lanier, missionary in Brazil, delivered moving speeches during the Women's Missionary Union's special Week of Prayer. Pastor Forrest Lanier was instrumental in the creation of Operation Touch which resulted in teams of dentists and medical doctors going on brief missions to Honduras, Jamaica,

Haiti, and elsewhere to relieve pain and suffering in impoverished areas. These firsthand visits and numerous mission support experiences kept the matter of missions uppermost in the minds and hearts of Savannah Baptists. It is no surprise that in both centuries the doctrine of the church frowned on the antimission movement and judged it to be in grave error in its interpretation of the whole mission of the Christian church.

On the local scene, Savannah's First Baptist Church has been alert to the expansion of the city and to religious needs in new sections of the city. As early as 1868 and as late as 1956, this has been the continuing experience of the congregation. First Baptist Church is the mother of a number of daughters—Bull Street Baptist Church, Riverside Baptist Church, and Immanuel Baptist Church. More recently in 1956 the Savannah Baptist Center was supported in its founding days as a special mission in the downtown area and has enjoyed evolving encouragement and support.

In addition to missions-becoming-churches on the local scene, a number of "intentional" service projects have been undertaken to deal with unique needs in the downtown area. Though discussed earlier, these efforts would include the Counseling Center, Congregations Responding to You (CRY), Emmaus House, the Union Mission, the Thomas D. Austin House, and AIDS Interfaith Network. In these ways, a wide diversity of mission needs have been met through the years.

In 1984 yet another mission opportunity presented itself in the form of Habitat for Humanity which itself had emerged from the Christian commune near Americus, Georgia, Koinonia Partners. Pastor Austin had been invited to serve on the board of the Coastal Empire Habitat for Humanity but felt that he had too many other commitments and could not accept. Urging Jim Miles to serve on the board as First Baptist's representative, Austin was successful and Miles served in that capacity until 1996. In 1989 the local Habitat board was requested to consider building a house for one of the families whose membership was in the Savannah Baptist Center. First Baptist Church and Bull Street Baptist Church agreed to combine forces and support the project with funds and labor. They would renovate an old house located on 34th Street which was owned by Habitat. In spring 1991 work began and the renovation was completed in late 1993, with the house being dedicated as a home on November 14. Millard Fuller, the founder and president of Habitat for Humanity International, was present and made the major speech. The parents and their five children proudly and thankfully moved into their new residence. In addition to working on this house, young people and other members of First Baptist Church have worked on additional Habitat houses in a truly local-mission-ministry. The relationship with this truly worthy organization continues.

Crew for Habitat for Humaity. Front row volunteers L to R: unidentified volunteer, Melissa and Janis Lewis. Middle row L to R: seated, Caroline Creaser, Trina Dodd, unidentified volunteer, Todd Monfalcone, Patrick Skutch. Standing L to R: Julie Skutch, Brother Francis, Charlie Waldrop, Emily Richardson, Jim Miles.

From beginnings onward, the women of First Baptist Church have been "on mission," whether as individuals or acting as an organized group. Prior to the founding of the Women's Missionary Union in the Southern Baptist Convention in 1888, the women of the church had founded their own WMU, probably in 1879 (though 1874 is also given as a possible date). Since then this group has ably been the major mission and social arm of the church in the dimensions of support, action, and study. The organization changed its name to Baptist Women in 1969 and then to Women on Mission in 1996. (See appendix O for a listing of the twentieth-century presidents of this organization.) A partial listing of the numerous mission and social services of this long-term organization is as follows: operating a cafeteria on the corner of

The Women's Missionary Union has sponsored a variety of activities to raise awareness amd offerings for missions. In 1949 a group of WMU members and some male volunteers performed an elaborate biblical pageant.

Bay Lane and Bull Street in 1920–22 so that new pews for the church could be purchased; hosting Sunday dinners for the church and certain other visitors, such as members from Mickve Israel Synagogue; support of the publication of the church paper named *The Messenger*; bringing a number of missionaries as special speakers to the church; support of the Baptist Center, Union Mission, Grace House, jail ministry, children's homes, Baptist Student Union at Armstrong College, and many different types of mission programs; and the financial support for black women to attend special institutes for women. For two centuries the women of First Baptist Church have been at the heart of virtually every mission effort. In 1988 the church celebrated the one hundredth anniversary of the WMU in the SBC with numerous meetings. Wright, Richardson, and Austin paid special and deserved tribute to the women of the church. As the most recent member of the pastoral team, Wright affirmed: "Without question the WMU organization of this church and its affiliate women's groups provide both a core of leadership and a strong reservoir of support for the missions and ministry of this church." Richardson remembered that through the years the women had led in the study and support of mission both at home and abroad, turning mission study into mission action. He continued: "Were it not for the Baptist Women, we would be hard pressed to find the volunteers to carry out the social ministries so important to this community. Because you care enough to give of yourselves to these endeavors, we come somewhat nearer to living out our Lord's great command." The senior minister, Tom Austin, named the women of the church as "pacesetters and doers"—always true but not always officially recognized. Austin reflected: "Much of what this church has done in this community would never have been accomplished without the unflagging support of Baptist Women." As they celebrated history, Austin urged the women to "be aware that this church, at least by 1813, had a group of women who were vitally concerned for extending the Christian witness in this community and beyond. . . . It is important to keep traditions vital and alive." Indeed, the *permanent* watchword of the Women on Mission at First Baptist Church is "For we are labourers together with God" (1 Corinthians 3:9a).

More recently the youth of the church, directed by Kristin Andreason, have participated in Group Workcamp, a nondenominational organization. They have spent a week

L to R: Melissa Lewis, Betsy Davis, and Julie Skutch cooking spaghetti to raise money for work in West Virginia.

in each of the last few summers on mission in Arkansas, West Virginia, and New Hampshire. These weeks were basically work weeks for the youth and their chaperones as they performed hard labor in improving the housing of those less fortunate than the laborers. New roofs and porches, new bathroom tile, the installation of drywall, extensive painting, and more were accomplished by these young "missionaries" as they acted out in word and deed the love and grace of God with others. These young people continue to experience graceful moments at home and elsewhere as they define in their own way the meaning of mission and ministry.

Early in his tenure, John Finley reminded the congregation that it must be about the business of "reclaiming our identity as a church in mission." One important part of this reclamation was the development of a new relationship with Cuban Baptist churches.

On May 10, 1995, Kairos, a singing group representing the Fraternity of Cuban Baptist Churches, presented a spirited concert at First Baptist Church. They were enthusiastically received and in addition to giving them a love offering, a fax machine for use in the Matanzas First Baptist Church was presented. The first contact was thus made. Later in the year, Pastor Finley was invited by the Alliance of Baptists to join a group that would represent the Alliance at an annual meeting of the Fraternity of Cuban Baptist Churches. In early November this meeting took place in Havana, and Finley began the exploration of a sister church partnership with the newly constituted Alamar Baptist Church. First Baptist Church made an immediate monetary contribution toward this church's ministry and Finley himself covered some 1,500 miles on the island, distributing some three hundred pounds of medical supplies to Baptist physicians.

Later in November, upon Finley's return, the matter of the sister church relationship was referred to the Missions and Social Ministries Committee for careful consideration. The committee decided positively and the Diaconate and congregation accepted the recommendation. At this time First Baptist Church committed itself to giving $1,000 per year for the next three years to help Cuban Baptists purchase retreat property. The church also joined the Myers Park Baptist Church of Charlotte, North Carolina, in helping the Alamar

Bible School in Cuba. Standing top center L to R: Kristin Andreason, Elaine Adams, Vivian Rodriguez (wife of minister of Alamar Church).

congregation purchase an apartment for use by the church and its pastor, Eduardo Otero.

From September 4–12, 1996, First Baptist Church was represented in Alamar by a mission team composed of Cindy Schroeder and Judy Wilburn. This was a very positive experience for these two women, and the personal dimension of the sister church relationship now took on new and creative meaning.

In March 1997 First Baptist made it possible for Pastor Otero to come to the United States to attend the convocation of the Alliance of Baptists in Raleigh, North Carolina, and then to visit Savannah. Finley had met the people of Alamar; now, Otero would meet the people of First Baptist. The church partnership took on an important personal face, and the relationship arrived at a higher plateau.

L to R: Eduardo Otero, Kristin Andreason, and John Finley in Raleigh, North Carolina.

In May and June 1997 Finley, accompanied this time by Jim Flanagan, returned to Cuba with funds, medical supplies, and other items. A gift of $6,000 made possible the purchase of a larger building for the rapidly growing membership of Alamar Baptist. This contact was followed in August 25–September 2, 1997, with the visit of Kristin Andreason, Elaine Adams, Laurie Cox, and Kamala Rivera to Alamar for the purpose of conducting a Vacation Bible School. In addition, Andreason preached at an evening worship service. As on other trips, monetary contributions and various supplies were also taken. The personal dimension of the trip was enhanced by the fact that Rivera's father was a native of Camaguey, Cuba. All who participated had incredible experiences.

Also during 1997 First Baptist Church became the conduit for a gift of $25,000 contributed by Robert Pattillo Jr. and the board of directors of the Rockdale Foundation. These funds were delivered in mid-1998 for Baptist church-related causes in Cuba.

At the time of this writing, First Baptist Church has enjoyed two and one-half years of partnership with Alamar Baptist Church in Cuba and with other Baptist churches and causes on the island. In addition to the travel of members (self-paid) to Cuba, First Baptist Church has made contributions of between fifteen and twenty thousand dollars for Baptist work in Cuba. The financial relationship, however, is simply one part of a much deeper experience of ecumenical sharing of time, energy, mission, and person. This mission relationship will doubtless discover new dimensions of mutual service in the continuing partnership in the future. As of this writing, another trip by members of First Baptist Church to the Alamar sister church will take place in December 1998 or January 1999. Medical supplies and teaching aids will again be taken as the church partnership continues to evolve.

The twenty-first century will bring new opportunities for First Baptist Church in relation to ministry at home and elsewhere. The congregation and its leadership know that the fullness of God in Christ through the spirit is the basis and goal of mission for the whole creation. It is committed to the belief that the church as the body of Christ is called to be the vehicle of the fullness of God, who fills all in all. With these understandings, only the sky will be the limit in relation to mission in the twenty-first century of our Lord.

CHAPTER 10

THE ROLE OF EDUCATION

To hand on the living *traditio* (what is most real or authentic or descriptive of being in its history) of the Church and denomination from one generation to the next is probably one of the most difficult tasks of those who call themselves Christian, and in this case, Baptist. The task is accomplished in multifaceted ways, but certainly one of the most obvious of these is in the educational outlook and work of the church.

From the early days of 1800 to the last days of the twentieth century, First Baptist Church has had a wide-ranging commitment to education and has illustrated this in a constellation of ways. Both clergy and laity have shared this commitment and have believed that the believing Christian must also be a thinking Christian. Faith and reason are then not contradictory but complementary.

The general public has been made aware of this early educational interest by the plaque in the sidewalk at 22 Broughton Street, West, which marks the site of early Deacon Josiah Penfield's home and business. Placed there in 1950, it tells of Penfield's $2,500 gift to the Georgia Baptist Convention "to create a fund for the education of pious young men for the gospel ministry." In 1833 Mercer Institute (later, University) opened, and among the thirty-nine students, seven began to prepare themselves for the Baptist ministry. The first pastor, Henry Holcombe, was described as in the "progressive wing of the Baptist denomination" and believed strongly in a sound education for the church's ministry. In the nineteenth and even into the twentieth centuries in Baptist circles there would not always be this confidence in, and expectation of, an educated ministry; emphasis had been placed upon the "call" at the expense of the "educated." Indeed some Baptists still frown upon what they consider to be an overly educated ministry. Over 50 percent of Baptist ministers in the twentieth century have had no formal university or seminary/divinity school education. Many have attended "Bible schools" but nowhere else.

First Baptist Church has been served by a huge majority of well-educated pastors, some of whom either served before in institutions of higher learning or after in such schools—that is, "before" and "after" their tenure of service at First Baptist. Eight of the thirty persons (thirty-two pastorates) who have served the church, either before or after, were presidents of a college or university: W. B. Johnson, Anderson College; J. G. Binney, Columbian College (now George Washington University); Joseph T. Robert, Burlington University; Thomas Rambaut, William Jewell College; W. Lowndes Pickard, Mercer University; Joseph Judson Taylor, Georgetown College; John E. White, Anderson College; and G. Leroy Cleverdon, Judson College. Those with other close associations with and appointments to educational institutions would include Albert Williams, professor, Mercer University; J. B. Stiteler, professor, Baylor University; and W. Forrest Lanier, vice president, Shorter College. In addition, every pastor serving in the twentieth century had a university and seminary or divinity school education. The schools

Penfield plaque at 22 West Broughton Street.

attended include some of the finest in the United States such as Tulane, Yale, Furman, Mercer, Southern Baptist Theological Seminary, and Southeastern Seminary (prior to the latter two schools becoming simply mouthpieces of neofundamentalism). A select number of the pastors also earned doctorates (Ph.D.s and D. Min.s) in various fields and schools, and yet others were awarded the honorary Doctor of Divinity (D.D.) degree in recognition of their contributions in ministry, often in education. A large number of the twentieth-century pastors studied and traveled in Europe and the Near East, some attending world-class universities such as Oxford University, the University of Basel, the University of Heidelberg, and Edinburgh University. World travel by these ministers was also made to Cuba, Israel, Egypt, Sweden, England, Scotland, Germany, and Switzerland. Some have attended international meetings involving the Baptist World Alliance, the World Council of Churches, and the Faith and Order Movement.

Such widespread exposure to the wider world was in itself another kind of educational experience. Through the century the church encouraged and sponsored educational leaves for the various ministers, even including time to work on additional educational degrees. Built into the package for every minister presently is a sabbatical leave program wherein the minister is allowed six weeks each two years to "recharge his/her batteries" through some kind of educational experience. It is simply a truism that every search committee in relation to any of the ministerial vacancies in the past as well as the future carefully considers the educational background of the candidates. At First Baptist the "call" is primary in its importance, but that "call" is also expected to include the formal educational experience in its total commitment of loving God and serving the people. In 1905 the church refused to ordain B. A. Hurley because "he had not studied systematically." Within a few years he had fulfilled that commitment and was ordained. An educated congregation is satisfied with no less than a formally educated ministry. Due to recent developments in the SBC and in this denomination's educational institutions, future search committees will look even more carefully at educational credentials.

Special attention and gifts to institutions of higher learning have been perennially given by the church. Perhaps the most recent symbolic gift was in 1995 when the

Church library contains 2,570 books, videos, and tapes. The collection includes reference, fiction, nonfiction, biographies, and history. Volunteers have given much time to its operation under the guidance of Joan Fulcher, May McCall, and Evalyn Miles.

original Penfield one was remembered in a $2,500 gift for the new Mercer University School of Theology, which opened in the fall of 1996.

Passing on the *traditio* in any church depends on a vast number of sources and factors. Certainly the basic educational values of the congregation are first and foremost. Then comes the educated ministry, funds allocated, church library founded, continuously educated and informed congregation, and, of course, the various organizations, each of which contributes in its own way to the educational process. Of these organizations the Sunday School is central. With one of the oldest Sunday Schools in the SBC, First Baptist had perennially nurtured, matured, and enhanced this organization—as well, staying abreast of current educational methods and principles.

In 1926 the church took a major step by building a new Bible School building to house its growing Sunday School program. Fully 50 percent of the real estate of the church would be dedicated to this building. Pastor Cox at the time was aware that simply a new building was not enough. To assure excellence in teaching, he began an intense series of lectures for those who wished to teach. At the end of the series, those who attended would be tested and awarded, if passing, a "Normal Course Diploma." Cox knew that the "call" for a Sunday School teacher was much like his own as a minister and that it, too, involved the discipline of study and becoming educated to a level that could result in being a teacher. Not everyone in the congregation had that talent within the call. The next year, 1927, the spotlight was upon the Sunday School's numerous contributions to the church in the special centennial celebrations of its founding.

Sunday School had its ups and downs over the next decades but remained a vital source of education in the church with a predominantly positive thrust. By the late seventies the times within the denomination dictated new problems involving the search for appropriate educational materials committed to a moderate, ecumenical Baptist approach that would lend themselves to a true Christian education and not to neofundamentalist brainwashing. That search remains flexible and open to the best materials. Presently, some materials come from the Smyth and Helwys publishing agency in Macon which has developed excellent Sunday School curriculum literature from a moderate Baptist perspective. It was highly predictable that First Baptist would turn to such a capable and honest church-material publisher for its educational literature.

Chris Fuller served briefly as Sunday School director (superintendent) in the early nineties and at the close of 1993 submitted a report about the Sunday School under the title "My Philosophy of Christian Education and a Proposal." His proposal was that a full-time minister of education be employed and called for "increased emphasis, with staff and money, to its Christian education program." He concluded that church growth and collegiality depended on getting a minister of education as the leader for recruiting leadership as well as membership.

In 1995 young and energetic Kristin Andreason joined the staff as assistant minister and has since then played a major role in Christian education at the church, especially among young people. September 1995 was a special Sunday for celebrating the New Beginning for Sunday School. Andreason was encouraged with the beginning of several new classes and her enthusiasm was contagious. Her role in Christian education will certainly be a critical one in the next few years, for First Baptist does need a younger set of members who will carry on the constellation of needs in the early years of the twenty-first century. Lay leadership is obviously a major necessity in addition to Andreason's work. From Robert C. Brown, 1827 superintendent, to Barbara Creaser and Doug Craig, 1998 co-superintendents, the church has been able to supply energetic and creative lay leaderships for its Sunday School. This must continue. New horizons will be sought as the whole congregation wrestles with the perennial question of the most effective means of sharing the essence of its faith in a contemporary key.

It is clear that Christian education in any church is a requisite to ministry. It is also a fact that this education is far broader than Sunday School or whether a church has a minister of education. The greening of the church in relation to education must be a total-member endeavor and commitment. Pastoral leadership must be foremost as well. Seminaries and divinity schools in the last several decades have exerted untold creative energies in the direction of curriculum changes which should more adequately equip the contemporary minister in his/her role as Christian educator.

In the history of how Christian Baptists here and elsewhere have tried to hand on the essence of faith, both admiration and alienation, both love and understanding and dogmatism are to be found. The means have at times been mistaken for the ends and the relative has too often been absolutized. To speak in Catholic terms, essences have too often been neglected and accidents made central. The contemporary secular and religious situation has tremendously aggravated the problems of religious education as well. The vast amount of information and knowledge coming to light about humans and their environment is expected to be harmonized quickly and neatly with humans' spiritual heritage. Everyone seems to want a "quick fix." However, superficial answers have not proven themselves to be satisfactory and in-depth answers have not been easily nor quickly found. Doubtless, the crises to be faced in the next century by First Baptist call for bravery and creativity in the field of Christian education. The task is formidable, but if past history of a congregation is any indicator, First Baptist will again succeed in this aspect of its pilgrimage.

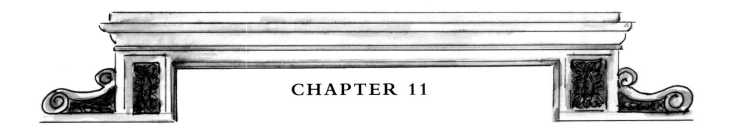

CHAPTER 11

THE PRIESTHOOD OF ALL BELIEVERS

The famous teacher and theologian, Robert McAfee Brown, correctly notes in his *The Spirit of Protestantism* that "the best safeguard against . . . institutionalized and individualized distortions of the meaning of grace is a proper understanding of the 'priesthood of all believers.'" From their beginnings Baptists submitted to this theological insight of the Protestant movement. More hierarchically oriented neofundamentalists such as W. A. Criswell have more recently rejected this doctrine in their "break" with their own Baptist history. Among moderates, however, it remains a centrally important doctrine. If Protestants in general have not always understood its meaning, they have continued to subscribe to its doctrinal value. The doctrine's correct meaning has to do with each believer's being a priest to every other person—the horizontal dimension which takes place in community, the church. It is not crass, self-centered individuality; it necessitates community and out-going service. This doctrine raises the whole *laos*, the whole laity, to the level of the priesthood. Luther called Christians to be a "Christ to your neighbor" and a long neglected New Testament maxim of the priesthood of all believers was restored for practice and discussion. It means that all members of the church participate in ministry both within and outside the actual buildings of the community. Priests of God come together on weekends but go everywhere in the secular world on weekdays—but they are ministers in both settings. For good theological reasons, recent pastors of First Baptist have preferred the title of "senior minister"—perhaps first, but first among equals. Perhaps the major contribution of the Protestant movement to world Christianity is this idea of one essential ministry in the Church—thus, the priesthood of all believers as participants in that ministry. In its total history, First Baptist Church has subscribed in word and deed to this primary Protestant doctrine.

All of this is to introduce a chapter that will simply look at some of these priests of God and their contributions in ministry both within and outside the church. A full presentation would include the full membership; this will be a selective presentation and doubtless, some important priests will either be overlooked or not mentioned. No offense should be taken for none is intended, nor should a true servant of God suffer pain because one's name goes unnamed. The joy of ministry is the ministry itself. This is a bit of an apology, however, because so many of these pilgrim-priests on the road do merit attention.

In this chapter few staff members will be given attention and only a cross section of priests from the twentieth century will be discussed. Until recently in religious circles, women generally did most of the work and men received most of the credit. These female priests will definitely receive attention here.

Too many pages to number could be included here and in the appendices of resolutions adopted in the Minutes of the church and Diaconate in honor of so many worthy priests of both centuries. The list would almost be unending but would certainly include the following: George Mosse, W. H. Mathers, John Rose (the first deacons), Mary Robert, all the various clerks (with clear as well as difficult script), Matthew Lufburrow, Josiah Penfield, Charles Watson West, Mrs. F. J. M. Baker, and John F. Sweat. To all these and others, a hearty "bravo" and kudos glowing are extended.

Those who record history usually labor unseen offstage while front-and-center stage is given to those who make history. If we did not have those who record and contemplate, however, those on center stage would not be remembered so well. The LaFar family produced two historians and one on center stage; all were members of First Baptist. Sanford Branch LaFar (1876–1965) married Mabel Freeman (1878–1947) at First Church in April 1901. The union produced two daughters, Margaret Freeman (1905–1987) and Mabel Branch (b. 1913). The mother and wife, Mabel Freeman, became the historian par excellence of the church. Her historical interests were broad and extended beyond the church and into the Savannah community. She had to have spent thousands of hours in her preservation and compilation of church records and archives. The two-volume set of materials which she completed, consisting of 1,044 pages, covered the first thirty-six years of the church's history and was divided into three parts—church organization, biographical sketches of the pastors, and abstracts of the Minutes of the congregation covering its first thirty-six years. She even included a detailed index of all the materials. Her dedication page is worthy of being presented in full—for prior to women even being accepted as deacons, she dedicated her volumes to them. She had observed multiple illustrations of the fact that the church would not have survived without their ever-present contributions. Her page of praise reads as follows:

> The early era of church history place[s] the responsibility for the church on the deacons and "male members." There is no written record to show how the women unofficially assumed their responsibility by serving as "home advisors," but it is most probable that this was so.

> Modern times reveal significant changes in church customs, for, instead of the men and women sitting on opposite sides of the meeting house, they have sat together for a number of years, and together they now take their places in assuming their responsibilities for the welfare of their church.

> And so, I have dedicated this work to the women who with a oneness of purpose, have even done the multitudinous little things which made possible and kept alive The First Baptist Church of Savannah, Georgia.

The contribution of Mabel LaFar in relation to the history of the church could not possibly be underscored too much—she remains the historian of the church. Her interests

Deacons, 1950. Bottom row L to R: Royce Thompson, Lee Rivers, John G. Kennedy Sr., ★ *Judge Saxton Daniel, Bruce Griffin, Otis Stubbs,* ★ *Dr. Leroy G. Cleverdon (Minister),* ★ *Branch LaFar,* ★ *Callie Helmly, Thomas Wren, J. Curtis Lewis Jr.* ★; *Second row L to R: Ray Alexander, Clyde Mixon, H. A. Moak, D. Boyd Yarley, A. U. Futrell,* ★ *D. G. Morgan,* ★ *Wade Layton, Roy Carr, Parker Dewberry, William C. Sutton Jr.* ★; *Third row L to R: H. R. Tarver, Fred Scholl, Hunter Via, Fred Haymans; Fourth row L to R: Charles W. McCall,* ★ *G. B. Bainbridge, P. O. Phillips, Francis M. Oliver,* ★ *J. A. Kelley, Dennis Harvey, D. D. Edwards, Howell Cone.*

★*Indicates there is a biographical sketch in the text.*

in preserving history were witnessed more broadly, as well. As librarian of the Lachlan McIntosh Daughters of the American Revolution, she was mainly responsible for assembling a bookshelf of genealogies and state archives in Hodgson Hall. With Carolyn Price Wilson she collaborated in compiling *The Abstract of Wills, Chatham County, 1773–1817,* published by the National Genealogical Society in Washington, D.C. A charter member of the Savannah Historical Research Association, she made major contributions to research projects having to do with the history of Chatham County, including the compilation of the *General Index to Savannah, Georgia Newspapers, 1763–1845.*

Mabel's husband, Sanford Branch, was also active in church and community. With both such active roles, some weeks they must have been like ships passing in the night. Elected as treasurer of the church in 1929, he served in that office for thirty years. It is sometimes presently said that during the difficult Depression years he and J. C. Lewis kept the church financially solvent. He was honored by the church by being voted a Life Deacon as well as treasurer-emeritus. He served as an executive officer of the Georgia State Savings Bank for fifty-eight years where his trademark was a flower which he wore everyday in his lapel. Also the treasurer of the Savannah Chamber of Commerce for many years, in retirement he was a board member of the Union Mission and for many years raised funds in Savannah for the mission's projects. Upon thirty years of service in the church, Branch made the cover of *The Calendar* (1959) and was honored with these words: "His genial personality, his high sense of responsibility and his noble Christian character are qualities which have endeared him to all."

Branch and Mabel's daughter, Margaret Freeman LaFar, lived in her parents' shadow, but gave her own unique service to both church and community. Following in her mother's footsteps, she was a historian and an educator. Never married, she devoted herself to her work and her family. First a teacher and then principal at Romana Riley Elementary School, she later became principal of Herty Elementary School. Remembered as a highly contributive teacher to students as well as colleagues, she became a loved and admired administrator who nevertheless ran a "tight ship" that practiced no favoritism, a quality generally desired by teachers. At Pastor Austin's urging, she picked up her mother's historical mantle in the early 1970s and wore it proudly and effectively. Doing a great deal of research herself, she also utilized her mother's volumes to make a major contribution to the 175th anniversary celebration of the church. Her *A Historical Sketch of the First Baptist Church, Savannah, Georgia* is a thirty-six page pamphlet loaded with valuable historical information concerning First Baptist. She opened her work with these descriptive words about her church, "Established in faith; nurtured in hope; continuing in love." Mother, father, and daughter had indeed given of themselves as priests in faith, hope, and love.

Francis M. Oliver (1872–1954) led a discussion in the deacons' meeting of October 12, 1938, favoring the ordination of women as deacons. His discussion was tabled, but he had shown his prophetic spirit and insight and his courage to support what he thought was right even when he was probably a minority of one. He served for many years as a deacon and taught a Sunday School class for over thirty years. His Christian witness extended in numerous directions in Savannah. Oliver received his law degree from Vanderbilt University in 1896 and was admitted to the Georgia bar in the same year. He established residence in Savannah. Married to Juliet P. Ashurst in 1902, he was elected city alderman in the same year and served a four-year term. It is said that "he was a zealous alderman, alive to the problems of the city." He served when City Hall was built in 1906 and his name is inscribed on the marble slab in the rotunda. Achieving success as a lawyer in Savannah, he gave a great deal of energy to many projects which contributed to the community's progress. For example, he served as a director of the Savannah Motor Club, as president of the Oglethorpe Highway Association, and as vice president of the Georgia Highway Association, championing the cause for better roads in Savannah, Chatham County, and south Georgia. He early on agitated for a new bridge across the Savannah River to connect the city with the coastal section of South Carolina. A past president and very active member of the Kiwanis Club, he also became a booster for the raising of cattle and diversified crops in Georgia. Again as a prophet, he envisioned a sales tax in Georgia and parking meters in Savannah. Oliver was a staunch supporter of the Salvation Army, serving on the board for many years and at the time of his death was vice chairman of the board. When he died, he was publicly honored with these comments:

It was characteristic of Frank Oliver, that he gauged his decisions and acts in life strictly upon a basis of what he sincerely believed to be the right thing to do. A man of vigorous conviction, he was never afraid to express them openly regardless of consequences.

Along with his pastor, Leroy Cleverdon, his character was tried in the crucible of grief and sorrow during World War II, for his son, Francis McDonald Oliver Jr., a West Point graduate, died in action in Europe.

The church named a Sunday School class for him and the Savannah Bar Association appointed him as their first chaplain in 1952. On March 27, 1954, the City Court of Savannah mourned his death and stood in recess during the hours of the funeral. The Superior Court of Chatham County adopted resolutions honoring him in its Minutes and stipulated that "the Staff of this court be draped for a period of thirty (30) days." Judge David Atkinson wrote: "I believe that Mr. Oliver's every act was motivated by an earnest desire to better his country and improve his fellow man." This priest of God had expressed himself effectively in the civic as well as the religious arena. Again, there had been interpenetration of the two spheres of church and state. Frank Oliver's religious faith was expressed in both his Sunday School class as well as in the civic halls of justice and government.

J. Marcus Stubbs (1893–1978) as remembered by J. Curtis Lewis Jr., and indeed by all who knew him, was a "doer"—an activist. James's injunction, "Be ye doers of the word and not hearers only," was taken literally and seriously by Marc Stubbs. Active from the start (in the early years of his membership he taught a boy's Sunday School class) in the church, Stubbs was a creative activist in numerous parts of the public arena where he served for over thirty-two years. A veteran of World War I, Stubbs served for twenty years as postmaster of Savannah (1942–1962) and at the age of seventy-four ran successfully for a term as alderman in the city. As postmaster he left a national legacy—he originated the snorkel-type street letter mailbox which is so useful to motorists. During his tenure as postmaster, two national commemorative stamps were issued which gave wide publicity to Savannah—the Juliette Gordon Low and the Steamship Savannah stamps. He also gave of himself in designing a plan that resulted in the erection of two high-rise apartment buildings for the elderly in Savannah. One of those was named in his honor, Stubbs Towers. In 1976 he was tabbed Veteran of the Year in Chatham County and in the same year received the highest honor of the DAR—the Medal of Honor. Stubbs was also the subject on two different occasions of nationally noted columnist Tom Coffey. Coffey called Stubbs the right kind of "busybody" and concluded his second column with these perceptive words: "That's the example Marc Stubbs set that I was referring to: Not only should we count our blessings, we should use them. The old gentleman who never was old used his wisely and constructively. He shared

The beauty of the sanctuary makes it a popular place for weddings. Mary Stubbs stands with her father Marcus in the narthex before her marriage to John Tyson in 1952.

those blessings." After his death, he was given full editorial coverage in the *Savannah Morning News* on February 18, 1978, and on April 30 the new church hymnal, *Hymnbook for Christian Worship*, given in honor of Stubbs by his friend J. Curtis Lewis Jr., was dedicated and then used weekly for two decades. It was in that service that Lewis named him a "doer" par excellence. Pastor Austin had at Stubbs's funeral referred to the heavily marked March calendar of this eighty-five-year old and observed:

> He taught us how to grow old. Marc did not see the future as an enemy. He did not spend his time wishing for the days past. Rather he saw the present as an opportunity. Although he was born in another century, he was at home in the age in which he lived. He did not believe the best had been. But he did believe that it could be. And with God's help, he would make it come to pass.

Commemorative resolutions upon his death were adopted by the state house of representatives and by the aldermen and mayor of Savannah. The major prongs of his service were nicely summarized by the latter resolution of March 9, 1978:

> He spent his energies to help improve this community, as is evidenced by his involvement in the establishment of a Naval R.O.T.C. unit at Savannah State College; by being an original proponent of the relocating of Savannah's railway passenger station from West Broad to Telfair Road, thus speeding up the building of U.S. [Interstate] Highway 16 along the old right of way leading to Union Station; by his pushing for construction of the Savannah Civic Center and leading the effort to place the Eternal Flame in front of the main entrance as a memorial to the area's war dead; by his promoting the Skidaway Island causeway bond issue and development of the marine and oceanographic centers there; and by his serving senior citizens; particularly for initiating a plan resulting in having two high-rise apartment buildings for Savannah's elderly. . . .

To his church, his family, and his beautiful city he left a legacy of numerous deeds and dreams. He was a faithful pilgrim who literally went all places during weekdays. Perhaps minor, but the present writer will always remember this man upon mailing a letter on a rainy day by means of the snorkel mailbox!

Henry Ludlow Ashmore (1920–1995) was an educator educated to the principle that one could be a believing as well as a thinking person. Faith and reason were defining parts of his person. After completing his doctorate at the University of Florida, Ashmore's career began and continued for four years at Georgia State Teachers' College (now Georgia Southern University) where he served as the director of student teaching. At the young age of thirty-three he and his wife, Clarice, moved to Pensacola, Florida, where he began an eleven-year tenure as the first president of Pensacola Junior College. Ashmore developed the small "family" of 325 students and eleven faculty within eleven years to 3,800 students and 165 faculty. Known for continuing the "family" spirit and for bringing the "town and gown" into a mutually encouraging and supporting relationship, he was honored in 1990 with the Fine Arts Center on campus being named for him in an impressive ceremony. Clarice remembered those years as the "honeymoon" experience and she was really reluctant to leave. She knew, however, that her husband was a "builder" and in the summer of 1964 they moved to Savannah where he became president of Armstrong College (now Armstrong Atlantic State University). He guided the school's move from a two-year school to a four-year college. During his eighteen-year tenure it grew from 500 students and thirty-five faculty to over 3,000 students and 155 faculty. Five academic programs expanded to the number of forty, and the first graduate program was initiated in 1971. When he left Armstrong in 1982, he became the associate executive director of the Commission on Colleges for the Southern Association of Colleges and Schools. When he retired in 1991 he continued work as a consultant in education and in 1994 served as interim president of Anderson College in South Carolina. To Ashmore, the word "retirement" was definitely a contextual term for he continued serving until his death.

Known as "Lud" to his friends at First Baptist, he was a respected Bible teacher as well as a long-term deacon who served terms as chair of the Diaconate as well. Ashmore was active through the years serving on numerous committees; he even filled the pulpit on several occasions. Ashmore is a good example that theology must not be left to the "specialists." If theology means loving God with the mind, then every pilgrim of God is called upon to do this. If faith must be in search of understanding, no one is exempt from the demand. The layperson must love God with his/her mind; laypersons must seek to understand their faith. This means that Christianity and education must travel hand in hand. To this truth, Henry Ashmore was committed and tried to tug numerous other pilgrims down the road of ideas where faith discovers understanding.

The Buckner/George/Scudder families stretch back in the church's history for six generations and to baptisms in 1853 and 1870. The fourth generation in this genealogical history sees the names of Frank Vreeland George Jr. and his wife Allene (Elizabeth Wilkie). Vreeland formally became a part of the congregation in 1934 at his baptism. Since then his name appears numerous times in the varied activities of the congregation and Diaconate. Voted a Life Deacon, Vreeland served on two occasions as chair. His well-rounded service also saw him as Sunday School director, serving numerous terms on committees, but especially as the Budget and Finance Committee chair as well as on that committee every layperson dreads—the Pastoral Search Committee. He has done yeoman's work on that committee on three different occasions. A consulting civil engineer for forty-five years with a "Ramblin' Wreck" degree, George has been active in the wider community within the Rotary Club and Chamber of Commerce, holding numerous leadership positions, as well as being a board member of the Royce Learning Center. George has expressed himself honestly through the years on prickly issues, but has also been open to new ideas. When Pastor Austin discussed the issue of "open membership" for the first time, George wanted to know whether this was truly "Baptistic." Education then took place through straightforward dialogue and discussion. To George's credit, it must be observed that he was more interested as a deacon in dialogue than diatribe, part of the description of the true pilgrim who is "on the way."

Ralph Francis Crutcher (1906–1988), as president of the Warsaw Lumber and Trading Company, was widely traveled and encountered many new ideas and cultures in his travels. He was, then, ecumenically educated through business and is remembered as a man of quiet loyalty. He, his wife, Eleanor, and his daughters have been described as deeply committed to the principle of loving one's neighbor as oneself and for serving within this construct of faith. They were "people persons." A Life Deacon in the church, he also taught young people in a Sunday School class. It will be remembered that it was he who interviewed Forrest Lanier in Edinburgh and was served delicious homemade coconut cake by Gene Lanier, thus sealing the call to Forrest, according to Gene. A Phi Beta Kappa graduate of the University of Alabama, Ralph had a winsome and charismatic personality and thus was very effective in fund-raising. In the community he was an active Rotarian and served on the boards of the Salvation Army and the

Science Museum. Since he took so many business trips he became an amateur photographer and was known for giving numerous slide shows at home and church. Whether inviting someone to a slide show or urging a member to do better in relation to stewardship, it was difficult to say "no" to this man. Crutcher was a world pilgrim and an excellent illustration of the "golden rule." At his funeral, Jody Wright reflected on his family loyalty: "He was a grateful man. He was grateful for life itself, and he enjoyed life as much as anyone could. He lived each of his almost eighty-three years with a zest which characterized his appreciation for life. He was grateful for his family, and held family as the dearest gift he had received in life." One might add to this that his church was his extended family and the second dearest gift he had received in life.

Jane Blakely Jennings, M.D., joined First Baptist Church by letter from the Wilmington Island Baptist Church in July 1982 with bookends of service to the community on both sides of 1982. Baptists do move around and the church was fortunate indeed to welcome such an unassuming, generous, respected, and loyal member such as Jane. Since becoming a member, she has taught Sunday School, sung in the choir, and achieved a hallmark in the Diaconate. In the year Tom Austin left, Jennings became the first female chair of the Diaconate and accomplished an unusually successful tenure, especially in light of just losing the senior minister and beginning a major capital fund campaign. Receiving her medical degree from the Medical College of South Carolina, she interned at Philadelphia General Hospital (1962–63) and did a first year of residency in Mobile, Alabama, completing her residency at Memorial Hospital in Savannah (1965–68). From 1973 to 1991 she was director of the pathology laboratory at the Memorial Medical Center and from 1977 to the present, a clinical assistant professor, Department of Laboratory Medicine, Medical University of South Carolina. Serving in numerous important capacities with the American Red Cross, in 1997 she became medical director of Southeast Region Blood Services. Certainly proud in 1977 of being president of the Georgia Association of Pathologists, perhaps she was even more proud in 1981 when she received the "Boss of the Year" Award from the American Business Women's Association in Savannah. Published widely, she is also a member of at least eleven professional societies. Medical pilgrims who give of themselves in such multifaceted ways are almost revered by the average layperson. In this case, the physician is worthy of the revering.

Julius Curtis Lewis (1876–1942) came to Savannah in 1894 at the age of eighteen with only $21 in his pocket. The story of his life is a "rags to riches" saga and a good illustration of a self-made person rising from an obscure background to one of leadership, financial security, and prominence. He started in Savannah as a clerk in the Savannah Guano Company. Later he worked for a loan company and then was a clerk with Foye and Morrison, a dry goods store. While there, he began to study bookkeeping at night at the Richards Business College. From this position, he went to bookkeeper for the automotive firm of Thomas A. Bryson and later rose to the level of manager. In October 1912 Lewis became associated with the Ford Motor Company and from that time on he steadily expanded his Ford dealership and at the same time he expanded his real estate holdings. The J. C. Lewis Motor Company became well-known in Savannah and beyond. In 1920 he married Lucy May Wiegand and they had one son, Julius Curtis Lewis Jr. Lewis Sr. was active in every aspect of the church and along with Branch LaFar virtually carried the church financially through the Great Depression. Voted a Life Deacon, Lewis was as loyal to his church as he was to his business. Here was one self-made man who did not forget his moorings.

Lewis Sr.'s only son was reared and nurtured from the start in the church, from the "cradle roll" to the Diaconate. Lewis Jr. was baptized on Easter Sunday, 1938, at the age of twelve. In later years he served as a Sunday School teacher as well as a member of the Diaconate, having two terms as chair. Elected Life Deacon he also was honored by having Lewis Hall named for him. Through the years his financial generosity to the church saw numerous fruits, more recently as he provided the Union Mission properties as well as the new and remodeled facilities for the new Baptist Center on Wheaton Street. Both facilities have made countless contributions to homeless as well as disadvantaged persons. One can only admire such illustrations of positive stewardship. This eminently successful businessman also made an important contribution to the church during the tension of the civil rights movement. He became good friends with W. W. Law, head of the NAACP in Savannah, and during the time Lewis served as mayor, he often greeted Law at the door of the church, welcoming him to service, for the church had an absolutely open door policy in relation to race—first, experientially, and then by formal vote. Lewis and Law actually bonded during those days and developed a friendship which resulted in their collaboration on many community activities.

An honor graduate of the University of Georgia in business administration, Lewis also served in the U.S. Navy, Coast Guard, and Merchant Marine. Well-known nationally in the automotive industry, Lewis is presently president and CEO of J. C. Lewis Enterprises, which includes companies in several fields such as broadcasting, automotive, equipment leasing, real estate, and insurance. His interests are multidisciplinary. On numerous fraternal and civic boards (for example Union Mission and Bethesda Home for Boys), Lewis has also received a medley of awards and recognitions. Among those awards for service are the Union Mission Golden Heart Award, the "Others" Award from the Salvation Army, and the Brotherhood Award from the Agudath Achim Synagogue. Active in politics, Lewis was elected mayor of Savannah for one term, 1966–1970. He was the first Republican to be elected mayor of a Georgia city since the days of Reconstruction. One of his aldermen that term was, of course, Marc Stubbs. First Baptist was represented in a major way in city government. It is a truism that political action and "holy worldliness" are integral parts of "sharing the good news." Lewis, Stubbs, and others who participate so actively in the political process take Christianity into the public arena with them. Surely they wrestle with the issue of conscience and compromise, but it is also a truism that society cannot expect evil persons to produce good government. These political pilgrims become representatives of the larger people of God as they instill their values into the political system. Politics and "holy worldliness" go together with witness, service, and community.

Tom Coffey, noted columnist, called John B. Rabun (1916–1991) "my x-ray doctor" and numerous others remember him for his gifts of beautiful flowers grown by his own "green thumb." Those who stopped for a moment to admire and smell the flowers in a small plot near the First Baptist Church's entrance were also unknowingly indebted to him, for he took the time and care to develop and nurture this small garden in the midst of concrete.

Rabun received his medical degree from the Medical College of Georgia in 1943 and within one year he was serving as a captain in the U.S. Army Medical Corps in the United States, England, and France. At war's end he entered general practice in Millen, Georgia, and then radiology practice in Fayetteville, North Carolina. In 1952 he moved to Savannah in radiology practice where he remained until his retirement in 1987. At the time of his retirement he was president of Savannah Radiologists. In 1972 he had been honored by being appointed a Fellow in the American College of Radiology. During his career he served on numerous boards, organizations, and societies, and was president of the Georgia Medical Society (local) and delegate to the Medical Association House of Delegates. His wide-ranging activities were recognized in two special awards. In 1990 he received the Medical Association of Georgia's Civic Endeavor Award for the outstanding service he had rendered in Savannah. The next year the Rotary Club of Savannah recognized him for being an example par excellence of the Rotary's Creed of Service. Indeed, the list of services by John Rabun to Savannah and the state reads like a true Who's Who list. Following his death he continued to be honored by the community when in 1992 the John B. Rabun Award was established to be given each year to a Georgia Medical Society member for contributions to the community. The very next year another John B. Rabun Award was begun by the Medical Association of Georgia (the state association) to be given yearly to a local medical society in the state for excellence in community activities.

At various times in its history, the church has turned over its leadership to the members of the youth group. Youth would fill a variety of positions in worship from song leader to minister. Here Forrest Lanier turns over his Bible to Youth minister John Rabun Jr.

John Rabun was certainly an activist in the civic community but not to the neglect of his church community. Honored as a Life Deacon, he served for four different terms as chair (1960, 1972, 1975, 1982) but also was president of the Men's Brotherhood, superintendent of a Sunday School department, and chair of multiple committees, including three different pastoral search committees. When he completed his Deacon Information Sheet and was asked to list the areas of his greatest interest in the church, he simply wrote one word—"serving." According to Jody Wright, this "serving" involved being "even tempered" and working quietly and effectively as a "peacemaker." Indeed, "blessed are the peacemakers, for they shall be called children of God." Rabun nurtured his flowers, his neighbors, his church, his family, and his patients.

At Rabun's funeral Wright called attention to the anonymous "The Physician's Prayer" as a true reflection of Rabun's attitude and efforts:

Lord, who on earth didst minister
To those who helpless lay
In pain and weakness, hear me now,
As unto Thee I pray.

Give to mine eyes the power to see
The hidden source of ill,
Give to my hand the healing touch
The throb of pain to still.

Grant that mine ears be swift to hear
The cry of those in pain;
Give to my tongue the words that bring
Comfort and strength again.

Fill Thou my heart with tenderness,
My brain with wisdom true,
And when in weariness I sink,
Strengthen Thou me anew.
So in Thy footsteps may I tread,
Strong in Thy strength always,
So may I do Thy blessed work
And praise thee day by day.

On November 15, 1992, the history room of the church was dedicated and named in honor of his life of service. This pilgrim physician had never failed to notice and attend to other pilgrims on the road in their difficulties and needs. One ecumenical footnote must be given. Sister Mary Faith of St. Joseph's Hospital in Savannah participated in Rabun's funeral ceremony and this was the first time that she had ever participated in a Baptist service.

Rabun's three loves were family and home, church, and profession. He was devoted and very proud of his wife, Alsie, and his son, John Jr. They, too, have made unique contributions. Alsie has served on a vast-ranging number of civic committees in Savannah and the state. For her numerous contributions to the PTA, she was honored with a life membership. In the church her contributions are also wide-ranging. In addition to serving effectively on two occasions as the president of Women on Mission (1956–57, 1981–82), she also was elected as a deacon. Alsie chaired the committee for the 175th anniversary of the church as well as the one to celebrate the one hundredth anniversary of the WMU. She presently is a member of the History Book Committee which has planned this present work and will yet plan the special bicentennial year of celebration. John and Alsie were always a servant team in their togetherness.

The Rabuns' son, John Jr., accepted graciously the "serving" mantle of his father and mother and has made unique contributions on an international level. John Jr. as a young child was active in the full range of activities in First Church following his parents' move to Savannah in 1952. Baptized as a member in 1957, he served as youth pastor of the church during his junior year in high school. During his senior year at Mercer University, he was ordained by First Church on January 1, 1967—the only young man who was ordained during Pastor Lanier's tenure. Upon graduation from Mercer, he continued his higher education at The Southern Baptist Theological Seminary and at the Kent School of Social Work at the University of Louisville, completing his work in 1971. Working in social service units in Louisville, Kentucky, by 1978 he rose to the position of program manager of field services with the Department for Human Services. From 1980 to 1984 he was program manager with the same department for the Exploited and Missing Child Unit, building a national reputation in the investigation of cases involving sexually victimized and exploited children. In 1984 he moved to his present position of Vice President and Chief Operating Officer of the National Center for Missing and Exploited Children, in Arlington, Virginia. Widely published and with guest appearances on national television and radio talk shows, Rabun Jr. has a national reputation on the subject commitment of the center. Widely honored, his awards include the 1985 Distinguished Alumnus Award from the University of Louisville, the 1993 Presidential Award from the International Association for Healthcare Security and Safety, and the 1991 Russell L. Colling Literary Award by the same association. Following in his father's footsteps in relation to worthy and widespread service, he is a deacon in the Columbia Baptist Church of Falls Church, Virginia. Pastor Lanier could never have predicted on that New Year's Day of 1967 that he was leading the ordination for a young man who would be so far-reaching in his own service and ministry to missing and exploited children. The seeds of John Rabun Sr.'s flowers were widely sown by his as well as his wife's and son's dedicated service.

Four generations of the Usher family are and have been members of the church. Rose Smith Usher is the "mother" of these generations and made religious history at First Baptist in 1974 when she became one of the two first females voted onto the Diaconate. Later, she made history again as the first female Life Deacon in the church's history. Prior to that she had a long tenure as teacher of the young girls in a Sunday School class as well as serving as president of Women on Mission, 1964–1965, and as chair of the Outreach Committee. In the community she was instrumental in the founding of the original auxiliary of the Georgia Medical Society in Savannah and was on a number of local and state committees. Her son, Jack Holmes Usher Sr., has had a distinguished career as a jurist in Savannah, especially in his service from 1966 to 1970, first as assistant city attorney and then as city attorney. Baptized in the church in 1938, Jack served as chair of the Diaconate on three occasions and as chair of the Finance Committee six times. Serving as attorney of the church for twenty years, he chartered the Savannah Baptist Center and was also attorney for the Florence Crittendon Home (for unwed mothers). His wife, Joan C. Usher, looks upon herself as more of a team player. However, she "led" for years as a Sunday School teacher on several levels, has served as president of the Garden Club of Savannah, and was for twenty years a part-time docent for the Juliette Gordon Low National Center in Savannah. In marriage, church, and community she has indeed been both leader and team player. As of this writing she is co-chair of the History Book Committee and has done yeoman's work in collecting materials and interviews for the project. The dimensions of humanness and "common life" experience in the book will have benefitted tremendously due to her contributions. Family commitments in church and society loom large as contributive factors to the special ministry of such a downtown church as First Baptist.

The McCall family of Alice, William, Charles, and then Kelsy, Frank, and May, children of Charles and Annie, made continuing contributions in the total life of the church. Kelsy, for example, wrote beautiful script, and so as church registrar he entered numerous beautifully done resolutions in the Minutes. May served two terms as president of Women on Mission and was active in developing and expanding the church library. Charles as well as Kelsy also served as deacons. Service of various types intertwined the McCall family.

The Huff/Sutton family's creative legacy from four generations of service includes four ordained deacons. Frank and Lucile Huff, upon moving to Savannah, joined the First Baptist church in 1916. One of their four daughters, Cilie, married Bill Sutton, a Life Deacon, and their two children, Billy and Suzy, are presently deacons. Billy married Nancy Harrison, who prior to the marriage had been chosen by the Savannah Jaycees in 1987 as Lay Person of the Year. She, too, was later ordained as a deacon. Their own three children introduced the fourth generation of this productive family to the larger congregational family where genuine and Christly service has been rendered.

Political action has always marked the congregation and in this relation, two more persons should be briefly highlighted. Charles Harold Carter (1919–1972) was one of those who was active not only on the Diaconate but in city politics as well. Elected to the city council in 1954, he was mayor *pro tem* for a full decade and an alderman for twelve years. John Groover Kennedy (1882–1955) was another deacon who entered the political arena as well as practicing law in the city from 1910 to 1955. A member of the Georgia State Legislature in 1933, in 1937 he was appointed by Governor E. D. Rivers to the Georgia State Board of Regents (the body which governs the colleges and universities in the state system), where he served as vice chair. From 1947 to 1948 he served as mayor of Savannah. Again, politics and religion meshed; church and state met one another in the public halls of justice.

Staff persons are often the unsung heroes of a congregation—they are the glue of mutually cohering parts. Anna Law was senior secretary for many years for pastors Cleverdon and Lanier. She and her family were loyal members. Pastor Austin initiated a new policy when he employed Cathy Parrish, for she was not a member of the congregation. He believed that confidentiality was not so easily compromised if such staff were not part of the membership. At the time of this writing she has been with the church for twenty-one years and is valued for her high professionalism, knowledge of membership, diplomatic personality, loyalty, and expertise in her position. Finally, Albertha Washington, known as "Boss," is another long-time member of the staff—twenty-nine years at present, a much longer tenure than any pastor or present staff member. When extra custodial employees come to the staff, they are certainly informed of their responsibilities but they are also told that they must get along with "Boss"!

Through the years she has done such a wide number of jobs that she is considered virtually indispensable and irreplaceable at First Baptist.

As reflected earlier, presented here is simply a cross section of the priests and pilgrims of First Baptist. Each person's list might be a bit different, but the ones reported upon here are definitely an interesting variety and a cross section.

The image of the pilgrim on a pilgrimage is as old as Abraham leaving Ur of the Chaldees. When one of his friends shouted, "Hey, Abe, where are you going?" Abraham shouted back, "I don't know, but I'm going!" The Builder of the City, the Christ, has given all of us poor priests of God our marching orders and instructions. Sometimes the air is so clear that we see the very spires of the city. At other times we wonder whether the city even exists as we continue our journey. But we are not alone. We are with a congregation of others, some of whom at times see better than we see and are "pilgriming" better than we "pilgrim." It is also our belief that the Builder himself is with us. And when he joined our group he took the form of a servant. In this way He taught us that to be a pilgrim is to be a servant. Success is not the goal, however; service is, as well as prophetic vision.

This chapter has presented a variety of persons—banker, lawyers, postmaster, educator, engineer, businessmen, medical doctors, housewives, and staff persons. They have all been part of the warp and woof of Baptist history at First Church. Each, in his/her own way also had a vision—whether realized or unrealized. They all fit that beautiful description by Thomas Merton:

> What choice remains?
> Well, to be ordinary is not a choice.
> It is the usual freedom
> of men [and women] without visions.

These pilgrims were and are men and women of outstanding vision who also know that the pilgrim of God is a servant of all folk for Jesus the Christ's sake. In reality all of their vocations (*vocatio*=calling) have been and are sacred callings with the Christian vocation spelled out in a daily life of service.

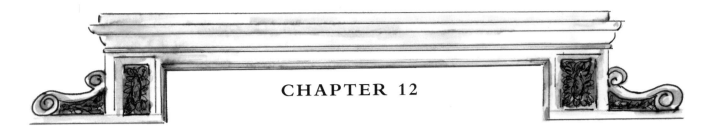

CHAPTER 12

A DOWNTOWN CHURCH
WITH AN ALTERNATIVE WITNESS

The Protestant movement has always subscribed to the principle of *ecclesia reformata sed semper reformanda*—the church reformed but always to be reformed. Protestantism cannot be static; it never completely arrives for it is always "on the road," in transit toward the City of God. The Reformation always remains unfinished, especially in its institutional forms. The spirit of Protestantism must never sanctify the status quo or else it breaks with its own history and genius. The Baptist movement in its own history has faithfully adopted this commitment of the larger Protestant movement especially in its insistence on local autonomy, the priesthood of all believers, and the separation of church and state. Thus far this cluster of commitments has witnessed a great deal of variety within a common, shared history of servanthood mission.

Times and contexts change for every congregation, but downtown churches since the 1950s have been especially hard hit. As populations in urban centers moved outward in suburban clusters, dozens and dozens of new community suburban churches were created. First Baptist Church itself faced the issue of whether or not to move elsewhere in 1953–1954 and decided to remain in its downtown setting. The easy way out would have been to relocate in the suburbs, but the congregation made the hard decision to stay where it was. Since then, the ongoing struggle has been the adaptation and response to the ever changing downtown context and to do so "faithfully." How to find out what "faithfully" really means in each case is a challenging and sometimes grievous task. It is not surprising that the church's last mission-become-church was in 1953. After this, all the downtown churches experienced drainage of membership to the suburbs and a changed kind of charge and mission in the downtown setting of tourists, street people, and changing social times. In 1967 Pastor Lanier publicly said: "There's no doubt about it, it is much more difficult to have a downtown church than a community [suburban] church. People just naturally gravitate to a community church. But we feel that a witness should be maintained downtown." He and other contemporary downtown ministers agreed that if the challenge of drawing members widely from the city could be met, that the resulting congregations would be made up of persons from many different walks of life who could enjoy rich fellowship together. They definitely believed that such a congregation would be spiritually richer and more electrically vital than any suburban church ever could be. Downtown churches and the hub of the city itself could share a common electrical experience not even available out in the boondocks! How to meet this challenge "faithfully" was something else, of course, beyond this most appealing idea.

First Church has from the start had high expectations for the education of its senior ministers. These men have been educated in the twentieth century in some of the leading seminaries and divinity schools in the United States and some have done post-graduate work in leading theological centers abroad. Since the 1950s theological education has made some major directional changes not only with the continuing theme of the goal of the churches "to comfort" but also with the striking addition of the theme "to challenge." As the nation entered a period of dramatic social change and "future shock" (defined by Alvin Toffler as "dizzying disorientation brought on by premature arrival of the future"), its seminaries and divinity schools were graduating a new breed of "challenge" ministers who saw the local church not simply as a place of refuge and changeless outlook and doctrines. These graduates saw a world of people who were not nearly as bad as John Calvin depicted them but not nearly as good as Pelagius pictured them. It was a world of good and evil, sometimes messy, but a world outside the structures that must be engaged in a number of ways if the church completed its mission of service. Additionally, a "flourishing" congregation was certainly no longer necessarily to be defined in relation to numerical growth. This would doubtless be the case with downtown churches as the population had fled the inner city.

First Baptist Church as a historic downtown church has had to adapt and adopt and retain in this comparatively new situation. It has had to find its alternative witness to suburban flight as well as to remain faithful to its historic witness within the Southern Baptist Convention and to downtown Savannah. Conflict has of necessity been a part of this search for ministry and identity. Lewis Coser in *The Functions of Social Conflict* has correctly observed that "intensity of conflict is related to closeness of the relationship." Congregations are always closely knit, and therefore conflicts are sometimes intense. Congregations are "struggle" groups and continuously select and reselect those they consider to be "worthy leaders" at a given point in their pilgrimage. These persons lead and tug a congregation in new ways which are often, however, rooted in essential principles of the past. When the process is truly salvific, the congregation is finally strengthened and the umbrella approach can lead to creative cooperation, witness, and mission.

No one factor describes "alternative witness" for First Baptist Church. There is a constellation of factors, some of which overlap with one another much like the Olympic rings of world competition. These factors all together describe the historic witness of this church.

This twentieth-century congregation has fortunately had a vital and active sense of its own history and has been faithful to early and valuable commitments. Early as well as late, Savannah has been a mission-field setting for its historic churches. Though increasingly denominationally aware, Episcopalians, Methodists, Presbyterians, Lutherans, Baptists, and others were from the beginning ecumenical in experience and commitments. Certainly, along the way, there have been a few exceptions to this, but definitely, "exceptions." This ecumenism even extended to the Jewish faith and has continued. Since the Second Vatican Council (1962–1965), Catholics have also been more forthright in joining hands with Protestants and Jews. Cooperation in total mission marks the downtown churches. This more liberal social and religious attitude has at times caused denominational tensions as well as the practical and theological question—"What does it mean to be a Baptist?" First Baptist in its illustrations and answers has at times been far more faithful to the essence of Baptist history than those who have questioned or criticized them.

First Baptist has been fortunate to have an intelligent and well-educated ministry which has led the church to historic awareness, theological identity, and self-understanding. The longer tenures of Pastors Cleverdon and Austin certainly made their unique mark on congregational style, but the others in their own way have been equally important. These men were more than adept in the pulpit but also successful in the numerous other roles which a pastor must play in the total ministry.

The style of these well-educated ministers has in the main been open and accepting. Even Taylor was no fundamentalist, though he may have described himself that way. The pastors have ranged from evangelical conservative to evangelical liberal. None have even approached the style of neofundamentalism. They all have been ecumenical in their commitments, some more than others. Rubbing shoulders with the cross-section of downtown humanity in religious and secular settings can only lead to greater acceptance of one another. These sometimes lonely Baptists found numerous avenues for spiritual expression down many other religious avenues than the rigidly separatistic denominational ones. Cleverdon experienced firsthand the World Council of Churches and the Faith and Order Movement. Pastors and members through the years attended the Baptist World Alliance. Austin made best friends with Rabbi Rubin, and John Finley visited Communist Cuba and participated in founding a new Baptist congregation there. Ecumenical acceptance and experience mark the essence of pastoral leadership as well as the congregation at First Baptist. It is historically Baptist but also has historical awareness that the Baptist way of life is only one of many down pilgrim's road toward the City of God.

These senior ministers, as well, have in each tenure found an energetic and capable laity and have been successful in engendering high levels of commitment—even in the midst of change and conflict. Through the century this laity has also been brought to a deeper self-understanding as well as to a new awareness of theological identity. This has taken place on several different levels. The ecumenical level finds virtually weekly illustrations in a downtown setting but has been highlighted with lay participation in ecumenical gatherings, education in both Sunday School and pulpit, and *face à face* dialogical exchanges with other denominations and faiths. Minister and laity alike have experienced evolutionary doctrinal changes, always with historical precedent in the church in addition to loyalty to denominational principles if not to the individual contemporary denominational leaders and their separatistic views. Inclusivism rather than exclusivism has marked these changes and new awarenesses. From Pastor Taylor to Pastor White, the congregation learned to accept strongly held minority views from different pastoral leaders—in this case the principle of pacifism. Taylor had been rejected; White was embraced. The broad and educated views of Cleverdon, Lanier, and Austin resulted in numerous doctrinal evolutionary changes. Cleverdon was the ecumenist par excellence; Lanier uttered a *cri de coeur* concerning social changes related to the years of integration; and young Austin challenged the congregation in numerous doctrinal directions.

All three of these ministers led the congregation to a fresh understanding of denominationalism in the new era of ecumenicism—especially for downtown churches. The principle of "detached-attachment" was presented and experienced as legitimate in the Baptist experience. Though the SBC was still racist in its practices in the main and the Savannah religious community was wracked with pain over the social issue of integration, First Baptist was led by Lanier to be open to all who truly wished to worship and serve. However tense those days were, the church carefully worked through the problem and did the Baptist and Christian act. Actually, the church had been open to all for years; in 1967 by formal vote it recognized this. True, forced integration by a group whose first intention was apparently not worship had been opposed by a few, but even this was accepted as part of what must take place for the process to be completed. The church was open to other denominations and now to all races. Joint services later with the First African Baptist Church gave positive witness to mutual acceptance and appreciation.

Young Tom Austin with stars in his eyes developed openness in yet other doctrinal ways, really in keeping with the church's history as well as with certain parts of the Baptist tradition. Early on, he, as had other pastors, opened the Communion table to all who would come in clear Christian conscience. The ordinance, he and the congregation knew, was a Christian ordinance first and a Baptist practice second. Viewing the future, it will be interesting to see whether this church "remembers" its earliest history as well as the Christian tradition well enough to the point of beginning to use wine again instead of grape juice, or, as some churches do, offer both at the same table. Also useful might be a procession of freshly baked unleavened bread and congregational wine or juice brought to the table as a congregational act to be shared later and invested with the new memory of body and blood. This, too, would be "open" congregational participation.

During Austin's tenure the church also began to practice "open membership." Again, normative baptism for Baptists was to be believer's baptism by immersion, but those coming into the church with "meaningful baptism" from other denominations were now received without being required to be rebaptized. This, too, recognized baptism as a Christian act first and as a Baptist ordinance second. Both evolutionary understandings of the doctrines of the ordinances were definitely ecumenically grounded and pragmatically important for downtown churches with wide-ranging denominational appeal. Both practices also had numerous Baptist precedents as well as strong contemporary and affirming biblical interpretations. The church and Diaconate might have to be reeducated from time to time about these doctrinal insights, but they are now part of the *traditio* of First Baptist Church.

From Frank Oliver in the 1930s onward, there was the lurking issue of equity for women in the church. The haunting question emerged from the principle of the priesthood of all believers that far more than

Seniors enjoy a holiday trip of Christmas shows at Myrtle Beach. First row L to R: Betty Waldrop, Nelly Jones, Mary Waters, Anna Seyle, Margaret West, Catherine Scholl, Vic Kennickel, Jack and Joan Usher. Second row L to R: Charlie Waldrop, Ola and Harry Skinner, Julian and Doris Thomas, Charles Seyle, Grace Burke, Allie McDonald, Amelia Dreese, Carolyn Upson, unidentified tourguide, and Billy Jones.

a mere church vote was the right of every female to serve as ordained deacons and ministers. Only a patriarchal chauvinism stood in the way of such a development, both in culture and church. Neither unbiased biblical interpretation nor Baptist principles barred the way; in fact, both supported such equity of the genders. Austin, committed to the ordination of women, led the church further down the road to self-understanding and discovery and two females were elected to the Diaconate in 1974. Their number has multiplied several times since then and they form a strong minority on the board. A few years later in 1981 Peggy Stout was ordained as a minister by the church and took her place alongside a small number of well-qualified female ministers in the SBC. By 1993, the church had heard its first female preach from the pulpit—Cathy Cole. Since her arrival as Assistant Minister, Kristin Andreason has preached a number of times. Inclusiveness had reached all the way to the pulpit. Long overdue, women were receiving their due and full opportunity to service and ministry. Meanwhile, the bulk of the SBC was taking all its cues from a culture of the past and from a stultified religious outlook.

Another important factor for downtown churches is so simplistic that it often goes unsaid or overlooked. The different constituencies that make up the downtown church find a great deal of their bonding in inclusive worship experiences but also in simply eating together. There is a special bonding that takes place when persons of different background and vocation simply sit down and "break bread" together. Inclusive eating, in its own way, is just as important as inclusive worship. It is not surprising that Jesus was with his closest friends for the last time at a meal. It was there that lasting revelations were given. However trite this may appear to some, its importance to congregational internal growth cannot be overestimated. Playtime and field work experiences together also create the glue of the mutually cohering parts. First Church gives weekly opportunities for all of this congregational bonding.

It has often been observed that the church hymn offers one of the most powerful means for promoting the unity of the faith and the communion of the saints. The musical and liturgical programs of the church from Sunday to Sunday offer a weekly menu of possibilities for the total interests of the congregation. The expertise of organ performance and the carefully structured service itself offer the universally relevant experience of the mystical moment for each person in the congregation. It is not a matter of entertainment; it is a matter of God-fulfilling worship. This in itself is an alternative to the hustle and bustle of the concrete jungle outside. One is replenished within to go and serve without.

Gifts to denominational missions and the establishment of a number of missions-become-churches (Bull Street, Ardsley Park, Immanuel, Morningside and Riverside), the last in 1953, have been and are wonderful projects, but the downtown church must seek to do more than others in its total ministry to special downtown problems and needs. Since 1956 and the founding of the Baptist Center under Pastor Cleverdon's leadership, First Baptist has been sensitive to the unique needs of certain segments of the downtown population. All of the pilgrims of the church have joined in one way or another in these missions and services. Already mentioned in historical context and now listed, these include the following: counseling programs (with Chris Wilburn contributing so freely), the ecumenical CRY services, Emmaus House (keeping so many members hustling), the Union Mission (directed by Mike Elliott, a member, author, and national authority on street people and homelessness), Habitat for Humanity projects, and the AIDS Interfaith Network. No member committed to service and mission would be left without a choice on this broad menu of possibilities.

This story of faith began in a simple structure. Through the years we have built, repaired, increased, and refurbished God's church. Now two hundred years later we continue on the pilgrims' way from sidewalk to rooftop and all in between.

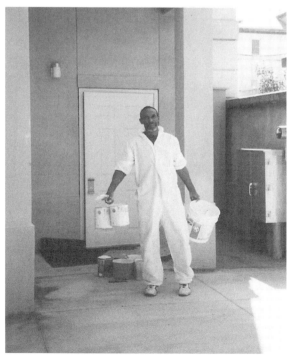

All these wide-ranging factors combine to offer the multifaceted alternative witness of this downtown church. Perhaps each alone is not unique; however, the combination of all of them is and within a special historic tradition offers alternatives to special persons living both near and far from the church structures themselves. Neither First Baptist nor any of the other downtown churches are "flourishing" in the sense of outstanding numerical growth. First Baptist is "flourishing," however, in the sense of providing for all of the spiritual needs of its congregation which includes all the service projects as well. The principle of the *dynamique du provisoire* has been actively at work. The "dynamic of the provisional" experience of the church is its strength. The "provisional" is the fact that as congregations continue their pilgrimage, there will always be change; all is provisional. The "dynamic" of the principle is the fresh openness to the ever-renewing hand of God in relation to this change. With such a principle actively at work, the institution itself is never idolized and the reformation keeps happening.

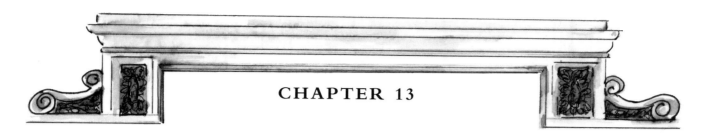

CHAPTER 13

IN SEARCH OF CHRISTIAN
AND BAPTIST IDENTITY

Since 1800 First Baptist Church has considered itself both Christian and Baptist. Since 1845 First Baptist Church has been an active and contributing member church of the Southern Baptist Convention, presently the largest Protestant denomination in the United States. Half-humorously, it has sometimes been said that there are more Baptists in the South than people—or sparrows! From 1845 onward the SBC membership grew by leaps and bounds in this grassroots denomination. For years the twin themes of evangelism and missions kept this diverse folk under one large umbrella. Acceptance of diversity was practiced and love for one another was expressed even in the midst of disagreement. Controversy in close-knit religious families certainly takes place, but in this case there was usually the final scene of forgiveness and "kissing and making-up." Pluralism within the SBC was actually an essential part of its vitality. It was really its own little ecumenical movement. Pastoral leadership and membership ranged mainly between fundamentalists and evangelical conservatives. Only a handful of liberals were to be found, and even they would want to be known as evangelical liberals for they subscribed to what they considered the essence of the gospel to be. But they all sang "Amazing Grace" and "How Great Thou Art" together and jointly wept to think of God's grace for such sinners as themselves. They also shared that common history which had been going on since 1845.

But something began to happen in the 1970s that caused a certain number of churches, pastors, and members to feel like round pegs being forced into square holes. A "broken history" began to evolve involving a new breed—neofundamentalists. "Broken history" refers to a rejection of historical beliefs and practices of Baptists in favor of a kind of religious monopoly. The word Baptist had meant freedom first; it subtly began to mean something else with this new breed. Though they decried what they considered to be modernism and liberalism all around them, they were actually the modernists, for they were making a break with their own history. "Neofundamentalist" in the context of the SBC simply refers to the fact that this new breed was "neo" in the sense that it had now become politically adept and had an actual plan to take over the SBC politically and push its agenda and belief system onto the entire denomination. The umbrella over the family would be replaced by the single-cell outlook and the family would be kept in tow by guards committed to a religious monopoly. No longer would Baptist mean freedom with these folk.

Up to this point, if these people were dissatisfied with things in the SBC, they had simply founded their own seminaries and Bible schools and looked beyond the SBC press and teaching materials for their own books and educational materials. They kept their affiliations with the SBC but complained of "liberalism" and sometimes went their own way in relation to certain alternative programs.

By the 1970s, however, these neofundamentalists had a new plan of political takeover. It would take a while, but they figured correctly that within a bit more than a decade, they would be successful. The mechanism to be used would be the presidency—since the days of W. B. Johnson a very powerful office. If they could elect a neofundamentalist each year for the next decade as president, those persons could use their powerful appointive rights to stack every board of control in the Convention with like-minded individuals, instead of with a broad selection of persons as had been the case since 1845. Starting with the election of Adrian Rogers in 1979, this was done; by the early 1990s the neofundamentalists completely controlled every aspect of the organizational life of the SBC—the seminaries, the publishing house, the mission boards, other boards and commissions, and the powerful Executive Committee of the SBC. Judge Paul Pressler, Paige Patterson, W. A. Criswell (the "patron saint" of the takeover), Adrian Rogers, and others now had their political machinery in place to push their social, political, and doctrinal agenda. Their palace takeover was completed and the purging of all those who even slightly disagreed with them continued to take place. The SBC had now completely broken with the genius of its own denominational history and headed in foreign directions.

There was and is mass confusion in this denomination. A loud *cri de coeur* echoes across the mammoth Convention as persons and churches wrestle with decisions concerning their first commitment—being Christian—and their second experience—a specific Baptist denominational history reaching back to 1845.

Two kinds of groups have evolved presently, each with sub-groups within it. The SBC in the main has remained conservative and evangelical. One group of these, however, are neofundamentalists who want to be considered conservative and evangelical, but they are not open and accepting of other positions and label all who disagree with any of their ideas as "liberal." They use all the same language as conservatives, but they are separatistic, anti-ecumenical, and harshly judgmental. On the other hand, the conservatives are more accepting and, to a point, less judgmental—but they seem to be willing to leave the denominational machinery in the hands of those who use the same language they love, and they are loyal to the historical relationships since 1845 without really confronting the issue of a changed direction. These are the two kinds on the right of the religious spectrum.

On the left side of the religious spectrum are conservatives who range more broadly from conservative evangelicals to evangelical liberals and they have been labeled as "moderates." Two kinds of moderates have evolved. One group of moderates is willing to seek alternatives in addition to their involvement in and support of the SBC. They are, however, not interested in joining or founding another denomination—they at this time are too committed historically to this denominational relationship. Another group of moderates is perhaps more realistic about the present and future situation in the SBC, however, and less historically committed in the face of the "broken history." They are reforming enough in their understanding of what being Christian and what being Baptist mean to be willing to leave the SBC for another Baptist denomination or to found another Baptist denomination which will carry on what they consider to be the legitimate and historical SBC tradition. Both sets of moderates are also ecumenical in their outlook but are criticized with words and actions by the neofundamentalist leaders that have to be interpreted as anti-ecumenical. To these leaders ecumenical is an unorthodox word.

Local congregations with lay and pastoral leadership that is moderate in character and with a history of long-term ecumenical relationships have suffered grievously of late in relation to their own pilgrimage and simply in what route to take. First Baptist Church of Savannah, Georgia, is an illustration par excellence of this kind of congregation. In addition to wrestling with the issue of offering an alternative witness in a downtown setting, the church is conflicted with the present chaos in the Southern Baptist Convention. At this point, its own historic awareness has been and should be of some assistance in its decisions. Ecumenical from the start and with a leadership both lay and pastoral that identifies more with the several moderate positions, the church has re-directed itself accordingly.

As Bill Leonard, dean of the Divinity School of Wake Forest University, has so correctly observed, for moderate Baptist churches there has been a loss of a denominational "center." Most of these churches still support the SBC to a point, but it is only one of many organizational centers. Moderate churches at the present time have actually reverted to pre-SBC history and their style is more reflective of the "society" kind of cooperation. Since the politics of the SBC has expressed itself in ways absolutely opposed to what First Baptist thinks are more Christian and Baptistic, it has sought out other avenues of expression *in addition to* its continued historic and financial support (however less) of the SBC.

These new "centers" of organizational support offer a medley of opportunities. The two most obvious new centers for moderates are the Alliance of Baptists and the Cooperative Baptist Fellowship (CBF). First Baptist has supported these two new centers from the start. Mission, education, and publications in both centers have afforded alternatives to SBC organizations and entities controlled by the neofundamentalist agenda. The CBF has developed rapidly and been so financially successful that the question is often posed as to whether it will eventually evolve into a new Baptist denomination. One of the major problems, of course, is that local congregations are so "mixed" in their loyalties that if this took place there would be numerous local schisms and/or drainage of members to other SBC congregations. At present, CBF churches seem content with remaining officially in the SBC while at the same time supporting other "centers." This presently is the case with First Baptist Church.

There are other "centers" as well. Smyth and Helwys Publishing, Inc. based in Macon, Georgia, was established to publish books and educational materials appealing to the commitments and interests of moderate Baptists. Teaching materials from this publisher are presently used by First Baptist in its educational program. The last two hymn books adopted were not published by the SBC Press. Since the takeover of all six seminaries of the SBC by neofundamentalists and the purging of moderate professors, many new seminaries and divinity schools have been founded aimed at Baptist students but with greater commitment to the principles of diversity, ecumenism, and academic freedom within bounds. Some of the fundamentalist-dominated schools have been placed on censure lists due to their violation of the principle of academic freedom as well as that of professional collegiality. The new moderate schools offer alternative theological education for Baptists in virtually every Southern state. First Baptist has shown special support for two of these new schools—the Baptist Theological Seminary of Richmond, Virginia, and the Mercer University School of Theology. The many changes in theological education among Baptists in the South will certainly lead to the development of more carefully discerning pulpit committees in the future. These committees must ask new questions as well as make careful explorations of educational credentials. The future remains open as to what kind of denominational organization and identity will finally result from these educational changes.

Another changing center has to do with state Baptist conventions. The takeover on the national level has led to efforts on the state convention levels as well. In Texas and Virginia, for example, neofundamentalists have been unable to take over the state Baptist machinery and have founded separate state conventions subscribing to the same theological, moral, and political agenda as the national takeover. Other conventions have tried to retain their own identity as cooperative Baptist bodies. Various plans of giving to various "centers" have been devised by a number of state conventions. As well, Baptist colleges and universities in the various states have redefined themselves in such a way that their own history as institutions of higher learning cannot be interrupted by any neofundamentalist takeover. This has generally been done by restructuring the boards of governance. This route has been taken by such leading institutions as Furman, Baylor, Stetson, Samford, Wake Forest, Mercer, and Meredith. Each school has attempted to remain true to its Baptist heritage while becoming distanced from the politics of the state Baptist conventions.

The local congregation in Southern Baptist circles has witnessed, and is witnessing, a great deal of transition. A new definition and underscoring of local autonomy are being widely seen. The politics of the SBC in the last two decades resulted in a new committee being formed at First Church—the Denominational Relations Committee. The folders of this committee covering the last seven years are crowded with materials illustrating every facet of local change in the new context—from letters of protest concerning political developments which have disenfranchised moderates to refreshing efforts to educate the entire congregation concerning unfortunate developments. Wrestling, struggling, searching, experiencing pain—all this and more jam the records of the committee.

First Baptist in the last two decades has been faithful to its ecumenical heritage as well as to the pilgrimage mentality found within the essence of Baptist history. It has come to practice open communion and open membership and has ordained women as deacons and, in one case, as a minister. It ordained its organist to the gospel ministry. The church has supported all the institutions of higher learning supported by moderate churches. There certainly still exists denominational loyalty especially among those over fifty years of age, but even among these members it has become a moderated loyalty especially due to the long history of the church to different commitments. First Baptist knows that it is Christian and Baptist, but is no longer completely sure that it is Southern Baptist in a contemporary understanding of that denomination. It is only one of many Baptist churches facing the question of identity. As it and many other Baptist churches change their connections to the various changed "centers," they must reevaluate themselves as to their intentionality, identity, and purpose not only within the Baptist tradition but also within the Christian tradition. Denominational exclusivity may become a thing of the past for many churches as a result of their reevaluation. First Baptist as a downtown SBC church has already given a number of answers about what it means to be Baptist in such a setting and is hard at work deciding which elements of the Baptist heritage should be retained and shared. On the other hand, she has rejected in her own longer history so many things that seem to be so important to the new controllers of the SBC. The only present option for her is the reversion to the early Baptist society approach as she searches to support the principles to which she has been so loyal in her own history—missions, education, social work, and ecumenism.

The twenty-first century early on will be a difficult time for the neofundamentalists, conservatives, and moderates in Southern Baptist circles—whether the result is yet a new denomination on the American religious scene or the maintenance of an old one that has so recently changed directions.

Pilgrims and sometime wayfarers, the members of First Baptist Church are convinced that somewhere down that pilgrim's road there is to be found the essence of the Christian as well as the Baptist way. They pray with the true twentieth-century prophet, Pierre Teilhard de Chardin, as they bravely walk into the next century:

> Jesus, Saviour of human activity to which you have given meaning, Saviour of human suffering to which you have given living value, be also the Saviour of human unity; compel us to discard our pettinesses, and to venture forth, resting upon you, into the uncharted ocean of love. (*The Divine Milieu*)

CHAPTER 14

UNSCIENTIFIC POSTCRIPT

Congregational history can help congregations find their
identities in a pluralistic and rapidly changing context.
　　　　　　　　　—James Wind, *Places to Worship*

Until fairly recently, the local congregation has been one of the most overlooked aspects of American religious history. Within the last few years more and serious attention has been directed to this critical segment of religious experience in such excellent works as James Wind and James Lewis's two volumes, *American Congregations* (Chicago, 1994). Like mirrors of the congregational soul these works have reflected the corner-stones of American religious life. To tell a congregational story involves far more than simply rehearsing historical materials in order to celebrate special birthdays, such as a two hundredth one. Granted, this may be reason enough to produce a local history, but it is only one of many reasons. Celebration is not all there is.

For one, it is the *basic* institution to be observed if one wishes to understand religion and society in the United States. Such a study touches on both the public and private spheres of religion in the numerous intersections of the two. Witness the numerous lives of the members of this present congregation who go everywhere during weekdays acting upon the many values heard and adopted during weekends. This is "common, nearby history." This is warp and woof of daily life in Savannah. If historical awareness brings these members to a deeper understanding of their own *vocatio* in life, then the whole community and not just the congregation is better off as a result. A genuine Christian witness is thereby made to the world.

Not only is there celebration and greater self-understanding for the individual, but also the entire congregation understands itself better and contributes to its ongoing history. As Wind has been quoted above—such a history helps local congregations to "find their identities in a pluralistic and rapidly changing context." Valuable roots, traditions, and themes are recovered which give hints, meanings, and values that assist the contemporary decision-making processes in relation to mission, ministry, and denominational affiliation. As a downtown church, First Baptist has perennially sought its identity in a "pluralistic and rapidly changing context" and is presently and additionally challenged by the rapid and radical changes which have taken place in its own denomination, the Southern Baptist Convention.

First Baptist has been blessed in the main since 1800 with excellent though varied pastoral leadership and by bright and active laypersons. Through the years the congregation has been sensitive and open to numerous changes and adaptations as it has actively searched for the most effective kind of ministry in the varied contexts of the years. When it rejected moving to the suburbs, it found numerous avenues of service and mission in the downtown area. It must continue to struggle simply with "place"—where it is—as it attempts to adapt and transform itself in addition to its own surroundings.

First Baptist's warp and woof are saturated with ecumenical experiential illustrations along with its denominational affiliation. It has sensed no problems within itself in relation to being ecumenical as well as Baptist. Throughout its history it has experientially expressed itself to the realities of the autonomy of the local congregation as well as the priesthood of all believers. The illustrations of this are legion. It has found a way to mesh loyalty and criticism in its expressions of denominational affiliation. From nearly producing a pastoral president of the Southern Baptist Convention to the ordination of women as deacons and ministers, the congregation has shown expressions of majority as well as minority positions in its chosen denomination. In the future it will be critically important to see whether this will be allowed by an increasingly separatistic position by the denominational leadership. The church will also face even more decisions concerning its own intentionality being in sharp tension with that of a denomination that has changed course in midstream. If the church does change its denominational affiliation, it may even open up new vistas of mission in a downtown setting that will expand its own membership toward the future. Moderate Baptists in the next century will be forced to stop dwelling and brooding on the past and move into the future, building upon the Christian and Baptist principles which have brought them as far as they have traveled in their own pilgrimage. The downtown church must continue to move beyond individual piety to faith expressed in social and political contexts, from emotional fervor to emotional-intellectual-liturgical excitement about a pluralistic mission, and from a personal orientation of faith expression to a continuously healthy congregational witness in the city. The past is only prelude to the future, and as progress has been made in the past with conflict, so must it be in the future. No change is ever effected without undergoing conflict. Any congregation that systematically avoids conflict is not going to be able to change. As in the past, the church as a family must absorb any pain in conflict and move on to a healthier understanding of mission in the future it chooses. This will require engendering high levels of commitment from the member pilgrims who themselves will deal with such pain as involved in the racial and feminist search for justice and mission. As in the past, so in the future will mistakes be made. Congregational progress must allow the possibility of mistakes for thus a creative congregation learns and creativity is not stifled. One backs up sometime and starts over, learning from mistakes. The principle of the "dynamic of the provisional" demands this kind of freedom. The twenty-first century early on will witness both successes and failures if any eventual progress takes place.

Thus far in its history, First Baptist Church has illustrated all of the above principles. It must continue on its Baptist and ecumenical road toward contextual faithful Christian witness. It will struggle at times, as it has in the past, but it will "flourish" as it offers costly grace to all who join in this congregational pilgrimage.

May this history turn a sometimes amnesia of the congregation into magnificent recollection and celebration of graceful mission in the new century of our Lord. As we enter a kind of twilight zone of our civilization, the future of our lovely planet will depend on having such contributive and sensitive congregations in these critical yet challenging times. All heaven stands on tiptoes waiting to see how we are going to turn out! The next century will witness many providential events—new Pentecosts and reformations as great as any that have gone on before. The twenty-first century has stupendous surprises in store for both the church and the world.

CHAPTER SOURCES

Since this volume is directed primarily to a general readership, notes will be kept to a minimal level. For those interested in more comprehensive reading, all of the major primary and secondary sources are listed here. Though based on a solid acquaintance with the major sources, this book is not intended for teaching scholars but, on the other hand, it is dedicated to intelligent church members who do not prefer to be weighed down with heavy sentence-by-sentence notations. What is presented in this section, however, could certainly lead anyone to such in-depth scholarship. The effort here is to make this book "reader friendly."

THE FIRST CENTURY

Chapter 1: Baptist Beginnings in Europe and the New World
Chapter 2: Baptists in the South and Especially Georgia
This general material would be elaborated upon in the following useful volumes:

Ahlstrom, Sydney E., *A Religious History of the American People*, New Haven, 1972.
Armstrong, O. K. and Marjorie Moore, *The Indomitable Baptists*, New York, 1967.
Baker, Robert A., *A Baptist Source Book*, Nashville, 1966.
Barnes, W. W., *The Southern Baptist Convention*, Nashville, 1954.
Brackney, William Henry, *The Baptists*, Westport, Conn., 1988.
Coleman, Kenneth, *A History of Georgia*, Athens, Ga., 1991.
Duncan, Pope, *Our Baptist Story*, Nashville, 1958.
Hays, Brooks and John E. Steely, *The Baptist Way of Life*, Macon, Ga., 1981.
Leonard, Bill, *Dictionary of Baptists in America*, Downers Grove, Ill., 1994.
_____, *A History of the Baptists*, forthcoming.
Lester, James Adams, *A History of the Georgia Baptist Convention*, Nashville, 1972.
Lumpkin, W. L., *Baptist Confessions of Faith*, Valley Forge, Pa., 1959.
Torbet, Robert G., *A History of the Baptists*, Valley Forge, Pa., 1963.

Chapter 3: Origins and Early Days of the Baptist Church in Savannah
All of the above volumes will expand upon many issues covered in this chapter. In addition, there are two other major sources. The first is the helpful work of Mabel Freeman LaFar, *The Baptist Church of Savannah, Georgia: History, Records, and Register*, volume 1, 2 parts. This was compiled in 1941 and "dedicated to the women of the church" by this congregational historian, par excellence. Every church should be so

fortunate! These two parts summarize important material from the Minutes and Register of the church between 1805 and 1836. The other major sources are the Minutes themselves, found in the archives of the Georgia Historical Society. Within my text, references to these materials can be easily located in the sources due to my specific dating of matters. This is a much simpler form for the average reader and does not overburden the text with redundant footnotes. The dates are the key ingredients.

 First Fruits by Henry Holcombe, 1812, was donated to the church archives by Mr. and Mrs. Hugh Tarver.

Chapter 4: Pastoral Leadership and Building Changes

Again, the major sources for this chapter are the multivolume Minutes of the church. References to dates are keys to locating material in these sources. The Register of the church is also a major source as are the Minutes of the New Sunbury Association whose more complete information can also be located by reference to dates. In addition to all the works listed above, for this chapter the following volumes will also prove to be helpful:

 Gardner, Robert G., *Baptists of Early America*, Atlanta, 1983.
 McDonogh, Gary Wray, *Black and Catholic in Savannah, Georgia*, Knoxville, 1993.
 Raboteau, Albert J., *Slave Religion*, New York, 1978.

Chapter 5: Church Discipline

As in chapter 4, the major sources in chapter 5 are the multivolume Minutes of the church for the nineteenth century as well as the Register of the church. The Minutes of the New Sunbury Association have also been used. Internal references to dates are keys to locating material in these sources. In addition to all the other sources listed for other chapters, the following volumes will also prove to be helpful:

 Littell, Franklin H., *The Free Church*, Boston, 1957.
 Wills, Gregory A., *Democratic Religion*, New York, 1997.

Chapter 6: Doctrine, Liturgy, Worship, Education

All of the previously mentioned sources would be useful to pursue these subjects, but the multivolume Minutes of the church as well as the Register of the church have been most helpful. Internal references to dates are keys to locating material in the sources. In addition, the following materials were most useful:

 LaFar, Margaret Freeman, "Lowell Mason's Varied Activities in Savannah," *Georgia Historical Quarterly* (September 1944).
 Manual of the First Baptist Church of Savannah
 Record Book of the Sunday School of First Baptist Church

Chapter 7: Ecumenical Roots—Unity within Diversity

All of the previously mentioned sources would be useful to pursue the subject of ecumenism, but again the major primary sources have been the Minutes as well as the Register of the church. Internal references to dates are keys to locating material in the sources. In addition, the following items would be most useful:

 Brown, Robert McAfee, *The Spirit of Protestantism*, New York, 1968.
 Estep, William R., *Baptists and Christian Unity*, Nashville, 1966.

Hays, Brooks and John E. Steely, *The Baptist Way of Life*, Macon, Ga., 1981.

Rubin, Saul Jacob, *Third to None: The Saga of Savannah Jewry*, Savannah, 1983.

THE SECOND CENTURY

Chapter 8: Pastoral Leadership

The major sources for this chapter have been the Minutes of the church conferences and the Minutes of the Diaconate. Minutes of the New Sunbury Association were also used. In addition, thousands of pages of *The Messenger* and *The Calendar* have been read and used. Numerous interviews kindly done by members of the church have also been appropriately employed. They are included below. Works listed in earlier chapter bibliographies have also been consulted.

Austin, Thomas, Series of historical sermons on pastors of First Baptist Church, 1986.

Fletcher, Jesse C., *The Southern Baptist Convention: A Sesquicentennial History*, Nashville, 1994.

Interviews, letters, and statements (taped or written):

Fred Andrea, letter, 1997.

Thomas Austin, taped statement, 1997.

Shirley Cleverdon Solms, interview by Joan Usher, 1997.

Gene Lanier, interview by Jack Usher, 1997.

Julian Quattlebaum Jr., interview by Joan Usher, 1997.

James Richardson, written statement, 1998.

Bill Sutton, written statement, 1998.

LaFar, Margaret Freeman, *A Historical Sketch of the First Baptist Church on Its 175th Anniversary*, Savannah, 1975.

Leonard, Bill J., *God's Last and Only Hope: The Fragmentation of the Southern Baptist Convention*, Grand Rapids, 1990.

_____, *A History of the Baptists*, forthcoming.

Manual of the First Baptist Church, n.d.

Rubin, Saul Jacob, *Third to None*, Savannah, 1983.

Shriver, George H., ed., *Dictionary of Heresy Trials in American Christianity*, Westport, Conn., 1997.

_____, ed. *Encyclopedia of Religious Controversy in the United States*, Westport, Conn., 1997.

_____, "Southern Baptists Ponder 'Open Membership'—An End of Rebaptism," *Journal of Ecumenical Studies* (summer 1969): pp. 423–430.

Shurden, Walter B., ed., *The Struggle for the Soul of the Southern Baptist Convention*, Macon, Ga., 1993.

"The Southern Baptist Convention, 1979–1993: What Happened and Why," *Baptist History and Heritage* (October 1993).

Chapter 9: Doctrine, Liturgy, Worship, and Mission

The Manual, Congregational Minutes, and Minutes of the Diaconate are basic sources as well as *The Calendar*. Other helpful sources are following:

Austin, Thomas D., James C. Richardson, and Jody C. Wright, "Worship Planning at First Baptist Church, Savannah, Georgia," *Review and Expositor*, 85 (1988): pp. 63–70.

Richardson, James C., "Personal Reflections," 1998.

Smith, Harmon C., *Where Two or Three Are Gathered*, Cleveland, Ohio, 1995.

Chapter 10: The Role of Education

In addition to the Minutes of the Diaconate, Minutes of the Congregation, *The Calendar*, and earlier volumes already listed, recent volumes in relation to religious education will be helpful.

Chapter 11: The Priesthood of All Believers

The major sources for this chapter are materials gathered on congregational lives by Joan Usher, Cilie Sutton, and others as well as the Minutes of the Diaconate, issues of *The Calendar*, and selected newspaper articles.

Chapter 12: A Downtown Church with an Alternative Witness

The following works will be useful:

Bliese, Richard H., "Communities that Change, Congregations that Adapt," *The Christian Century* (January 7–14, 1998).

"Congregations in the Midst of Change: An Interview with Nancy Ammerman," *The Christian Century* (January 15, 1997).

Hill, Samuel S., *Southern Churches in Crisis*, New York, 1967.

Shriver, George H., ed., *Encyclopedia of Religious Controversies in the United States*, Westport, Conn., 1997.

Wind, James P. and James W. Lewis, eds., *American Congregations*, 2 vols., Chicago, 1994.

Chapter 13: In Search of Christian and Baptist Identity

All of the following volumes will be found useful:

Aldridge, Marion D. and Kevin Lewis, eds., *The Changing Shape of Protestantism in the South*, Macon, Ga., 1996.

Bland, Thomas A., Jr., ed., *Servant Songs*, Macon, Ga., 1996.

Carey, John J., *Carlyle Marney: A Pilgrim's Progress*, Macon, Ga., 1980.

Copeland, E. Luther, *The Southern Baptist Convention and the Judgment of History*, Lanham, Md., 1995.

Cothen, Grady, H., *What Happened to the Southern Baptist Convention?*, Macon, Ga., 1993.

Farnsley, Arthur Emery, II, *Southern Baptist Politics: Authority and Power in the Restructuring of An American Denomination*, University Park, Pa., 1994.

Ferguson, Robert U., Jr., ed., *Amidst Babel, Speak the Truth: Reflections on the Southern Baptist Convention Struggle*, Macon, Ga., 1993.

Furr, Gary A. and Curtis W. Freeman, eds., *Ties That Bind: Life Together in the Baptist Vision*, Macon, Ga., 1994.

Hill, Samuel S., *Southern Churches in Crisis*, New York, 1966.

_____, ed., *Varieties of Southern Religious Experience*, Baton Rouge, 1988.

Morgan, David T., *The New Crusades, The New Holy Land: Conflict in the Southern Baptist Convention, 1969–1991*, Tuscaloosa, Ala., 1996.

Teilhard de Chardin, Pierre, *The Divine Milieu*, New York, 1968.

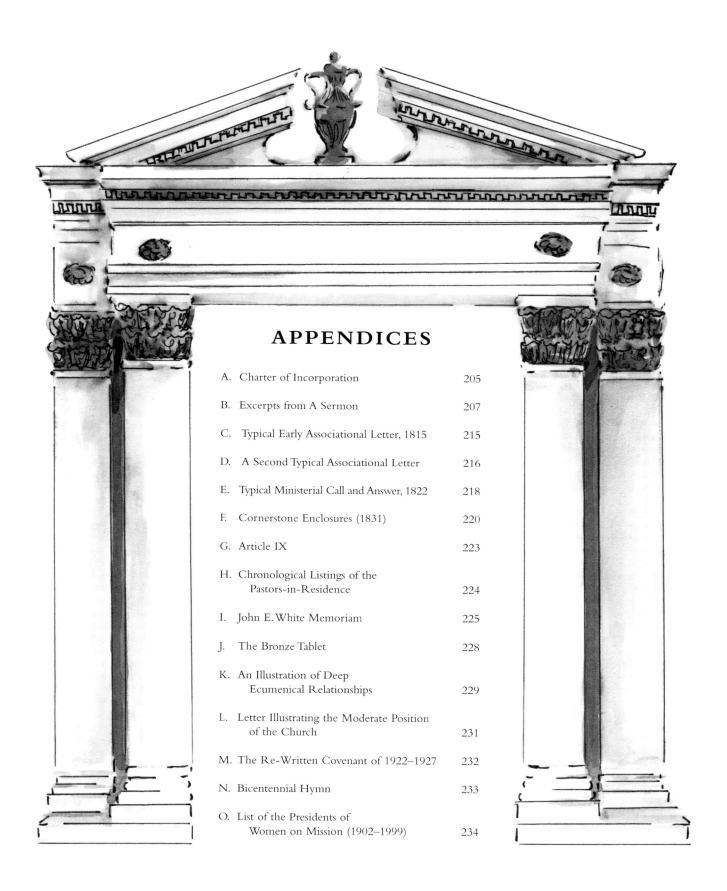

APPENDICES

APPENDIX A

CHARTER OF INCORPORATION

BY HIS EXCELLENCY, JOSIAH TATTNALL, JUN.,
GEORGIA: GOVERNOR AND COMMANDER-IN-CHIEF
OF THE ARMY AND NAVY OF THIS STATE, AND
OF THE MILITIA THEREOF:

To All, to Whom These Presents Shall Come; Greeting:

Whereas, Application in writing hath been made to me, signed by H. Holcombe, George Mosse, William H. Mathers, John Rose, Elias Roberts [sic], Joseph Wiseman, Theodore Carlton, Joseph Davis, Isaac Sibley, and William Parker, by order, and in behalf of the Baptist Church in the City of Savannah, praying that the customary Charter of Incorporation, may be granted to the same, and that George Mosse, William H. Mathers, and John Rose, and their successors in office, may be known and distinguished by the name and style of THE DEACONS OF THE BAPTIST CHURCH IN SAVANNAH; Now KNOW YE, That I, the said Josiah Tattnall, Jun., Governor and Commander-in-Chief of the Army and Navy of the State of Georgia, and of the Militia thereof, by and in virtue of the powers in me vested, and of my own good will and pleasure in consideration of the premises, have incorporated, founded, and erected the Baptist Church in the City of Savannah, and I have hereby nominated, constituted and appointed and I do by these presents, nominate, constitute and appoint, George Mosse, William H. Mathers, and John Rose and their successors in office, under the name and style of THE DEACONS OF THE BAPTIST CHURCH IN SAVANNAH, and the members of the said Baptist Church, and their successors, to be a body politic or incorporate, hereby giving and granting to them, the said George Mosse, W. H. Mathers, and John Rose, and their successors, in office, and the members of the said Baptist Church, and their successors, to have, hold, exercise and enjoy, the right of electing or otherwise appointing all and every of the officers of the said association, under such restrictions as they, or a majority of them, shall devise and ordain; and also, to sue, or be sued, implead or be impleaded, Grant or receive by their corporate name of THE DEACONS OF THE BAPTIST CHURCH IN SAVANNAH, and to do all other acts as natural persons may, and also hereby investing them with all manner of property, both real and personal, all monies due, donations, gifts, grants, hereditaments, privileges, and immunities whatsoever which may belong to the said Church, or which may hereafter be made or transferred to them or their successors, by gift, grant or purchase, to have and to hold the same for the proper use, benefit and behoof of the Baptist Church as aforesaid, and also to have and to use a common or corporate seal; and lastly, to make such rules and regulations for the better government of the said Association as they, or a majority of them shall devise and ordain.

In Testimony whereof, and in pursuance of the afore-cited act (of 1789) I have to this instrument put my hand and caused the great seal of the State to be affixed thereto:

Done at the State House in Louisville, this tenth day of December, one thousand, eight hundred and one.

JOSIAH TATTNALL, JUN.

GEORGIA SECRETARY'S OFFICE, 10TH DECEMBER, 1801.
Examined and recorded in Book Dz, Folio 230, 231, 232, and 233.

HOR. MARBURY,
Secretary.

GEORGIA CLERK'S OFFICE, CHATHAM COUNTY.
Recorded in Book X., Folio 66, 67, and 68, and examined this 18th day of October, 1802.

By Bulloch,
Clerk.

APPENDIX B

Excerpts from A SERMON
OCCASIONED BY THE DEATH OF
Lieutenant-General GEORGE WASHINGTON
Late
PRESIDENT
of the
UNITED STATES OF AMERICA;
WHO WAS BORN, FEBRUARY 11TH, 1732, IN VIRGINIA, AND DIED,
DECEMBER 14TH, 1799, ON MOUNT VERNON, HIS FAVORITE
SEAT IN HIS NATIVE COUNTRY; FIRST DELIVERED
IN THE BAPTIST CHURCH, SAVANNAH,
GEORGIA, JANUARY 19TH, 1800,
AND NOW PUBLISHED AT
THE REQUEST OF THE
HONORABLE CITY COUNCIL,

By HENRY HOLCOMBE, Minister of the Word of God in Savannah.

"Mark the perfect Man, and behold
"the upright: for the end of that Man is peace." David

Printed by SEYMOUR & WOOLHOPTER, on the Bay

A SERMON, & c.
2d of Samuel, 3d Chap. And part of the 38TH Verse.
"KNOW YE NOT THAT THERE IS A GREAT MAN FALLEN?"

In these words David refers to Abner, a distinguished officer of his day, who fell an unsuspecting victim to the well known traitorous scheme, and by the bloody hand of Joab, whose brother Aahel, to save his own life, Abner had reluctantly slain in a battle at Gibeon. To awaken a correspondent sense of their great loss in the afflicted Tribes, David and Saul, to them the pathetic inquiry adopted on this melancholy occasion, as applying with the most forcible propriety to the late Lieutenant General GEORGE WASHINGTON. Know ye not that in him a great man, a much greater than Abner is fallen? The sufficiently visible effects of this penetrating conviction render a comparison of these great men unnecessary, would the dignity of my subject, and the solemnity which reigns over this unexampled and overflowing concourse admit it. Their coincidence in point of greatness, established by the highest authorities, whatever disparity as to the degree of it, may exist, is all that is requisite to my purpose. In reliance therefore, on the plentitude of candor to which I am already greatly in arrears, however inadequate to the important service which has unexpectedly devolved on me, and with all the unaffected diffidence which overwhelms me, I shall make immediate advance towards the awful ground on which our greatest orators sink unnerved, and giants in literature stand and tremble! And though I am not about to deliver an oration, not to pronounce an eulogium; but to preach a sermon, and briefly touch on one of the greatest merely human characters, I am fully apprised of the delicacy of my situation, and too sensibly feel the pressure of difficulties.

My feeble soul take courage! A *Demosthenes* or a Cicero might fail here without dishonor; and though the famed Caesars, Alexanders, Pompies [*sic*] and Marlboroughs, must resign their inferior laurels to the more famous *American General*, he was but a man; all his greatness was derived from his and thy *CREATOR*, and thou wilt be assisted in the execution of thy arduous design by the prayers, candid allowances and liberal constructions of thine audience, who will deem it very pardonable on thy theme to be defective. The first doctrinal observation which our text, and the occasion of our assembling, unitedly suggest, is seriously important: Great as ABNER was, he fell; and WASHINGTON is fallen, it, therefore, undeniably follows *that great men, as well as others*, must fall. Though it would be absurd to attempt a formal proof of this doctrine, and have the appearance of an insult on dying man, there is nothing that merits more frequent, or more serious consideration; and a few explanatory remarks on it are so far from being amiss, that they are indispensible. The Heathens and Deists, of all descriptions, believing the immortality of the human soul, consider their bodies as falling by death into corruption and dust, never to rise; and their notions of the state, exercises, and enjoyments of the soul after death are so vague, indistinct and unimpressive, that they have little or no visible effect on their practice. Atheists, and such Deists as believe the soul of man to be mortal, consider all who are fallen, and our immortal WASHINGTON among the rest, as plunged into undistinguished and irretrievable ruin! As consigned to their original nonentity: happily for our various interest, few, if any, of these gloomy monsters disgrace or infest the United States: They are chiefly, if not altogether, confined to the smoke and flame in which they have involved miserable Europe. Let Americans never suffer their nature and its author to be insulted and degraded by the influence, or existence of such detestable sentiments.

This natural and laudable, as well as ancient and universal custom of honoring the pious and eminent dead, may be further justified by quotations from the New Testament. At the grave of Lazarous [sic], "*Jesus wept;*" devout men buried Stephen, who had the honor to be the first martyr in the christian [sic] cause, with great lamentation; and Paul mentions a number of the illustrious characters of antiquity, with the highest respect, and warmly recommends their noble and heroic conduct to the imitation of posterity. After bestowing on many the encomiums proper to their respective merits, he adds, "And what shall I more say? For the time would fail me to tell of Gideon, and of Barack, and of Sampson, and of Jepthae, of David also, and of Samuel, and of the prophets; who through faith subdued kingdoms, wrought righteousness, obtained promises, stopped the mouths of Lions, quenched the violence of fire, escaped the edge of the sword, out of weakness were made strong, waxed valient in fight, and turned to flight the armies of the Aliens." So warm a panegyrist of these great men was the Apostle, that he avers, "*Of them the world was not worthy.*" And though many of these failed of obtaining the attention due to their merits in, and immediately after their respective generations, by having their names and worthy deeds enrolled in the volume of inspiration, God has plainly shewn us that the fall a [sic] of a great good man should excite respectful and public attention. Encouraged, therefore, and in some degree assisted by such precedents, I will proceed to what is *finally* incumbent on me; and that is, *to evince the applicability of my text to the illustrious deceased. . . .*

Divine Providence gave him opportunities and dispositions to add great *acquired*, to the greatest *natural* abilities. If his education were not classical, it was profound: If he had not the comparatively superficial knowledge of all *names*, he possessed an universal knowledge of *things*: and tho' no great proportion of his previous time was spent in the study of dead languages, it was because the beautious objects of all kinds of useful and ornamental knowledge invited his attention and persuit [sic], in all the copious elegance of English attire.

His great mind was occupied with correspondent objects. He had well arranged and distinct ideas of all essentially interesting, and truly important facts, domestic and foreign, ancient and modern, temporal and spiritual. Among the subjects which WASHINGTON investigated, and the objects which he regarded with an assiduity and seriousness becoming their importance, were science; morality and religion; civil and religious liberty; agricultural commerce and navigation; tactics and the different forms of civil government; the rise of revolutions and falls of empires, in connection with their causes and consequences; and the religions, laws, customs, characters, and origin of nations.

With a singular felicity of perception, he comprehended the subjects of his knowledge in all their extensions and relations; and we well know, that in his conversation, public speeches, and admirable writings, ease and strength were united with all the beauty and simplicity of precision. But it would require talents brilliant as his own to do justice to a subject of such extent and sublimity, I shall conclude these imperfect remarks on his great literary merit, by observing that the honor of conferring on him the degree of L.L.D. was reserved for Rhode-Island College.[*]

From the economy observable in all the variety and profusion, if I may so express myself of Heaven's bounties, we are led to conclude that such mental strength and excellence as WASHINGTON possessed, must have been properly deposited, furnished with suitable organs, and intended for appropriate and important purposes: And our expectations are fully answered when we view him as entitled to the application of our text, *by the disposals of an all superintending Providence . . . .*

But his well-tried, and sterling merit, united to the splendor of his talents, and the unbounded confidence of his fellow-citizens, soon rendered it necessary, from the inefficacy of our Governmental arrangements, that he should again embark on the stormy sea of politics. Summoned by his country, to whom he could deny *nothing*, to assist in forming, and adopting our present energetic, yet free and happy constitution, he readily obeyed; and after the accomplishment of these important objects, he was called by the unanimous voice, of, at least, three millions of people to preside over these Sovereign and Independent States. To the Presidential chair he continued a noble ornament, by the united wish of his grateful country, who delighted to honor him, *eight years*, and discharged the important duties of this high station with his usual wisdom and firmness, integrity and rectitude. And after retiring the second time, in full possession of the affections and confidence of the people, to the solitude when he was capable of enjoying, as of adorning public life, he was prevailed on, tho' hoary with years, and covered with glory, to accept the command of our armies, when the political hemisphere wore a most menacing and wrathful aspect. Behold the greatest General in the world, tho' on the borders of three score and ten, in obedience to his much indebted country, ready, again, to take the field against her insulting foes!

And so obvious was the policy of this appointment, that it was anticipated, as well as ardently wished by every intelligent citizen. His martial and August appearance, the sound of his *name* and *voice*, the glance of his experienced eye, and the lightning of his sword at the head of our armies, rendered them gloriously enthusiastic, and absolutely invincible! But great as he was by nature, a liberal education, and the display and perfection of his superior powers, natural and acquired, in spheres of action the most conspicuous, elevated and important, he was still *greater* by the invaluable *gifts of the GOD of grace*. Considered as aggrandized by *these*, or text applies to him with the *utmost* propriety and force!

Know ye not that a great man, the greatest of men, is fallen?. . . .

His piety, though like his other shining excellencies unaustentatious [*sic*], was genuine and exalted. Through the veil of all his modest reserve, it was discoverable in the whole tenor of his conduct, and especially in his admirable and appropriate answers to the numerous addresses of his almost adoring fellow-citizens, where he uniformly, and with glowing gratitude ascribes all the glory of his unparrelled successes to GOD.

How high *christianity* [*sic*] stood in his estimation, and how near its interests lay to his heart, every one may see, who has read his excellent answers to the congratulatory addresses of various religious bodies, on his first election to the chief magistracy of these United States. And his opinion of religion in a *political* view, I will do myself the honor to give you in his own words; so that though alas! He is dead, he still to his weeping country thus speaketh:

> Of all the dispositions and habits which lead to political prosperity, religion and morality are indispensable supports. In vain would that man claim the tribute of patriotism, who should labor to subvert these great pillars of human happiness, whose firmest props of the duties of men and citizens. The mere politician, equally with the pious man, ought to respect and cherish them. A volume could not trace all their connections with private and public felicity. Let it simply be asked, where is the security for property, for reputation, for life, if the sense of religious obligation desert the oaths which are the instruments of investigation in courts of justice? And let us with caution indulge the supposition, that morality can be maintained without religion.

Whatever may be conceded to the influence of refined education on minds of peculiar structure, reason and experience both forbid us to expect that national morality can prevail in exclusion of religious principles. It is substantially true, that virtue or morality is a necessary spring of popular government. The rule indeed extends with more or less force to every species of free government. Who that is a sincere friend to it can look with indifference upon attempts to shake the foundation of the fabrick! Promote then, as an object of primary importance, institutions for the general diffusion of knowledge in proportion as the structure of a government gives force to public opinion, it is essential that public opinion should be enlightened.

Ye winds, waft these sentiments on your swift pinions; and ye sun-beams record them in more than golden characters, throughout the political world!

American, English, French, and all other politicians, hear him who was as famous in the cabinet, as formidable in the tented field! In proportion as he is regarded, will be prevented the effusion of blood; hostilities will cease, and order and confidence between rulers and the ruled, individuals and nations, will ensue.

The essential advantages of religion, in a political light, were discovered clearly, and felt impressively by the American sage, whose eagle eye distinguished plainly betwixt vain *pretenders* to religion, and its real *possessors*; and whose cool deliberate sagacity, discerned the difference between genuine religion, as delineated in the holy scriptures and the empty forms, gross adulterations, and shameful abuses of it. And it is difficult to determine, whether he were most correct and eminent in religious theory or practice. But one thing, and that of vast importance, is evident: Bright as this sun of human glory shone, with the sweetly blended rays of morality and religion, through every stage, and in every condition of life, like the cloudless star of day, gently and with increasing majesty, sinking beneath the western horizon, his mild effulgence was greatest in death!

> *"His mind was tranquil and serene,*
> *No terrors in his looks were seen:*
> *A Saviour's smile dispelled the gloom,*
> *And smooth'd his passage to the tomb."*

O Death! Never hadst thou, but in one astonishing instance, such a prisoner before! . . .

And permit me to observe, that the greatest honor of all that we can do to his memory, and the best improvement that we can make of his life and death, is to imitate his virtuous and pious examples: and this may be done by those of the tenderest capacities, and in the lowest ranks of society.

> *"Honor and fame from no condition rise,*
> *Act well your part there all the honor lies."*

My fair hearers, may I not hope that you will do more than weep? *This* is natural, it is becoming, it is unavoidable. Many of you could not refrain from tears when, some years ago, you saw the face of the hero who had, for you, endured so many painful years of fatigue, and hardships of all kinds, amidst dangers in all forms: Much more abundantly must your tears flow, now you hear your great friend and benefactor is *no more*. *Mourn* with his venerable *relict*, sinking under stupendous grief, for him who has slain your enemies, saved your country, "and put on ornaments of gold upon your apparel:" But I am persuaded you will do *more*; you will, like the great and virtuous WASHINGTON, in your measure, increase the dignity and happiness of human nature; you will adorn, by your solid, though private virtues, social life, of which you were intended to be the brightest ornaments.

War-worn veterans! Venerable fathers! You must feel the most pungent grief for him who led you in battle and to victory: And having enjoyed the advantages of his glorious examples, both in the peaceful cabinet, and on the hostile plains, you need not be reminded of your special obligations to patriotic virtue, and genuine piety.

He has taught you how to live and how to die.

Painfully tender, on this solemn occasion, must be the feelings of you, my fellow citizens, who lately, at the appearance of danger stepped forward, with an honorable zeal, in your country's defence. Your great commander in chief, is fallen! I see you feel the shock, and you need not wish to conceal it.

> Masculine cheeks bedew'd with tears,
> Become the August occasion;
> Nor need they blush, should heaving sigh
> Escape the manly breast, to day.

We have sustained, our country, and the world have sustained *no common loss.* Nations should mourn. *Our nation does mourn.* Our *venerable* and *much beloved chief* MAGISTRATE, the supreme council of the land, our bereaved armies, rising navy, cities, towns and villages, exhibit a widely-extended, endlessly-diversified, and most melancholy scene of deep mourning! All christian [*sic*] and masonic societies with an honest pride and exultation claiming WASHINGTON as their Brother, are laudably ambitious of making the most emphatical expressions of their fraternal regard and affection. The *Cincinnati*, after these, in particular, and all other societies in general; and in fine all descriptions of the American people, have variously, and yet as with one voice, testified their high respect, and most cordial affection, for the dear and illustrious object of their common attachment. "*Know ye not that there is a great man fallen?*" Methinks I hear the honorable City Council, and the rest of the worthy magistrates present, the officers of all grades, the reverend clergy, the congregation who statedly meet here, and the respectable residue of this vast mourning concourse, *reply*—Alas! Too well we know it! The most callous heart feels it! WASHINGTON is indeed fallen! The awful report is propagated in thunder along the North American coast, and reverberates in tremendous accent from the distant hills! The shock of Mount Vernon, trembling from the summit to its affrighted center, shakes the continent from New Hampshire to Georgia! O *fatal*, and *solitary* Mount! Vernon is an appellation that no longer becomes thee and may thine appearance correspond with thy situation! No more let cheerful green array thee!

---

*Sept. 1st, 1790, the degree of doctor of Laws, was conferred on GEORGE WASHINGTON, President of the United States of America. Soon *afterwards*, it appeared from the Baptist annual register for 1790, of which Doctor RIPPON of London is the editor, that "In a conversation between several friendly gentlemen, which turned chiefly on the confinement of LEWIS the little, who, like an absolute sovereign, had said to five and twenty million people, I will *be obeyed*; contrasted with the popularity of WASHINGTON THE GREAT—it was mentioned, that the Baptist College, in Rhode Island, had conferred the degree of doctor of Laws, on the President of the United States; while it seemed to be the general mind that this distinguished character in the history of man, would prefer the laurels of a college to a crown of despotism, one of the company, it is said, quite impromptu, gave vent to the feelings of his heart, in the following effusion:

> When Kings are *mere* sovereigns or tyrants, or tools,
> No wonder the people should treat them as fools;
> But WASHINGTON therefore presides with applause,
> Because he *well merits* the DOCTOR OF LAWS.
> I'll ne'er be a ruler till I'm L. L. D.
> Nor England, nor Scotland shall send it to me,
> I'll have my diploma from PROVIDENCE HALL,
> For WASHINGTON had, or I'll have none at all.

THE PRAYER

Rightful Sovereign of the universe! divinely awful Jehovah! we approach thine exalted Majesty with supreme veneration, and thy most profound awe!

That the Lord our God is infinitely worthy of religious adoration, we acknowledge that the deepest prostration of soul. All truly enlightened creatures, from the weakest of frail men, to the most illustrious in moral strength and excellence, worship thee as the unoriginated and essential source of being, perfection, and felicity! Eternity is thy time! Commensurate with immensity is thy presence! and the united powers of the whole creation are incapable of rendering thee adequate praise! Thine essence is love: wonderful thy Council, excellent thine operation, and infinite the expanse of thine ability! Supreme intelligence infinitely wise design, and boundless benevolence, are gloriously displayed in all thy works, and in all thy ways! Thine eyes pervade the essences, relations and properties of all things, and survey futurity's dark abyss!

With dread serenity thou walkest on the wings of the wind, and the clouds are the dust of thy feet! Thou hast thy way in the whirlwind, and in the storm, and thy foot-steps are in the deep waters! But judgment and righteousness encompass thy throne. When we behold thee arrayed in these sublimely awful perfections as the uncontrolable arbiter of life and death, we are constrained to acquiesce in thy righteous dispensations. Reason and experience render it probably, and thy word, which is truth, assures us, that all things, however distressing in themselves, are interesting in their issues to all who love and serve thee. This is our consolation under the bereavement and great loss suffered by our nation, in the removal of thy servant, the commander-in-chief of her armies, from time to eternity. It is the Lord of Hosts, and judge of the whole earth, who hath done it. Though we mourn, we do not murmur; nor is our sorrow like theirs who have no hope. By the light of divine revelation thou hast graciously enlarged our mental prospects, and enabled us to discover thy kind superintendence of our affairs.

With unfeigned gratitude we acknowledge that thou hast done great things for, and by our deceased brother: We render thee our united thanks for his creation; for the amiable and excellent disposition, sound principles and uncommon abilities which he possessed; for his wonderful preservation thro' an awful series of dangers; for the many essential services he rendered our country; and more especially for the hope and fortitude, serenity and composure, with which he resigned his soul to thee.

We praise thee as the God of Grace for the fair examples of public and private virtue, and of eminent piety which he has left for our imitation. And permit us to beseech thee of thine infinite goodness, to sanctify his dissolution to this weeping country. May a double portion of the admirable spirit which he possessed, rest on our Rulers! that all who are clothed with either legislative, judicial, or executive power, may be instrumental in preserving our many and distinguished blessings, and in effectually promoting all the important interests of these United States. And may that firm persuasion of the importance of Religion, which eminently distinguished the invaluable deceased, so pervade and penetrate our own, and the minds of our fellow-citizens, that the blessed Gospel may diffuse its divine influence, and exert its transforming efficacy throughout this favored land! that all vice may be suppressed, virtue and piety promoted, our excellent government perpetuated, and our civil and religious liberties and privileges, transmitted unimpaired to the latest posterity!

Grant these inestimable blessings, and speedily extend, not only thy providential, but special, goodness and mercy to all men, we humbly entreat thee, o God! for the sake of Jesus Christ, our only and divine Mediator, to whom with thee, and the spirit of all grace, be cordially ascribed all honor and dominion, by men and angels, world without end! Amen.

APPENDIX C

TYPICAL EARLY ASSOCIATIONAL LETTER, 1815

The Savannah Baptist Church to the Savannah River Baptist Association, to convene at Spring Town in So. Carolina on the Saturday preceeding the fourth Lord's day in the present month.

Beloved Brethren in the Lord, we feel great pleasure to address you once more in a church Capacity, and to inform you that thro divine goodness, after much sickness, we again begin to resume our health generally. The great Shepherd and Bishop of souls has deigned in mercy to give us a pastor, Brother Benjamin Screven, whom [sic] was solemnly Ordained to the pastoral Charge over us on the last Lord's day in October last, and whom we have the pleasure to delegate to your body at your approaching Session. Religion is not in such a state of progression as we could desire, nevertheless we meet and part in peace, & greatly hope for a revival in some short time, for the [fruits of] which we also request your prayers to God for us. Our numbers remaining are 69: one withdrawn from our communion, and six valuable members deceased since our last Association. Owing to a recent circumstance taking place among us and may occur in other parts of our union, we would state to you the following query which we hope you will decide on when you are together: It is this, Should a minister who has been regularly ordained, withdraw his membership and pastoral care of the flock committed to his Charge on account of the principles held in such Church from when he withdrew, tho' formerly warmly espoused by him and still continue to Baptize persons with whose experience he is satisfied, and if such persons should wish to become members of a Baptist Church can they be admitted to fellowship in such Church without being Baptized in a due and regular manner.

We have made the following Collection of money for the use of the missionary fund which we leave to your choice in distributing among the Candidates, it amounts to $12.50 twelve dollars and fifty cents—hoping that the Lord will meet with & bless you in all your deliberations for his Glory and the good of those you represent. We subscribe ourselves,

Dr. Brethren
Yrs ever in Gospel Bonds
Elias Robert C.S.B.C.
Signed by request and in behalf
of the whole Church
18TH day of Nov. 1815

APPENDIX D

A SECOND TYPICAL ASSOCIATIONAL LETTER
SAVANNAH NOVEMBER 3RD 1821

The Savannah Baptist Church of Christ to the Sunbury Association appointed to meet at the upper Black Creek Church, on the 2ND Saturday of this month send Christian Salutations—

Beloved Brethren.

Since we enjoyed the pleasing satisfaction of participating in the privileges of your last session amongst us another year has nearly passed away and it becomes our duty as well as our privilege again to address you in an associate capacity, and to acknowledge with unfeigned thankfulness the spiritual & temporal blessings which has pleased our God to confer upon us; for which we would adore and bless his holy name forever—In reviewing the Lord's dealings towards us the past year tho' we are not able to speak of having experienced the copious showers of refreshing grace which he hath found upon some parts of his vineyard, yet we trust our hearts have felt something of the Joy which pervaded the pure Spirits of the heavenly host, who are represented by the divine Saviour as rejoicing over one Sinner that repenteth, we have had 25 added to our number of such as we hope the Lord will save with an everlasting Salvation.

We are still favoured with the regular administration of divine ordinances, tho we have to lament that many seats in our house of worship are unfortunately empty which we desire to see filled with earnest hearers of "the word of truth."

We have been comforted in hearing that Bro. Southwell[,] the Missionary of the Association continues to prosper and increase in usefulness; and we cannot but hope that while the Churches are thus manifesting their love & Obedience to the Saviour in Caring for the Souls of their fellowmen who are destitute of a preached Gospel, they will receive a recompense in their own bosoms by the bestowment of more copious effusions of the divine spirit to refresh their withering graves, so that they may unitedly pray 'thy kingdom come thy will be done on Earth as it is in heaven' then may they hope to see his great power in the Sanctuary, causing Sinners to cry out in the anguish of their Souls, 'What shall we do to be saved.' The great Watchman of Israel hath truly watched over us in mercy the present year; and tho' our Sins have deserved his wrath and indignation, yet hath he pitied us as a father pitieth his children— hath remembered our frame that it is but dust—He hath preserved from the pestilence that walketh in darkness and the destruction that wasteth at noon day; we desire in remembrance of his mercy to shew forth his praise from day to day—we shall cordially concur in any measure that may come before you having for their object the furtherance of the Redeemer's Kingdom and the increase of vital piety in our several Churches—We have elected our worthy Pastor and our Bro. Collins as our delegates to your body & send by their hands $50 for the Missionary fund and $5 towards printing the Minutes.

Praying that all your deliberations and resolves may tend to the great object of promoting the glory of God—In behalf & by the direction of the Church.

Baptized	12
Rec'd by letter	3
Dismissed	2
Dead	1
Restored	0
Excommunicated	0

For and in behalf of the church—
J. Penfield
Acting Clerk

APPENDIX E

TYPICAL MINISTERIAL CALL AND ANSWER, 1822

The Baptist Church in Savannah
to the Rev. Thomas Meredith,
    sendeth Christian Salutation—Whereas through the interpretation of divine providence we have been favoured with an opportunity of becoming acquainted with your gifts as a Gospel Minister, and having full fellowship with you as a man of piety and possessing correct views of the important doctrines of the Gospel and believing that the Lord had directed us in our deliberations, we have unanimously resolved by a solemn vote of this church, to present you with a call to become our Pastor, and as we deem it important that the will of the Lord should in all our transactions be consulted, and for the mutual benefit of Pastor & People and have thought it more advisable to limit our call to the first of January 1824, with a full expectation and anxious desire that at the close of that period we may be well convinced that the Lord approves your labors amongst us, that we may review our call with the hope that your mind may be so operated upon by the spirit of our God, as to induce you to continue among us & we trust that a lasting benefit may be experienced by our Church & congregation through your instrumentality and that we may long live & dwell together in christian [sic] love & unity—we have this day disposed of Pews to the amount of Seven Hundred & Sixty Dollars which we pledge to you for your support until any additional amount we may receive for Pew Rent previous to that date. It is our intention the first day of December next to rent the Pews for twelve months, the proceeds of which we consider pledged for your support for that period—hoping that the Lord may by his holy spirit influence you to accept the call & meet the views of the church, we are dear Brother Yours in Gospel Bonds.

    Savannah
    April 24th 1822
    John Shick
    Josiah Penfield
    Jas. Postell
    Church Committee

On the following day the committee received from the Rev. Thomas Meredith the following reply:

To the Baptist Church at Savannah

Beloved Brethren:

A short period has elapsed since I have had the pleasure of receiving a Call from your body to become your pastor. I trust I have submitted the matter to the Lord and considered it well.

It now gives me pleasure to say that I feel a freedom in accepting your call, and hope that the great head of the Church may approve and bless the compact—Most affy yrs in Gospel Bonds.

Thomas Meredith

April 25, 1822

APPENDIX F

CORNERSTONE ENCLOSURES (1831)

The original of which the following is a true copy was placed under the corner stone of the new Baptist church now erecting in this City

DEDICATION TO THE WORSHIP OF ALMIGHTY GOD
The Corner Stone of this House of
Worship for the use of the Baptist
Church in Savannah is laid on the
2ND day of February, A.D., 1831.
The following are the names of the several
Pastors who have labored with this society—

Rev. Dr. Henry Holcombe . . .   1800–1811
Rev. William B. Johnston [sic] . . . 1811–1814
Rev. Benjamin Scriven [sic] . . .   1815–1818
Rev. James Sweat . . .   1819–1822
Rev. Henry O. Wyer . . .   1825–
continues to be the pastor at this time.

Number of members admitted up to this time . . 381

The funds for the erection of this Edifice have been raised
    By a Legacy of the late Josiah Penfield $2500.00

By Fair undertaken by Ladies of various
    Denominations 2125.00

And by subscriptions of benevolent citizens—
The following Gentlemen have served as Building Committee:

Deacons

John Shick	Abram Harman	Michael Brown
Homes Tupper	Thomas Clark	William Rahn
Horace Blair	John Huguemen	John J. Dews

COVENANT

We whose names are under written having been baptized upon our profession of Faith in Christ and believing it to be our duty to walk in all the ordinances of the Gospel; do declare our belief of all the doctrines of the Old and New Testaments, preferring the explanations of them by the Author of the Baptist Confession of Faith, and such as agree with them to any that we have seen, and we are very sensible that our conduct and conversation both in the church, and in the world ought to correspond with this sublime and holy system of Divine Truth.—To exercise a conscience void of offence towards God and Man, to live soberly, righteously and piously in the world endeavoring by all lawful means to promote the peace and welfare of Society in General; We consider as important and indispensable duties—

As to our regards to each other in our church communion we feel ourselves bound to walk with each other in all humility and brotherly love, to watch over each other's conversations, to stir up one another to love and good works, not forsaking the assembling of ourselves together as we have opportunity to worship God according to his revealed will; and when cases require such measures to warn, entreat, exhort, rebuke, and admonish in the spirit of meekness according to the rules of the Gospel—At the same time that we think ourselves obliged to sympathize with each other in all conditions, bearing with other's weaknesses and other imperfections, we view it as absolutely necessary to our peace and prosperity, and the honor of God to carefully maintain a strict gospel discipline; all which duties together with those which respect the most peaceful and charitable conduct towards all who love our Lord Jesus Christ in sincerity and a zeal according to knowledge for the propagation of his gospel. We desire and engage to perform to our humble abilities, through the gracious assistance of God, while we both admire and adore, the grace that has given us a name in his house so much better than that of sons and daughters —

In testimony of our unanimous consent to the aforesaid Doctrines, Duties and Covenant we most cheerfully subscribe our names.

CONSTITUTION

I. This body shall be denominated agreeably to its charter of incorporation—The Baptist Church in Savannah.

II. It shall be composed of such members only as have been baptized by immersion upon profession of their faith in the Lord Jesus Christ and who generally embraced the confession of faith adopted by the Baptist Denomination.

III. There shall be chosen and properly ordained two or more or less Deacons for the purpose of taking the charge of the temporal.

IV. There shall be elected annually a Secretary who shall be required to keep a correct list of all the members and to preserve a register of all transactions of the church in a volume kept for that purpose.

V. There shall be elected annually a Treasurer who shall hold the monies of the body and render a correct report concerning the state of the funds every twelve months.

VI. The members of the body shall be subject to the foregoing constitution, the subsequent code of Bylaws and the discipline generally observed by the churches of the Baptist order.

VII. Any of the preceding articles may be subject to amendment whenever propriety may dictate.

Bylaws

1. At every Church meeting the pastor, if present, shall take the chair, when absent a moderator shall be chosen from the members.

2. Every Church meeting shall be opened and concluded by singing or prayer.

3. The church meeting shall be composed of the members of this body and such as may be invited to confer with the church.

4. After the opening of conference the Covenant shall be read and the minutes of the last meeting shall be read, reviewed, and confirmed.

5. Every person who speaks during the sitting of conference shall rise from his seat and address the moderator.

6. Every motion properly made and seconded shall be free for discussion and for the consideration of the body.

7. Every question before the Church shall be decided by a majority of members present and in case of tie, the moderator shall give the deciding vote.

8. No person shall be allowed to speak more than twice on the same motion without special permission from the moderator.

9. Any person manifesting levity of mind, or whispering during conference shall be liable to be called to order by the moderator. [Repealed in 1826]

10. No person shall leave the meeting previously to adjournment without permission from the moderator. [Repealed in 1826]

11. Every person who is absent without sufficient reason from the regular meetings of the church shall be liable to admonition or censure as the case may demand.

12. The minutes of the present meeting shall be read subsequently to the motion for adjournment.

13. The meeting shall not be adjourned until a resolution to that effect shall have been regularly adopted.

APPENDIX G

ARTICLE IX "OF DISCIPLINE" IN THE
RULES AND BYLAWS OF 1860

While the minute rules to govern the exercise of discipline are too numerous to allow, and too obvious to require mention, the church deem it proper to specify the following:

1. In all cases of grievance between members, or offense against the church, the offending member shall be dealt with according to the rule laid down in the eighteenth chapter of Matthew.

2. No complaint shall be preferred in church conference against any member until after the course recommended in the preceding rule shall have been pursued towards him; and any charges preferred against a member in church conference, shall be in writing.

3. No person shall be excluded, until he or she shall have been cited to appear before the church, and shall have had an opportunity to reply to any charges that may have been preferred; except in cases where gross immorality or dishonesty is clearly proved, and in cases where circumstances render an interview impracticable.

4. When the dismission of a member from the fellowship of this Church results from a change of views in reference to our articles of faith or principles of gospel order, and not from any immorality or unchristian deportment, this Church may give a certificate to the member dismissed as to the Christian propriety of his or her conduct up to the time of separation from our communion.

APPENDIX H

CHRONOLOGICAL LISTING OF THE PASTORS-IN-RESIDENCE

1. Henry Holcombe, 1800–1811
2. William B. Johnson, 1811–1815
3. Benjamin Screven, 1815–1818
4. James Sweat, 1819–1822
5. Thomas Meredith, 1822–1824
6. Henry O. Wyer, 1825–1833
7. Josiah S. Law, 1834–1835
8. Charles B. Jones, 1836–1837
9. Joseph G. Binney, 1837–1843
10. Henry O. Wyer, 1844–1845
11. Albert Williams, 1845–1847
12. Joseph T. Robert, 1847–1849
13. Thomas Rambaut, 1849–1855
14. Joseph B. Stiteler, 1856 (Died in Office)
15. Samuel G. Daniel, 1856–1859
16. Sylvanus Landrum, 1859–1871
17. Timothy Harley, 1872–1879
18. Sylvanus Landrum, 1879–1881
19. J. E. L. Holmes, 1881–1891
    (Died in Office)
20. S. A. Goodwin, 1892–1897
21. John D. Jordan, 1897–1906
22. W. Lowndes Pickard, 1907–1914
23. J. J. Taylor, 1915–1918
24. Luther R. Christie, 1918–1921
25. Norman W. Cox, 1922–1927
26. John E. White, 1927–1931
    (Died in Office)
27. Arthur M. Jackson, 1931–1941
28. Leroy G. Cleverdon, 1942–1961
29. W. Forrest Lanier, 1962–1969
30. Thomas D. Austin, 1970–1988
31. Fred W. Andrea III, 1989–1993
32. John M. Finley, 1994–

PASTORS OF THE SCHISM OR SECOND BAPTIST CHURCH

1. Henry O. Wyer, 1847–1849
2. J. P. Tustin, 1849–1854
3. Henry O. Wyer, 1854–1855
4. M. Winston, 1855–1859

APPENDIX I

IN PRAISE OF JOHN E. WHITE UPON HIS DEATH, JULY 26, 1931

The Messenger

Our Pastor, Dr. John Ellington White

When word came to our Church that our beloved pastor was indisposed, no one was seriously apprehensive. He was physically so vigorous, mentally so alert, spiritually so steadfast—so strong and active in every way—with such wonderful zeal and enthusiasm for the work always at hand and by him so easily accomplished, that no one thought of his affliction as being more than temporary. Reports from his bedside gratified us in our hope for his speedy and complete recovery.

But we reckoned not of the strain to which his vitality had been subjected. For forty years and more he had driven his physical body to do the work of many men. With face forward, body erect, a high purpose in his heart, with faith and hope to persevere, and a resolution to succeed, he had been always in the forefront of the strife. In the service of Baptist denominational organizations, in striving with might and main for the education of the youth of our land, in the building of schools, orphanages and hospitals, and in proclaiming the Gospel of his Lord and Master for the redemption of sin-burdened souls, he had ever the Crusader's zeal. But flesh and blood are not without limitations. The human heart and nerves can stand so much strain and no more. When the source of supply is exhausted, the end is at hand.

And so it was that on last Tuesday afternoon, a hush fell upon the city of Savannah. Over the telephone wires the message was borne, "Dr. White is dead." Impossible! It cannot be!

But why not? Pale Death with impartial tapping comes knocking at the earthly temple of all. Why not at the door of one who, throughout his entire ministry, had proclaimed with triumphant faith, "There is no death to them who die in the Lord"?

Why should not our Pastor obey the last and final call? In the mutations of time, was it not for him to realize:

Sunset and evening star,
And one clear call for me,
And may there be no moaning of the bar,
When I put out to sea.

But such a tide as moving seems asleep,
Too full for sound and foam,
When that which drew from out the boundless deep,
Turns again home.

Twilight and evening bell,
And after that the dark,
And may there be no sadness of farewell,
When I embark;

For tho' from out the bourne of Time and Place
The flood may bear me far,
I hope to see my Pilot face to face
When I have crost the bar.

To those of us who have heard fall from his lips, in silvery, cheering tone, the acclaim, "Death is swallowed up in victory," we know that he went triumphantly to meet his Maker. We also know that while he lay upon his bed of sickness he said to the loved ones about him, that if his Father willed that his earthly labors be at end, he was ready for the call. And we know that from his lips came the submissive words, "Father, not my will but Thine be done."

And so we have buried his mortal remains in the cemetery in Anderson, South Carolina. But we have not buried and cannot bury the immortal part of his being— His Good Name, His Good Deeds, His Consecrated Christian Life.

Howe'er it be, it seems to me,
'Tis only noble to be good.
Kind hearts are more than coronets,
And simple faith *than Norman blood.*

We would not if we could, bury from our Church the minister whose service to us will be surpassed by none. We would not if we could, bury the foremost minister of Savannah, for truly he was their leader. We would not if we could, bury the foremost Baptist of the South, for truly he was, by common consent, the acknowledged head of our denomination. We would not if we could, bury the love and esteem in which he is held by men of all denominations, for truly he labored for that church which is circumscribed only by the limitations of Love.

With the faith of Abraham, the fortitude of Moses, the zeal of John, the Baptist, and the winsomeness of John, the Beloved, he was above and beyond denominational lines in the service of his Master.

No, we have not and cannot bury the good which he has wrought, for,

True happiness, when understood
Is found alone in doing good.

We would not if we could, bury the rare and radiant spirit which has lived among us, for he was without malice, speaking ill of none. We would not if we could, bury his conquering optimism, bottomed as it was upon his abiding faith in God.

His life was beautiful beyond the tender words spoken at his funeral and dearer than the harmony of the hymns wafted upon southern breezes. Those for whom he labored, to whom he gave of his best, and for whom he died, literally the embodiment of love, mingled their voices in the triumphant songs.

And at that funeral there was no hint of doubt, no note of despondency, no wail of gloom. Over that vast assemblage was the benediction of the everlasting triumph of God's Coming Kingdom. In the heart of the assembled throng was the conquering paean,

The strife is o'er, the battle won!
Alleluia.
THE BOARD OF DEACONS

APPENDIX J

THE BRONZE TABLET, NOVEMBER 26, 1950

A beautiful bronze tablet setting forth the basic history of the First Baptist Church and dedicated to the memories of the Reverend Henry Holcombe, the first pastor, and those who succeeded him in the Church's ministry is presented and dedicated at the afternoon service today. The tablet, the text of which is given below, is placed on the outside wall at the right of the center door of the Church.

1800 SESQUICENTENNIAL 1950
FIRST BAPTIST CHURCH
SAVANNAH, GEORGIA

On November 26, 1800 the Reverend Henry Holcombe and fifteen other Baptists organized the Savannah Baptist Church. As early as 1795 a group of interested Baptists had erected a House of Worship on Franklin Square where the congregation worshipped for thirty-three years. The Sunday School was organized there on April 29, 1827.

During the pastorate of the Reverend Henry O. Wyer the cornerstone of the present church on Chippewa Square was laid on February 2, 1831 and the building was completed in 1833. The Church House was enlarged in 1839, improved from time to time and completely renovated in 1921. Since 1847 the Church has been called the First Baptist Church. In 1926 the Educational Building was erected and dedicated to the memory of John J. Cummings.

The Church has had a long line of distinguished deacons and members who have given it their support, devotion and prayers. The pastors have been Henry Holcombe, William B. Johnson, Benjamin Screven, James Sweat, James Meredith, Henry O. Wyer, Josiah S. Law, Charles B. Jones, J. G. Binney, Albert Williams, Joseph T. Robert, Thomas Rambaut, J. B. Stiteler, G. S. Daniel, Sylvanus Landrum, Timothy Harley, J. E. L. Holmes, S. A. Goodwin, J. D. Jordan, W. L. Pickard, J. J. Taylor, L. R. Christie, Norman W. Cox, John E. White, Arthur Jackson, and Leroy G. Cleverdon.

This tablet is given in grateful recognition to God for His divine blessings of the Church and is dedicated to the memories of the Reverend Henry Holcombe and those who succeeded him in its ministry. Done with appropriate exercises on this the Twenty-sixth Day of November One Thousand Nine Hundred and Fifty and the One Hundred and Fiftieth Anniversary of the organization of The First Baptist Church of Savannah, Georgia.

APPENDIX K

AN ILLUSTRATION OF DEEP ECUMENICAL RELATIONSHIPS

Congregation Mickve Israel
20 East Gordon Street, Savannah, Georgia 31401
May 28, 1986
Clergy, Diaconate and Members of First Baptist Church
Chippewa Square
Savannah, Georgia 31401

Dear Friends;

I rejoice in the magnificent gift that Tom Austin presented to Elsie and me at the retirement ceremonies. The Lenox Elijah's Cup is both a splendid art object and sacred symbol. It is placed at the Passover table as representation of the universal hope that one day the harbinger of the Messianic era, Elijah, the prophet, will walk among us. I believe that long awaited day will dawn when human beings learn the ways of love, integrity, and peace, and act in accordance with the Divine image within them. Then we shall all be worthy of a redemptive age. I trust that you sense how richly the Elijah Cup speaks to my spirit, even as it inspires joy by its intrinsic beauty.

Over these years an uncommon bonding has passed between the people of First Church and my Temple. I believe it was a natural response to the trust, affection and mutual concern of the spiritual leaders. I remain Tom Austin's (and Edna's too) greatest fan. He has known my support and encouragement in all the humane causes to which he has provided direction. His presence in this community remains one of its choicest assets. How blessed are you to have James Richardson as your chief musician. From time to time, he honored our congregation with music, impressing all with his refined talent. Would that I had the poise, skill and good sense of Jody Wright at a comparable stage in my ministry! From your ranks, we have recruited Sheila Ferrell whose numberless gifts we have relied on, day after day. I wish more of you knew what kind of a witness she is to the nobility of your faith! Cathy and Albertha and all the others have made your staff an impressive professional unit, worthy of praise. I have only pleasant memories of my associations at First Church. Yours is a remarkable congregation; my earnest prayer is that growth and shalom may be its destiny, generation after generation.

Finally, one must marvel at the bridge building process that has occurred in a relatively brief span. It seemed unlikely, in 1972, that an historic Southern Baptist congregation in a setting like Savannah would develop friendship, yea spiritual linkage, with an equally historic and venerable community of Jews. Where understanding is limited, suspicion abounds. There is enough difference in matters theological between us that we may overlook that rich strata which constitutes our common heritage. I have been excited at the prospect that year after year more and more of that layer has been mined in your church. It will only deepen and intensify your appreciation of what is ancient and strengthening in your faith. Whatever triumphalism was within me has diminished over the years. I am a devotee of religion; the God Whom I cherish is the God of all humanity. I worship Him in the way of my forebears because that is comfortable to me and has led to levels of fulfillment and tranquility. I believe that all that I have derived from my faith is open to you in yours. I treasure your friendship because we are steadfast affirmers of Deity and that makes us profoundly one. If the gift of Elijah's cup is your way of showing friendship, we feel blessed, my wife and I, beyond the power of language to express.

Thanks to each of you for many kindnesses received over the years. May blessing sustain you in all your ways.

B'shalom (in peace),
/s/ Elsie and Saul
Rabbi and Mrs. Saul Jacob Rubin

APPENDIX L

LETTER ILLUSTRATING THE MODERATE POSITION OF THE CHURCH IN THE MIDST OF DENOMINATIONAL TURMOIL JUNE 20, 1990

WHEREAS the First Baptist Church of Savannah, Georgia, established forty-five years prior to the founding of the Southern Baptist convention, is wholeheartedly committed to the singular purpose for which our convention of local churches exists, namely, voluntary cooperation for the cause of Christian missions, evangelism, education, and benevolent service; and

WHEREAS our congregation, constituted one hundred twenty-five years before the creation of the Cooperative Program, unreservedly supports free, reverent biblical scholarship and boldly exemplifies contemporary Christian faith in an historic setting; and

WHEREAS this local church has been served, nurtured, and challenged for more than a century by outstanding ministers trained effectively in Southern Baptist seminaries; and

WHEREAS Savannah's First Baptist Church treasures the rich tradition of excellent theological education provided through The Southern Baptist Theological Seminary;

BE IT THEREFORE RESOLVED THAT we urge each of the Seminary's trustees to maintain her historic nature, to exercise responsible trusteeship, and to demonstrate Christ-like behavior in conducting assigned duties; and

BE IT FURTHER RESOLVED THAT we pledge our continuing and prayer concern for the Seminary's administration, faculty and support staff, and her student body; and

BE IT FURTHER RESOLVED THAT we oppose the emerging politico-theological agenda of the Board of Trustees and we deplore the innuendo, half-truth, and personal attacks directed toward Seminary President Roy L. Honeycutt and various members of the faculty; and

BE IT FURTHER RESOLVED THAT we declare our unequivocal desire and unalterable determination to ensure the preservation of superior theological education in the historic tradition and spirit of The Southern Baptist Theological Seminary; and

BE IT FINALLY RESOLVED THAT we convey a copy of this resolution to President Honeycutt, and the trustees, appropriate officers of the Southern Baptist Convention, and representatives of the Baptist Press.

APPENDIX M

THE RE-WRITTEN COVENANT OF 1922–1927

Having been, as we trust, brought by Divine grace to embrace the Lord Jesus Christ, and to give ourselves wholly to Him, we do now, solemnly and joyfully covenant with each other to *walk together in Him with brotherly love*, to His glory, as our common Lord. We do now, relying upon His gracious aid, solemnly covenant with each other, and promise that we will exercise an affectionate care and watchfulness over each other, and faithfully admonish and entreat one another as occasion may require: that we will not forsake the assembling of ourselves together, nor neglect to pray for ourselves and others: that we will endeavor to bring up such as may at any time be under our care, in the nurture and admonition of the Lord, and by a pure and holy example, to win our kindred and acquaintances to the Saviour, to holiness and to eternal life: that we will rejoice at each other's happiness: and endeavor with tenderness and sympathy to bear each other's burdens and sorrows: that we will not bring forward to the Church a complaint against any member for any personal trespass against us, until we have taken the first and second steps pointed out by Christ, in the 18th Chapter of Matthew, and that all private offences, which can be privately settled, we will never make public: that we will live circumspectly in the world, "denying ungodliness and worldly lusts" setting a worthy example, and remembering that as we have been voluntarily buried by baptism, and have been raised up from the emblematical grave, so there is on us a special obligation, henceforth to lead a new and holy life: that we will strive together for the support of a faithful Evangelical Ministry among us: that according to our ability and opportunities we will, as faithful servants to the Lord, do good to all men, especially in helping to extend the Gospel in its purity and power to the whole human family: and that through life, amidst evil report and good report, we will humbly and earnestly seek to live to the glory of Him, who hath called us out of darkness into His marvelous light.

"And may the God of Peace, who brought again from the dead our Lord Jesus, that great Shepherd of the sheep, through the blood of the everlasting covenant, make us perfect in every good work, working in us that which is well pleasing in His sight, through Jesus Christ: to whom be glory, forever and ever. AMEN."

APPENDIX N

BICENTENNIAL HYMN BY JAMES C. RICHARDSON

Written for the Bicentennial Celebration of First Baptist Church, Savannah, Georgia, founded November 26, 1800

To God, Our Help in Ages Past

WORDS and MUSIC: James C. Richardson, quoting fragments of "Our God, Our Help in Ages Past" by Isaac Watts, 1719, and ST. ANNE, attributed to William Croft, 1708.
© 1999 James C. Richardson

CHIPPEWA SQUARE
8.7.8.7.4.4.7.11.7

APPENDIX O

LIST OF THE PRESIDENTS OF WOMEN ON MISSION (1902–1999)

Mrs. W. C. Powell	1902	Mrs. J. Harry Duncan	1954
Mrs. C. D. Baldwin	1903	Mrs. W. Harold Cordray	1955
Mrs. W. R. Powell	1904	Mrs. John B. Rabun	1956–57
Mrs. W. S. Wilson	1905–06	Mrs. W. Harold Cordray	1958
Mrs. H. W. Way	1908	Mrs. Robert C. Daniels	1959–60
Mrs. J. M. Gannon	1909	Mrs. W. Ray Alexander	1961–62
Miss Alice W. Wheatley	1913	Mrs. Wheeler E. Chapman	1963
Mrs. James R. Cain	1914–15	Mrs. Charles Usher	1964–66
Mrs. J. J. Taylor	1916–17	Mrs. James R. Upson	1967–69
Mrs. M. E. Stacey	1919	Mrs. J. Harry Duncan	1970
Mrs. Hartman	1920	Mrs. Henry L. Ashmore	1971
Mrs. E. T. Whatley	1921	Mrs. George A. Blood	1972
Mrs. Edgar J. Oliver	1922–24	Mrs. John B. Ferguson Jr.	1973
Mrs. E. T. Whatley	1925	Mrs. Louise C. Underwood	1974
Mrs. Roy Chalker	1926–28	Mrs. Brevard F. Law	1975–76
Mrs. Tiffany Wilson	1929–30	Mrs. John B. Ferguson Jr.	1977–78
Mrs. Charles D. Ellis	1931–32	Mrs. B. Robert Miller	1979–80
Mrs. Albert M. Dixon	1933–34	Mrs. John B. Rabun	1981
Mrs. Almon U. Futrelle	1935–36	Mrs. William J. Saseen	1982–84
Mrs. A. O. MacDonald	1937–38	Mrs. William I. Waller	1985–86
Mrs. William M. Roberts	1939	Mrs. William C. Sutton Jr.	1987
Mrs. Tiffany Wilson	1940	Miss May McCall	1988
Mrs. Edgar J. Oliver	1941–44	Mrs. Joseph V. Adams	1989
Mrs. Thomas C. Helmly	1945–46	Mrs. Mitchell Palles	1990–93
Mrs. Henry M. Meadors	1947–48	Mrs. Earl Kirkley	1994–95
Mrs. David W. Pearson	1949–50	Mrs. George Worthy	1996–97
Mrs. A. T. Garrick	1951	Mrs. Mitchell Palles	1997–98
Mrs. D. W. Hoffman	1952	Mrs. Mitchell Palles and	
Mrs. Edgar J. Oliver	1953	Mrs. Charles L. Davis	1998–present

SELECTED BIBLIOGRAPHY

I. PRIMARY SOURCES

The Calendar, 1942–1998.

Holcombe, Henry. *The First Fruits in a Series of Letters*. Philadelphia, 1812.

LaFar, Mabel Freeman. *The Baptist Church of Savannah Georgia, 1805–1836: History, Records, and Register.* Volume 1, 2 parts, 1941.

Manual of the First Baptist Church, n.d. and 1860.

Messenger, 1922–1941.

Minutes of the Congregation and Diaconate, 1805–1997.

Minutes of the New Sunbury Association, 1818–1938.

Record Book of the Sunday School, n.d.

Register of the First Baptist Church.

II. SECONDARY SOURCES

Ahlstrom, Sydney E. *A Religious History of the American People*. New Haven, 1972.

Aldridge, Marion D. and Kevin Lewis, eds. *The Changing Shape of Protestantism in the South*. Macon, Ga., 1996.

Armstrong, O. K. and Marjorie Moore. *The Indomitable Baptists*. New York, 1967.

Austin, Thomas D. Typescript. Series of historical sermons on pastors of First Baptist Church. Savannah, 1986.

Austin, Thomas D., James C. Richardson, and Jody C. Wright. "Worship Planning at First Baptist Church, Savannah, Georgia." *Review and Expositor*, 85 (1988): pp. 63–70.

Baker, Robert A. *A Baptist Source Book*. Nashville, 1966.

Baker, W. W. *The Southern Baptist Convention*. Nashville, 1954.

Baptists Today. (Periodical voice of moderate Baptists.)

Bliese, Richard H. "Communities that Change, Congregations that Adapt," *Christian Century* (January 7–14, 1998): pp. 21–23.

Bland, Thomas A., Jr., ed. *Servant Songs*. Macon, Ga., 1994.

Brackney, William H. *The Baptists*. Westpoint, Conn., 1988.

Brown, Robert M. *The Spirit of Protestantism*. New York, 1965.

Carey, John J. *Carlyle Marney: A Pilgrim's Progress*. Macon, Ga., 1980.

Childers, James S. *A Way Home: The Baptists Tell Their Story*. New York, 1964.

Coleman, Kenneth. *A History of Georgia*. Athens, Ga., 1991.

"Congregations in the Midst of Change: An Interview with Nancy Ammerman," *Christian Century* (January 15, 1997): pp. 48–51.

Copeland, E. Luther. *The Southern Baptist Convention and the Judgment of History.* Lanham, Md., 1995.

Cothen, Grady H. *What Happened to the Southern Baptist Convention?.* Macon, Ga., 1993.

Duncan, Pope. *Our Baptist Story.* Nashville, 1958.

Estep, William R. *Baptists and Christian Unity.* Nashville, 1966.

Farnsley, Arthur Emery, II. *Southern Baptist Politics: Authority and Power in the Restructuring of An American Denomination.* University Park, Md., 1994.

Ferguson, Robert U., ed. *Amidst Babel, Speak the Truth: Reflections on the Southern Baptist Convention Struggle.* Macon, Ga., 1993.

Fletcher, Jesse C. *The Southern Baptist Convention: A Sesquicentennial History.* Nashville, 1994.

Furr, Gary A. and Curtis W. Freeman, eds. *Ties That Bind: Life Together in the Baptist Vision.* Macon, Ga., 1994.

Gardner, Robert G. *Baptists of Early America.* Atlanta, 1983.

_____. *A Decade of Debate and Division.* Macon, Ga., 1995.

Gilmore, A., ed. *Christian Baptism.* Chicago, 1959.

Goen, C. C. *Broken Churches, Broken Nation: Denominational Schisms and the Coming of the American Civil War.* Macon, Ga., 1985.

Hays, Brooks and John E. Steely. *The Baptist Way of Life.* Macon, Ga., 1981.

Hill, Samuel S. *Southern Churches in Crisis.* New York, 1966.

_____, ed. *Varieties of Southern Religious Experience.* Baton Rouge, La., 1988.

LaFar, Mabel Freeman. "Henry Holcombe, D.D.: Minister, Humanitarian, and Man of Letters." *Georgia Historical Review* (September, 1944).

LaFar, Margaret Freeman. *A Historical Sketch of the First Baptist Church* (175th Anniversary). Savannah, 1975.

_____. "Lowell Mason's Varied Activities in Savannah," *Georgia Historical Quarterly* (September, 1944).

Leonard, Bill J. *Dictionary of Baptists in America.* Downers Grove, Ill., 1994.

_____. *God's Last and Only Hope: The Fragmentation of the Southern Baptist Convention.* Grand Rapids, Mich., 1990.

_____. *A History of the Baptists* (forthcoming)

Lester, James Adams. *A History of the Georgia Baptist Convention.* Nashville, 1972.

Littell, Franklin H. *The Free Church.* Boston, 1957.

Lumpkin, W. L. *Baptist Confessions of Faith.* Valley Forge, Pa., 1959.

McDonogh, Gary Wray. *Black and Catholic in Savannah, Georgia.* Knoxville, 1993.

Morgan, David T. *The New Crusades, The New Holy Land: Conflict in the Southern Baptist Convention, 1969–1991.* Tuscaloosa, Ala., 1996.

Mueller, William A. *A History of Southern Baptist Theological Seminary.* Nashville, 1959.

Patterson, W. Morgan. *Baptist Successionism: A Critical View.* Valley Forge, Pa., 1969.

Raboteau, Albert J. *Slave Religion.* New York, 1978.

Rubin, Saul Jacob. *Third to None: The Saga of Savannah Jewry.* Savannah, 1983.

Shriver, George H., ed. *Dictionary of Heresy Trials in American Christianity.* Westport, Conn., 1997.

_____, ed. *Encyclopedia of Religious Controversies in the United States.* Westport, Conn., 1997.

_____. "Southern Baptists Ponder 'Open Membership'—An End of Rebaptism." *Journal of Ecumenical Studies* (summer 1969): pp. 423–430.

Shurden, Walter B., ed. *The Struggle for the Soul of the Southern Baptist Convention*. Macon, Ga., 1993.

Smith, H. Shelton. *In His Image, But . . . .* Durham, N.C., 1972.

Smith, Harmon C. *Where Two or Three Are Gathered*. Cleveland, 1995.

"The Southern Baptist Convention, 1979–1993: What Happened and Why." *Baptist History and Heritage* (October, 1993).

Stealey, Sydnor L. *A Baptist Treasury*. New York, 1958.

Teilhard de Chardin, Pierre. *The Divine Milieu*. New York, 1968.

Torbet, Robert G. *A History of the Baptists*. Valley Forge, Pa., 1963.

Wills, Gregory A. *Democratic Religion*. New York, 1997.

Wind, James P. and James W. Lewis, eds. *American Congregations*. 2 vols. Chicago, 1994.

III. INTERVIEWS AND PAPERS

Andrea, Fred. Letter. 1997.

Austin, Thomas. Taped statement. 1997.

Dated materials in *Baptists Today* and *Savannah Morning News*.

Lanier, Gene. Interview by Jack Usher. 1997.

Numerous reflections from various members gathered by Joan Usher. 1997.

Quattlebaum, Julian, Jr. Interview by Joan Usher. 1997.

Richardson, James. Written statement. 1998.

Solms, Shirley Cleverdon. Interview by Joan Usher. 1997.

Sutton, Bill. Written statement. 1998.

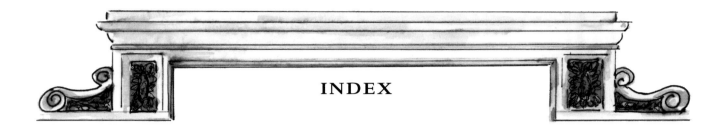

INDEX

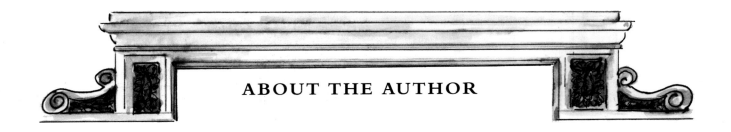

ABOUT THE AUTHOR

Graduate of Stetson and Duke Universities, Dr. George H. Shriver is Professor of History, Emeritus, Georgia Southern University. Professor for forty-one years, he has been given numerous awards such as Professor of the Year and the GSU Ruffin Cup. The present volume is his tenth book, and he is well known in the U.S. as an expert on religious heresy, dissent, and controversy. Member of Phi Beta Kappa, he has published dozens of articles, numerous chapters and essays in books, and hundreds of book reviews. He makes his home in Statesboro with his wife, Cathy. World traveler, he also enjoys hiking and tennis.